♀ Basic Philosophies of Education

Holt, Rinehart and Winston
New York · Chicago · San Francisco
Toronto · London

CHRISTIAN O. WEBER

Wells College

BASIC PHILOSOPHIES OF EDUCATION

for

SALLY, JIMMY, DONNA, and CAROL

PREFACE

Living creatures need frames of reference for their activities. Even ants use them in their homing excursions. This book covers six basic frames of reference in educational thought: religion, political control, traditionalism and essentialism, idealism, realism, and instrumentalism. Man's frames of reference tend to become cosmic in scope, having their origins in the distant past. The effects produced by Plato as a physical person, the echoes of his footsteps, have long since died away. But our remembrance of his thoughts leaps centuries of time to provide, among other things, part of the modern educator's frame of reference. The six points of view covered in this book, although originating in past eras, are still very much alive both as conceptual frames and as guides to educational practices. The main matters of aim and design of the book are as follows:

1. The practical aim of the book is to provide adequate material for a semester course on educational philosophies which are "classic" without having lost contemporary significance. Good college courses should involve reading in multiple sources, and this is especially necessary in the philosophy of education. Assuming sufficient supplementary reading, this book provides the structural outline for a year's course. The main users intended by the author are undergraduate college juniors and seniors working under the guidance of mentors well grounded in general philosophy and education. It is hoped that graduate students of education and teachers in service will find the book profitable even though their college preparation in philosophy has been scanty. The book itself gives the historical and systematic information needed for a critical understanding of each philosophy of education presented.

2. The literature on philosophy of education is often warped by taking statements of writers out of context and then praising or blaming them accordingly. To avoid miseducation from this source this book gives rather full expository accounts of each philosophy, followed by its application to education. The views of selected leaders of each school of thought are presented as *integrated wholes*. Such comparatively full treatment of relatively few writers helps to dispel some chronic misunderstandings. This method applies especially to discussions of Alfred N. Whitehead, Bertrand Russell, G. Stanley Hall, and William H. Kilpatrick.

3. A third aim, always challenging, is to integrate as closely as possi-

ble the more sweeping and abstract principles of philosophers with the down-to-earth problems of education. The author was pleased to find that psychology (to which a good share of his training and teaching has been devoted) often bridges gaps between philosophical theory and educational practice. This type of integration especially appears in Chapters 5 and 6, dealing with certain doctrines of essentialism, and in the disputes between Herbartians and Progressives regarding the role of interest in education.

Regarding personal aid from others, special mention should be made of the generous help of Professor Jacob Loewenberg in clarifying Hegelian and other forms of idealism. I am also grateful to Professor Frederick C. Neff, Chairman of the Department of Educational Philosophy at Wayne State University, for reviewing the entire manuscript and making a number of valuable suggestions. And I owe a debt to various authors and publishers for permission to quote materials. This permission is acknowledged by references to sources. The publishers who thus extended their generosity are The Bruce Publishing Company; Charles Scribner's Sons; Dial Press (for materials reprinted from *Education for Modern Man* by Sidney Hook, copyright 1946 by Sidney Hook); Harcourt, Brace and Company; Harper & Brothers; Holt, Rinehart and Winston; The Macmillan Company; New York University Press; Philosophical Library, Inc.; Prentice-Hall, Inc.; Simon and Schuster, Inc.; Bureau of Publications, Teachers College, Columbia University; The University of Chicago Press; and the Yale University Press.

CHRISTIAN O. WEBER

Aurora, New York
January, 1960

CONTENTS

⚥ Basic Philosophies of Education

book 1

RELIGION, POLITICS, AND PHILOSOPHY IN EDUCATION

C. The current Demand in Education and Thought
D. Value of Philosophy in Education
E. Traditional Positions of Philosophy
F. Current Trends in Philosophy and Educational Thought
G. Table of Contents Figures

A. The Domain of Education

$\overset{\bullet}{\triangledown}$ *chapter 1*

DOES EDUCATION NEED A PHILOSOPHY?

Philosophies are crossroads through the realm of reflection. This book is devoted to the exposition and criticism of six philosophical highways which lead through the terrain of education. Highways of philosophy resemble geographic ones in that they afford various perspectives of what is presumed to be the same territory. Highways also point in two directions, and crossroads offer more possibilities of getting lost! While searching for the proper directives for education we shall try not to be misled by the directions specified by the philosophies to be reviewed in this book. We shall not regard certain goals of education as good merely because they accord with familiar wants—we shall want them because they are good.

Philosophy is related to education in the usual way in which branches of knowledge are related to their practical applications. A hypothesis that is not verified by the tests of practice should not be seriously entertained. A philosophy of education should not be regarded as valid until educational practice has shown its validity. However, we cannot wait for a philosophy to be fully validated before applying it in practice because such practice is one of the chief ways of validating it.

The present preliminary chapter gives the blueprint of our journey throughout the book by considering seven subjects, as follows:

A. The Domain of Education
B. Philosophy as the Basis of Education

C. The Current Ferment in Educational Thought
D. Values of Philosophy in Education
E. Traditional Problems of Philosophy
F. Current Trends in Philosophical and Educational Thought
G. Prelude to Future Chapters

⚥ A. The Domain of Education

Education is said to be an activity in which everyone is engaged while awake. While awake, we are supposedly having experience; and experience, by general consent, is the Great Teacher. Of course, it is sometimes alleged that certain individuals do not learn from experience, but in this case it is doubtful whether they are sufficiently awake! To be alive at all implies learning from life. Conditioned responses have been set up in the snail and even in lower forms of life, but this sometimes takes "some doing." Indeed, the capacity to learn is perhaps the chief mark which distinguishes the living from the nonliving.

Material sciences like physics and chemistry owe their exactness, at least in part, to the inability of material objects to learn from experience. No matter how often heat causes a piece of metal to expand, its coefficient of expansion remains constant. The usefulness of the clock rests on its inability to run faster as the result of practice. But a living being, to use Henri Bergson's image, is like a rolling snowball, gathering up its path as it moves along, and thus never perfectly repeating its past states.

Experience has two main educative ingredients: action and reflection. Learning from action becomes indispensable in the case where the consequences of a given situation cannot be gauged by mere reflection. But action must be supplemented with reflection to make experience educative. We have here one of the main keys to the origin of educational institutions. The fruits of reflection are subject to rapid and easy transmission from one individual to another. Institutional education thus arises as the medium for transmitting accumulated wisdom to the young.

Institutional education is the medium of learning with which this book is chiefly concerned. We shall not, however, lose sight of the fact that education is carried on outside the portals of the school. In the home, instruction is freely handed out by parents and offspring alike. Radio and television vie with newspapers and magazines in conveying information, although they are often diluted in the interests of entertainment or warped in the interests of propaganda. Social life, work, and play repeat their grave or cheerful lessons endlessly. But there is no substitute for the school fired by the motive attributed to philosophers—pursuing knowledge for the sheer love of it; from which, as is fitting, the best practical fruits may be expected.

▽ B. Philosophy as the Basis of Education

Education, like all conscious and deliberate action, seeks for a basis of demonstrated principles. In this quest for certainty man turns to philosophy, the supposed fount of knowledge about the eternally true and precious. Some three hundred years ago education rested on trusted religious convictions (12, pp. 3-12). But education has become secular in the Anglo-Saxon world; control has shifted from church to state. Having lost its religious moorings, education turns to philosophy for guidance— at the risk of discovering that philosophers are far more skillful in questioning answers than in answering questions.

1. Implicit and Explicit Philosophy

It is said that everyone has an implicit philosophy even though it is not formulated in words. Thus, the enterprising individual who speaks of "putting ideas to work" might be astonished to learn that he is a "pragmatic philosopher." This discovery might please him, as was one of the characters in a Molière comedy when told that his daily speech was "prose." Many men might be regarded as physicists in the same Pickwickian sense, confining their physics to the mysteries of household gadgets. As has been observed, one might even regard those who invoke the devil in expletives when things go wrong as "theologians" of a sort. But it should be our aim in this book to be more than philosophers of sorts, whose ideas are piecemeal and implicit.

Implicit beliefs have a startling character when put into words. It has been observed that it is a unique privilege of citizens of the United States to drive their automobiles to the office where they get unemployment benefits. Stated explicitly, this says that Americans look upon automobiles as personal necessities in the same class as food and shelter. Implicit philosophies, being uncritical and unvoiced, are typically piecemeal, disorganized, and full of inconsistencies. They are often hybrid mixtures of elements from different official philosophies. John L. Childs (5, pp. 49-50) calls attention to the unconscious influence on our thinking of early Greek philosophers. Many unvoiced assumptions of our thinking reflect the views of Socrates, Plato, and Aristotle. The very words we use are imbued with unconscious assumptions. For instance, we speak of the "weight" of a physical object as though weight belonged to it as an absolute and intrinsic property. The truth is (as Newton discovered) that every object owes its weight to other objects around it. Indeed, this relativism—this reference of everything to things beyond it—is so universal that wisdom is rapidly taking the form of defining each thing in terms of something else! A philosophy of language is now emerging, having as one of its aims the exposure of hidden meanings lurking in the structure of language. This enterprise is becoming one of the new byways of educational thought (see section F, this chapter).

We should not conclude that the unschooled philosophy of the layman is necessarily unsound. There is at least one reason why it may be more trustworthy than the views of professional philosophers. A familiar aim of philosophers and scientists is to discover a few simple principles which will explain numerous if not all things. Henri Poincaré somewhere writes that the belief that ultimate truth is simple has its roots in our unconscious suspicion that the human mind is simple, and hence that the world must be reduced to simplicities if it is to be understood at all.

William James declared that philosophers try to reduce all phenomena to one principle because it takes great ingenuity to do this, and hence gives them the comfortable assurance that they are earning their salaries! Consider now the educator who is well aware of the complexities of education but innocent of philosophy. In seeking a total view of education he may mix up different schools of thought, but he comes out with a better view of his profession than any one philosophy would give. For reality is not simple. It conceals unknown abysses and tides. A single philosophy covers all experience in somewhat the same inadequate fashion as a short blanket covers a sleeper on a cold night—pulling the blanket over the head exposes the feet, and vice versa.

2. Ideas and Destiny

Whether technical or casual, one's philosophy of life is important—important even because it reflects feelings and attitudes as well as conscious ideas. Many if not most ideas are powerful agents in human affairs. If beliefs have any bearing on action they tend, as it were, to leave the head and enter the hands. Ideas are sometimes viewed as purely cognitive, and lacking in urgency or power. This view supposes that the energy which sustains action comes from the hormic forces of the organism—the emotions, appetites, drives, ambitions, and so on. Assuming this to be true for the sake of argument, ideas would still play an important role in conduct. They exert *directive* influences on behavior, if not *urgent* ones. Felt hunger may drive a man to seek food but his ideas direct him in the search for it, especially when means-end habits fail in the situation. The immense toil of the pyramids of Egypt manifests the directive power of ideas. The ideas of Christ turned the tides of history. When Bismarck declared, "Might makes right," this also expressed the power, not of might alone, but of an idea.

Error, of course, may guide action as much as truth does. The idea of world conquest in the mind of a megalomaniac may create havoc on a world-wide scale. Addison W. Moore writes: "If a madman thinks you are his enemy and therefore to be destroyed, you will scarcely feel safe on being told that you are 'really' not his enemy and that his idea is false" (13, p. 95).

⚡ C. The Current Ferment in Educational Thought

Ideas, whether sane or mad, may direct the course of destiny. But in view of current turmoil in educational thought, what guiding ideas should we select? We must, first of all, avoid deception by the mere appearance of agreement in answering this question.

1. Specious Agreements

Education, like other activities, seeks to discover valid objectives. There is a deceptive appearance of agreement when the aims of education of various authorities are listed. If you say, "The aim of education is to develop a sound mind and character in a sound body," you will at once win the assent of most hearers. This ideal of sound minds in sound bodies occurs in the first sentence of John Locke's classic *Some Thoughts Concerning Education* (1693). It has served as the slogan for educational solidarity ever since!

Sidney Hook notes that, despite apparent agreement about the aims of education, controversy continues unabated, and even grows more bitter (11, pp. 1-14). Hook finds explanations for the paradox of continued disputes in spite of verbal agreements. Educational aims, like moral aims, are *plural,* and they may conflict with each other or even with themselves in different situations. Thus, when a choice has to be made between an individual and a group need, values will be weighed differently by different people. Again, people may agree about a word but the word may have different meanings for different individuals. Stuart Chase (4) wrote an entire volume on such spurious agreements where there are differences of belief. Hook proposes that *practice* is the best criterion for deciding whether or not people mean the same thing. We mean the same thing when we agree to the same program of behavior or action in a given situation. (Words given as synonyms in the dictionary may have similar meanings in one context, opposed meanings in another. Thus, the terms *vision* and *sight* mean the same thing in psychology. But to describe a young lady as a "vision" is quite unlike describing her as a "sight.")

2. The Battle of Ideologies in Education

John S. Brubacher (3, pp. 4-7) notes that before the twentieth century, Plato (in his *Republic*) produced the only notable philosophy of education. But the twentieth century has produced a welter of conflicting publications on education. Brubacher attributes this ferment of ideas to various causes. The rise of progressive education alone would account for much of the dialectical warfare among educators. In addition, the twentieth century is characterized by political and economic strife. The quarrel of democratic with fascistic and communistic ideologies still engulfs the world with patriotic and bloody fervor. Within the nation, winds of doctrine produce ceaseless turmoil: federal or state paternalism versus rugged individualism, moral integrity versus corruption, national economic recovery sought through individual extravagance, the dual worship of God and of Mammon. No wonder our "moral texture" is under strain. At this juncture, men turn to the sour bread of philosophy for sustenance. And philosophy is really no more than devotion to serious thought. But, as C. I. Lewis noted, man thinks, not by preference, but only as a last resort!

D. Values of Philosophy in Education

Philosophers are rather notorious for their persistent disagreements. Their attempts to answer questions about reality and how we should live in it appear merely to stir up more questions. What, then, is the profit of trying to answer "ultimate" questions about things which have baffled the best minds? No school of thought, although some have sought to do so, has produced a philosophy that ends all philosophizing. If the pronouncements of philosophers in general are contradictory and therefore uncertain, will not education based on philosophy be equally uncertain? We shall here note several gains to be expected from philosophizing about education.

1. Certain *Versus* Probable Knowledge

Philosophy, as Neitzsche observed, is man's bad conscience—it is the gadfly which drives men to think. Strangely enough, the history of thought shows that progress dispels about as many certainties as it produces. Scientists of the past viewed the laws of nature as absolutely specific, but now these laws are regarded as having only statistical certainty, as in

Heisenberg's "principle of indeterminacy" in physics. If this is the state of affairs in the exact sciences how can one reasonably expect certainties of an absolute sort in the political, economic, moral, and educational aspects of life?

Ross L. Finney (7, pp. 1-28) points out the extent to which we have to rely on guesswork. We cannot escape this in most practical phases of life any more than in philosophy. We are not absolutely certain about how we should nurture the young, budget expenses, make investments, arrive at moral decisions and religious commitments. The "principle of indeterminacy" also holds sway in the realm of government. Such problems as taxation, immigration, tariffs, penal laws, and international treaties are one and all subject to action in the light of probable conclusions derived from "facts" no less probable. In education, as in the other major areas of practical life, we *must* act, and if perfect knowledge is not available we must act in the light of probabilities. On a dark night, weak illumination is better than none. We do not reject meteorology because it often results in unreliable weather predictions.

But probable conclusions have to be questioned in education as much as elsewhere. Many teachers become so absorbed in routine duties that thought about their mission becomes casual and piecemeal or may vanish entirely. When this occurs, as Sidney Hook notes (11, Preface, p. xi), education yields to various and clamorous demands from without —the inertia of tradition, the insistent demands of pressure groups, the false economy which insists that everything, including education, should pay for itself. Even colleges may continue certain courses because the professors concerned can teach nothing else!

However uncertain they may be, advances in education are usually reactions against existing evils. Rousseau's stress on a "return to nature" in education was a wholesome revolt against the artificial and tyrannical formalism which beset education in his day. Current pupil-centered education is a similar revolt against rote book learning in traditional schools. The role of sane feelings is no less than the role of sane ideas in educational reform. The large-hearted Pestalozzi undertook his first ventures in education out of pity for destitute children. Maria Montessori did her first work to alleviate the drab lives of the mentally deficient in her day. The ancient doctrine of mental faculties, which ruled education for centuries, was full of errors. But, thanks to the freedom to criticize nonsense, discussion of the doctrine of faculties (as we will see in Chapter 5) led to important research concerning primary mental abilities, the possibility of their training, and the question of transfer of training. These are samples of the gains to be expected from the philosopher's habit of questioning answers.

2. Free Inquiry in Democracies

We have now to consider our second justification of philosophy in education, namely, its indispensable role in a political democracy. It supplies the main root which nourishes a liberal education in a liberal democracy. The original conception of a liberal education was that of an education worthy of a free man. This version of liberal education, according to Benjamin F. Wright (15, pp. 13-14), is still the best. It takes the words "free man" in the sense of one who is politically free, not necessarily free from the need of earning a livelihood. In its original Greek usage the phrase "liberal education" had reference to the education of the gentleman who, since he was free from economic needs, had no use for vocational training.

The two meanings of a liberal education (a) for the politically free man, and (b) for the "gentleman" are not mutually contradictory. We can accept both as essential aims of a liberal education. The citizen of a genuine democracy is politically free whether or not he earns his own living and hence needs cultural training which preserves and is preserved by political freedom. The fact that a man works for his living is no reason for giving him only vocational training, like that accorded by ancient Greeks to their slaves. The laborer in a democracy is given periods of leisure and needs the cultural training presumed to make possible the enjoyment of leisure.

But the chief justification of liberal education which approaches all knowledge critically is that it preserves democracy. James Madison held that a representative government presupposes: (a) diversity of opinion, and (b) the right to express opinions. Diversity of opinion and its free expression are similarly necessary for a democratic education. Every teacher is an entrepreneur in philosophy, taking the risks of applying new ideas to education. To realize the validity of Madison's view, one has only to notice what happens to education when free inquiry is suppressed. Germany under Nazi rule will serve as an instance, although fascist Italy and communistic Russia would do about as well. Communism illustrates the principle that in dictatorships schools will be ruled by ideologies whether the citizens like them or not.

It is significant that no one school of philosophy is dominant in a democracy. A single national philosophy would be as tragic as a single political party. No one philosophy is dominant in France, not even the existentialism of Sartre, nor the old positivism of August Comte, nor neopositivism. The same is true in America where winds of doctrine blow freely. These situations in France and America contrast sharply, for instance, with the official dialectical materialism, conditioned-reflex psychology, and Michurinian genetics of Russia.

Liberal education, like liberal democracy, depends on a system of checks and balances between conflicting convictions. If it were not for the restraints exercised by essentialists in education, progressives intoxicated by the doctrine of individual differences might tend to forget the common humanity present in all pupils, and hence overlook the common essentials of training needed by them. On the other hand, if it were not for the progressives in education striving to extend the curriculum to the diverse practical interests of students, the essentialists might establish in the schools a curricular diet as restricted as the trivium of scholastic times. If it were not for the pragmatists and realists, idealists might make education a preoccupation with eternal aims and "realities" lying quite beyond the mundane world. But thanks to the idealists, pragmatists are not allowed to turn education into mere training for vocational survival without giving the pupil convincing reasons why he should wish to survive.

It is therefore a healthy sign that criticism is rampant in education at the present time. This ferment of criticism has its storm center in philosophical and religious questions about education. Sidney Hook writes:

American philosophers, until now largely indifferent to educational issues, have been rediscovering the truth of John Dewey's claim that philosophy in the largest sense is a "general theory of education" (11, Preface, p. x).

⑂ E. Traditional Problems of Philosophy

Philosophy is the basis for our examination of education. In setting forth the prior analysis of philosophy we will move from the general to the specific. The present section accordingly sketches the most generic features of traditional systems of Western philosophy. In the chapters to follow we shall first tease out the main traits of special schools of philosophy and then sketch the personal convictions of individual thinkers whose educational ideas are under scrutiny.

Philosophers of the past endeavored to integrate all human knowledge and thus erect a systematic view of the nature of the universe and the place of gods and men in it. The human experience which philosophy embraced included not merely what is known but what is felt and done; not merely what exists but what could and what should exist. The philosopher examined the facts, principles, and hypotheses of all special fields of investigation. In fact, the philosophy of ancient Greece included all special branches of knowledge which broke away one by one to become such separate fields as physics, mathematics, and psychology. These special fields are now so numerous and full of content that philosophers have given up the hope of being encyclopedists and storming the heights of Mount Parnassus. They now address themselves to areas and problems of narrower scope which are still quite enough to tax genius and fortitude to the utmost. But the current problems of philosophers still relate to the three great areas of inquiry established by traditional philosophy.

1. Three Fields of Inquiry

a. METAPHYSICS. This concerns problems of the nature of reality, and of man's place in it. What is matter in its essence, and how does it form the vast material cosmos, ordered in time and place (cosmology)? What is the essential nature of the mind or soul? What about the existence and nature of God? What does it mean to exist—what is the criterion of existing (ontology)? What are the ultimate causes of things being what they are (causality)?

b. EPISTEMOLOGY. Epistemology has to do with the problem of knowledge. Grant, for the sake of argument, that we have knowledge, how is this possible? What does knowledge mean? Can all knowledge be traced to the great gateways of the senses, to the senses plus the activity of reason, or to reason alone? Do feelings render wordless but true knowledge? Does true knowledge ever come in the form of immediate intuitions, so often viewed with fear and awe as the special gift of the female mind?

c. AXIOLOGY. This branch of philosophy is concerned with the problems of *value*. There are two main traditional fields of value inquiry: *ethics*, which is concerned with the problems of good and evil, right and wrong, and their bearing on moral conduct; and *aesthetics*, the problem of beauty and ugliness. Axiology is extended to include inquiry about values of any kind whatever, such as religious, social, or economic values.

The three classic problems of philosophers, stated baldly as they are above, appear all too simple, and as barren as the Nubian Desert. But we shall see them taking on bewildering complexities in later chapters. For one thing, we shall learn that the three problems do not exist in isolation but have tangled relations with each other. Thus, the nature of reality (metaphysics) is not merely "discovered," but is to a degree "made" by man, and how he makes or remakes it will depend on his values (axiology). Further, the theory of knowledge accepted as valid depends on the nature of the realities and values which that theory of knowledge is to illuminate. Already we encounter one of the puzzling but charming dilemmas of philosophers: We must select a reliable method of inquiry before we can explore reality, but we must know what reality is like in order to select a suitable method of inquiry! Undaunted, the philosopher wrestles with both problems simultaneously, beginning with "trial and error," and arriving by a series of approximations at a theory of reality and a theory of knowledge which suit each other. In this intellectual wrestling match no holds are barred!

Conflicting systems of philosophy have arisen from different initial choices among the ways of knowing. It will be well to have in advance some ideas about the main ways in which knowledge could be related to the things known. We shall distinguish six theories in the field of epistemology, again stated rather baldly.

2. Six Theories of Knowledge

a. THE REVELATION THEORY. This view holds that the final test of the truth of assertions is their consonance with the revelations of authority. We recognize this as one of the views, but not the only one, favored in religious thoughts (Chapter 2). However, weight of authority has played its part in areas other than religion. Aristotle's utterances, for instance, were depended upon for centuries as the *sine qua non* of wisdom. It is said that even scholars of Galileo's time refused to look through the telescope because Aristotle had not indicated this as permissible!

b. THE COHERENCE THEORY. This theory says that a statement is true if it is consistent with other statements accepted as true. Statements, of course, must be "true" to the particulars to which they refer, just as revelations accepted as valid in religion are not necessarily extended to other areas of belief. But on the hypothesis that the entire universe expresses a single unified and rationally consistent order, each statement accepted as true must be congruent with *all* other statements accepted as true. Thus, in a system of geometry all propositions are congruent with all other statements accepted as true in that geometry. But geometers do not usually assume that such congruence is to be found everywhere outside of geometry, nor even as between different systems of geometry. Certain idealists in philosophy, however, as we shall see in Book III, have held to the view that the whole universe is a perfect façade of reason in which all particular truths are united into one congruent whole.

c. THE PRESENTATIVE THEORY. This view holds that reality as presented to the mind in perception is known directly and without alteration. Errors of perception occur, but further observation is able to detect and explain them. This view is favored by realists, specifically the neorealists, whom we shall discuss in Book IV. The presentative view is typical in common-sense thinking; although common sense, with admirable impartiality, may adopt all six of our theories of knowledge as convenience requires. The presentative theory regards such traits as the colors, shapes, and odors of objects which appear to our senses as true objective characteristics of the objects, except for the occurrence of detectable errors.

d. THE REPRESENTATIVE THEORY. This view, again favored by certain realists, holds that our perceptions of objects are not identical with them. This differs from the presentative view sketched above which goes the length of saying that when we perceive truly, our perception is identical with the object perceived. This implies that the object perceived literally enters the mind which perceives it—a rather startling conclusion. The representative realist tries to be more cautious on this point. What we see when we look at a tree is only its image. The tree cannot be identical with this image. The image is in one's mind, and the mind is somehow located in the brain; if the tree is fifty feet high there is not room enough in one's brain to accommodate it. Although the representative realist does not identify the perception with the object, he believes that the perception usually *represents* the object with accuracy. The image is usually a reliable replica of the object. Again, we consider that the tree continues to exist whether or not we are seeing it.

e. THE PRAGMATIC THEORY. This view holds that statements are true if they work successfully in practice. If an idea or principle is effective in organizing knowledge or in the practical affairs of life then it is true. The belief of the pragmatist that the function of knowledge is to guide thought and action successfully is at the root of the important development in American education known as the progressive movement. This is the view to be considered in Book V, dealing with pragmatic philosophy, the instrumentalism of John Dewey, and their influences on education.

f. THE INTUITION THEORY. This view, which hardly concerns us in this book, varies so much in its definition that it sometimes becomes identical with some of the other theories sketched above. At one extreme, intuition refers to a mysterious and immediate inner source of knowledge apart from both perceptual observation and reasoning. In this sense intuitionism is encountered in some philosophies (e.g., neo-Platonism and Bergsonism), in religion, philosophic spiritualism, and in the twilight areas of mysticism in general. At the other extreme the term intuition has been used to designate generally accredited and immediate ways of knowing, such as in immediate sensation, or the immediate awareness we may have of some self-evident or axiomatic truth. Thus Aristotle's principle in logic that any object A cannot at the same time be *not-A* is said by some to rest on an immediate intuition. It does not arise from proof because all proof presupposes it. A related concept denoted by the term "insight" occurs in the literature of modern gestalt psychology.

The sketch given above of the classical problems of philosophers is far too simple for current times. Philosophers sometimes unite in "schools" in defending their ideas against other schools, while continuing their genial disagreements with each other, with each Horatio defending his own bridge. This marked individuality of philosophers gives the reason for devoting this book, not so much to the educational philosophy of each school, but to representative philosophers who belong, with many qualifications, to certain schools. Theodore M. Greene (9, pp. 1-45) may serve as an instance of the "rugged individualism" of American philosophers. Greene is essentially an idealist in philosophy but a Christian in religion. He devotes considerable space to the matter of his agreements and disagreements with other idealists, and this is truly necessary in order to understand his philosophy of education (10, pp. 93-107).

☿ F. Current Trends in Philosophical and Educational Thought

Moving ahead to current times we still find philosophers engaged with the basic problems previously noted, but they follow narrower and less ambitious paths. This book is concerned with traditional philosophies which are still significant in theory and educational practice. That this is the case is made amply evident in the last chapter of this book (Chapter 18) which analyzes the vast ferment in current educational thought. As for the ultracurrent interests of philosophers, which are also being applied to education, brief notes are here offered for the guidance of readers wishing to press inquiry beyond the limits of this book.

For a review of current trends in philosophy the symposium edited by Vergilius Ferm (6, Part II), or the recent revision of Benjamin A. G. Fuller's work (8, Part II), and other relevant works may prepare the student for an examination of newer and more tentative approaches to philosophy of education. The diverse trends in present educational philosophy are set forth in a number of compact sources. The Fifty-Fourth Yearbook of the National Society for the Study of Education, published in 1955 (10), contains contributions reminiscent of earlier schools (realism, Thomism, idealism, pragmatism, Marxism) and adds to these the ideas of such newcomers as existentialists, logical empiricists, and semanticists. Another anthology, published in 1958 (14), does not set forth systems of educational philosophy but examines education in the light of contemporary analytical thought in philosophy. The most extensive current compendium, the Year Book of Education of 1957 (1), has forty-four contributors, representing many nations of the world. Only the first two sections of the book consider philosophical questions, the remaining four sections dealing with such practical matters as national systems of education, historical examples of schools, experimental institutions, and the teaching of philosophy of education.

It should be noted that one tendency in current philosophy is to turn away from questions about the nature of being and to explore more fully the nature of inquiry. To this end logical positivists and empiricists and philosophers of language in general, although at odds regarding many issues, are centering attention on the role of language in thinking, the communication of thought, and the verifiability of propositions. Attacks are being centered on such problems as: (a) the unwitting meanings and assumptions ingrained in words, their syntactical union in sentences, and in the structure of grammar in general; (b) vagueness, tautology, and contradiction in language, masking under a false façade of clarity and cogency; (c) the linguistic requirements which must be met so that assertions may be verified empirically (logical positivists).

Although setting aside for the time being the old problems of the nature of being, there is hope that, equipped with the results of this analysis of language, we may attack earlier metaphysical questions with more success. Max Black (2) considers that linguistic analysis promises better if not conclusive answers to some age-old problems, such as the free-will controversy, the problem of the reality of time, the possibility of knowledge of other minds, the physical world, the future, and the solution of certain paradoxes of skepticism. Dr. Black applies his ideas to education considered as art and as discipline (14).

The bearing of these linguistic studies on education is clear. Essentialists (see Chapters 3 and 4) hold that the chief aims of education are to develop the capacities to think, read, listen, write, and speak. Other theories of education would not reject these aims, but would make qualifications regarding *how* the capacity to think is developed, and *what* the subjects of reading, listening, writing, and speaking should be. It should be noted that all of these skills, with the possible exception of thinking, are linguistic activities. But the relation of language to thought is so intimate that one might agree with Emerson's assertion that no belief is clearly understood until it is adequately stated. At any rate, it would be difficult for the educator to try to develop skill in thinking in isolation from linguistic skill. We should acclaim the efforts of the philosophers of language to further the use of language to *express* thought and not to *conceal* it, as Talleyrand declared was the case in international politics.

⍗ G. Prelude to Future Chapters

The sort of explorations to which future chapters invite us is now fairly clear. We shall take up, one at a time, the main philosophies which have been offered as the foundations of education. The first of these, to which we accord the distinction of being the first in time for our culture, is religion. The Christian religion is hardly a philosophy in the strict sense of the word, although it lays claim to an organized set of doctrines subject to rational and empirical criticisms and defenses. For the great mass of

Christian laymen, Christianity is not a matter of systematic deductions from evidences—it involves *faith* based on "evidences of things unseen," having as much to do with ways of living as with ways of knowing. In this sense religion has mightily influenced the history of man, including the development of education.

But education has been secularized in most areas of the Christian world. When this occurred, the winds of philsophical speculation began to blow in earnest over the fields of education. The common faith and appreciation derived from religion gave way to searching inquiry with its "critical appreciations," which are perhaps one part appreciation and nine parts criticism. In this way, man got rid of blind faith by replacing it with enlightened doubts.

References

1. Bereday, George Z. F., and Joseph A. Lauwerys (eds.). *Education and Philosophy,* The Yearbook of Education. Yonkers, N. Y.: World Book Co., 1957.
2. Black, Max. *Language and Philosophy, Studies in Method.* Ithaca, N. Y.: Cornell University Press, 1949.
3. Brubacher, John S. "The Challenge to Philosophize about Education." *Modern Philosophies and Education* (Part I, N. B. Henry, ed.). Chicago: University of Chicago Press, 1955.
4. Chase, Stuart. *The Tyranny of Words.* New York: Harcourt, Brace, 1938.
5. Childs, John L. *Education and the Philosophy of Experimentalism.* New York: Century, 1931.
6. Ferm, Vergilius (ed.). *History of Philosophical Systems.* New York: Philosophical Library, 1950.
7. Finney, Ross L. *A Sociological Philosophy of Education.* New York: Macmillan, 1928.
8. Fuller, Benjamin A. G. *A History of Philosophy* (3rd ed. revised by S. M. McMurrin). New York: Holt, 1955.
9. Greene, Theodore M. *Liberal Education Reconsidered.* Cambridge, Mass.: Harvard University Press, 1953.
10. Henry, Nelson B. (ed.). *Modern Philosophies and Education,* Part I, Fifty-fourth Yearbook of N.S.S.E. Chicago: University of Chicago Press, 1955.
11. Hook, Sidney. *Education for Modern Man.* New York: Dial Press, 1946.
12. Meiklejohn, Alexander. *Education Between Two Worlds.* New York: Harper, 1942.
13. Moore, Addison W. *Pragmatism and its Critics.* Chicago: University of Chicago Press, 1910.
14. Scheffler, Israel (ed.). *Philosophy and Education.* New York: Allyn and Bacon, 1958.
15. Wright, Benjamin F. "The Independent College of the Future." *Decade of Decision for Higher Education.* Fifth Annual Barnard Forum, New York: Barnard Forum Office, 1953.

⍗ *chapter 2*

FROM CHURCH TO STATE IN EDUCATION

Etymologically, the word *philosophy* means "the love of wisdom." **It** should be noticed that philosophy in this generic sense is not coldly intellectual—it is still moved by love. The aphorism that "The love of God is the beginning of wisdom" shows that religion stands close to philosophy, sharing with it the master motive of the love of wisdom. Philosophy, like religion, has had its martyrs, such as Socrates and Bruno.

This chapter renders an account of the shift from church to state in the guidance of education. This account will also introduce us to the shift from religion to philosophy as a guide in education. These transitions will be discussed under seven headings, as follows:

A. The Main Doctrines of Christianity
B. Early Dominance of the Church in Education
C. The Legal Secularization of Education
D. Religion as Cultural Subject Matter
E. Current Issues in Religious Education
F. Public Support of Religious Instruction
G. Education and the State

⍗ **A. The Main Doctrines of Christianity**

Christianity shares with Buddhism the tendency to great variation in form. The essential doctrines of Christianity have varied with time and locality. To sketch these variations in full would be a task of monumental proportions. With respect to ritual alone there is on the one hand the great elaboration characteristic of the Greek and Roman churches and on the other hand the simple worship of the Quakers. These prolific variations in doctrine and the sectarian prejudices which sustained them became, as we shall see, one of the causes of the alienation of religious instruction from the public schools in America.

If we ask the fundamental questions of philosophers the essential beliefs of Christianity will stand out in sharper relief. Religious attitudes and beliefs have much in common with idealistic philosophy, and their views on education show harmony. Our later more exhaustive study of idealism and its application to education (Book III) will serve as an adjunct to the present chapter on religion. Since education has been secularized in American education, our interest in religion as the basis of education is more historical than systematic.

We shall attempt to tease out the most common answers which Christianity offers to the philosopher's questions.

1. Metaphysics

The account of creation given in the Bible (in the opening chapters of Genesis) makes it clear that: (a) the universe originated from God as the first and sole cause, (b) that God was real before the universe existed as an orderly cosmos, (c) that the creation of man was the final and most important step in creation, and (d) that man was made in God's image, i.e., as a spiritual being. It is not made clear whether God created the cosmos out of a "waste" or "void" which existed with God before creation, or whether these words are intended to convey the idea of nothingness. The word "waste" suggests a preexisting stuff (matter) having an existence of its own, like the "primal gas" or nebula from which certain astronomical theories derive the cosmos.

The conceptions of the nature of God and of man's relations to Him are rather complex, but conform essentially to the analogy of the relations of a father to his children. In the Gospel of St. John we encounter the Platonic idea that God is reason. But the God of Christianity is not the pure element of reason in the universe as held by certain idealistic philosophers. He is the God of Abraham and Jacob. He is holy but does not remain aloof from man. God loves man and seeks man's love. Man is a sinner, fallen from grace. The only hope for man and his fallen world is to restore contact with and allegiance to the Father. God amply provided for man's regeneration, for the return of the prodigal to His boundless loving-kindness. Another metaphysical doctrine of Christianity is that the spirit (soul) is distinct from the body and will survive death without loss of individuality.

2. Epistemology

A common misconception of the Christian religion is the notion that its sole avenues to knowledge are mystical revelation and authoritative pronouncements. No doubt such revelations and pronouncements exist, but many of the moral pronouncements, at least, are verifiable in individual experience. In fact, the average layman has to yield to authority in science far more than he does in religion. For example, we have to accept it on the authority of physicists that light travels at the incredible speed of about 186,300 miles per second. Christian morality, on the other hand, contains injunctions which even the most ignorant can verify in daily life. This will appear more fully when we come to the question of Christian morality.

As far as authority per se is concerned, Jesus occupies a preeminent position. Christ is the accredited revealer of such things as the nature of God, God's relations to man, the nature of man, and the ideals of conduct. Some stress the authority of Jesus so much that even portions of the New Testament are rejected on the ground that they do not specifically concern the teachings of Jesus. A second and more liberal view is to accept the entire New Testament as religious authority. A third view is to accept the New Testament and add to it the decisions of certain councils and formal dogmas of the church. But the church cannot alter the basic teachings of Christ—it can only interpret them in the light of well-considered judgment.

3. Christian Ethics

The basic questions of philosophers are related to each other, and cannot be answered in isolation. Thus, the verities about nature and human nature (metaphysics) determine in part what rules of conduct should be observed (ethics). The Christian view that man is created by God and in God's image but still with an individual autonomy or will of his own has the utmost import for conduct. This view makes the individual precious because he is in essence a spirit or soul, and not a mere thing.

Where materialistic "dialectic" gains ascendancy, as in communist Russia, there is inevitably the tendency to regard the individual as the property or chattel of the state. As materialistic ideology spreads, human individuality becomes like that of physical objects, which are sorted and summed up in inventories. At this level "individuality" is established by any *individual difference,* which billiard balls possess in the same way as human beings. No matter how much alike the balls may be, they are "individuals" because there are still two of them.

In the view of Christianity and of democratic states, the individuality of a person derives, not alone from his occupancy of a separate pair of shoes, or from his specific name, traits, and social position, but includes the idea that he is a *creative* and *purposive* being. *Men are capable of free choice and action* whether or not they are accorded the right to such action. If the individual is accorded liberty, as he is both by Christianity and by democratic philosophy, he now becomes *responsible* for his behavior. These are the basic tenets of Christian ethics.

The Christian view of human personality has had the most profound effects on human history. Since our major interest is in education we may take as our sole illustrative case the effect of Christianity on the status of children. Ancient historians have strangely neglected the child. One might conclude that there were no children, so seldom are they mentioned. A few modern historians (A. F. Chamberlain, B. Kidd, G. H. Payne) have given attention to the history of the child as part of human history in general. The story they tell is largely one of appalling neglect and cruelty.

Infanticide was not confined to ancient Sparta but existed in the nineteenth century in such non-Christian countries as India and China. Ancient Romans and Gauls had the right to sell their children. Although this, at least, has its counterpart in child slavery during industrial expansion in our own land, the status of the child of today is vastly better in Christian lands than in many others. Prophets preceding Jesus, notably Isaiah, revered children; and the exaltation of childhood by Jesus and the Christian church in general is well known. On the other hand it is true that some branches of the Christian church, e.g., Calvinism, viewed children as primordial sinners, and the punishments used to correct the child were often very inhumane.

▽ B. Early Dominance of the Church in Education

Despite persecution, or because of it, by the end of the first century A.D. Christianity had spread throughout the vast Roman empire. Within three hundred years it became the official religion under Constantine I. A new culture, that of Christianity, was taking shape in the monasteries, and classic learning became less and less important. During the Middle Ages education centered in universities under the auspices of the great cathedrals. Grammar schools were fostered by monasteries and by parish priests. The Reformation gave new impetus to education, especially at the elementary levels.

1. The American Colonies

It was natural for the colonists to put education in the hands of the church, as was the practice in their former homelands. The minister in each community usually had the best education, had the most leisure, and hence often became the local teacher. The Bible and the Shorter Catechism served as the "core" curriculum. Massachusetts created the first American tax-supported schools in 1647.

2. Sectarian Quarrels in the Colonies

Although the search for religious freedom was one of the chief causes which brought colonists to America, colonial religious history is one of excessive bigotry and intolerance. Massachusetts especially was the storm center of religious strife. In 1800 Massachusetts had only eight different religious sects. By 1936 there were fifty-six denominations in this state (2, p. 18). Even the origin of some New England states is attributed to quarrels about religion in Massachusetts.

⚥ C. The Legal Secularization of Education

Alexander Meiklejohn observed that the shift from church to state in the control of education was made with the consent, even with the initiative, of churches themselves (6, p. 7). Massachusetts enacted the first law concerning religious instruction in the schools in 1826-1827. This law was as follows: "The school committee shall never direct to be purchased or used in any of the town schools, any books which are calculated to favor the tenets of any particular sect of Christians" (2, p. 29).

It is clear that this ban was against sectarian instruction in the schools, not against religious instruction as such. Horace Mann was intrusted with the task of administering the new law. Mann did not seek to exclude religious teaching in the schools, but only sectarian religion. He refused petitions to use books which were flagrantly sectarian, and became a much maligned and unpopular man as a consequence. Other states followed Massachusetts in passing laws against sectarian religion in the schools. The number of such states had reached a total of about forty in the year 1950.

The Massachusetts law of 1826-1827 was enacted on the assumption that the question of religious instruction was under the jurisdiction of the states. This interpretation was regarded as validated by the First and Tenth Amendments to the Constitution, both declared in force in 1791. The Fourteenth Amendment of 1868 also concerns the question of the right of states to interfere with the "privileges or immunities of citizens," but we confine our attention to the First and Tenth Amendments.

The First Amendment reads: "Congress shall make no law respecting an establishment of religion, or prohibiting the free exercise thereof; or abridging the freedom of speech, or of the press; or the right of the people peaceably to assemble, and to petition the Government for a redress of grievances."

The meaning of the phrase "establishment of religion" soon became an issue. Religious groups contended that Congress was forbidden the right to establish any *one* sectarian faith. James Madison agreed to this version of the Amendment. Thomas Jefferson interpreted the Amendment as delegating prescriptions regarding religion to the states. The Tenth Amendment supports Jefferson's version of the intent of the First Amendment. The Tenth Amendment reads: "The powers not delegated to the United States by the Constitution, nor prohibited by it to the states, are reserved to the states respectively, or to the people."

The famous Champaign, Illinois, case of 1948 once more made the issue of religious instruction in the schools a national one. Clyde L. Hay (2, pp. 54 ff.) describes the incidents at Champaign as follows: Religious weekday classes had been held in the schools of Champaign since 1940. Catholics, Protestants, and Jews cooperated with school authorities in this work. The classes were conducted in public school buildings, using school facilities, and utilizing "released time" from other academic work. No public expense was incurred for books, materials, and teachers. Attendance was wholly voluntary. The pupils, however, were divided into sectarian classes instructed by sectarian teachers.

Mrs. Vashti McCollom appealed to the courts to stop this practice on the ground that her son, who did not attend the religious classes, suffered criticism and embarrassment on that account. The lower courts and the Illinois Supreme Court decided against Mrs. McCollom. The case was appealed to the U. S. Supreme Court. The Justices rendered a decision of eight to one in favor of Mrs. McCollom, with Justice Reed dissenting.

The action of the Supreme Court gave rise to polemical disputes on a national scale. It is usually conceded that the Justices of the Supreme Court had some justification for their decision. Many approve the condemnation of the sectarian nature of religious instruction as it was given at Champaign, despite the seeming cooperation of Catholics, Protestants, and Jews. Others regret this interference with the attempt of antagonistic religious groups to cooperate, even though it was no more than an armed truce.

⚐ D. Religion as Cultural Subject Matter

It must not be supposed that mere sectarian jealousies are always at the root of quarrels concerning religious education. There are some partisans to the dispute who are concerned with the salvation of education rather than of either religion or atheism. Sidney Hook (3, pp. 108-110) contends that those who wish to establish religious and theological studies in the schools desire to convert the student, to induce belief, to teach the Bible as revealed truth, not as truth derived from inquiry and free criticism. Hook charges that this runs counter to the method of critical inquiry followed by all other studies in the curriculum. To require or even give courses aiming at religious indoctrination would revive the dangerous religious controversies of the past.

Few educators would challenge the value of the study of religion as subject matter. Sidney Hook objects to religious indoctrination but approves exploration of the cultural and explanatory value of religious history (3, p. 107). Jacques Maritain declares that theology is necessary for the understanding of numerous writers (5, p. 74). He submits a sample list of over a score of famous authors including even Karl Marx!

Indeed, so many subjects require the study of religion for their complete grasp that it appears impossible to separate the secular from the religious in education. Mr. Justice Jackson, in a supplementary opinion filed in the Champaign case (2, p. 97) suggested that such subjects as mathematics and physics could be "secularized," but an attempt to do this with other subjects would result in their serious emasculation. We could not achieve an adequate study of music without including sacred music, of architecture without cathedrals, of paintings excluding those with religious themes, of English literature without the Bible. To forbid instruction about religion in the schools would render a decision in favor of paganism in the study of cultural development.

▽ E. Current Issues in Religious Education

The Champaign incident and decision have not ended attempts to find ways of introducing religious instruction in the schools. Two major aims of such attempts may be distinguished.

1. Sectarian Education

The most uncompromising religionists hope to establish religious instruction and indoctrination in the public schools along sectarian lines. To accomplish this impartially the system used at Champaign or some variation of it is proposed. That is, various denominations, basically Jews, Protestants, and Catholics, would be represented. The parents would have the option of deciding which group, if any, their children would be required to attend. This position rejects two arguments against religion in the schools which were involved in the Champaign case: (a) Excluding religious instruction from the schools because it might lead to "isolation" and "embarrassment" of the irreligious is at once trivial as an argument and exalts the comfort of an atheistic minority above the will of a majority who represent our cultural tradition. (What about religious people being "embarrassed" by their irreligious neighbors? Would we take a thief seriously who complained that honest men "embarrassed" him? To feel embarrassed by others is a private right and luxury, but can always remain mutual. To make a legal issue about harmless or even beneficent beliefs and practices which are not mandatory is an ill omen in a democracy.) (b) Furthermore, the Champaign plan did not abrogate the constitutional proscription against establishing *a* religion in the schools since three basic faiths were represented and attendance was voluntary. Sectarian religion is still legal in private and parochial schools. Many thus consider it an unjust penalty to exclude religious study from public schools. Another sore point is the claim sometimes made by parochial schools to public financial support. This claim is vigorously opposed by denominations having no religious schools or only a few of them.

2. Interdenominational Education

The moderate wing of religionists aims to tease out the common elements of religious faith and culture. These essentials are proposed as the core of religious instruction, to be embodied (a) in special courses in religion, or (b) in other courses of instruction to which they are relevant. The ideas of this rather ill-defined group of moderates may be illustrated by two studies sponsored by the American Council on Education. The first study (7) gives the opinions of a group of educators representing our three major faiths from both private and public schools, and from elementary, secondary, and higher levels. This group did not favor "common core" studies of religious beliefs. Such distillation of what is common to several faiths is deplored. The general position is that religious instruction falls within the control of the states, and that such control is largely delegated by the states to local communities. Such communities, it is implied, would have the right to institute almost anything deemed wise in the way of religious instruction.

Yet the participants of this report deny that public education should try to win adherents to any one religious system. It should give such instruction as will enable the young to attain a personal reaction to the challenge of religion. It is suggested that religious instruction could be embodied as essential parts of the study of such things as government, welfare, and even industry. The Bible would have its place in the study of literature. This second way of implementing religious study seems to make it a cultural pursuit, lacking the dynamic and positive aim of securing religious conversion. It may well be true that the pupil might be converted to a faith of his own choice after an impartial survey of the contributions of each faith (not their "common core") to the enrichment of culture and of personal life.

A more recent plan for religious education in the schools (4) is the result of the work of fifteen educators and religious leaders headed by F. Ernest Johnson. The plan is based on sixteen months of study. The aim was to work out a plan of religious education in public elementary and secondary schools, and in the training of teachers. The plans proposed, like the sources covered in the study, were designed to be suitable for three major faiths (Catholic, Protestant, Jewish); and were to be consonant with the accepted principle of the separation of church and state.

☙ F. Public Support of Religious Instruction

If an acceptable plan of religious instruction could be worked out and adopted in our public schools, whether along denominational lines or in terms of a "watered-down" core curriculum, several troublesome current issues would be allayed, but no doubt other issues would be raised.

Some protagonists of parochial schools clamor for public support. The denial of such support, they contend, is itself a form of sectarianism. It is pointed out by James B. Conant that parochial schools in other countries receive financial aid from their governments (1). Thus, Scotland provides for secondary education in Roman Catholic and Episcopal schools (1, p. 150 and elsewhere). It should be noted, however, that all national schools in Scotland are denominational. That is, the great mass of the Scottish people are Presbyterian and so are the public schools. It is therefore in the interest of justice that public support be given to Catholic and Episcopalian faiths. England, too, has denominational schools largely supported by tax money (1, p. 146). Conant notes the amazing contrast between the English and the American attitudes in this matter. In America it is felt that the support of sectarian schools curtails the freedom of religion of the people as a whole. For the English, there is restriction of religious freedom unless tax money supports both denominational and other schools (1, p. 147).

There are questions about private schools, whether denominational or not, which outweigh the mere problem of their support by taxation. James B. Conant may serve as spokesman against public support for private schools in America (1, pp. 80-82). Conant notes that for seventy-five years our public schools, attended by all but a few of our children, have served all creeds and classes and have likewise promoted assimilation of the various cultures which came to America. If our high schools should lose popular support, private schools and religious schools would become the logical recipients of tax money. This would pose a threat to democratic unity. It would accent and perpetuate class distinctions. Any dual system of education will cause and maintain social cleavages. Conant declares, "To use taxpayers' money to assist private schools is to suggest that American society use its own hands to destroy itself. This is the answer I must give to those who would advocate the transformation of the American pattern into that of England" (1, p. 81).

♻ G. Education and the State

The continued struggle to keep a foothold for religion in education is by no means mere partisan ax-grinding on the part of pressure-groups. There is more to such persistence than meets the eye. The major conclusion usually held by comparative psychology is that man, being superior to animals in mental endowments, is able to achieve his ends with superior effectiveness. This, however, overlooks another important difference: Man is the creature that expends more energy seeking for and justifying ends than in attaining them. In short, man is an incurable philosopher. He must give meaning to his place in the cosmos, whereas an animal is content to adapt itself to its local habitat. Man must find basic meanings for what he does—even a tenuous theory about it is better than dumb silence and acquiescence. This is perhaps the chief reason which leads religionists to restore the religious foundations of education despite legal enactments against such attempts. When education became secular, many felt that it had lost all security and orientation.

But there are those who seek moorings other than religious ones. One of the most challenging of these is the thesis that the state, which took over the educational prerogatives of the church, may also have a philosophy which can vindicate education. In Nazi Germany, fascist Italy, and other more current dictatorships education became a tool for the regimentation of the masses. But in these cases education is founded on expediency, becoming, not an end in itself, but a strategic tool for attaining other goals. Such states may claim consonance with an "ideology," but this is not to be confused with a system of philosophy.

On the other hand, democracy as a form of the state may rightly claim grounding in basic principles subject to logical and empirical validation. Attempts to found education on a democratic philosophy is one of the striking phenomena in contemporary America. No doubt this impulse is inspired to a great extent by the potential threats to democracy inherent in two World Wars, both blamed on predatory dictatorships. Dozens of books on education with the words "democracy" and "freedom" blazoned in their titles have appeared in recent times. The authors include such outstanding leaders in education as John Dewey, James B.

Conant, Edmund E. Day, Benjamin Fine, L. Thomas Hopkins, and Robert M. Hutchins.

Our spokesman for a political philosophy of education will be Alexander Meiklejohn, a philosopher, one-time college president (of Amherst), and an educator of repute (6).

1. A Crisis in Education

The early church in Europe, which had charge of education, had convictions about the nature of man and his world. The church's authority to instruct man and guide his behavior was regarded as derived from God. Religion supplied a philosophy of democracy, based on the doctrine of the fatherhood of God and the brotherhood of man. This religious sanction of democracy is apparent in the histories and constitutions of great democracies, including the United States. But now education has become secular in the greater part of the Protestant world. The control of education is under the jurisdiction of government—national, state, provincial, local. Education is not only secular, it has become political. In Germany and Italy, and now in Russia, the state became the rival of the church. Meiklejohn calls attention to the vast significance of this change:

Do we realize what we have done? This is revolution. . . . As compared with it, changes in the gaining and holding of property, the making and enforcing of laws . . . are secondary and superficial. . . . We have changed our procedure for determining what kind of beings human beings shall be (6, p. 4).

2. Does the State Have a Purpose?

Meiklejohn unerringly poses the crucial questions arising out of the shift to the state control of education. What beliefs and moral values do governments represent? What is the philosophy of the city of New York, any other city, town, or village which prepares youth for living? "What lessons have they to teach? Does New York City believe anything?" This, says Meiklejohn, is the "most terrifying question" which our education faces (6, p. 5). Meiklejohn goes on to detail our fears and doubts about the state as an agency of understanding (6, pp. 8-10).

Many question whether the state has moral convictions, and regard political control as hostile to individual freedom. Witness the widespread and persistent suspicion of federal infringements of states' rights, of local distrust of the state, etc. This is why we say that the government which governs least is the best government. Another suspicion is that the state is *negative* in function—it tells us what we must *not* do—it fails to tell us what we *should* do in many areas of conduct. In short, says Meiklejohn, we suspect that the state is a "brute," yet we authorize it to teach our children! This whole situation, he says, is intolerable. Education has a *positive* function which should be based on solid reflection. It is the task of education to fashion human beings, and thus modify the whole of society in the direction of ideal ends.

Meiklejohn, instead of advocating a return to the control of education by the church, proceeds carefully to demonstrate that a democratic political philosophy can provide ample sanction for a broad and secure basis for education. Meiklejohn's search for the roots of our democratic philosophy leads him to a detailed examination of the political ideas of John Locke and of Jean Jacques Rousseau. The ideas of these men played an important part in the establishment of our form of government. Both of them are also considered classic writers on education. Meiklejohn contrasts and evaluates the ideas of Locke and Rousseau. Locke turns out to be the villain of the piece, and Rousseau the true prophet of democracy.

3. Locke's Philosophy of the State

Locke was not a "villainous" man, personally. He was merely the spokesman for a villainous, self-contradictory, and self-destructive ideology into which Christian culture had fallen: namely, that of *Christian capitalism.* This ideology has two gospels, one the Bible, the other the capitalistic state (6, p. 57). Locke was deeply religious. He held that God created the universe and created mankind. When God created men he endowed them with eternal, inalienable rights to such things as freedom, equality, property, justice. God had authority over conscience and moral law.

But, according to Locke, *God did not create the state.* Locke wrote two works on civil government. The first purported to show that God did not create the state, the second maintained that the state was created by man. Before the state was created, man lived in a state of nature in which he was not able to enjoy the rights God had bestowed upon him. This was because the rights of men were violated by the selfish actions of other men. In time, men created the state on the basis of a "social contract," dictated by prudence and maintained by force. The situation is, then, that the citizen is responsible to God in matters of conscience, but in matters of prudence, he will find it wise to keep an armed truce with other men, respecting their rights so that they will respect his own. He fears the legal penalties entailed if he violates legal enactments (6, pp. 63-65).

Both Locke and Rousseau spoke of a "state of nature" from which the state emerged. If this view be regarded as nonsense, the score between Locke and Rousseau is "even." Probably neither Locke nor Rousseau believed that man had ever lived in a state of nature shorn of all group regulation. Both writers use this notion as an illustrative device for inferring what life would be like without social control of any human form, whether resting on unwritten taboos or on formulated civil laws.

Some of Locke's ideas may strike the reader as lofty and idealistic. The rights of men were established by God; individual conscience and responsibility to God are exalted above obedience to the civil laws established by men. But it is precisely here that Meiklejohn finds the basic duplicity in our Protestant-capitalistic world. The trouble is that men confuse conscience with prudence and no end of avid desires. Meiklejohn could have rallied the support of both psychoanalysis and the psychology of the laboratories to support the thesis that human beings notoriously deceive themselves regarding their own motives (rationalization), repress memories which hurt their egos (protective amnesia), make the wish father to the thought (dereistic thinking), and are even capable of seeing what they want to see (autistic perception).

A free interpretation of what Meiklejohn means might run as follows: The individual who wishes to be religious on all days of the week can accept the urges of prudence and prejudice as the voices of conscience. Another way of living in the Christian-capitalist society is to serve conscience and God on Sundays and be a "rugged individualist" on other days on the ground that it is not wrong to do what the state does not forbid. Meiklejohn writes: "It is by mental jugglery such as this that a disintegrating religion has tipped the moral balances of the Anglo-Saxon world. It has enabled us to combine righteousness in morals with success in business" (6, p. 83).

4. Rousseau's Philosophy of the State

Meiklejohn is fully aware of Rousseau's personal weaknesses and knows that his thinking is often flagrantly inconsistent and dictated by passion. Yet, the flashes of insight of this man, when carefully sifted and ordered, yield the framework of a sound philosophy of the democratic state, one enabling that state rightfully to assume the direction of public education.

Like Locke, Rousseau spoke of the state as arising, not from God, but from a "social contract." By means of this contract men raised themselves from a state of nature in which there were no rights, but only the rule of strength. Locke had supposed that God endowed men with rights which belonged to them whether or not they were able to enjoy them in practice. But Rousseau does not in any sense grant rights to man in a state of nature, not even the abstract rights flowing from divine intentions. Without a state, no property can be held on legal grounds. The holding of property implies a contract. In a state of nature there is no justice for there are no laws. There is no equality, for men differ in the ability to appropriate what they want. In the state of nature there is no freedom and there is no morality.

In short, for Rousseau, both individual rights and the hegemony of the state were made by man. The moral rights of individuals are validated by the moral perceptions of the group, sustained by the "general will" (6, pp. 79-85).

The political relation of the individual to the state, according to Rousseau, is that the individual places himself and his possessions under the direction of the common will, which in return protects the rights and freedoms of the individual. Here is a paradox which confronts a democracy or any rational government: How can an individual "give his all" to the state and have any freedoms left which the state can guarantee for him? Locke solved this problem by assuming that the nonmaterial rights of the individual are guaranteed by God and by individual conscience. The individual thus makes reservations where the state is concerned: he will not "give his all" to it—he must fight for his rights against the possible encroachments of the state; as, for example, his right to "free enterprise" in business. Locke, says Meiklejohn, is responsible for the popular notion that the state is the individual's enemy, that the best state governs least. In Rousseau's schematism it is the duty of the state to protect *all* individual rights, even the rights of conscience and religious worship. The Bill of Rights in our Constitution does demand that the state ensure the individual's rights of worship, free thought, and the free expression of opinion (6, pp. 215-218).

Meiklejohn concludes that if Rousseau's conception of democracy is correct then any state which embodies his conception is qualified to teach. Education should conform to the best moral ideals of a people, and a democratic state has both moral convictions and a basic procedure for realizing them in practice. The moral convictions are made quite clear in the Constitution. Above all, the ideal of freedom must be sustained and furthered. Free intelligence and enlightenment are at once moral ideals and the chief implements for attaining other moral goals. It is therefore the right and duty of the state to maintain education whereby intelligence and enlightenment are cultivated.

5. Final Comments

Students of the history of political theory might question the accuracy of some aspects of Meiklejohn's account of Rousseau's political theories. For our purpose, it does not matter much whether Rousseau really held to the full theory of democracy attributed to him by Meiklejohn. The important point is that it is a challenging conception of the state whether it be the inspiration of Rousseau, or of Meiklejohn, his interpreter.

As Meiklejohn notes, there is analogy between Rousseau's idea of the relation of the individual to the state and the traditional Christian view of the relation of the individual to God. The individual gives his soul to Christ—only to get it back again, much ennobled. He who serves Christ will realize his own life in richer measure. Similarly, in

Rousseau's democracy, the citizen pledges himself and his possessions to serve his state, and gets in return spiritual freedoms worth much more than his sacrifice (6, p. 215). In both religion and in democratic theory *à la* Rousseau the individual is motivated by the challenge of service to something greater than himself—God in the one case, the democratic community in the other.

Meiklejohn does not stress Rousseau's model of democracy as something superior to religion for the purposes of education. He accepts Rousseau's thought as a workable substitute for the church to meet the crisis of education sundered from its religious moorings. Whether the new moorings are better or worse than the old is a tangled problem we cannot pursue further. But since the church has lost official status as the lamp and staff of education, we may at least ask some poignant questions which may point to values which education has lost. Is man so constituted that he will serve temporal powers in the way he would serve God? Does not Christianity enjoin men to serve each other more because they also serve God? Is not the philosophy of Rousseau itself the expression of centuries of Christian thought and culture rather than a substitute for it? Would Rousseau have spoken without the liberty of conscience which the church fostered?

But there are philosophies other than purely political ones which might support, illuminate, and inspire that vast ferment we call education. We have now to explore these one by one in the rough order of their historical dominance. The first of these will be essentialism and traditionalism, to which the four chapters of Book II are devoted.

References

1. Conant, James B. *Education and Liberty. The Role of the Schools in a Modern Democracy.* Cambridge, Mass.: Harvard University Press, 1953.
2. Hay, Clyde L. *The Blind Spot in American Public Education.* New York: Macmillan, 1950.
3. Hook, Sidney. *Education for Modern Man.* New York: Dial Press, 1946.
4. Johnson, F. Ernest. *The Function of the Public Schools in Dealing with Religion.* Washington, D.C.: American Council on Education, 1953.
5. Maritain, Jacques. *Education at the Crossroads.* New Haven, Conn.: Yale University Press, 1943.
6. Meiklejohn, Alexander. *Education Between Two Worlds.* New York: Harper, 1942.
7. Zook, George F. "The Relation of Religion to Public Education." *American Council on Education,* Series I, No. 26, April, 1947.

book 2

ESSENTIALISM AND TRADITIONALISM IN EDUCATION

⇳ *chapter 3*

ESSENTIALISM AND TRADITIONALISM:
POSTULATES AND DEVELOPMENT

The preceding chapter briefly portrayed the early grounding of education in Christian doctrine, traced the shift from church to state in education, and ended with an examination of Meiklejohn's contention that Rousseau's theory of the state can serve as the basis of education in a democracy. We now turn to certain great academic philosophies which are neither exclusively religious nor political in their world views. The earliest philosophies of education to assert themselves in the United States as replacements for purely religious sanctions of education were traditionalism, essentialism, and idealistic philosophy. These three approaches to education existed long before the shift from church to state in the control of education. Since each one of the three has a lineage of religious ideology, they were natural successors of the church as bases of education.

We set aside idealism for a series of chapters to constitute Book III of this volume. Traditionalism and essentialism will be the subjects of the four chapters of the present portion (Book II). A brief survey of the contents of the four chapters may serve as a preview of the manner in which the intricate problems of essentialism and traditionalism will be explored. Chapter 3 (the present one) defines the most basic tenets of essentialism and traditionalism, traces their origins briefly, and then sketches their development in American education. Chapter 4 portrays the educational thought of leaders of essentialism, both radical and moderate. Chapters 5 and 6 deal with technical issues growing out of essentialism. The strength of essentialism depends in part on modern evidences bearing on two of its original doctrines, faculty psychology, and formal discipline. Chapter 5 discusses faculty psychology. It may be stated in advance that modern experimental psychology (a) forces a modification of the ancient doctrine of mental faculties, and (b) rigorously qualifies the old claims made regarding formal discipline (Chapter 6). We shall find, however, that a revision of the basic postulates of essentialism in order to harmonize them with psychological findings is possible without destroying, so to speak, the "essentials of essentialism." The claims of any philosophy of education are confronted with criticisms and counterclaims of other points of view. Throughout this book all criticisms and countercriticisms will be taken up after the exposition of the matters in dispute.

The main divisions of the present chapter are as follows:
A. Basic Postulates of Essentialism and Traditionalism
B. Essentialism in Catholic Education
C. Essentialism in Secular Education

⩒ A. Basic Postulates of Essentialism and Traditionalism

Essentialism and traditionalism are not major systems of thought ranking with the great historical schools of philosophy. They are essentially philosophies of education having historical roots in the philosophies of the past and present, especially in historical realism. The philosophical roots of essentialism begin with certain Platonic and Aristotelian doctrines which attained great currency in later centuries, especially true of Aristotle's realism.

The Platonic roots of essentialism are mainly recorded in Book VII of Plato's *Republic* where Socrates and his friends discuss the kind of education best suited for rulers of the state. They conclude that only reason is able to penetrate beyond the changing world of the senses and grasp the eternal archetypal forms or ideas which are the models of the imperfect and changing realities found in immediate experience. The ruler, above all, needed to grasp the great ideal of the *absolute good,* and this requires the rigorous cultivation of pure intelligence. Plato describes the type of rigorous training needed as *dialectic,* and selects arithmetic, music, geometry, and astronomy as the best subject matter for developing intelligence. Plato clearly held to the principle now referred to as "formal discipline," namely, that some studies, irrespective of any practical values they may have, are preeminently valuable for developing intellectual power.

In the *Politics* of Aristotle, Plato's ideal of devoting education to the cultivation of intelligence is given further supports, as we shall see. Various writings of Aristotle suggest that his favorite curriculum consisted of metaphysics, physics, rhetoric, and poetry.

Through the influence of St. Thomas Aquinas and other early church fathers, Aristotle's ideas were embodied both in scholastic philosophy and in the educational practices of the Middle Ages. In the Middle Ages the liberal arts consisted of the lower trivium (grammar, logic, and rhetoric) and the higher quadrivium (Plato's four subjects, consisting of arithmetic, music, geometry, and astronomy).

The terms *essentialism* and *traditionalism* have reference to the subject matter of education, but as full-fledged points of view they cover many issues which determine what the curriculum should be. Traditionalism finds the essential subject matter of education in our cultural inheritance, and places less stress on knowledge won in contemporary times. The critics of traditionalists sometimes call them "perennialists" to call attention to their conservatism. Essentialism and traditionalism are harmonious points of view but are not necessarily identical. The "essential" studies of the Middle Ages became traditional. Hence the modern essentialist also tends to be a traditionalist, except that essentialists of today might put their faith in studies other than traditional ones. For example, recent forms of material science might be favored in place of grammar and logic. From now on, in the interests of brevity, we shall employ the term *essentialism* to include traditionalism except when the difference between them becomes significant.

We shall try to grasp essentialism as a point of view in education in terms of its five basic postulates. These postulates came into existence gradually, and were modified with passing time. An educator need not subscribe to all five of the postulates in order to qualify as an "essentialist." Perhaps adherence to the fifth postulate, the postulate concerning "essential subjects," would be enough for such classification. The fifth postulate confines itself to the proposition that there are a few essential studies which should form the basic curriculum for all students.

We shall first give the historical versions of certain postulates of essentialism. Thus, the postulates concerning the mental faculties and their formal discipline are quite ancient, and have fallen into desuetude. The reader must be especially careful not to assume that essentialists of today hold literally to these archaic ideas. They hold to equivalent principles which have grown out of criticisms of old concepts in the light of modern knowledge. For a full and clear account of the five postulates of essentialism indicated below and their influence on modern education the reader is referred to Walter B. Kolesnik's work of 1958 (9).

1. Postulate of the Rational Nature of Man

Aristotle's famous view of man as the "rational animal" occurs in a number of his writings. In the *Politics* he wrote: "Now reason or intellect is the end or *complete development* of our nature. . . ." (1, p. 210). This view of man, together with other Aristotelian ideas, became basic in scholastic philosophy, especially through the influence of St. Thomas Aquinas. Important elements of Aristotle's philosophy, as modified by St. Thomas and others, survive in the philosophy of the Catholic Church. The Aristotelian concept of *Homo sapiens* is accepted by the so-called neoscholastic wing of essentialists in education, including such men as Robert M. Hutchins, Mortimer Adler, and Stringfellow Barr. If man is essentially the creature of reason, Hutchins concludes that the chief business of education is to cultivate the "intellectual virtues," as he calls them.

We may note that other pronouncements about the essential nature of man are less flattering than Aristotle's view. Freud viewed man as Homo sexualis. In the midst of recent international political strife and warfare, many will favor the view of Thomas Huxley, who held that man is best distinguished from other animals by his excessive ferocity.

2. Postulate of Mental Faculties

Having declared that man is the rational animal, the essentialist wishes to specify more closely the nature of man's rationality and of his mind as a whole. Essentialists of the past favored what is known as a *faculty* psychology. A faculty theory of mind refers in general to any view that regards the mind as composed of separate powers which, acting singly or together, account for most if not all mental activities. Even the enumeration of such mental capacities as sensation, perception, memory, reasoning, attention, and feeling is said to involve the grievous error of faculty psychology.

The reader may feel rather dismayed and astonished by the suggestion that the seemingly innocent phrase, "He has superior intellectual powers," conceals grave errors as old as the Pythagoreans! If it is erroneous to use such terms as perception, memory, and the like, as referring to distinct mental operations, it is puzzling to know how one is to discuss mental activities at all. The reader who uses such terms in characterizing mind may take comfort from the assurance that he has, so to speak, good company in disrepute; because all psychologists use these terms— even write separate chapters or books about them. The problem of the validity or invalidity of a faculty psychology is not only very old but is particularly intricate. In evaluating the sense and nonsense of faculty theory we shall make an excursion later on into experimental psychology bearing on the question of the abilities of mind and the mind's organization (Chapter 5).

3. The Postulate of Formal Discipline

This is the doctrine that each mental faculty or power can be strengthened by exercises or studies appropriate to its development. Since some studies are considered far better than others for developing the powers of mind, of which the power of reasoning is the chief, such studies should become the required curriculum.

In fact, the enthusiasts about formal discipline went so far as to assert that the subject matter learned in a course of study was less important than its power for developing the faculties. Thus, spelling books of the past showed accumulations of ten thousand or more words where four thousand were amply sufficient for the student's needs. In geography and history students were required to memorize arrays of locations, names, and dates. Why? Because such work was assumed to develop the faculty of memory. The very difficulty of study became a special virtue. The more vigorous the exercise, the greater the resultant development. In this respect the faculties and the muscles were regarded as in the same category!

4. The Postulate of Transfer of Training

This is the assumption that a faculty once developed by an appropriate series of studies will show benefits in other tasks involving the action of that faculty. Thus, reasoning power developed by the study of geometry could be applied to all problems of life where reasoning enters in, as in business, farming, politics, and science. Thanks to childhood practice in memorizing numerous dates and names in history, the adult man can be a model of efficiency in learning the numerous details of his business or profession.

The question of the transfer of training may be investigated experimentally, as it has been, without accepting any advance theory whatever regarding mental faculties or powers. In fact, such research on transfer should serve to test the claims of the faculty theorist. This consideration will lead us to our second digression into experimental psychology—the research on transfer of training (Chapter 6).

5. The Postulate of Essential Subjects

Essentialists hold that education should be devoted to the thorough study of a few subjects selected for their universal and basic importance. This postulate is the end result which follows logically from the first four postulates. A study will have basic importance if it addresses itself to man's basic rational nature (postulate 1), and the subordinate faculties of man's mind (postulate 2). Again, essential studies will be the ones which best develop the faculties through disciplinary exercise (postulate 3). Finally, the mental powers developed by the pursuit of essential studies will yield benefits in subjects other than the ones in which training was given (postulate 4).

There remains only the problem of discovering the identity of the essential studies. This, so the essentialist supposes, should not be difficult, for we know in advance that they must be studies which tax the higher intellectual powers. In Chapter 4, which details the views of some leading essentialists, it will be seen what studies are proposed as "essential."

When it comes to enumerating essential studies, teachers and even opposed philosophers of education show some agreement. Some subjects which essentialists stress, such as reading, speaking, writing, and arithmetic, are familiar "tool" subjects cultivated in all schools. But the essentialist adds to these some rather "intellectual" subjects, such as grammar, rhetoric, logic, and languages; and opposes so-called practical and vocational subjects. For some essentialists, as we shall see, even reading is considered a highly intellectual and rigorous activity when one studies famous classics in place of materials supplied by the popular press.

⚥ B. Essentialism in Catholic Education

Hutchins and his friends are called "Neo-Scholastics" and "neo-Thomists" to indicate their penchant for Aristotelian thinking and their partiality to the philosophy of St. Thomas. Since scholastic philosophy, especially that of St. Thomas, is the official philosophy of the Catholic Church, we should naturally expect Catholic writers on education to favor essentialism. That this is indeed the case is apparent from the writings of Bishop Fulton Sheen, Jacques Maritain, John D. Redden, Francis A. Ryan, and others. Catholic writers on education join the essentialists in attacking pragmatism in education. Jacques Maritain writes that pragmatists in education, having lost sight of ultimate ends, give exclusive attention to the student. Thus, in order to teach John mathematics, the pragmatist begins by studying John, and "will so perfectly succeed in knowing John that John will never succeed in knowing mathematics" (10, pp. 13-14).

We shall review the educational thought of Catholic educators as synthesized by William F. Cunningham, Professor of Education at the University of Notre Dame (5), and test Cunningham's careful crystallization of Catholic opinions on our five postulates of essentialism. One rather surprising result is that the average Catholic educator appears to be more liberal and less unyielding in his scholasticism than is Hutchins. In fact, Cunningham reports (5, pp. 3-5) that Hutchins, on being invited to address a group of Catholic leaders, took them to task for not being Catholic enough! Hutchins noted that Catholic colleges have a long tradition of liberal arts to uphold; yet he finds them succumbing, like secular colleges, to anti-intellectualism. Anti-intellectualism for Hutchins includes such vices as athleticism, vocationalism, and "collegiatism." Collegiatism consist in producing "well-tubbed" young Americans who, although mentally undistinguished, are acceptable at house parties and become ornaments of political groups!

1. On the score of Aristotle's conception of man's rational nature and destiny, Cunningham is one of the "faithful." Catholic education seeks to perfect the intellectual virtues (cf. Hutchins), especially to develop priceless wisdom. Wisdom, following St. Thomas, embraces *understanding*, which grasps principles in themselves, and *science*, which moves from principles to further conclusions (5, p. 45).

2. But there are other capacities of man to be developed, such as his feelings and emotions, his conscience, citizenship, and Christian life. There is little concern in Cunningham's book for outmoded doctrines about mental faculties.

3. What about development through discipline? Here the modern Catholic has much to say. Any study can have three possible values for the student: utilitarian, cultural, and disciplinary. To merit a place in the curriculum each course of study should possess all three of these values. Thus, Latin has practical use in that it makes it easier for the student to master the large number of English polysyllabic words which give "beauty and ornamentation to English" (5, p. 131). The cultural value of Latin will appear when it is joined with such things as the study of the history of the Roman Empire. The disciplinary (discriminative) value of Latin appears in the study of syntax, as in comparing Latin with other languages.

Cunningham now lists a set of "categories of discipline" (5, pp. 135-149). Self-development is achieved through self-discipline. Morally, self-development through discipline implies denials imposed upon urges which are antagonistic to development. The discipline of the intellect therefore has moral significance. How is the discipline of thought to be achieved? The study of history is of value here because it develops the student's sense of perspective. Philosophy disciplines the mind to unification, to synoptic thinking. Mathematics disciplines precision of thought. The natural sciences discipline thought in the direction of objectivity, adherence to facts, and freedom from bias.

The second great category of discipline is that of the feelings and emotions. In this sphere discipline consists in cultivating aesthetic appreciations through the study of literature and art.

The third category is the discipline of action through the study of

the social sciences. The social studies should be more than merely in-
formative. They should lead to the student's appreciation of good things
in his culture. Further, they should lead to the student's appreciation of
the importance of social action, which preserves what is good and elim-
inates what is bad in social life. Under the third category also belongs
the study of Christian ideals and theology.

The fourth and last discipline is that of language. The arts of language or expression are various, but the basis of this discipline consists
of the trivium which begins with grammar, proceeds through logic, and
then through rhetoric.

4. What about transfer of training? Cunningham refers to the studies
of Professor Thorndike which led to the conclusion that all capacities are
specific, and that the training of one capacity will improve another one
only if they have elements in common. Accordingly there can be no
general transfer of training from one skill to another. Cunningham approves the pronouncement of Nicholas Murray Butler (4, pp. 110 ff.),
who described this entire development in psychology as "errant nonsense" (5, p. 133). Cunningham charges that the notion that all learning
is *specific*, that training improves only the skill being trained, led to a
deplorable multiplication of courses in all areas of education.

5. Finally, the list of disciplines indicated above gives us an answer
to the question of the essential curriculum for Catholic education. Cunningham also expresses a distrust of elective systems of courses. He refers
to the Harvard elective system introduced by former President Eliot as
a bit of "sophomoric enthusiasm" (5, p. 2), which was apologetically
rejected by Harvard in 1945 (8). The elective system, says Cunningham,
is responsible for the abandonment of traditional liberal education.

Cunningham, however, allows some freedom for taking elective
courses. There should be some choices in all disciplinary areas except
in philosophy; and even here there will be choice if philosophy becomes
the student's field of concentration. What about vocational training? With
true essentialist instinct, our Catholic friends urge that every student
should culminate his general education by concentrating on one of the
liberal arts or sciences (not in vocational or professional courses). But
the financial needs of students may lead the college, regretfully, to allow
professional training during the last two college years. This departure
from austere intellectualism will win the approval of progressive educators, but it led Hutchins to chide Catholics for being lax in upholding
their intellectual traditions.

A physician is said to have exclaimed that Janet's theory of hysteria
was so elegant that it would be a pity if the disease did not exist! The
postulates of essentialism form such an articulate whole that one might
view with regret the discovery of any flaws in them. But the postulates

of essentialism are surrounded by pitfalls, real and imaginary, which the supporters of other philosophies of education delight to point out. The essentialist called upon to defend his convictions must indeed be alert and wary. One ought not be discouraged by the veritable jungle of charges and countercharges of school against school. This may look like chaos to the faint of heart, who may prefer agreement even at the cost of accepting a dictatorship in the philosophy of education. But this is not the healthy way of life in a democracy, which derives fuller life and growth from the constant and gradual resolution of clashing opinions.

We have so far considered only the barest outlines of essentialism, and are still leagues away from its adequate appreciation or criticism. Having given essentialism's postulates in skeletal outline, we shall next briefly trace its history and status in American secular education.

⇳ C. Essentialism in Secular Education

As an educational practice, essentialism is at least as old as the trivium and quadrivium of the Middle Ages. Even the use of the Bible and Shorter Catechism as the essential curriculum by our colonial schools seems old to the present generation. The doctrine of mental faculties is very old, being at least contemporary with the ancient Pythagoreans. Beliefs are not, of course, to be regarded as invalid merely because they are ancient. It is not the business of this book to give details regarding the history of ideas in education. Yet, some brief notes on the origins of contemporary essentialism will be of help both in understanding and evaluating it.

1. Some Historical Notes

Essentialism existed in practice long before it acquired its present name. The term "essentialist" was first introduced by Michael Demiashkevich in 1935 (6). Essentialism existed along with idealism in education at the turn of the present century. Essentialism has more in common with idealism in education than it has with a new rival appearing on the educational horizon. This new rivalry began with the founding of pragmatic philosophy by Charles S. Peirce and William James. John Dewey, an important philosopher of education (Chapter 16) applied pragmatic philosophy, under the title of "instrumentalism," to education. Deweyism in education was at once part of and a cause of the rise of the progressive education movement.

The Progressive Education Association was founded in 1918. By 1930 it had become very influential as the opponent of essentialism. Progressivism did not hesitate to replace the traditional "essential" subjects with an "experience" curriculum, in which life in school is made to resemble practical life outside of it, thus preparing the student for adult life and work. In fact, progressivism gathered power and influence to such an extent that in 1938 American essentialists formed a special committee to defend their views and practices against the spread of progressivism and against the system of elective courses introduced by President Eliot at Harvard University. Essentialists deplored the spread of elective courses in higher education and elsewhere. Elective courses tended to vary from place to place and even from one instructor to another in the same department. Observing this mushroom growth of varying courses under the same labels, Edward J. Fitzpatrick was led to observe that pure-food laws did not hold in education (7).

2. Leaders of American Essentialism

There are numerous spokesmen for essentialism. Although essentialists stress the "common humanity of men," which points to the need for uniformity in their education, they show differences in other matters. In Chapter 4 brief biographical and ideological accounts will be given of the more stalwart and militant leaders of essentialism in contemporary American education. These include Robert M. Hutchins and his friend Mortimer J. Adler, John Macdonald, Edmund E. Day, and Alfred W. Griswold. To attain fuller measure, the reader may wish to explore the clear defense of essentialism given by William C. Bagley (2), and the grim thoroughness with which Stringfellow Barr and Scott Buchanan introduced traditionalist essentialism at St. John's College, Annapolis, Maryland (3).

References

1. Aristotle. *The Politics of Aristotle* (J. E. C. Welldon, tr.). London: Macmillan, 1912.
2. Bagley, William C. "The Significance of the Essentialist Movement in Educational Theory." *Classical Journal*, 1938-1939, Vol. 34, pp. 326-344.
3. Barr, Stringfellow. "A College in Secession." *Atlantic Monthly*, 1941, Vol. 168, pp. 41-49.
4. Butler, Nicholas M. *The Faith of a Liberal.* New York: Scribner's, 1924.
5. Cunningham, William F. *General Education and the Liberal College.* St. Louis, Mo.: B. Herder, 1953.
6. Demiashkevich, Michael. *An Introduction to the Philosophy of Education.* New York: American Book Co., 1935.
7. Fitzpatrick, Edward J. *How to Educate Human Beings.* Milwaukee, Wis.: Bruce, 1950.
8. Harvard Report. *Education in a Free Society.* Cambridge, Mass.: Harvard University Press, 1945.

9. Kolesnik, Walter B. *Mental Discipline in Modern Education*. Madison, Wis.: University of Wisconsin Press, 1958.
10. Maritain, Jacques. *Education at the Crossroads*. New Haven, Conn.: Yale University Press, 1943.

♀ *chapter 4*

SOME PROTAGONISTS OF ESSENTIALISM AND THEIR VIEWS

Samuel Johnson once declared, "When speculation has done its worst, two plus two still make four." In the philosophy of education, assuming that everything got said and done, we would still not be certain what things would add up to in the future. This is because education changes with changing times—it is as much in the process of *becoming* as in the state of *being*. Education will be what we make it to become.

To get things done in the schools in accordance with a favored theory of education, other educators must be converted to that point of view; and to accomplish this, very much has to be done. In such spheres as morals, politics, and education we have not as yet succeeded in founding beliefs upon complete demonstration. In this predicament we seek to compensate for the dubious status of the evidences by trust in the individuals who utter them. This is why leadership is important in all reform movements. This chapter portrays the ideas of representative leaders of essentialism. We shall consider examples of rather militant advocates of essentialism in order to see in sharp relief the philosophy they defend. Some of the comments of the writer of this book are enclosed in parentheses to avoid the danger of confusing them with the views of the educational leaders being discussed.

The main divisions of the chapter are:

A. Robert M. Hutchins and Mortimer J. Adler

B. John Macdonald on Interest, Effort, and Moral Discipline

▽ A. Robert M. Hutchins and Mortimer J. Adler

1. Hutchins' Personality and Career

Robert Maynard Hutchins (1899-   ) was trained at Oberlin and Yale. After becoming a professor of law and dean at Yale, he then became president of the University of Chicago at the early age of thirty-one years. He continued in this position until recently when he was appointed as director of the Fund for the Republic of the Ford Educational Foundation. Hutchins and Adler made the University of Chicago a stronghold of essentialism.

The force of Hutchins' personality is shown by the eminence he enjoys in education despite views which are out of harmony with strong trends in contemporary education. Hutchins advocates the study of logic, mathematics, grammar, and rhetoric as basic in the "permanent curriculum." This is because such subjects, in his view, teach the student how to think, write, and speak. Hutchins supplies a good example of this sort of education. His readers may reject his views, but his laconic and incisive sentences leave little doubt about what he means. His writing is polemical, but contains flashes of good humor in the midst of irony and sarcasm.

Hutchins' writings on education are modest in quantity. Our account will be based almost entirely on three of Hutchins' books, each one of which gives a forceful defense of essentialism. Indeed, in the first book, *The Higher Learning in America,* 1936 (11), an almost complete account of Hutchins' views is given by the single chapter entitled, "General Education." Our second source will be his *Education for Freedom,* 1943 (12), and the third one is the little volume, *The Conflict in Education in a Democratic Society,* 1953 (13). Hutchins' views have remained quite constant throughout the years. The last book (1953) gives once more approximately the same convictions and aversions found in the work of 1936.

To get the full measure of Hutchins' faith in essentialism, it will be well to determine how faithfully he adheres to the five postulates of essentialism given in the previous chapter. It can be stated in advance that Hutchins accepts all of them, but gives detailed attention only to the final one concerning the essential contents of education. Criticisms against his opponents and certain practices in education have occupied Hutchins' interest quite as much as or even more than the defense of his own views.

2. Hutchins and the Postulates of Essentialism

a. OUR COMMON HUMANITY. Hutchins believes that in order to decide what education should be we must first ask, "What is the essential nature of man?" This theme, occurring in the book of 1936, is explicitly stated in 1953 (13, p. 68). Human nature shows essential constants which should determine the nature of education in all places and times where an educational system is possible. The aim of education is to improve man's essential nature.

What, then, is the essential nature of man? Hutchins and other so-called Neo-Scholastics trace their views back to Aristotle's famous thesis that man is the rational animal, that intellect or reason represents the final end of man's complete development. Hutchins sees profound significance in the thesis that reason represents man's essential nature. He concludes from it that the aim of education is to cultivate the "intellectual virtues" which are good in themselves and good as means to happiness for all men in all societies. The intellectual goods are the ones for which all other goods are only means. "Material prosperity, peace and civil order, justice and the moral virtues are means to the cultivation of the intellect" (11, p. 67). This citation is important in showing that Hutchins, like Aristotle, holds to a broad, inclusive conception of reason or intellect, which terms are commonly used to designate the "cold" processes of logical inference with no reference whatever to virtue. But for Hutchins, to develop peace and civil order, justice and the moral virtues, is to develop intelligence.

b. FACULTIES, DISCIPLINE, AND TRANSFER. Without specifically defending the faculty theory of mind, Hutchins uses this term and a similar one, "mental powers." As for formal discipline, Hutchins clearly accepts the view that mental powers can be developed by exercises which are appropriate to strengthening them. The following citation illustrates Hutchins' acceptance of all three of the postulates now being considered: "Grammar disciplines the mind and develops the logical faculty. It is good in itself and as an aid in reading the classics" (11, p. 82).

3. Criticism of the Doctrine of Man's Essential Rationality

While Aristotle's view of man is fresh in mind, we shall review several criticisms against it. Professor Sidney Hook's criticisms are complete and forceful (10, pp. 15-27). Hook severely attacks the "metaphysical rationalism" which holds that the ends of education can be deduced from the true nature of man; and that since man is a rational animal, the aim of education should be the cultivation of reason. Hook's main criticisms are as follows:

(a) Man's potentialities are multiple. Man is like the egg which might develop into a chicken, but which might also, among other things, become an egg sandwich! Thinking is no more natural to man than eating, singing, and numerous other activities. Man is not unique among animals merely because he is so rational. He is also the only animal that commits suicide, and that laughs. Benjamin Franklin and Karl Marx defined man as the tool-making animal. Should we conclude from this that man's education should be entirely vocational?

(b) If it be argued (as against *a* above) that rationality is the *important* essence of man, this overlooks man's emotional and other needs, which also require development. The training of reason cannot, in fact, be carried out independently of the education of the emotions.

(c) The mere existence of natural capacities is no cogent reason for developing them. What should be developed depends upon some ideal of appropriateness or need-fulfillment in the present and future, growing out of past experience. Feelings, emotions, rationality, and the like are good or bad depending on social contexts and outcomes.

(d) The conclusion of Hutchins and Adler that human nature always and everywhere is rational, irrespective of culture and epoch, is unrealistic. They speak as though human nature were completely independent of physical nature, even independent of the human body and all social contexts. The only entity that has such aloof independence is the soul of Christian theology.

4. Replies to Criticism

The replies of Neo-Scholastics to Hook's criticisms would very likely be as follows:

(a) Man's potentialities are indeed multiple, but they are not all of the same order of importance. It is quite evident from the data of biologic evolution and cultural history that man's superior intelligence is far more crucial for his advancement than his capacity to sing or to feel emotions. Intelligence is more universal in the species than the occasional liability to suicide. As for making tools, without man's intelligence there would be no tools worth mentioning.

(b) To be sure, man has an emotional and moral as well as an intellectual nature. But, as noted earlier, Aristotle, St. Thomas, and their modern spokesmen do not sharply separate reason from feeling and virtue. The cultivation of the intellect includes the discipline of the emotions. We discipline and curb certain emotions because we have the intelligence to see that their results will be bad. Man can safeguard his present and future needs for good feelings and moral actions only by using his intellectual resources.

(c) Assume with Hook that what is good and what should be developed depends on numerous aspects of the current scene viewed in the light of the past and desired future outcomes: But what is the source of the "light" which supplies all this guidance if not from man's intelligence? It may happen in individual or group experience that reason proves to be a poor guide, as when one tries to be reasonable with a man who is criminally insane. But it is later rational reflection which discovers this inefficacy of rationality! It is important to cultivate good feeling and sterling qualities of character, but it is intelligence which decides which feelings and qualities of character are desirable. If one were to deny the importance of cultivating the intellect, this would be self-contradictory because only intelligence could arrive at and validate the denial.

(d) What now of the charge that it is unrealistic to hold that human nature is always and everywhere rational irrespective of all physical, social, and other circumstances? This charge expresses a misunderstanding, if not of the neoclassicists, then of Aristotle, who inspired them. For Aristotle, the nature and significance of a thing is to be looked for in the end toward which it moves. For Aristotle, says W. D. Ross, "the explanation of things is to be found, not in what they have developed from, but in what they are developing into; their nature is seen, not in their origin, but in their destiny" (16, p. 237). Nonliving things can be defined in terms of their origin—an ornament of brass never can be an ornament of gold. But living things *evolve*. Human beings are not to be defined solely in terms of what they now are; they are partly understood in terms of what they may become.

Essentialists, like earlier faculty theorists, tend to view intelligence as a *substantive* entity—it exists whether or not it is active. The progressive critics of essentialists view intelligence as an *activity*, and have the support of modern psychologists. The faculty theorist did not usually hesitate to *infer a thing from a function*. This seems sensible enough when we are dealing with material things. When the clock stops running it still exists and is still a clock. But on the assumption that such faculties as memory and intelligence are nonmaterial, the question of whether or not they still exist when not being exercised is puzzling. This gives one reason why modern psychologists prefer to view mental capacities from the *functional* rather than the *substantive* point of view. In this respect the modern critic of essentialism is a better disciple of Aristotle than are the Aristotelians of essentialism. Aristotle held that the part of the soul we call reason (which thinks and judges) "is not actually any existing thing before it knows" (16, p. 212).

5. Hutchins' Revolts Against Current Evils

Hutchins inveighs against the evils of materialism in education and elsewhere. In all three of the books mentioned the love of money is considered the first and most vulgar cause of confusion in education. To appeal for money, whether from legislatures, donors, or students, a college runs the risk of selling its soul—and not getting the money. The surrender to materialism and outside pressure groups result in two related evils:

a. OVERSPECIALIZATION. We must always have specialists, but neither the world nor our knowledge of it shows the excessive departmentalization to be found in our universities. Specialization is so great that professors are scarcely able to speak intelligibly with other specialists in their own departments. This breakdown of communication is too serious to be remedied by such palliatives as roving professorships, interdivisional fields of study, and Institutes of Human Relations (as at Yale).

b. VOCATIONAL EDUCATION. The second evil, related to overspecialization, is the spread of no end of practical, vocational courses in our schools and colleges. Such courses inevitably result when the schools become the tools of that popular and perverse sense of "utility" to be found in America: That the only knowledge worth while must be of service in making money and in "getting ahead."

It must be noted that Hutchins does not regard material prosperity as an evil in itself. It is good because it enables us to live at all, but it does not guarantee that we shall live well. Man is a rational, moral, and spiritual being, and living well implies the exercise of the powers implied by these traits. (When material prosperity becomes an end in itself cultural decadence, strife, and moral eclipse are likely to set in. In the end, purely material progress cheats man of its primary use—healthy survival. In place of such survival prosperity brings insatiable demands for more and more luxurious living. Of these, the automobile alone kills more citizens than the mortality rate to be expected from downright poverty.)

The great pity is that many so-called vocational courses are quite inadequate as means for fitting students for jobs. With outmoded equipment and instruction the schools are usually behind the methods in actual use in business and industry. Schools are vainly endeavoring to train infinitely varied individuals for infinitely varied jobs. It is foolish to try to master knowledge suited to the current scene which refuses to remain current (13, pp. 51-54).

Hutchins counts on experience outside the schools to teach practical wisdom. We forget that students have homes, churches, newspapers, clubs, and jobs to educate them in practical matters while away from the campus. Industry has often demonstrated that it can train technologists more efficiently than can high schools and colleges.

There is only one remedy for these evils of a materialistic culture. This remedy is to achieve a radical and uncompromising return to Aristotle's dictum that man's full stature will appear with the full development of his rational, moral, and spiritual powers. What course of essential studies will deliver education from the worship of Mammon, and develop the pursuit of ideals which are ends in themselves and ways to the fullest realization of the humanity shared by all men?

6. The Essential Curriculum

The basic skills listed by Hutchins appear deceptively simple. He wishes merely to develop the abilities to think, read, write, and speak. These skills are the most practical—they will be valuable no matter what vocation the student enters. More important still, these skills are the bulwarks of democracy. Democracy requires the unflagging vigilance of intelligent, well-informed, and vocal citizens. Mortimer Adler holds that the trouble with democracy is that most people have not learned to read, or even to want to read, worthwhile books. Stringfellow Barr, former president of St. John's College, says that the bulwarks of democracy are reading, writing, talking, listening, and thinking (6, p. 9). But there is more than meets the eye in acquiring such skills. What studies develop them best?

a. CLASSIC BOOKS. Reading as a skill, in the views of Hutchins and Adler, is no merely pleasant and lazy "eye bath" mediated by comic strips, the yellow press, or even the best-seller list. Serious reading involves the study of great classics of past centuries, including the ancient and medieval periods. Classic books are significant for every age (11, p. 78). The dialogues of Socrates are perhaps more urgent today than when Plato wrote them. A man cannot be considered educated who has not read some of the great books of our Western tradition, yet many students graduate from college without having read any of them except perhaps Shakespeare. (The graduates of St. John's College have read a hundred or more of them.)

Of course, students learn about these books from textbooks. But Hutchins declares that textbooks have done more damage to education in the United States than has any other force (11, p. 78). If students want to know about Cicero, Milton, Galileo, or Adam Smith, why not read them in the original? We cannot understand the contemporary world without these books. The student should read Newton's *Principia* to see a fine genius in action, producing a book of great simplicity and elegance. This great work will give a basic understanding of modern science, Plato's *Republic* will introduce the student to the essentials of law, and Aristotle's *Physics* is important for natural science and medicine.

Mortimer J. Adler, Hutchins' associate while he was at the University of Chicago, also puts his leading faith in the reading of great books (1 and 2). Adler is not concerned with reading for amusement. He declares that reading is so dynamic a process that two hours of it leaves him exhausted!

b. GRAMMAR. It will now be clear that learning to read, in the opinions of Hutchins and Adler, is no sinecure for the languid or faint of heart. But this redoubtable art requires still another preparation in the form of grammar. Grammar is the scientific analysis of language and is the basis of being able to read. It develops the logical faculty.

c. RHETORIC. Rhetoric covers the rules of speaking and writing. Hutchins deplores the lost arts of speaking and writing. The great classical rules governing these arts are not to be found in popular courses in English composition (11, p. 83).

d. LOGIC AND MATHEMATICS. Logic is the study of the technical rules which govern valid reasoning. Mathematics, too, shows the operation of pure reason as it occurs universally in human thought. Correct thinking is acquired more impressively through the study of mathematics than in any other way. Mathematical study should be of the type found in Euclid's geometry. Arithmetic and geometry are usually presented to the student as having great practical value. This practice, says Hutchins, is a mistake. For now the student will resist the study of mathematics until its practical value is shown. Mathematics and logic have a higher utility than to serve greed—they develop the power of thinking which, since it is man's nature, has its own justification and satisfactions.

7. Required *Versus* Elective Studies

Essentialism is at opposite poles from child- or student-centered education as favored by progressives. Essentialism *prescribes* the course of study. In progressivism, especially of the "projects" variety, the present interests and preferences of the child are never disregarded in selecting the course of study.

Hutchins says that we cannot allow the child to dictate the course of study, with the teacher playing the role of chaperon. A free elective system is a confession that educators themselves do not know what contents are basic for education (11, pp. 70-71). This is why the curriculum becomes crowded with trivia, including such things as courses in "cosmetology" and courses for drum majors.

Adler's most recent utterances (3) grant certain contentions of progressives but without giving up the core ideas of essentialism. It is true that the student whose interest has not been aroused cannot be adequately taught. But we cannot be guided by the interests which the student happens to have because they are poor guides to what he *should* know. It is the business of the teacher to develop desirable interests in the student and then to satisfy them. How is the student to decide what he should know if the educator himself cannot answer this question? The teacher offering the student a variety of studies from which to make a selection which is considered interesting is behaving like a doctor who should offer his patient a variety of treatments and then ask him to select the one he likes best! (To improve this similitude, the doctor might first ask the patient what affliction he prefers.)

Adler proposes to reconcile the warring principles of required *versus* elective courses as follows: Determine what the course of study should be from a consideration of our common human needs—the humanity shared by all men. But apply this education differently in individual cases in recognition of individual peculiarities. That is, we should vary the *methods* of instruction to suit the individuality of the learner, but not give up the essential subject matter of instruction (3, p. 179).

8. Criticisms of Traditionalism

It will be noted that the essential curriculum as seen by Hutchins is also a *traditional* curriculum, all the way from the reading of classic books, through the study of grammar, logic, mathematics, etc. It will be well at this point to consider the main criticisms against the traditional curriculum.

The reaction against traditionalism naturally takes the form of a plea for the needs of the present and of the future. Alfred N. Whitehead has written some eloquent passages which underline the great importance of the present. He rejects the essentialist's view that the mind is an instrument which is first sharpened in school and then used during adulthood (18, pp. 8-9).

Sidney Hook justifies "presentism" in education with force and eloquence:

> Whatever other world an individual will inhabit, his life will be spent in this one. . . . Whatever we teach, whether it be a tale of glory, the procession of the seasons or the mystery of the atom, we teach ultimately for the sake of the present. We teach our children reading, writing and arithmetic not because they are skills that were once acquired by man—there have been many skills developed in the past that were better forgotten (10, pp. 70-71).

Hook's further criticisms of traditionalism, which express the views of many dissenters, are as follows (10, pp. 68-83):

(a) It is an error to suppose that because one criticizes traditionalists one means to reject all traditional knowledge. On the contrary, knowledge of the past throws light on present problems. We cannot, for instance, understand the present problem of totalitarian states without studying earlier writers like Plato, Aquinas, Nietzsche, and Hegel. For the analysis of propaganda, what text would serve us better than Hitler's *Mein Kampf?* The problem of conserving natural resources involves the study of many sciences which were developed in the past.

(b) But although traditional knowledge has relevance for the present, education should center attention on present problems. These are the great social, political, intellectual, and spiritual problems which confront us today. We do not have to study grammar, rhetoric, and logic in order to be intellectual—this end is accomplished as well by studying other things, such as the modern sciences. To hold up "visions of greatness" is excellent, but not all great heroes have lived in the past. We should study great books, but not all of them are historic.

(c) Consider now the absurdity of a classical curriculum devoted to the social, political, and other problems of antiquity—of every age but the present age! Traditionalists object when we give courses dealing with modern waterways and sanitary systems. But they "regard it as perfectly proper to study and glow about the marvels of Roman aqueducts, plumbing, and roads" (10, p. 76).

(d) It is true that traditionalists often argue that knowledge of the past will help solve present problems. Thus, Alexander Meiklejohn defends the classical curriculum at St. John's College on this ground. But Hook thinks it better to center education on present problems, and to draw on tradition where it will be of help. To study the cultures of Greece and Rome *as wholes* in the interest of their present use is like swallowing a barrel of chaff to get a grain of wheat (10, pp. 78-79).

(e) A common misunderstanding of those who wish to center education on the problems of today has to do with the rate or tempo of historical change. Thus, Hutchins wishes to study only permanent things, and accuses modern educators of the cult of immediacy. But if we insist on studying only the permanent, we should not study such things as feudalism, capitalism, and the rise and decline of empires because they will eventually come to an end. To attack the study of present problems because they are transitory implies a false disjunction. It implies that things are either unchanging or ephemeral, so that a course of study is either profound or superficial (10, p. 74). Hook denounces these alternatives as absurd. The problems of our day have come into existence gradually, and will not vanish in a fortnight (10, p. 74).

9. Education and Democracy

Benjamin Fine and others have charged that essentialism stands for "aristocratic education," which they compare unfavorably with the democratic education supposedly nurtured by progressivism (6, p. 10). It is true that higher education during earlier times was the gentleman's prerogative, and it did consist largely of traditional and cultural subjects considered appropriate for the life of leisure.

Yet, from another point of view, Hutchins is the democrat for he wishes to extend the "gentleman's education" to all; not as an ornament of snobbery, but as a safeguard of the democratic way of life. Vocational high schools and professional colleges face the danger of becoming mere training schools for wage earners. To safeguard democracy our people must learn to govern as well as to work. They must learn to cherish the values and ideals for which democracy stands, and these are revealed in our history and cultural inheritance. The citizen must realize that liberty is painfully won. It is easily lost to those who are "factory-wise" but uninterested and unversed in learning how to read, listen, write, and speak.

Thomas Jefferson wrote, "If a nation expects to be ignorant and free . . . it expects what never was and never will be" (15, p. 89). In similar vein William E. Hocking declares that freedom cannot be legislated for a man who has no head for it. "Give him a vote, and he will use it if he has an idea. If he has none, he will ask his boss, his friend, his club, and then where is his liberty?" (9, pp. 13-14).

Of course, no philosophy of education has a monopoly on the aim of developing vigilant intelligence in the citizenry, but essentialism may claim that it accents the development of higher intelligence as opposed to vocational training; which training taken alone or made primary may spell industrial slavery with consequent class warfare to restore the rights which were lost when liberal education was sacrificed.

10. The Administration of Essentialism

Essentialism in the lower grades and in the high schools is too familiar to need description, at least not for the older generation of citizens. It consisted of a curriculum of standard courses, given in definite sequence from easier to more difficult levels of study. The colleges have been and still are the strongholds of essentialism, and their requirements for college admission have held the high schools to an "essential" program of studies. The impact of progressive education, however, has partially disrupted the old pattern of fixed and essential courses, and has led to a relaxation of requirements for college admission. Hutchins gives his own account of the aims and practices at the University of Chicago (12, Chapter 4).

Both at St. John's College and at the University of Chicago students have been admitted to the freshman class after the completion of the second year of high school. Those who entered college as high-school graduates have been granted the Bachelor of Arts degree after two years of college work. Other colleges have severely criticized this practice. Thus, the New York State Department of Education declined to accept Chicago's Bachelor's degree, and credited it as no more than two years of college work. The student's work at Chicago under the administration of Hutchins was comprehensive and rigorous, well calculated to "cultivate the intellectual virtues." The qualification for the Bachelor's degree did not consist in the usual accumulation of course credits. The graduating student had to pass about a dozen comprehensive examinations in basic areas of the social sciences, humanities, physical sciences, biological sciences, and English. Integration was stressed, the seniors taking a special integrating course covering earlier studies.

⩔ B. John Macdonald on Interest, Effort, and Moral Discipline

John Macdonald is selected as our third proponent of essentialism because his emphases supplement those of Hutchins and Adler. The ideal citizen in Aristotle's view is the individual who has developed to the utmost those qualities which define man's nature: namely, reason and virtue. Macdonald applies essentialist ideas in a convincing way to the problems of character development. The power or faculty involved is the will or what might be termed "will-character." The issue concerns the respective educative merits of doing things by voluntary effort or doing them through spontaneous interest. Macdonald proposes to show, as against John Dewey, that effort in the pursuit of goals has educative values which are not found in goal-seeking under the drive of spontaneous interest.

We confine our analysis to a single chapter of Macdonald's recent book, *Mind, School and Civilization*, 1952 (14, Chapter 4).

1. Is General Character Training Possible?

It is the traditional belief of mankind that qualities of character are subject to training. *General* qualities of character are such relatively permanent traits as perseverance, endurance, the power of sustained concentration, and self-control. A trait is *general* if it operates in all or nearly all situations to which it is relevant. Thus, generosity is general when it governs its possessor in all situations which call for generosity. But a father who is generous only to his own children shows it as a *special* trait. General traits are assumed to provide for *transfer* in the sense that the individual can use them, once they are developed, in subsequent situations. The problem is this: Do *general* qualities of character exist; and if they do exist, can they be developed by deliberate training in the schools? Unfortunately, says Macdonald, there are no experimental findings on these questions, hence we must depend on general psychological considerations (14, p. 24).

Macdonald is in error about the lack of experimental work on the problems in question, as will appear in Chapter 6. For the present mention may be made of the three volumes of work of H. Hartshorne and M. A. May (8). The experimental studies of Hartshorne and May were mostly of the "performance" type, and were made with school children.

One general result of these studies was the conclusion that such traits as honesty, cooperation, and generosity are largely specific for specific situations. This finding is adverse to Macdonald's belief that there are general character traits that function in many life situations to which they are relevant. An excellent critical examination of this whole problem is given by Gordon W. Allport (4, Chapters 9 and 10).

2. Interest *Versus* Effort in Education

Educators are of two minds regarding appeals to interest in instruction. The proponents of interest hold it to be obvious that when children are interested they learn quickly. It is therefore the duty of the teacher always to keep the interests of her charges in mind. The opposite view puts its faith in effort rather than interest as a sound educative principle.

John Dewey regarded this opposition of effort and interest as one of the false dualisms which bedevil education. Other dualisms which Dewey berates are the separation of work from leisure, culture from vocation, and means from ends (see Chapter 16). For Dewey, effort and interest are but two aspects of the same activity. Interest has reference to the needs which motivate an activity and the satisfactions which accompany success. Effort refers merely to the energy output during activity. Dewey concludes that the curriculum must appeal to the pupil's needs and satisfactions, for only these can arouse the interest which accompanies dynamic effort and effective learning. In time, these ideas led to "child-centered" education in America. The basic ideas involved had been sketched by Rousseau over a hundred years earlier.

3. Immediate *Versus* Remote Goals

The distinction between immediate and remote goals and interests is obvious. Consider the child engaged in any favorite pursuit: Interest is immediate and strong. The energy expended may leave the child exhausted, yet this is not experienced as effort. If one wants a paradox one can say that while the child is playing there is "effortless effort." In this case, Macdonald concedes, Dewey is quite correct—there is here no conflict between interest and effort.

On the other hand, consider the child at school learning the multiplication tables or other material he finds abhorrent. As the child sees it, even being in school is not his or her purpose—it is the purpose of parents and teachers. The need for knowing the multiplication tables is *remote*. In this case a real dualism occurs between effort and interest. The child is forced to pursue a remote goal with effort, and is unable to tap the "effortless effort" which is so effective when an immediate and interesting activity engages attention. The question is, can the effortful pursuit of remote goals develop general character traits? Macdonald thinks that an affirmative answer can be given to this question (14, pp. 26-28).

4. Effort, Remote Goals, and Character

Without invoking an entire prolegomenon to morals it appears obvious that many remote goals which do not arouse spontaneous desire and interest in the present are nevertheless worth pursuing. Actions leading to such goals have one thing in common besides the value of attaining the goals: namely, *resistance to present inclination*. This is the general trait present in deliberate or voluntary forms of such behavior as perseverance, concentration, and self-control. Persistence in denying present inclination when a remote goal must be attained will tend to become habitual. Such habitual discipline develops will-character, which will yield transfer effects to other situations where present sacrifices must be made in order to attain a remote goal. (In terms of a picturesque expression encountered among laymen, this way of life "develops the backbone instead of the wishbone.")

Macdonald declares that there is nothing wrong in requiring the child to pursue goals which he does not as yet understand and which he must accept from others (14, p. 29). He regards as dubious the notion that such moral discipline of the child is contrary to the interests of mental hygiene. Sometimes the attempt is made to support this view by the questionable assertion that primitive peoples are free from nervous disorders because their lives are free from inhibitions. Even if this bit of anthropology be accepted as true, Macdonald notes that the end product, after all, is a savage! "Civilized society needs a very different product" (14, p. 30).

Macdonald concludes that it is possible to develop generalized and transfer-bearing character traits through that discipline which selects present effortful action in the service of remote interests in place of spontaneous action in the pursuit of immediate interests. Such moral discipline is an essential part of education. Those without it will fail to attain many of the precious things of life which require present self-denial.

The fact is that those who advocate the basing of education on the pupil's needs often use language which has the effect of obscuring the greatest need of all, the need for a discipline that will put him in the way of attaining the most deeply satisfying of life's experiences. This is not a plea for a return to a hard and joyless puritanism in education. It is simply a reminder of a fundamental fact of the moral life. Any theory of education which tends to obscure this fact, or to make us forget it, is bad (14, pp. 31-32).

‡ C. The Moderate Essentialism of E. E. Day and A. W. Griswold

The late Edmund E. Day served as president of Cornell University for a period of over twelve years. His philosophy of education has some points in common with the ideas of Hutchins (5).

1. Traditionalism

Day, like other essentialists, stresses the role of education in maintaining social solidarity by teaching the convictions, loyalties, and cultural appreciations which, as Hutchins would say, belong to the "common humanity" of a democratic society.

2. Essential Subjects

With something of the beguiling but rather deceptive simplicity of the essentialists, Day tells us that the essential skills consist of speaking, hearing, reading, and writing. That the "reading" Day has in mind is not to be confused with restful recreation becomes clear when we are told that education should cultivate the intellectual powers, establish good intellectual habits, enthusiasms, and moral attitudes (5, pp. 6-13).

3. An Over-all Program

Like Hutchins and some other recent writers Day favors a period of general education shorter than the present one by two years. There should be six years of elementary schooling in place of the traditional eight years. This should be followed by four years of high school devoted fundamentally to a common and general education for all students. During this period, however, the special interests and capacities of students should be determined for possible future vocational education. Following high school there would be differentiated institutions for vocational education, in addition to colleges and universities.

4. Vocational Training

Day does not propose to exclude vocational and professional training from the university. Most of the colleges at Cornell where he served as president are vocational or professional. The essentialist flavor of Day's thought appears, however, in his insistence that vocational and professional training should not be given in the form of highly specialized routine skills which are required by many jobs. Vocational instruction can and should be given in terms of basic subject disciplines upon which the vocations rest. If this is done vocational training will remain intellectual (5, pp. 56-57).

Alfred W. Griswold, president of Yale University, is a liberal essentialist, along with Edmund E. Day and numerous college presidents of the past and present. In his recent *Essays on Education* (7) Griswold notes that the trivium and quadrivium have been properly broadened to include language, literature, philosophy, the fine arts, and history.

These subjects can and should be taught in a context that includes the sciences and social studies. I do not suggest shrinking them down to their hard medieval core and offering that as the whole apple. My point is that in our national educational system they have already shrunk to a brown and seedy core which the janitor has picked up and is about to drop in the wastebasket, and that unless we rescue this and plant it and cultivate it, its fruit will be lost to a society that desperately needs it (7, p. 125).

As indicated in this passage, Griswold believes that the liberal arts are in danger of being lost, and his essays give good evidence in support of this fear. The two World Wars brought a general impoverishment which leads the overtaxed citizen to look upon liberal arts education as a luxury which we cannot afford. At the same time, wars stress technological training in the schools and colleges as an emergency measure. When once intrenched, such technical training does not easily yield to the more liberal education which it has replaced. Again, the great increase in the school population expected in the future, together with a growing shortage of adequately trained teachers, will lead to lowered admission requirements in the schools, to "accelerated" programs, and lowered scholarship.

In addition to the threats against liberal education noted above, there is the disturbing enmity of totalitarian nations which is hostile to all freedom of thought. But Griswold has Plato's faith in the eternal power of ideas.

Books won't stay banned. They survive burning. Ideas won't go to jail. In the long run of history, the censor and the inquisitor have always lost. The only sure weapon against bad ideas is better ideas. The source of better ideas is wisdom. The surest path to wisdom is a liberal education (7, p. 96).

☿ D. Prologue to Future Chapters

Controversy rages about the five postulates of essentialism. But three of these postulates in particular are so obscure that even essentialists tend to mention them gingerly and hasten on. These troublesome dark spots are: (a) the faculty psychology, (b) the doctrine of formal discipline, and (c) the principle of transfer of training. Many critics regard these as three "skeletons in the closet" of essentialism—as three defunct traditions of traditionalism. But not all has been "said and done" about these dark regions of inquiry, and they will be discussed in Chapters 5 and 6 which follow. The statement that "two plus two equals four" may be regarded as a "closed incident." But questions which have not been properly answered are never closed incidents to a true philosopher or educator. He will probe them, if not in the hope of finding an answer, then with the grim determination to discover the range and depth of our ignorance. It is only after discussing the related problems of mental faculties, their discipline, and transfer values that we can properly evaluate essentialism and traditionalism as points of view in education.

References

1. Adler, Mortimer J. "The Crisis in Contemporary Education." *Social Frontier,* 1939, Vol. 42, pp. 141 ff.
2. ————. *How to Read a Book; The Art of Getting a Liberal Education.* New York: Simon & Schuster, 1940.
3. ————. "Doctor and Disciple." *Journal of Higher Education,* 1952, Vol. 23, pp. 173-179.
4. Allport, Gordon W. *Personality, a Psychological Interpretation.* New York: Holt, 1937.
5. Day, Edmund E. *Education for Freedom and Responsibility* (M. R. Konvitz, ed.). Ithaca, N. Y.: Cornell University Press, 1952.
6. Fine, Benjamin. *Democratic Education.* New York: Crowell, 1945.
7. Griswold, Alfred W. *Essays on Education.* New Haven, Conn.: Yale University Press, 1954.
8. Hartshorne, Hugh, & Mark A. May. (With Maller, J. B.) *Studies in Deceit,* New York: Macmillan, 1928. *Studies in Service and Self-Control,* New York: Macmillan, 1929. (With Shuttleworth, F. K.), *Studies in the Organization of Character,* New York: Macmillan, 1930.
9. Hocking, William E. *What Man Can Make of Man.* New York: Dial Press, 1942.
10. Hook, Sidney. *Education for Modern Man.* New York: Dial Press, 1946.
11. Hutchins, Robert M. *The Higher Learning in America.* London: Oxford University Press, 1936.
12. ————. *Education for Freedom.* Baton Rouge, La.: Louisiana State University Press, 1943.
13. ————. *The Conflict in Education in a Democratic Society.* New York: Harper, 1953.
14. Macdonald, John. *Mind, School and Civilization.* Chicago: University of Chicago Press, 1952.
15. Padover, Saul K. (ed.). *Thomas Jefferson on Democracy.* New York: New American Library, 1946.
16. Ross, William D. *Aristotle.* London: Methuen, 1923.
17. Van Doren, Mark. *Liberal Education.* New York: Holt, 1943.
18. Whitehead, Alfred N. *The Aims of Education and Other Essays.* New York: Macmillan, 1929.

chapter 5

MENTAL ORGANIZATION: FROM FACULTIES
TO PRIMARY MENTAL ABILITIES

It has been stated that the air in rural regions is so fresh because the farmers shut up the bad air in their houses! This somewhat scurrilous pleasantry resembles another one authored by Jules Henri Poincaré who said that the clarity found in books about nature is often secured by leaving all of the darkness outside! In education there are similar certainties in the midst of a vast darkness. Each philosophy of education boasts of a basic course of studies which, when pursued by the methods specified, will develop the mind, personality, character, and even the body. But these aspects of the pupil developed by tutelage are themselves dark mysteries. It is rather astonishing that we can agree so readily that growth has taken place in a given individual when we are not sure what is doing the growing. Essentialism, which especially stresses mental discipline, encounters the oddity that the mind, which clarifies other things, is itself a mystery that parries attempts to fathom its innermost nature.

There are roughly three types of essentialists: (a) There are the radicals, now almost extinct, who insist on a course of studies which will develop the powers of mind. If the subject matter involved is useful and interesting, so much the better; but a course which will develop the mental sinews is not rejected by this group because its contents are relatively useless. (b) Another group of essentialists goes in for breadth and moderation. Its members want a course of studies which will both develop the powers of mind and impart essential knowledge. (c) The members of the third group use the word *essential* to refer only to useful subject matter.

In this chapter we are concerned with essentialism in the first two senses. The first group regards the development of the pupil's mental powers as a "must," and the second group also gives mental development a high rating. What, then, is the nature of the mental abilities we seek to develop? Since one of the aims of every teacher is to develop the minds of pupils we should make every effort to determine the nature of the mind that is being developed. Historic essentialism held to the faculty theory of mind. This theory is hoary with age and full of superficialities. As W. H. Cowley notes, faculty psychology has had no important defenders for half a century (1, p. 9). But the issues raised by faculty psychology form an excellent introduction to the problem of the nature of mind and its organization. This is a basic problem for every philosophy of education.

The purpose of this chapter is to explore the dark regions of the mind and its mysterious "powers." We shall divide our inquiry into the following steps:

A. Faculty Psychology: Its History and Concepts
B. Modern Research on Mental Abilities
C. Modern Research and Faculty Theory
D. Summary: Bearings on Essentialism

▽ A. Faculty Psychology: Its History and Concepts

There are many historical faculty theories. The first problem is to find a definition of the faculties that is fairly representative. Faculty psychology was present in the writings of ancient philosophers and became more explicit in the eighteenth and nineteenth centuries, and still exists implicitly in modern psychology. Whatever their differences, all faculty theories hold that there are distinct and general powers of the soul (mind) which enter into and explain the mental and even bodily performances of the individual. Faculty theorists took functional terms in common use, such as perception, memory, imagination, reasoning, instinct, and feeling. These were called the "faculties" of the soul. Then, by "armchair" analysis, these activities were reduced to a few principle faculties to which the others were subordinated, thus often given a hierarchical conception of the "powers of the soul." Reason or the intellect usually stood at the head of the hierarchy as the most important of the faculties.

Faculty theories are numerous and contradictory, and their authors are generally unknown individuals who existed long ago. As a result, modern ideas about faculty psychology often fall wide of the mark, take liberties with history, and repeat hearsay on the subject. There are two misunderstandings about faculty psychology which deserve special mention. They are as follows:

(a) Did the faculty psychologists hold that the soul is constituted entirely of its faculties, so that there is no remainder when all the faculties are enumerated? The answer is "No" for most faculty theories. The faculties were conceived as only powers *possessed by the soul*, after the manner in which current thinking regards the mind or ego as something over and above its aptitudes. Thus, the faculty theorists for the most part held that when the soul acted through any faculty it nevertheless had an existence of its own.

(b) The faculties were regarded as distinct from each other: They were distinguished and counted. Many critics erroneously take this to imply that the faculties were thought to *act independently* of each other. But the fact that two things are regarded as *distinct* implies only that they are *distinguishable*, not that they are necessarily *separate* or causally *independent of each other*. The color and shape of an apple are distinct but they do not exist in isolation—the apple unites them. The brain is both distinct and separate from the muscles, but they show causal interaction. The reader no doubt distinguishes between such mental functions as perceiving an object, remembering it, and reasoning about it, but realizes that these three activities interact.

Without perception there would be little or even nothing to remember. Without memories (knowledge) reason would not have materials to reason about. Practically all faculty theorists of the past considered that the mental faculties interacted with each other at the mental level. It is true, however, that they simplified this interaction far too much. Again, faculty theorists realized that the powers of mind are thrown into joint action by the outside task which engages them. Thus, to perform the work of a carpenter or merchant at once requires alert perception, accurate memory, and good judgment. This is very similar to the view which prevails among modern psychologists engaged in mental testing and among teachers in giving and grading examinations. They realize that a task or test may involve the activity of a number of mental capacities. Even Thomas Hobbes (*Leviathan*, 1651), an early critic of faculty theorists, credits them with teaching that the senses supply materials to be retained as memories, and that memory supplies the materials for reflection.

It would take us too far afield to examine in detail the writings of early faculty theorists with a view to showing that they were not guilty of the two errors commonly charged against them. (a) They realized that all of the faculties taken together do not exhaust the nature of the mind. The faculties were viewed as "powers of the soul." In this same way the modern psychologist speaks of the "mind," "self," or "ego" as superordinate entities to which individual traits and abilities "belong." (b) Faculty psychologists on the whole were not guilty of holding that the powers of mind operated in isolation from each other. Outstanding faculty psychologists of the past, such as Aristotle (384-322 B.C.), St. Thomas Aquinas (1225-1274), and Christian Wolff (1679-1754) did not hold to these errors.

Catholic writers on the philosophy of education deny that scholastic philosophers held to the doctrine of independent faculties. John D. Redden and Francis A. Ryan write:

> Some writers have falsely ascribed faculty psychology to scholasticism. Aristotle and the scholastics did use the term "faculties" in reference to the ways in which the soul manifests its activities, but they never taught that these "faculties" were separate and independent, or that they were air-tight compartments of the mind, as it were, each carrying out its particular role in its own peculiar costume (3, pp. 172-173).

There were two closely associated faculty theorists of the past who were guilty of gross errors regarding the nature of the mind, and they deserve the condemnations which are usually charged against all faculty theories. Franz Joseph Gall (1758-1828) developed a physiological version of faculty theory: *phrenology*. Gall and his collaborator Johann K. Spurzheim set forth their views in their *Introduction au cours de Physiologie du Cerveau* (1808). The mind or self, Gall held, has a number of distinct functions, each one located in a specific area of the brain. Gall recognized a total of about thirty of such faculties and his followers extended the list. Thus, such things as imitation, the poetic faculty, destructiveness, and veneration were regarded as located in special areas of the brain. Gall's followers added the notion that the degree of development of an individual's faculties could be determined from prominences or "bumps" on the skull. (Psychologists of today enjoy a little pleasantry to the effect that the "bumps" on a man's head tell more about his wife's characteristics than about his own.)

Phrenology no doubt supplies the deserving "whipping boy" of criticism against faculty psychology. It put the faculties into separate compartments. The faculties were held to interact only in the rather spurious sense that they might be simultaneously active, each one doing its part, in some outwardly defined task. Modern neurologists, knowing vastly more about the cortical localization of functions, do not pretend to know where veneration is "located." We are rather sure that Gall's thirty faculties and their locations are armchair fictions. Modern psychologists, aware of the complex and subtle interrelations between mental functions, find Gall's notions merely childish.

Chiefly to be condemned was the *method* of discovering the faculties. Whenever some new function of mind was noticed, a new "faculty" was at once invented to explain it. This led to the inordinate multiplication of faculties—or say, rather, the multiplication of *labels.* The story is told that early pharmacologists wished to explain why opium induced sleep. This action of opium, they decided, was due to its "dormative potency." Such invention of labels gives neither adequate description nor adequate explanation. It does not usually give even adequate *identification,* which is the most we can expect from a label.

The brief tale of errors given so far about faculty psychology has some practical values. The educator must beware of the vagaries of faculty theory and the fallacy of labels. It is easy to fall into the error of supposing that since a course of study may be contained in a single book, it demands the exercise of some one capacity of the mind, and then teach in accordance with this idea. The teachers of history, geography, and languages, noting that these subjects bristle with itemized facts and words, teach them primarily as exercises for the memory. The teacher of mathematics, noting the beautiful and sweeping principles it affords, may teach it *abstractly,* without applying it to concrete problems.

In diagnosing the handicaps of learners, there is a whole catalogue of labels to draw from. Thus, "strephosymbolia" and "word-blindness" are labels for "explaining" difficulties in reading, but this baptism does not cure the condition and seldom prescribes a good remedy. The capacities of mind interact so fully that each one has some responsibility for a task-defined handicap. Learning, as William H. Kilpatrick is wont to say, is never single. Defined in terms of the outward task, adding or multiplying numbers seems to be a single activity. But psychologically almost the entire mind takes part in each of these activities. More, the zestful mastery of arithemetic can lead to development of attitudes and character. There are always concomitant learnings.

Although official psychology has shunned a theory of mind which the doctrine of faculties favors, educators of the past or even of the present have shown no such aversion. W. H. Cowley cites evidences of the currency of such terminology occurring as late as the latter half of the nineteenth century (1, p. 9). The use of such terms as *faculties* and *mental powers* will be found in some of the most recent writings in education. Such functional terms as memory, reasoning, and the like are so indispensable that without them intelligible discussion of either psychology or education is seriously handicapped if not impossible. It must be remembered, however, that the terminology used by a writer is not always a reliable index of what he means. If one speaks of a man's capacity for veneration, that does not imply that one believes veneration to be located in a phrenological bump. In short, whether or not the use of the term *faculty* is to be criticized depends on what is meant by it.

Our acquaintance with historical faculty theories is now sufficient for undertaking a far more searching criticism of any attempt to understand the mind and its activities. Our interest in this matter is far from being merely historical. We shall see in what follows that modern psychology and educational philosophy are heirs to the redoubtable problems faced by the faculty theorists of the past. Yet a sound philosophy of education must come to grips as best it can with the problem of the nature of the mental capacities which education seeks to develop. We shall attack this problem by probing further into the difficulties faced by the faculty theory of mind. These difficulties turn out to be the very ones we face today, and they are not solved by merely dropping the terms "faculties" and "powers" of the mind and replacing them with the terms "abilities" and "aptitudes."

▽ B. Modern Research on Mental Abilities

Modern literature on mental abilities and their organization is very extensive, and involves highly developed experimental procedures and mathematical methods of analysis. We shall deal with the subject only to the extent necessary to answer two main questions: (a) Are there problems which both ancient faculty psychology and modern mental analysis fail to answer? (b) Do the positive discoveries of modern analysis suggest the complete falsity of the doctrine of essentialism that distinguishable and general powers of mind exist, or do modern discoveries suggest a revision of essentialism without destroying it?

1. Origins and Methods

Beginning with the work of Carl Spearman in 1904, a modern approach to the problem of mental abilities and their organization was carried forward. The new approach was developed chiefly in England and in the United States. In the 1920's and 1930's technical journals of psychology abounded with research studies, and lively debates centered on such questions as the number, nature, and interrelations of mental abilities. The main method of experimentation was to give batteries of tests to groups of subjects, score the tests, perhaps revise the tests and give them again, meanwhile controlling the variables in the experimental situation and in regard to the testees used. The nature of mental abilities was inferred from the test results, not from mere speculation about the "powers of mind." The existence of an ability was inferred from evidences showing that scores on given tests tended to remain constant for given individuals but varied from one individual to another.

Test results are analyzed mainly by two mathematical methods. Carl Spearman, Godfrey H. Thomson, and other earlier workers depended on correlational analysis. Instead of seeking for the faculties of mind the modern psychologist seeks for "factors" which determine test results. In a similar spirit, the physicist thinks it more sensible to observe what electricity does to his instruments before he tries to answer the question, "What is the nature of electricity?" What are the factors of mental ability as determined by their effects on the psychologist's instrument, the tests? To answer this query simply and briefly, the procedure is as follows: (a) If two sets of test scores correlate positively it is concluded that there are mental factors which these tests measure in common. That is, the positive correlation implies that there are certain (as yet unidentified) factors of ability which entered into both test performances. (b) If two tests show zero or nearly zero correlation it is concluded that they have no factors in common. (c) If two tests show negative correlation this means that one test measures degrees of the presence of a factor, the other test measures degrees of its absence.

Besides the method of correlation and its adjuncts, which need not here be described, newer methods are widely current under the title of *factor analysis*. Various methods of factor analysis have been developed by such men as Louis L. Thurstone, Truman L. Kelley, and Cyril Burt. This method begins with a set (matrix) of all possible correlations between scores from a battery of tests. These correlations are then subjected to mathematical analysis which we need not describe. Such factor analysis shows, for each battery of tests, the number of mental factors of ability which are necessary to explain the test intercorrelations. Stated in another way, factor analysis indicates the number of factors which must be assumed to account for all variances of test scores. It shows the degree to which each factor entered into each test. These are called *factor* weights or *loadings* of the test. The greater the loading of a test with a certain factor, the greater the influence of that factor on the score earned in the test.

It will be noticed that factor analysis indicates *how many* mental factors are operating in the minds of the testees. It is not immediately revealed *what* the factors are or *how* they function. But factor analysis answers first questions first. It is first necessary to know whether or not a given factor *is* affecting test scores before asking how it does its work. Put bluntly, this is a way of avoiding superstitions. It would be wise to discover whether or not pixies exist before concluding that they sour the milk!

2. Results of Factor Analysis

Without giving the special views of individual workers, we may say that there is agreement regarding the existence of three main classes of factors:

a. GENERAL (g) FACTORS.   When a large number of tests show positive intercorrelations, and especially when the intercorrelations form a pattern known as hierarchical order (Spearman), it is concluded that a g, or general factor, exists. In this way Carl Spearman validated the concept of general intelligence. Later on, other g factors were found, such as perseveration (p), which refers to the general inertia of mental processes —their resistance to change. Thus, the individual who finds it difficult to shift from one activity to a different one is said to be a perseverator. Another g is called the will (w) factor. This factor appears in studies of personality and character, and is shown by tests of such traits as persistence, decision, and self-control.

b. SPECIAL (s) FACTORS.   These are narrow factors or "specifics" which affect score results of particular tests. Thus, color vision is a factor which determines most of the score on a color-blindness test.

c. GROUP FACTORS.   Sometimes a group of related tests show something in common which is not accounted for by some g factor which may also be present. This is called a *group factor*. It is apparent that group factors occupy a position intermediate between g and s factors of ability. Most investigators of today favor the view that batteries of test results are best explained by a relatively small number of group factors.

3.   From Factors to Mental Abilities

After our modern research worker has given his tests and analyzed them for the factors they involve, he is inclined to turn to the question, "What are the primary abilities in the minds of the subjects to which the factors correspond?" When the factor analyst asks this question he is tempted, like the faculty psychologist, to borrow labels from current psychology. When factor analysts do this they often list the names of "abilities" which are often found in ancient lists of the "faculties." This holds for such functions as intelligence, linguistic ability, number comprehension, and perception. Thus Spearman identifies the g factor which he discovered as *general intelligence*. As for the inner nature of g Spearman tentatively suggested that it is the general mental energy of an individual.

The conception which regards intelligence as mental energy reminds one of the faculty theorist's talk about mental "powers." Intelligence, which Spearman calls a g factor, was called a faculty by Aristotle and by St. Thomas. St. Thomas concluded that reason (intelligence) gets at the essences of things—it abstracts and generalizes. Spearman voices a similar opinion when he declares that the best tests of intelligence are those dealing with abstract relations.

4. The Work of L. L. and T. G. Thurstone

Basing their conclusions on their own extensive research and that of others, the Thurstones distinguish about twelve primary abilities or "facilities" as they sometimes call them. Those best established include such facilities (essentially group factors) as the following:

1. Verbal comprehension
2. Number (or number manipulation)
3. Associative memory (as in rote learning)
4. Perceptual speed

5. Philip E. Vernon's Hierarchy of Mental Factors

P. E. Vernon, an English investigator (4, pp. 22-23), analyzed thirteen tests given to one thousand army recruits. He came out with a hierarchical pattern of mental abilities. General intelligence stands at the head of this hierarchy. This means that general intelligence accounts for most of the test intercorrelations. When the effects of g are ruled out, two main subgroups of factors appear. The conclusions of the Thurstones and of Vernon given above are indeed reported in scanty fashion, but they suffice for the purpose of indicating the effects of modern research on faculty theory.

⊽ C. Modern Research and Faculty Theory

The general aim of this chapter has been to explore the dark regions of the mind to discover what faculties, powers, or abilities inhabit it. There remains the task of considering results in terms of their effects on essentialism as a philosophy of education. We turn now to consider our first question: Are there any problems of mind which both ancient faculty psychology and modern factor analysis fail to solve?

1. General Mental Powers Cannot Be Described

The modern psychologist, although he shuns such terms as "faculties," "powers," and "potentialities," does use terms with somewhat similar meanings; namely, "abilities," "skills," and "aptitudes." The question is, can *general* mental entities or powers, whether we call them "faculties" or "abilities," be described? We can indeed describe *particular* mental processes, but not the general functions which underlie them. For instance, one can report on some particular idea which arises in the mind and indicate how it is associated with other ideas, but we are at a loss when asked to describe the "faculty" or "aptitude" to ideate. We may experience and report on a particular feeling, but what awareness have we about a general faculty of feeling? We can report on our memories but do not know how to describe memory as a pure or general act of the mind apart from the contents of memory.

William James gave an illustration of the difficulty encountered when we try to penetrate too deeply into the "pure" nature of the mind. James distinguished a number of "selves" in each individual, such as the conscious self, the bodily self, the social self. At the core of these we have the pure ego. This innermost entity owns all of the others. Thus, your mental processes are not the ego, they are only its activities. Such things as your memories, hands, feet, social position are not *you*—they are your *possessions*. The dilemma is that the possessions can be described but not so the pure ego to which they somehow belong. William James once declared that after "mistrusting consciousness" for twenty years he had the courage to deny its existence! (2, Chapter 1). Such a denial appears to be unmitigated nonsense until we reflect that James meant to deny the existence of *general* consciousness as an entity, apart from *particular* conscious activities. We can observe and describe particular images, feelings, memories, thoughts. But when all particular processes vanish consciousness does not continue its existence like an empty stage waiting for more players!

The points made above are not intended to prove that pure, abstract, and general powers of mind do not exist. No doubt the reader experiences activities of perceiving, remembering, and reasoning as *acts*, to be distinguished from their *contents;* namely, *what* is perceived, remembered, or thought. But one cannot erect a science of psychology about mental processes which are not subject to introspective description. This consideration is one of the main reasons why modern psychology has rejected faculty psychology.

What is more, the psychologist feels that concepts about such general entities and powers of mind are useless when it comes to *causal* explanations of the mind's activities. Consider the faculty psychologist at work: In place of studying the concrete processes of memory experimentally he dubbed it the "faculty of memory." When special activities of memory were noticed (such as memory for numbers versus memory for words) he invented subordinate faculties to account for them. The term *memory* is, so far, merely a label which neither describes nor explains how one remembers. To say that a man suffers from lumbago does not explain his illness—it *is* his illness. Similarly, one may say that recalling the past is an act of memory; this merely identifies it but does not explain *how* the mind recalls the past. As R. S. Woodworth said, one might as well try to explain the flight of birds by crediting them with a "faculty of flight."

2. Modern Psychology and the Dilemma

The modern experimental approach to mental processes does not escape the difficulties set forth above, which confronted faculty psychology. Examples will make this clear. Thurstone speaks of "verbal comprehension." We are sure that this factor appears when verbal materials are being studied, as in tests or courses of study. But the tests tell us very little about the "comprehension" exercised by the testee while dealing with verbal materials. Factor analysis uses only test scores—after the process which earned the scores has ended. Thurstone speaks of "associative memory." This too is identified in terms of the concrete memorization of rote materials. How the testee does the "associating" is not revealed by the test score.

The same may be said of Vernon's uses of such terms as *verbal, mechanical,* and *numerical* to identify his factors of mind. That is, they differentiate mental activities in terms of outwardly defined tasks and materials. The mental operations themselves escape description.

As regards our first query, then, the findings suggest that neither faculty theorists nor modern factor analysts throw much light on the nature of general powers of mind, whether they be called "faculties" or "aptitudes." On this score, one school cannot accuse the other of poverty because both are beggars. When the factor analyst wishes to identify the mental activity corresponding to a factor he draws on common psychological terms such as intelligence, memory, mechanical skill, and the like. This is what the faculty theorist did. Vernon calls attention to the resemblance between Thurstone's primary abilities and nineteenth-century faculties (4, pp. 19-20). Thurstone might reply that Vernon's hierarchy of abilities, with general intelligence at the head of subordinate abilities, was quite common in the history of faculty theory. But we must not forget that the modern student backs up his claims with research. If the psychologist is still ignorant about primary mental abilities it is at least, to borrow the badinage of Pascal, "a learned ignorance!"

ⵥ D. Summary: Bearings on Essentialism

The course of our explorations all the way from ancient faculty theories to modern factor analysis touched educational problems at many points. What are the main consequences of this chapter for an essentialist philosophy of education? We have in mind the full-blown and bold essentialism which says that education should be confined to those studies which, as subject matter, give the common cultural heritage of our civilization, and which as discipline develop those intellectual powers which represent the essence of our common humanity.

So far as this chapter carries us, there is no reason for supposing that essentialism has sustained a mortal blow at the hands of factor analysts. On the contrary, a modernized and strengthened essentialism is possible by exchanging the highly conjectural faculty psychology of the past for modern evidences regarding mental abilities. An essentialist educational program which sets out to cultivate the "powers of mind" would surely do better to switch from medieval faculties to the twelve "primary abilities" listed by the Thurstones.

What of the finding that we can better understand mental activities in terms of their concrete processes and the materials on which they act than in terms of pure powers and potentialities? It implies that essentialism in education should give emphasis to the acquisition of essential knowledge. In fact, essentialism has largely abandoned the idea that the function of education is to sharpen the "pure" intellect by exercising on concrete material and then discarding the material as of no further use. The definable general ideas and principles established by the exercise of intelligence are not merely *won* by its power, they *are* its power for meeting future problems.

But this prospect of a revised essentialism must be qualified. For we have said very little about two other important claims of essentialism. Essentialism does not stop with the claim that there are distinguishable powers of mind. It adds that these powers can be developed by certain disciplinary studies appropriate to them, and that such development yields dividends in the form of transfers of skill to other activities. These are the claims regarding which modern psychology has much to say, as we shall see in Chapter 6, which follows.

References

1. Cowley, William H. "Freedom and discipline." *Educational Record,* 1944, Vol. 25, pp. 5-20.
2. James, William. "Does Consciousness Exist?" *Essays in Radical Empiricism.* New York: Longmans, Green, 1912, Chapter 1.
3. Redden, John D., and Francis A. Ryan. *A Catholic Philosophy of Education.* Milwaukee, Wis.: Bruce, 1942.
4. Vernon, Philip E. *The Structure of Human Abilities.* New York: Wiley, 1950.

§ *chapter 6*

THE NATURE OF LEARNING: FORMAL DISCIPLINE AND TRANSFER OF TRAINING

In the last chapter we examined the nature of mental abilities. When confusions were cleared away some positive findings remained. Modern psychology validates the belief that there are primary abilities of mind. Chief of these is *general intelligence,* well established by research and having great significance for understanding the cognitive aspect of mind in general. An enlightened and progressive essentialism has only to accept the well-established forms of primary abilities and embody them in an essentialist program of education. Moreover, the striking generality of intelligence, operating as it does in abilities of narrower scope, producing positive correlations among them, invests it with the significance attributed to it by Aristotle and by his contemporary followers, the essentialists.

The next task is to consider the two remaining postulates of essentialism: (a) the doctrine of formal discipline, and (b) the more recent problem of the transfer of training. These two doctrines show a nice articulation, holding out the enticing promise of an "unearned increment" in education. Assuming that courses of study will develop the mental capacities which they involve, an additional increment can then result from the transfer of training. That is, after a given capacity is developed it will yield extra returns in areas of endeavor other than the one which developed it.

As in the case of the doctrine of faculties, modern psychology has subjected the doctrines of formal discipline and transfer of training to the searching scrutiny of experimental work. After modern research and judicious criticism have done their work will there be any formal discipline and transfer of training left on which to build an essentialist philosophy of education?

The main divisions of the present chapter are as follows:

A. Formal Discipline
B. The Transfer of Training
C. Transfer in Academic Education
D. Transfer in Character Education
E. The Role of the Teacher in Transfer

A. Formal Discipline

1. The Concept of Formal Discipline

The prevailing view of psychologists and educators takes formal discipline to mean that each capacity of the mind can be developed by special exercises or studies appropriate to it. It will be well to note at least two basic ways in which training may be brought about: (a) by the elimination of useless and wrong responses in any complex activity and the selection of the right responses. The infant, for instance, acquires motor skills by a long process of eliminating wrong responses and in coordinating useful ones. (b) There is training in the sense of increasing the *speed* and precision of any activity irrespective of any further selection from random trials. We wish to know whether training can improve an ability in either or both of the two senses given.

The reader may consider it quite obvious that training can develop an ability, and that it is a pedantic waste of time to discuss the matter. This is true enough for *particular* abilities. Psychologists would agree that practice improves narrow and special skills. There are multitudes of such skills which practice will improve in accordance with the famous "negatively accelerated" curve of learning. Also in learning *contents* as distinguished from increasing *skills* the amount learned and the duration of its retention are roughly proportional to the amount of practice. But essentialists hold that there are *general* capacities of mind which can be developed through discipline. For such capacities the effects of training are not clear. We shall not be surprised by this when we recall that it is rather a strain on credulity to believe that "pure" faculties or abilities, abstracted from concrete performances, can even exist, let alone improve with practice! William James had concluded that an individual's general memory capacity is given once and for all—practice could not improve memory per se. All that practice could do was to improve the special techniques of memorizing. (In this same way, a man with but average muscular strength may perform great feats in lifting weights because he has mastered the "tricks" of using his muscles.)

The issue of whether or not training can improve general ability becomes a storm center of dispute in the case of general intelligence, the development of which is stressed by essentialists. In the past the view has prevailed among psychologists that general intelligence is native; and that, except for the effects of marked deviations from normal conditions of health, training, and environment, the intelligence quotients of individuals tend to remain constant. The principle of the constancy of intelligence is still held by the majority of psychologists. But in recent times this doctrine has been challenged, as by Beth Wellman, George D. Stoddard, Irving Lorge, and others. The problem is quite intricate. The effects of schooling on intelligence is in itself a vast problem (1, pp. 205-212). However, the experimental ramifications of this problem do not much concern this chapter.

2. The Function of General Intelligence

Essentialists never tire of stressing the importance of "cultivating the intellect." What conception of the intellect is most suitable for the contention that it can be "cultivated"? Essentialists might well adopt the following thesis: General intelligence always expresses itself in subordinate activities. Let it be admitted that it is something like a ghost which must take on special forms in order to be seen, or rattle chains in order to be heard. Now, the numerous concrete activities "haunted" by general intelligence (as shown by positive intercorrelations among tests not accounted for by special skills) do improve with practice. One has only to regard special abilities as special techniques which are in part in the service of general intelligence, enabling it to manifest itself in the individual's thinking and doing.

Does this leave general intelligence with nothing to do which is *peculiar* to it, so that it remains that bogey of philosophy, a "thing-in-itself"? No, for the special task of intelligence is to abstract the common attributes of things and events, establish generalizations (class concepts and laws), and apply its general concepts to further instances. This service of intelligence is of course impossible without the help of lesser activities such as perception, attention, memory, which supply the data upon which intelligence acts. It may be meaningless to ask whether general intelligence, conceived as a pure and disembodied power from the "valley of the shadow," is improved by practice. But intelligence operating on concrete materials can derive general principles from them. The laws of science are such general principles and they represent very potent achievements of intelligence. Also, knowing a general principle is potent from the practical point of view for, as Poincaré noted, the general is that which occurs the most frequently! A generalization belongs to intelligence because intelligence alone derives, understands, and applies general principles. The more principles it masters the easier it will be for it to discover additional ones and to reduce multiple principles to single ones. The more plentiful the data which observation supplies for general principles the more effective will such principles become in pointing to other sources of significant data.

We then arrive at the conclusion that from the point of view of practical consequences intelligence *is* improved by training. As we shall see later, the general concepts grasped by intelligence are the chief media through which the transfer of training is secured. But we have so far been speaking of the general meaning of training. What about training in the special sense of "formal discipline," and are the aims of education which it suggests valid or invalid?

3. Discipline for the Sake of Discipline

Formal discipline means training, but it also means other things. It was formerly assumed that the function of discipline was to develop the faculties. The word *formal* refers to the use of special exercises which are considered suitable for the specific purpose of developing the faculty in question. Gymnastic exercises are "formal" in this sense—they develop the muscles but have no further use. Some studies, it was thought, would develop a given faculty more than others. This led to the educational doctrine of discipline for the sake of discipline, an idea which is abhorrent to the devotees of interest-centered education. In the application of formal discipline the process of learning is more important than the materials learned. The school is regarded as analogous to the gymnasium where the athlete "formally disciplines" his muscles.

4. Summary Criticism of Formal Discipline

On the score of adverse criticism of formal discipline there appear to be two major counts against it:

(a) It is unwarranted to stress the disciplinary (developmental) value of a subject to the detriment of its subject matter. Modern essentialists no less than adherents of other schools of educational thought favor certain *contents* of knowledge aside from the value of the mental gymnastics involved in securing such knowledge.

(b) A second important charge is against the doctrine of effort for the sake of effort, to the exclusion of interest. If interests could be ruled out, no doubt difficult studies, because of their very difficulty, would develop the mind best of all. But learning is better when effort is leavened with interest. The essentialist admits this, but holds it to be the responsibility of the teacher to make an essential study interesting. If the teacher fails in this, let the student study the necessary subject with boredom in place of interest! This idea has its salutary aspects. Society should not be expected, for example, to tolerate surgeons who were not trained in anatomy because the subject bored them at college.[1]

⫯ B. The Transfer of Training

Broadly defined, transfer of training means that training in one activity improves performance in another subsequent activity. A survey of the rich experimental literature on the subject of transfer would in itself cover a college course or two. We shall seek abbreviation by dealing with the methods of research in this area briefly, and by confining our review of experiments to those which bear directly on the problems of education.[2]

1. Research Methods

Early experimenters, E. Ebert and E. Meumann in particular, got evidences of huge transfer effects in memory training. Today we are quite sure that their evidences are spurious because they failed to observe certain experimental precautions, such as using control subjects or control series of observations. Others have repeated their experiments and found that the evidences in favor of positive transfer were too weak to be convincing (14, p. 744).

There are at least five different procedures for studying transfer experimentally. We shall describe but one of them, a standard method with experimental and control groups of subjects. It will be found convenient to use a few symbols and idioms which are conventional in this field of research. The letter x will symbolize the activity in which training is given, and y designates the subsequent activity to which transfer of training may extend. We shall speak of *positive* transfer when training in x does lead to improvement in the y activity. If training in x reduces skill in the y activity we speak of *negative* transfer.

The plan of the standard method to serve as our model is indicated in the diagram on the next page.

[1] Walter B. Kolesnik, in his *Mental Discipline in Modern Education* (Madison, Wis.: University of Wisconsin Press, 1958), gives a full and impartial analysis of the issue of formal discipline, with concrete recommendations for educational practice.

[2] The following sources give excellent surveys of fuller scope on the subject of transfer of training: R. S. Woodworth and H. Schlosberg. "Transference and interference." *Experimental Psychology* (rev.). New York: Holt, 1954, Chap. 24. L. W. Webb. "Transfer of learning." *Educational Psychology* (C. E. Skinner, ed.). Englewood Cliffs, N.J.: Prentice-Hall, 1951, Chap. 16.

Groups	Initial Test	Practice	Final Test
Control	y^1		y^2
Experimental	y^1	x	y^2

y^1 and y^2 represent initial and final tests given to both control and experimental groups of subjects. These tests are carefully equated and are selected to indicate as sharply as possible the effects of training in th x activity. The experimental and control groups should be equal ("matched") for all traits likely to affect the results of the experiment, and should avoid the effects of chance selection of subjects. The logic of the method is clear from a study of the diagram. We wish to know how much the experimental subjects will improve their y^2 scores over the y^1 scores because they were trained in the activity x. Some of the gains in y^2 may be due to their initial experience with y^1. The amount of this gain will be shown by the gains of the controls. If we subtract the gain of the controls in y from the gain of the experimentals in y, the residual gain of the experimentals, if any, will show the effects of practice with activity x.

2. The Domain of Transfer

If activities x and y were entirely identical, then there are indeed not two of them, unless we think of them as occurring at two different times. If they occur at two different times but are otherwise identical, and practice in x leads to improvement, we would have *learning*, not *transfer*. On the other hand, if x and y are entirely unlike, and practice in x leads to improvement in y, transfer would be a miracle! This would be like the feat of Aladdin who rubbed his lamp—an act which ordinarily would only polish it—but finds that this causes a jinni to appear!

The research on transfer is thus confined to the terrain in which activities x and y are neither wholly identical nor wholly different. This mid-region of activities is vast. Perhaps even opening the same door on successive occasions will vary in important ways, e.g., as when a boy is arriving at school or leaving it! On the other hand, there may be hidden resemblances between instances of x and y which superficially seem quite unlike. As instance of this, consider two languages like French and Latin, which at first seem quite unlike until inner evidences of genetic relationship are seen.

3. The Mediators of Transfer

Transfer of training from one activity to another is said to be "mediated" (made possible) by something they have in common. These media of transfer are of many degrees of generality. They may be quite narrow or specific elements which occur in both activities x and y. Examples of specific elements are isolated facts, elements of skill, and narrow habits. On the other hand, the media of transfer may be broad or general factors, such as common patterns of activity, general methods, common principles, attitudes, ambitions, and ideals. It will be noted from these instances of transfer media that they form different classes, each class having both specific and general media as just defined. The main classes are: (a) common features in the x and y activities themselves (facts, principles, materials); (b) factors in the learner (habits, attitudes, ideals, sensory and motor elements involved); and (c) common factors in the situation where x and y are exercised. An example of the last type is afforded by William James's story of the actor who could not recall his lines on the stage because a certain trunk was missing which was in full view in his home while he was learning the lines.

We turn now to two general theories of the transfer of training which are very crucial for our evaluation of essentialism in education.

4. Transfer via Identical Elements

This theory holds that transfer of training occurs between two activities because they have certain elements in common, such as identical facts, isolated habits, and simple mental or motor skills. This theory was based on extensive experiments made by Robert S. Woodworth and Edward L. Thorndike. The experimental work of these leaders and their associates indicated that the amount of transfer from one activity to another is quite small. Practice will improve the activity exercised, but the hope of securing large gains even in related activities is doomed to disappointment. The experiments seemed to show that skills are remarkably isolated, each one having a local existence without much interaction with other activities despite the sharing of some common elements.

5. Bearing on Faculty Theory and Essentialism

The results noted above were interpreted as adverse to any theory that there are broad or general "faculties" or "primary abilities" of mind. In place of belief in the existence of broad categories of ability the conviction grew that the mind consisted of a vast aggregate of *special* abilities. There is no general memory capacity but only the capacity to remember this or that! There is no general acuteness of vision but only the ability to see the narrow scope of things which one was trained to see. John Dewey clearly held this view (4, p. 76). Curiously enough, it is now the modern critic, not the faculty psychologist, who multiplies mental abilities inordinately.

The transfer studies of Woodworth and Thorndike were also considered blows to essentialism in so far as this point of view claims that there are certain essential studies which show large transfer effects to other studies and occupations. The Woodworth-Thorndike researches seemed to indicate that studies do not differ enough from each other in transfer value to justify setting up some of them as essential studies. Hence, even essentialists shifted emphasis to studies desirable for their contents rather than for their transfer values.

6. Transfer via Generalization

The theory that transfer is best mediated by general principles was first set forth systematically by Charles H. Judd in 1936 (6, especially p. 201). Judd held that the main purpose of education was to bring about the mastery of systematic knowledge which could be extended from the learning situation to other situations. To accomplish this end the knowledge acquired by the student must be understood by him in terms of the abstract principles and concepts which integrate and give cognitive unity to knowledge.

Judd's defense of the transfer power of generalized principles was verified in a simple experiment of his own (5). Some boys were taught the principle of refraction of light which, in this particular experiment, explained why a target under water is not in the position where it appears to be. After the boys had had some practice in shooting at the target, its depth in the water was changed, thus altering its apparent location. As a result, the boys who had learned the principle of refraction did better in the new situation than the boys not so instructed. It is now the view of the majority of authorities that larger transfer effects result from training in general principles than from training in elementary skills or isolated facts.

With these two theories of transfer in mind we now turn to some experiments on transfer which have special significance for education.

C. Transfer in Academic Education

Experiments bearing on transfer of training in education are very numerous. We will report only a few representative instances of transfer under each of two headings: transfer in the academic aspects of education, and transfer in the sphere of traits of personality and character. We will select experiments which bear on the claims of essentialists, and those which illustrate the opposition between the theory of identical elements and the theory of transfer by generalization.

1. Transfer in the Sphere of Learning

We will contrast the experiments of W. G. Sleight and H. Woodrow. W. G. Sleight's experiment (11) bears significantly on the theory of transfer via common elements. Sleight used a control group and three experimental groups, equated on the basis of several memory tests. Six tests measuring learning skill were given initially and finally to all groups. The controls received no special training in memorization between initial and final tests. One experimental group practiced rote memorization of poetry, the second group practiced with prose, the third practiced with mathematical tables.

The results of Sleight's experiment showed that the residual gains of the experimentals over the controls were quite small. The law of proportionality was atrociously violated. That is, the kinds of memory improvements obtained were not consistently related to the kinds of memory training received.

The procedure and results of H. Woodrow's experiment were quite different (13). Sleight's experimentals had tried to improve memory by practice in rote learning. In Woodrow's experiment we shall see the beneficial effects on transfer of utilizing general principles, as advocated by Judd. The control group took the initial and final tests but engaged in no practice work in memorizing prescribed by the experiment. There were two experimental groups. One group practiced memorizing nonsense syllables and poetry at certain periods covering four weeks. The second experimental group spent part of its time in mastering general laws of learning, and the remainder of the time in practice in memorization. The principles of learning which they first mastered included such things as the value of self-testing during the process of learning, rhythmic grouping of the materials, making meaningful associations, and learning by wholes rather than by parts.

Woodrow's controls did about as well on the final as on the initial tests of learning ability. The experimentals who were instructed in the laws of learning were decidedly superior in the final tests to the experimentals not given such instruction.

2. Thorndike's Study of Mental Discipline

Thorndike's study of the values of various high school courses as mental disciplines is no doubt the most extensive and most important study in this area (3, 12). It must be noted that these were studies of *discipline*, i.e., of the value of high-school courses for developing general intelligence. They are studies of transfer in only a secondary sense.

There were two experiments, one in 1922-1923 (12) involving over 8,500 high-school students, the other in 1925-1926 (3) involving over

5,000 students. The procedures of the experiments are too intricate to review in detail. Suffice it to say that Thorndike was a past master of experimental work, and we shall not expect any great flaws of procedure. The purpose of the experiments mainly was to determine the effect on intelligence level of the study of various high-school courses. The initial and final tests were the I.E.R. Tests of General Mental Ability. These tests measured such capacities as relational thinking, generalization, and organizing. They contained a large linguistic component.

As for the result of this sweeping experiment we will take note only of the general finding that high-school studies as a whole do not have much "disciplinary" value in raising intelligence scores. The various courses did not differ much in transfer value. The students who had taken such courses as arithmetic, bookkeeping, chemistry, physics, algebra, and geometry made the largest gains, but even these were not noteworthy. Students who took such things as dramatic art, cooking, sewing, biology, botany, and agriculture showed small losses as between initial and final tests.

Why is there the wide-spread belief that Latin, geometry, and other so-called "disciplinary" courses will develop general intelligence? Thorndike's answer is as follows:

The chief reason why good thinkers seem superficially to have been made such by having taken certain school studies, is that good thinkers have taken such studies, becoming better by the inherent tendency of the good to gain more than the poor from any study (12, p. 98).

♀ D. Transfer in Character Education

One of the severest strictures of modern education is its failure to develop or even try to develop desirable aims, attitudes, ideals, self-control, and other traits that belong to the terrain of character and personality. This failure, in so far as it is true, is lamentable; for it is in this area that training shows gratifying effects. This sphere again vindicates Judd's contention that generalized factors yield the largest transfer effects.

1. Neatness and Accuracy

William C. Bagley, whom we recall as a champion of essentialism, made an experiment with third-grade pupils (2, p. 189). Neatness and accuracy were stressed in a class in arithmetic. In classes other than arithmetic nothing was said about the importance of neatness and accuracy. The results were that subsequent work in arithmetic did show gains in neatness and accuracy, but for papers in spelling and language there were actual losses rather than gains in these two traits! In this experiment neatness and accuracy were encouraged as *specific habits* in arithmetic. These habits failed to manifest themselves in other situations because they were not taught as *ideals of general conduct.*

Now compare the results of Bagley's experiment with those of the following experiment by William C. Ruediger (10): Great stress was placed on the importance of neatness in *all* papers handed in, and on the value of neatness in life outside the school. As a result, there was a gain in neatness in all classes, even in those in which neatness was not stressed.

2. Judd's Principle

These two studies and many others vindicate the soundness of Judd's thesis that the learning of generalized principles, attitudes, and ideals will produce larger transfer effects than the learning of specific elements. The child who, when he enters another's home, remains standing until invited to be seated has so far acquired an *isolated habit* of politeness. When he grasps politeness as a general ideal of conduct he will acquire other polite habits without specific instruction. The studies of Hartshorne and May previously referred to (Chapter 4) are chiefly responsible for the belief that traits of personality and character in children are largely specific for specific situations. But these studies merely show what happens when no effort is made to teach honesty, cooperation, etc., as generalized principles of conduct. To so teach them, instruction must be addressed to intelligence.

Here again the essentialist's faith in the "intellectual" is warranted. As Thorndike's experiments show, no great difference will be found in the transfer values of courses which differ merely in their subject matter. The differences found in the amounts of transfer favored the more intellectual subjects, such as chemistry, physics, algebra, and geometry. Fortunately for the cause of education such courses compel teachers and students to overcome their natural reluctance to think!

⋮⃕ E. The Role of the Teacher in Transfer

John Macdonald stresses the role of the teacher in securing large transfer effects (7, pp. 17-23). He alleges that many experiments which resulted in insignificant transfer are like the play *Hamlet* with the Prince of Denmark left out. That is, the presence or absence of the good teacher is not considered. Instruction should be multilateral, not unilateral. Good language training aims at general gains for all varieties of subject matter, such as poetry, history, and science. Mathematics should be taught so as to bring out its relevance to other studies and to daily life. Every subject has contributions to make to areas beyond itself. Macdonald rightly adds that if all abilities of human beings were really specific, education could not get beyond the methods used to train animals (7, p. 23).

Does teaching a subject so as to secure large transfer effects mitigate against teaching that subject for its own sake? No, if we assume, as is reasonable, that a subject is best understood "for its own sake" when it is studied in multilateral fashion. Thus, the full psychological understanding of the minds of pupils requires collateral knowledge regarding such things as the influences of heredity, environment, and physical health and maturation on mental processes. James L. Mursell, an authority on methods of instruction, holds that any capacity which is carefully developed for its own sake will also yield the best transfer effects to other areas (8, p. 104). To illustrate Mursell's statement, it is obvious that the competence with which physics is applied to such practical pursuits as engineering will be proportional to the mastery of the science of physics.

In conclusion, we can say that transfer of training is an established fact. Pedro T. Orata (9, p. 267) summarized research literature on transfer covering the period from 1890 to 1935. His findings, briefly stated, were as follows: Large transfer effects were found in 28 per cent of all studies. Some transfer was found in 48 per cent of all studies. Only 3 per cent of the studies showed interference effects (negative transfer). It is also the consensus of authorities that transfer effects are largest when training centers on the mastery of general principles, in accordance with Judd's formulation. Judd's principle suggests that proper teaching could increase transfer effects very considerably. Failure to embody Judd's principle in teaching probably explains the failures to secure significant transfer effects in the numerous studies reported by Orata. The small transfer values of high-school studies reported by Thorndike very probably reflect adversely, not on the principle of transfer itself, but on the prevailing inadequacy of high-school instruction.

Of all of the postulates of essentialism, the principle of transfer of training may claim the fullest validation. Not only this, but the experimental literature on transfer validates the essentialist's emphasis on the exercise of intelligence. According to the accredited principle of Judd, generalized principles, attitudes, rules of procedure, etc., acquired in an *x* activity are largely responsible for any transfer which takes place to activity *y*. *It is general intelligence which grasps and uses such generalized media of transfer.*

But vigilant essentialism, although it stands ready to modify the essentials of a liberal education for all, will continue to assume the universality and dominance of the life of reason in man. It will guard education against narrow, *ad hoc,* and stereotyped methods of instruction. It will warn educators against narrow vocational training and against transient fads supported by extramural pressure lobbies. At the heart of essentialism is the genuine love of knowledge for its own sake rather than for the sake of success in the practical aspects of life. Hence the uncompromising vigor with which Hutchins rejects the "service station" conception of the college.

References

1. Anastasi, Anne. *Differential Psychology* (3d ed.). New York: Macmillan, 1958.
2. Bagley, William C. *Educational Values*. New York: Macmillan, 1911.
3. Broyler, Cecil H., Edward L. Thorndike, and associates. "A Second Study of Mental Discipline in High School Studies." *Journal of Educational Psychology*, 1927, Vol. 18, pp. 377-404.
4. Dewey, John. *Democracy and Education*. New York: Macmillan, 1916.
5. Judd, Charles H. "The Relation of Special Training to General Intelligence." *Educational Review*. 1908, Vol. 36, pp. 28-42.
6. ———. *Education as Cultivation of the Higher Mental Processes*. New York: Macmillan, 1936.
7. Macdonald, John. *Mind, School, and Civilization*. Chicago: University of Chicago Press, 1952.
8. Mursell, James L. *Psychology of Secondary School Teaching* (rev.). New York: Norton, 1939.
9. Orata, Pedro T. "Transfer of Training and Educational Pseudoscience." *The Mathematical Teacher*, 1935, Vol. 28.
10. Ruediger, William C. "Indirect Improvement of Mental Functions through Ideals." *Educational Review*, 1908, Vol. 36, pp. 364-371.
11. Sleight, W. G. "Memory and Formal Discipline." *British Journal of Psychology*, 1911, Vol. 4, pp. 386-457.
12. Thorndike, Edward L. "Mental Discipline in High School Studies." *Journal of Educational Psychology*, 1924, Vol. 15, pp. 1-22, 83-98.
13. Woodrow, Herbert. "The Effect of Type of Training upon Transference." *Journal of Educational Psychology*, 1927, Vol. 18, pp. 159-172.
14. Woodworth, Robert S., and Harold Schlosberg. *Experimental Psychology* (rev.). New York: Holt, 1954.

☿ *book 3*

IDEALISTIC PHILOSOPHY
AND EDUCATION

♀ *chapter 7*

IDEALISTIC PHILOSOPHY: PLATO AND KANT

The four chapters of the present book are concerned with that sweeping outlook on life known as idealism, as preliminary to exploring its bearings on education. The opinions of idealists and other philosophers about the world do not have the certainty involved in counting eggs, but they are profoundly significant despite their alleged uncertainty. Aristotle noted that the same degree of exactitude is not to be expected in all branches of inquiry. Moreover, the *significance* of statements is as much to be desired as their exactitude. The number of letters printed on a page is subject to exact determination. But if the page was written by Aristotle the number of letters on it pales in significance compared to what Aristotle wrote, even though he hazarded no more than a guess.

When the student first hears the term "idealistic philosophers" he may conclude that they are the ones who pursue fine and lofty ideals which, by implication, are shunned by philosophers of other schools. This natural error must be dispelled at once. Idealists, unless they are Platonists, might better have been called "idea-ists." For, as we shall see, they regard ideas as independently real or even as the only ultimate reality. Idealistic philosophers are usually religious or at least sympathetic with religious outlooks. Idealistic philosophy is the best substitute for religion which was cut off from education by legal enactments. This is because to view the universe as a system of ideas is to regard it as something spiritual, or at least as something mental. All of this is much more agreeable with the view that God exists and that men are spirits than can be said for materialism or positivism, and perhaps other schools as well. The materialist considers that all reality consists of matter and its manifestations. Even your consciousness is a manifestation of bodily processes. The positivist refuses to believe anything that cannot be verified by observation. But religionists believe that God is a nonmaterial spirit, and the evidences of His existence are in part unseen.

But idealistic philosophers are not necessarily religious, if we assume that religion requires belief in the existence of God as a person. Thus, Plato supposed that there are eternal ideas which maintain their own existence irrespective of the existence or nonexistence of the gods, nor do these ideas require the minds of men to give them reality by knowing them. But idealisms are usually religious. Like religion, idealism finds the universe spiritual, having an intimate kinship with man's spirit, and being friendly toward him.

The more uncertain a field of inquiry becomes the more important it is to get expert opinions about it. Our spokesmen for idealism should also be as representative as possible of idealistic philosophies as a whole. This creates a problem for the authors of texts because there are many systems and strains of idealistic thought. Some are identified with their authors, as in the cases of Platonic, Kantian, or Hegelian idealism. Others are identified by their favorite areas of interest, such as religious idealism, voluntaristic idealism, personalistic idealism. Again, no two philosophers, even those flying the same banner, are entirely alike in their views. The need for brevity in this book permits only limited treatment of each philosophy considered, but still sufficient for our main task, which is to examine education from various philosophical points of view.

As a sampling of idealisms sufficient for our use we will briefly sketch the idealism of Plato and then more fully the idealism of Immanuel Kant. In Chapter 8 we give rather full consideration to the absolute idealism of George Wilhelm Hegel because he greatly influenced such philosophers of education as W. T. Harris, H. H. Horne, and G. Gentile. The main divisions of the present chapter are as follows:

A. Idealistic Philosophies: Their Main Postulates
B. Platonic Idealistic Realism
C. The Idealism of Immanuel Kant
D. Kant's Moral Philosophy
E. Idealistic Philosophy and Education
F. Post-Kantian Idealism

⊽ A. Idealistic Philosophies: Their Main Postulates

An idealism, like any thorough system of philosophy, deals with certain basic questions. We shall now sketch the main ways in which idealistic philosophy answers such questions.

1. Metaphysics, or Theory of Reality

All idealisms are impressed with the thought that the universe is ultimately something mental or psychic. It is a system of ideas, a façade of reason, or (as with Schopenhauer) a blind will. Idealists are the uncompromising opponents of materialism. The spiritual or mentalistic view of the universe favored by idealists has its roots in ancient animistic ideas, but it has subjected these ideas to systematic extension and constructive criticism.

a. THE SELF. Idealists stress the spiritual nature of the self and exalt its importance. This emphasis on selfhood has great importance for education. The idealist is usually of the conviction that the states and activities of the self, as we experience them inwardly through the "mind's eye" or introspectively, *are the only realities which we can know directly and incontrovertibly*. This view seems plausible enough to common-sense thinking. Thus, modern physics tells us that a white stone, for instance, which looks so solid and inert, is really neither white, solid, nor inert. The stone reflects mixed wave lengths of light to the eyes which cause us to see it as white. Far from being solid and inert, the stone consists of minute particles in violent motion in empty space. Such knowledge is *indirect* or *mediate*—man acquired it through prolonged research and thought. But your experience of the stone as white, solid, and inert is direct and immediate. No scientist, however clever, can demonstrate that your immediate experience of the stone as white, solid, and inert is a matter of doubt.

The idealistic philosopher carries the dispute further. He argues that the scientist's conception of the stone is also something mental—it is a conceptual construct. Idealism thus tends to find in the activities of the mind, its ideas, rationality, impulses, and purposes, the keys for understanding the nature of the world. *To the extent that we can understand reality it must be an expression of mind.* To the extent that reason can grasp the world, the world must be an expression of reason.

b. TRANSCENDENTALISM. Idealists have shown a strong tendency, shown by Plato's doctrine of ideas, to believe that there is a sphere of reality transcending our world and partly hidden from it. Our world becomes the world "of appearances." The transcendent sphere is not entirely inaccessible, for severe mental application (and, incidentally, volumes of print) can tease out the lineaments of the eternal. Sometimes this reality beyond our temporal experience is conceived as dwelling *immanently* in the world, not in isolation from it. All are familiar with a similar choice in Christian theology between a transcendent and an immanent God.

2. Epistemology, or Theory of Knowledge

In terms of the old and rather useless distinction between rationalism and empiricism, idealists in general keep to the rationalist side of the fence. Rationalism has taken different forms in the history of thought. To ancient Greek philosophers, especially for Plato, empirical knowledge derived through the senses was illusory, inconstant, and therefore untrustworthy. The knowledge to be prized came through reasoning, which revealed the constant and universal principles of being. Curiously enough, this ancient point of view pervades the popular idealogy of today, as when we think of the rationalist as the armchair philosopher who keeps his eyes closed while the empiricist dashes about his laboratory with his eyes open and wishing he had more of them. The picture is of course distorted and even ridiculous. For the rationalist requires empirical observations upon which to exercise reason—a general principle without instances is empty. As for empiricists, no one imagines that they merely pile up sense observations without ever reasoning about them!

A better conception of rationalism arose with such continental thinkers as Descartes, Spinoza, and Leibniz. Their rationalism consisted essentially in starting with certain axioms or assumptions, stated as general principles and then applying them deductively to the world of experience. This method had signal success when applied to such sciences as geometry, mathematics, physics and its subbranches, and to astronomy.

The idealist philosopher inclines to follow the path laid down by Spinoza and Leibniz: The objective world is regarded as pervaded by universal and constant principles or laws, and to discover these laws (Plato's "ideas") is to attain knowledge. These universals may be revealed to us intuitively, or may be set up as tentative hypotheses and then verified by observation, as in science. Most scientists and objective idealists hold that observation does not *create* principles, but only *discovers* them. Universal principles have objective existence whether or not man comes to know them. These universals are more than man's knowledge—they are the very framework of objective reality.

But the scientist and objective idealist may part company on the question of where universal laws subsist, or what sustains them. The scientist who inclines to materialism will say that natural laws are inherent in matter. Thus, the law of gravity is not a disembodied principle which physical bodies "obey." This law *describes* rather than *prescribes* the action of physical bodies. But the objective idealist supposes that universals are sustained by or inherent in a universal mind, the mind of God, who is the essence of reality. But this clash between scientist and idealist is not very serious. The scientist who is also an idealist (as many of them are) will not find research hampered by supposing that the universal laws he seeks express divine thought instead of mere properties of matter. The idealist on his part may view the world of matter as part of God's being, and welcome the discovery of natural laws as revelations of God's nature.

The "objective" idealist has a more serious quarrel with the "subjective" idealist than he has with the scientist. The idealist Kant, as we shall see, rejected the view that the orderliness of the world is imposed on man's mind from without. Kant believed that man's mind imposed its inherent orderliness upon the world. Whether universals are objective or subjective, what are the signs which tell us that we have encountered them? There are at least two reliable signs: (a) A valid universal is apprehended by the mind as perfectly clear and self-evident (intuition). (b) A true universal will be in perfect harmony or *congruence* with other universals known to be true. In the mind of God there are no contradictions. The scientist similarly supposes an absence of inconsistency among the laws of science. In general, then, idealists accept what is known as the *congruence* theory of knowledge (defined in Chapter 1). A statement is true if it harmonizes with the interlocking, mutually consistent, and logically necessary system of thought which, in the objective idealism of Hegel (Chapter 8) both *reveals* reality and *is* reality.

3. The Axiology of Idealism

Axiology, we recall, has to do with questions of *value* as opposed to purely factual questions. Axiology is concerned, not with realities as such, but with their goodness or badness, their beauty or ugliness, etc. Idealism has its favored beliefs regarding such basic questions as the nature of evil, of beauty, of duty. As we would expect, these problems are defined and dealt with by the method of intellectual reflection favored by idealists. Their views regarding value are complex and varied, and we postpone their consideration to the accounts which follow regarding special idealistic philosophies. For the present, the reader can discern that idealistic views could lead to lofty conceptions of morality, making a powerful appeal to mind and heart.

☿ B. Platonic Idealistic Realism

1. Plato's Realm of Ideas

The term *idea* has various meanings. In the realistic idealism of Plato ideas are conceived as eternal and timeless forms. Plato's idealism is called "realistic" because he regarded the eternal ideas as *objective* in the sense of being self-existent. They do not depend on men, gods, or the physical world to sustain them. They existed before we knew them and will continue to exist when we pass away. Ideas, Plato held, are the essences or archetypes of things in our world. An "archetype" is the original model from which copies are made. For example, in the eternal realm of subsistent ideas there is the archetype of the perfect circle, of the perfect oak tree, or the perfect horse, etc. In our experience we encounter only imperfect embodiments of the eternal ideas. (This may be said to have its advantages since we are not eager to encounter such things as the perfect nuisance, liar, or criminal.)

How can the human mind have acquaintance with the eternal forms since they are never encountered in their perfection in earthly experience? In his *Phaedrus* Plato gives his doctrine of reminiscence which depicts our souls as having dwelt prenatally in the realm of perfect forms. After birth, we remember them dimly, and feel a consuming love for them. Plato thus offers us an arresting thought about the role of ideas in human conduct. Psychology and physiology regard most of man's behavior as driven by antecedent causes. We are driven to act in certain ways by the forces of nature and the needs of our own bodies. We have here the familiar notion of cause-effect relationships: Causes exist prior to their effects and "compel" the effects to occur.

Plato offers a more congenial and sublime interpretation of man's behavior—at least when at its best. Such ideas as perfect goodness, beauty, and truth do not "drive" us. They *attract* us by the love we have for them, and this leads us to strive to realize them. Plato regarded the *good* as the greatest of all eternal forms. This Platonic view regarding the attractive power of ideals of perfection is not mythology.

It is a wise teacher and reformer who remembers the inherent or potential love of the human heart for ideal perfections. The teacher who strives to awaken the inner and vital interests of the pupil rather than to impose rigid requirements of rote learning from without is applying Platonism to her teaching. She presides, as did Socrates, the great follower of Plato, over the birth of ideas. To awaken interests the teacher holds up the tantalizing images of perfection which lurk in all ambitions. She awakens rather than communicates to the pupil the potentialities for development which lie fallow in him, not as things unknown but as things forgotten, as the poet Alexander Pope discerned.

Our very sketchy account of Plato does poor justice to the profound and fascinating utterances of this ancient scholar on almost every weighty problem under the sun. But even so we have teased out of Platonism the basic views which reappear again and again in later idealism. He exemplifies the belief of idealists in a transcendental realm of which our terrestrial experience is a dim and transient copy. Plato shows the idealist's trust in reason as opposed to knowledge derived through the senses. Reason grasps the principles which are always true—the senses acquaint us with inconstants which come to birth only to vanish again. Bodies fall for their brief moments, but the law of gravity is universal and constant. Again, Plato's philosophy shows the tendency of idealists to exalt morality. Plato's eternal ideas were true ideals or perfections. He regarded the form of the good as the greatest of all eternal forms. Finally, Platonic thought illustrates the agreements between idealism and religious thought. Plato's distrust of the senses and his exaltation of the mind over the body reappear in the ascetic and puritanic tendencies in the history of Christianity. As Hunter Mead notes, "Plato has been called a Christian four hundred years before Christ" (2, p. 70).

The Neo-Platonists and Christian philosophers made Plato's universe of ideas subservient to the mind of God. Ideas become the models or prototypes which God follows in constructing all earthly things. This view prevailed throughout the Middle Ages. According to this view the existence of an idea depends on the prior existence of a mind (that of God's) which sustains it. The view that ideas have a purely mental existence is the popular way of conceiving them today. That is to say, we think of ideas as existing only in minds, in the realm of consciousness. The notion that ideas can leave our heads, where the mind is somehow supposed to dwell, and continue an independent existence of their own may strike us as sheer nonsense. This current belief in the subjective status of ideas was largely established through the influence of a British group of philosopher-psychologists known as empiricists and associationists. We will examine the ideas of John Locke, who belonged to this school. We encounter him again later as an important philosopher of education.

2. The Status of Ideas in Empirical Philosophy

John Locke (1632-1704), a pioneer in modern ways of thinking, defined the idea as the immediate datum which the mind experiences when it perceives an object, remembers, or understands. When you perceive a tree, the tree does not literally enter into your mind. (The mind is supposed to dwell in the head, and this is obviously too small to receive the tree!) No, when you see the tree the mind gets an "idea" of it, says Locke. Later on this idea may return to your mind as a memory and take part in thought processes about trees.

Today, largely through the influence of David Hume, another British associationist, we make a distinction between an *idea* and a *percept* or *image*. According to this distinction when you see a tree you get a phenomenal (sensory) copy of it which is called a percept or *image*. Look at a building or any object and then close your eyes. You experience the persisting image of the object—you picture it in your "mind's eye."

An image may be quite meaningless. One gets visual images while looking at the printed words of a strange language or while looking at some unfamiliar machine of modern science, but we may be unable to say what these things "mean." It is the function of ideas to convey meaning. Looking at some novel object one asks, "Have you any *idea* about what it is?" Our ideas about bridges in general give meaning to London Bridge. When we entertain some generalized idea, such as that of furniture, tools, flowers, etc., we may at the same time have the image of some particular piece of furniture, a tool, or as the case may be. Such images may be the "carriers" of meaning.

It is clear that the term *idea* has undergone changes in usage in the history of thought. It has also undergone a degradation or reduction in status from the lofty place accorded to ideas by Plato. We turn now to a brief paragraph on ideas conceived in Plato's sense of *ideals*.

3. Conceptions of Ideals

We may distinguish three basic meanings of the term *ideal*. (a) There is the ideal in the sense of something excellent which can be realized, as when we speak of "ideal companions" or of "ideal weather." (b) Then there is the ideal as something perfect which can never be fully realized. For instance, we incline to think of perfect beauty and goodness, not as attainable goals, but as *directions* of endeavors which can never reach their final goals, not in earthly experience. This is the Platonic sense of the ideal. Ordinarily we imagine that to pursue unattainable goals is painful and frustrating. The clinical psychologists say that frustration creates neurotic and maladjusted individuals, as though getting "adjusted" meant realizing all goals and then lapsing into a peaceful coma! Plato points unerringly to the true source of mental and moral health. Striving for ideal perfections can never end in slumber, which in many respects is worse than a neurosis. The impossibility of completely attaining the ideals is their very glory and the force which keeps cultural progress on the move. (c) Finally, there is the ideal in the derisive sense of something wholly visionary or quixotic.

☼ C. The Idealism of Immanual Kant

Immanuel Kant (1724-1804) is regarded by many scholars as the chief philosopher of modern times. Kant's thought is intricate and our account of it will of necessity be synoptic and incomplete in detail.

1. Some Biographical Notes

Kant, professor of philosophy at the University of Königsberg, was a man of encyclopedic knowledge. He taught not only philosophy, but mathematics, physics, physical geography, anthropology, and education! His heavy teaching schedule, sometimes twenty-six or more lectures per week, explains why Kant did not publish his first book until he was fifty-seven years old. This was the *Critique of Pure Reason* (1781) on which our account of his philosophy will largely depend.[1] Two other books of first importance appeared later, *Fundamental Principles of the Metaphysics of Morals* (1785) and the *Critique of Practical Reason* (1788). Kant's originative genius and wide learning is shown by his published contributions to science; such as an account of how the earth and moon retard each other through mutual attraction, the nebular hypothesis of the origin of planets, and an explanation of the effects of the velocities of various zones of the rotating earth on the directions of the winds.

Kant was eclectic in his philosophical thinking. He especially sought to reconcile philosophy and religion. His chief problem was to reconcile his earlier rationalism with the new British empiricism of Hobbes, Locke, Hume, and others. This led Kant to examine the *conditions of valid knowledge:* that is, of what is required in order to have valid knowledge. This is indeed a basic problem for education as well as for science and philosophy, and we will give it some stress. The teacher who imparts knowledge should have some conception of the source of its validity; some doubt about the validity of human ways of knowing is better than blind credulity about it. A second aspect of Kant's philosophy which bears directly on education is his theory of morals.

2. Kant's Theory of Knowledge

The problem of knowledge presented itself to Kant as follows: Empirical knowledge, such as that of science, is *a posteriori;* is based on observation and direct experience in general. Such knowledge always comes *after* the evidences are in. The trouble is that the evidences are seldom completely in. Empirical knowledge thus tends to remain probable in its

[1] An authoritative translation of the *Critique* is that of Norman K. Smith, New York: Macmillan, 1929.

validity, approaching exactness and certainty but never quite reaching these goals. The progress of experimental science consists in discovering laws of nature which increase in scope and exactness but never embrace the entire universe and never become perfectly exact.

This holds especially for the realm of the living, namely biology. The proposition, "All swans are white," holds until someone discovers swans of another color. Indeed, the realm of the living is the sphere of *becoming*, the sphere of evolution. Nature herself is continually producing novelties which violate the neat formulas we just now regarded as absolutely valid. It was formerly supposed that the material sciences such as physics and chemistry could attain laws of absolute validity since they deal with the realm of *being*, "given once and for all," and free from the surprises arising in the topsy-turvy realms of becoming.

But most modern scientists regard the laws of material nature as having a *statistical* and approximate, but not an absolute validity. Thus, a confined body of gas exerts equal pressure on every square inch of its containing walls. This is because the particles of gas are constantly bombarding the walls. Since they do this in utterly random fashion, each square inch of the container gets approximately equal numbers of blows per second. The number of blows are not absolutely equal, not any more than tossing pennies can be counted on to result in an absolutely equal number of heads and tails. The more pennies we toss, the nearer we get to such equality. Similarly, the greater the number of particles involved in an experiment in physics, the greater the validity of the resulting generalizations. This situation holds, so most scientists concede, for all branches of physical science. History has vindicated Kant's judgment that empirical knowledge is always probable knowledge.

But the situation is quite different, so Kant held, in other branches of knowledge. In mathematics and logic we appear to have *a priori* knowledge which has absolute certainty. Future experience cannot violate it. Kant gives as an example of *a priori* knowledge in mathematics the proposition that $7 + 5 = 12$. This proposition has absolute validity. It validates observation rather than that observation validates it. Observation, of course, *agrees* with it. If the grocer adds 7 eggs and 5 eggs and gets 11 of them as a result, we regard it as an error in addition, not as a novelty in the behavior of numbers. Pure (formal) logic is like mathematics in this respect. If all A is B and all B is C, then all A is C.

Kant proceeds in the first part of his *Critique of Pure Reason* (the *Transcendental Aesthetic*) to tease out the *a priori* factors in perceptual knowledge. The mind has three ways of knowing: perception, understanding, and reasoning. Perception is meant in the conventional sense, as when we see a chair, hear a bell, etc. Understanding occurs when one notes such things as that the chair is made of pine wood, that it belongs to a class of objects called furniture, and that it is the result of certain causes. Kant restricts the term *reason* to the attempt of the mind to gain knowledge regarding the reality of things which have no sensory content, which lie beyond direct observation, such as the notion of abstract matter divorced from all qualities, the soul as soul, or of God as pure spirit. Kant's elaboration of these ways of knowing is regarded by many as the most famous of all faculty theories (discussed in Chapter 5).

a. THE *a priori* FACTORS IN PERCEPTION. Kant thought of the data of our senses as raw, chaotic, unorganized. This is like the view which some modern child psychologists take of the experiences of the infant, which sees the world as a "buzzing confusion." According to Kant, sensory data are organized by the mind which imposes the forms of space and time on sensory experiences. All outer objects must appear to us as deployed in space because the mind thus orders its data. Time is a similar mental form which the mind imposes on its inner processes and on the events of the outer world.

What were Kant's proofs that space and time are thus *a priori* forms of understanding rather than objective characteristics of things? We deal with his evidences very briefly. We can imagine a physical object moved from one space to another, but cannot even fancy doing this with a bit of space itself! Space means nothingness—no wonder it cannot be moved about! Space is a creature of the mind. It is not learned from perception —*it is rather the presupposition of all perception.* This is why geometry is so absolutely certain. Once the axioms are chosen, inferences follow from them, but with *logical* (mental) rather than material necessity. In the geometry of Euclid all triangles have 180 degrees and parallel lines never meet. Later on geometries were evolved in which these claims regarding triangles and parallels are contradicted. But in each geometry, the conclusions follow inevitably from the axioms. Which one of them is true to reality? This is a matter of empirical observation, and so far is a matter of dispute.

In Einstein's physics, space is "warped" away from Euclid's model. We hear that the geometry which best describes reality must have at least ten dimensions. As knowledge grows, the geometry needed grows in complexity. It is said that there are hardly more than a half-dozen mathematicians who fully understand Einstein. All of this reminds one of the pleasantry that Q.E.D. means "Quit and eat dinner!"

b. THE *a priori* FACTORS IN UNDERSTANDING. Kant examines understanding (in a portion of the *Critique,* the *Transcendental Analytic*) to see whether or not it too has *a priori* ways of understanding like those of space and time in perception. To be very brief, Kant examines the twelve basic forms of logical judgments. He discovers in them twelve categories of understanding which are *a priori* ways of thinking. This may be made clear by some instances.

The mind uses the categories of *unity* and *plurality* in understanding the world. We are using the category of unity, for instance, when we view a multitude of soldiers as forming one army. The category of plurality enters into the opposite type of comprehension, as when we note that an army is made up of many soldiers. Both of these ways of viewing the situation are merely the mind's ways of looking at the world. We remind ourselves of this when we speak of seeing the trees but missing the forest, or vice versa. Much good teaching consists, not in imparting new facts of perception, but in correcting narrow and inappropriate points of view regarding facts.

Kant further notes that the category of *substance* enables us to understand that a changing thing still retains its identity. A green leaf withers and changes into mold, but we view it as still made of about the same stuff (substance), and that it is in a true sense the same leaf which was formerly fresh and green.

The categories of understanding, Kant held, are purely mental ways of understanding things. They cannot of themselves give us experience. But when experience comes the mind applies the categories to it so as to yield understanding. Physical objects themselves give us much liberty in viewing them as one or many, and in other ways. There is the story of a man who claimed that he owned a right-hand glove, a left-hand glove, and also a pair of gloves! This illustrates the absurdity that may result if one takes mental points of view for objective existences.

c. KANT'S METAPHYSICS. In the third portion of the *Critique* (the *Transcendental Dialectic*) Kant asks whether or not reason can secure knowledge of things lying beyond experience, such as of matter, the soul, or God. Kant's answer is "No." Things-in-themselves, apart from perception and the categories of understanding, cannot be known. They are *noumena*—only *phenomena* can be known. It is futile to ask whether there is a unitary soul or ego "as such" which could exist independently and survive death. The self or soul is known only in terms of its observable activities—perceiving, remembering, feeling, thinking. The reader will recall that the attacks on faculty theories (Chapter 5), especially Herbart's, resemble Kant's logic in denying that we can know things-in-themselves. Herbart held that we can observe and describe particular processes of mind but not the "potential powers" which are presumed to underlie them. We cannot discover memory "as such" which lies beyond its observable manifestations.

The notion of a transcendental world lying beyond our experience is also futile, Kant held, from the point of view of pure reason. When one tries to prove the existence of such a world beyond experience one gets involved in one or more of what Kant called *antinomies*. We will not pursue the matter further except to note that by an antinomy Kant means a situation where you have two opposed arguments, equally plausible, which refute each other. The notion of God is another one of which pure reason can form no clear conception. Obviously, according to Kant, the reliance on pure reason alone will lead to serious skepticisms. Many present-day opinions heartily agree with this view.

In his *Critique of Practical Reason,* however, Kant proceeds to argue that with the aid of faith the skepticisms of pure reason may be overcome, and man may accept the reality of the soul, its freedom, and the reality of God. Kant does not validate such beliefs by appeal to blind faith. He rather appeals to man's practical experiences and judgments about morals, freedom, and the divine. The moral ideals which should govern man's life are so sublime that they imply the existence of God and the reality of man's freedom to pursue such ideals. Kant's arguments on this point almost say that God and freedom must be realities because the august and sublime commands of duty require their existence.

☿ D. Kant's Moral Philosophy

Kant's moral philosophy is mainly set forth in the *Fundamental Principles of the Metaphysics of Morals* and in the *Critique of Practical Reason.* Kant seeks *a priori* principles which will prescribe universal laws of conduct. Kant concluded that there are such principles, and he calls them *categorical imperatives.* We examine Kant's moral philosophy in some detail because it bears on past and also current controversies about the aims and methods of character development in the schools.

1. Good Will as Unconditionally Good

Since there are some disagreements about what Kant intended to say about morality, we will turn to Kant's own statements (3). Kant concluded that the only thing in the world which is good without limitation is the good will to do one's duty. There are no doubt other "gifts of nature," such as intelligence, courage, and perseverance which are desirable, but they may be pernicious if the will which directs them is not good (3, p. 539). To take some examples from contemporary life, *loyalty* is not so impressive as a virtue when we notice the loyalty of thief to thief. *Courage* may further evil as well as good ends, as the case of the intrepid gangster shows. *Patience* seems to be an unqualified virtue until we reflect that it is a great asset to the counterfeiter of money and to the authors of skulduggery in general, including Satan himself! But what determines the goodness of good will? Kant answers, the will is good when it is completely devoted to duty for the sake of duty. As for duty, it is prescribed by the moral imperatives.

2. Duty and the Moral Imperatives

The will is not good merely because it achieves desirable consequences. The value of good will is not altered by its success or failure in reaching desirable ends (3, pp. 539-541 and elsewhere). Popular common sense seems to be in accord with Kant on this point. We are willing to credit a foolish man with "good intentions" even though he does the wrong thing. Kant, however, includes something more sophisticated in the goodness of good will. Good will is reverence for duty and duty is founded on reason. Now, *reason seeks universal principles*. We will readily agree to this statement.

Reason generalizes—is always reaching out for broader principles which are always valid and valid everywhere. The progress of science is measured by its success in discovering fewer laws which still cover more and more territory. If this is the task of reason, what is the task of the will which is guided by reason? The will is doing its duty when it strives to put the moral dictates of reason into action. The laws of conduct prescribed by reason are moral imperatives. That is, they are unqualified demands which are good in themselves. Categorical imperatives must be distinguished from hypothetical imperatives. A hypothetical imperative has the form, "If you want certain results you must act in certain ways." For example, *if* you want a strong body you must observe the rules of health. But for the categorical imperative, there is no "if" about it! It declares, "It is your duty to develop a strong body and you are therefore under obligation to observe the rules of health." We will now consider three formulations of the categorical imperative. Kant tells us that they are not really three different laws of conduct but three ways of formulating one universal law (3. p. 557).

a. FIRST FORMULATION. "Act in conformity with that maxim, and that maxim only, which you can at the same time will to be a universal law" (3, p. 551). This imperative law is something like the golden rule. But the golden rule appeals to the heart rather than for rational universality in behavior. To illustrate the categorical imperative we take the case of borrowing money on the promise to repay but not intending to make repayment. This is wrong because if it became universal no one would loan money to anyone else, and this would cause many evils which such loans could prevent.

But for Kant there is a deeper reason why borrowing money on false promises is wrong. It is wrong because it violates reason. If men surrender the guidance of reason they become helpless pawns, buffeted about by their own rampant and momentary desires, while justice and equity become mockeries. Reason seeks universal laws which are consistent (congruent). It violates this function of reason to set up the rule of conduct which requires faith to promises and then at once allows our own conduct to be an exception to it. This is contradiction, and reason cannot tolerate contradictions. To behave morally means to be able to *justify* conduct. Such justification, Kant thought, can be rendered only by the court of reason. To violate reasonableness is the primary vice of conduct. When behavior is governed by desires not sanctioned by reason, reason itself becomes the tool of desires, and men justify their conduct by no end of sophistry and logic-chopping. There is the story of the robber who objected to being called a "thief," declaring that all he had done was to "misappropriate property!" This justification is scarcely less cogent than the logic of a nation which establishes a dictatorship and then calls it a democracy.

b. SECOND FORMULATION. Every human being, including yourself, is always to be treated as an end, not merely as a means toward further ends (3, p. 555). This formulation of the categorical imperative especially brings out the conviction held by idealisms in general that each individual has an intrinsic worth of his own. This formulation does not forbid that we use others as means—we must not use them *merely* as means. They should be served for their own inherent worth.

c. THIRD FORMULATION. Always act as though you were the member of a group where each individual is at once ruler and subject. This rule shows that Kant is rightly considered a philosophical champion of democracy. Kant favored a republican form of government in which all laws are established by an elected legislature. In view of the times during which Kant lived, when nations were usually under the despotic rule of royalty, his political beliefs appear bold and revolutionary. Kant heartily approved the American Revolution and the Constitution finally adopted.

3. Critical Comments on Kant's Ethics

Disaffection against Kant's views about morality comes chiefly from empiricists who hold that moral conduct cannot be governed in terms of abstract, *a priori*, and absolute rules. We shall encounter the views of the opposition in their most uncompromising form in Book V on pragmatism and education. William James and John Dewey and other devotees of the practical and down-to-earth philosophy of pragmatism hold that there is no absolute good, hence no absolute rule for attaining it. What is good and what is bad must be determined by the concrete outcomes of each concrete line of conduct, not by a sweeping imperative which is presumed to cover all cases. (In Alaska the spoilage of food is avoided by keeping it in heated ovens instead of in refrigerators!) The empiricist in morals finds that circumstances determine the proper course of conduct. The rationalist replies that this way of thinking nevertheless leads in the direction of values conceived as absolute. Telling a lie may often be regarded as "good." It will be noticed, however, that the empiricist justifies the lie by reference to some greater good which upon other occasions is better served by telling the truth.

The doctor may lie to his patient about the latter's condition because the truth might kill him quicker than the disease. But lies are not tolerated on the witness stand. "Human welfare" is the greater good which rules in these two opposed cases and in countless others besides. These "greater goods" tend to increase in scope, covering more and more acts until even the pragmatist finds himself defending moral rules which may not be "absolute" for the whole universe, but cover all human behavior. Even from the pragmatist point of view a finite rule is practically as extensive as an infinite one as far as finite man is concerned. The man sentenced to prison for life might as well, as far as he is concerned, have been given the sentence for all eternity.

Thus Dewey, uncompromising humanitarian, places the democratic way of life on such a high pedestal that its effect on human behavior is practically as absolute as the Kantian imperative. We must not forget, however, that no matter how "absolute" the empiricist's moral rules may be, he regards them as validated by experience of good and evil. Reason, of course, must be relied on to determine what rules are justified by experience. But reason bases its judgments on empirical evidences, not on *a priori* insights which prove themselves and thus have no need for experience to support them.

Other critics of Kant find it difficult to apply his imperatives to daily moral problems. Certainly the moral perplexities of life would be simplified if one could trust to a few rules to be followed without deviation. But Kant's general rules are not easy to apply in practice.

Using Kant's own example, let us suppose that a man wishes to borrow money from you but you are certain that he has no intention of returning the loan. Guided by Kant's first formulation, you refuse to grant the loan since it is wrong to follow a principle which cannot be universalized. But suppose that if you refuse to grant the loan his family will suffer. If you refuse to grant the loan his child who is very ill may die for want of medical attention. You are now at odds with Kant's second formulation which enjoins you to treat individuals as ends in themselves. The child can no longer be served as an end—you have used it entirely as a means for meeting the first formulation.

The pragmatist favors a different procedure. He decides each case on its own merits. He estimates as best he can the good and evil consequences of each course of action and then selects the one promising the greatest good and the least evil.

Kant's system of ethics finds it difficult to establish *a priori* validity for rules of conduct without reference to goods of an empirical sort. This is true of his own instance. He grants that being able to secure loans is good because it can prevent or alleviate suffering. Clearly, this appeals to the consequences of behavior as the justification of behavior. If these consequences are left out of consideration, then the only satisfaction in moral conduct would be purely rational, namely, the satisfaction of seeing principles of conduct universalized and having congruent unity.

But if the mere universality of a rule of conduct is a virtue we could achieve it in countless ways provided we ignore the consideration that these ways may be utterly useless as far as doing anyone any good is concerned. Each person might, for instance, agree to wear a feather somewhere on his or her person. Although this practice would be trivial from the moral point of view, it could attain a relatively painless universality which would eclipse the usually painful virtue of returning loans. It seems that we should first make sure that a given line of conduct has empirically satisfying results for the largest number of persons concerned and then universalize it if we can. The Kantian moralist, so his critic holds, finds it difficult to justify the universalization of a line of conduct without reference to goods other than its mere universality.

⇕ E. Idealistic Philosophy and Education

The application of idealism to education will be explored more fully in Chapters 9 and 10. We here sketch what may be anticipated from our study of Plato and Kant. Their views have a broad rather than detailed significance for education. Essentialism, since it is primarily a philosophy of education, offers detailed prescriptions regarding what should be taught, and why and how it should be taught. Idealism is led away from concrete particulars by its penchant for rational speculation. But it suggests general aims, attitudes, and values for education. The attitude of the teacher may affect the destiny of the student more than the subject matter of instruction which the teacher has to offer. What, then, are the broad implications of the idealism of Plato and of Kant for education?

1. Emphasis on Selfhood

With Plato and Kant, as with idealism in general, the self is made significant and precious. Plato pictured the soul as coming from the eternal realm of forms trailing reminiscences of sublime perfections. Idealists do not regard the mind of the pupil or student as the passive recipient of impressions from an overwhelming physical universe. In place of this, Kant portrays the mind as the creator of time and space and as the provider of its own categories of understanding.

It is not a mere coincidence that Kant was the champion of democracy. The concept of the dignity and worth of the individual, which forms the basis of democracy, is consistent with Kant's critical philosophy as a whole. Religious individuals especially will feel less alien in a world conceived as spiritual than in one made up of inscrutable matter inexorably obeying the seemingly blind and insensate laws of nature. The mind of the pupil conceived after the fashion of idealism becomes something toward which reverence is due. When we come to consider Giovanni Gentile's thoughts on education we will see this tender reverence for the mind of the learner expressed with eloquence.

2. Kant's Views on Education

Kant gave some lectures on education, published in 1779 under the title, *Essays in Pedagogy*. E. F. Buchner (1) has organized Kant's views on education.

Kant was no unyielding martinet on matters of duty. But his fame as the philosopher of "duty" led early American leaders who had heard about the great German doctor to welcome his moral teachings. Kant's ethics seemed to harmonize with the rigorous and puritanic attitudes of the colonists. Our forefathers believed in conveying moral wisdom via the catechism, and they surpassed Kant in being "categorical." There is good reason to believe, however, that Kant did not bring all conduct under the rule of the imperative. There are numerous experiences of daily life which do not involve the rule of duty. In such cases we are free to be governed by personal desires. Moreover, we desire to be reasonable and the imperative merely points the way. Kant taught that we should strive for the happiness of mankind. Indeed, obedience to the categorical imperative was intended by Kant to bring about general happiness. Kant held that we should not, unless absolutely necessary, force others to do their duty. To become truly moral, the individual must freely choose to follow the rule of duty. Kant opposed the theologians who wished to base morality on God's commands. Morality, Kant held, makes its appeal to intelligence, not to the edicts of authority. If morality makes its appeal to intelligence, then it can be acquired through instruction which does not require the rod.

Kant did not regard the human will as "naturally perverse" or "steeped in original sin." Initially, the child's nature is neither good nor bad. The will of the child needs guidance, and reason is the supreme guide. Children must learn to act as they ought, not merely as they want to act. But their instruction in moral matters should be *persuasive* rather than imperative. To be "imperative" is the prerogative of the rule of duty, not of the individual who advocates the rule! Showing the influence of Rousseau, Kant rejected austere discipline for the sake of discipline. Morality is something sublime. Kant felt that the child's sense of this sublimity might be degraded by punishment (1, pp 185-188). Education should utilize the spirit of play, for while playing the child disciplines himself.

Kant tried to solve the knotty problem of how to enable the individual to exercise freedom and yet subject him to restraints. Kant's solution was that the child should be given the insight that (a) to get others to sanction his legitimate aims he must sanction their rightful aims; and (b) that in order to realize his own freedom and benefit from it he must learn self-restraint (1, pp. 131-132). In place of giving moral instruction by use of didactic pronouncements Kant favored the method made famous by Socrates in which knowledge is conveyed to the child by wringing it from him through discussion! This dialectical method of instruction was emphasized by post-Kantian idealists. We will see its application to education in later chapters, especially the use made of it by William Torrey Harris (Chapter 9).

F. Post-Kantian Idealism

The main task of later idealists was to remedy the discords created by Kant's dualisms, such as the opposition of pure to practical reason, the breach between the phenomenal and the noumenal world, and the contradiction between the determinism posited by pure reason and the freedom posited by practical reason.

Gradually, through the work of such men as Fichte, Schelling, and Hegel, an "objective" idealism was established which sought to eliminate the subjective elements in Kant's thought, such as his view that space and time are inner forms of perception having no existence in the outer world. Hegel would be rated by many as the most important figure in the development of so-called objective idealism. We have an added reason for devoting the following chapter to Hegel: namely, that his philosophy supplied the foundation for leading idealistic systems of education, such as those of Croce and Gentile in Italy and those of Horne, Harris, and others in the United States.

References

1. Buchner, E. F. *The Educational Theory of Immanuel Kant.* Philadelphia: Lippincott, 1904.

2. Mead, Hunter. *Types and Problems of Philosophy* (rev.). New York: Henry Holt, 1953.

3. Rand, Benjamin. *The Classical Moralists.* New York: Houghton Mifflin, 1909, pp. 539-558; reprinted from *The Philosophy of Kant* (J. Watson, tr.). Glasgow, 1901.

⍗ *chapter 8*

OUTLINE OF HEGELIAN IDEALISM

During the last half of the nineteenth century idealism was the dominant philosophy of Western culture. It first became dominant in Germany through the prestige of Kant and his successors, Fichte and Schelling. Hegel, following the leads established by Fichte and Schelling and adding novel features of his own, further established the authority of idealism in the sphere of philosophy. German idealism spread to England, France, Italy, the United States, and elsewhere. It must be remembered that idealism had already been established in England, especially through the influence of Berkeley. Berkeley's idealism, however, differs from Hegel's in important respects.

We select Hegel as the key idealistic philosopher for education. This is because Hegel's philosophy had great influence on prominent philosophers of education and on the practice of education. We will consider three idealistic philosophers of education who have applied Hegelian idealism to education: William T. Harris and Herman H. Horne in the United States, and Giovanni Gentile in Italy.

The present chapter will cover the following matters relevant to idealistic philosophy in general but with emphasis on absolute idealism as expressed in the teachings of Hegel:

A. Hegel: Biographical Notes
B. Hegel's Theory of Knowledge and of Reality
C. Hegel's Theory of Morality

D. Hegel's Thoughts on Education

E. Prelude to Chapters 9 and 10

▽ A. Hegel: Biographical Notes

Some highlights regarding Hegel's career as philosopher and educator are as follows: George Wilhelm Hegel (1770-1831) served for six years as tutor and for eight years as director of a *gymnasium* (grammar school) at Nuremberg, Germany. His later important professorships of philosophy were held at the University of Heidelberg and then at the University of Berlin, where he occupied the position formerly held by Fichte.

Hegel's writings were voluminous. After his death his collected works appeared in eighteen volumes! Hegel's philosophy was so much like a vast labyrinth or like a structure with many facets that even professional philosophers find despair in trying to understand him. Loewenberg (9, Preface) declares that in order to understand what Hegel writes one must already know what he means! The exposition which follows seeks to give the consensus of agreement among authoritative interpreters of Hegel, among whom we may count Hegel himself!

▽ B. Hegel's Theory of Knowledge and of Reality

For Hegel, *reality and our knowledge of it are one and the same thing.* Our knowledge of reality is essentially *rational* and *reality itself is a rational system.* Even physical nature follows the laws of thought. Whereas for some other points of view, including that of common sense, reality is considered as separate from our knowledge of it, for Hegel reality and knowledge are only different facets of the same thing. In what follows, statements about Hegel's epistemology are at the same time statements about his metaphysics. In Hegelianism, thought and reality embrace each other without overlapping. Since reality is itself a rational system, man's knowledge embraces reality to the degree that knowledge becomes a congruent whole. So far, this seems to suggest that omniscience is possible for man—a glorious prospect for education for those who think of it as exclusively the battle against ignorance. Unfortunately for this view, Hegel considered that the universe continually develops. Man's knowledge, so to speak, would then have to travel very fast in order not to lose ground.

1. Criticisms of the Congruence Theory of Knowledge

The congruence theory of knowledge (see Chapter 1) holds that the crucial test of truth is the degree of harmony or congruence which holds between propositions regarded as true. The congruence test of truth is important in science. If two propositions about nature contradict each other one of them must be false. Of course, both of them may be false despite the fact that they are in harmony with each other. The congruence theory of truth appears in many schools of thought, but is especially favored by absolute idealism as set forth by Hegel and some of his British and American followers. Man's knowledge is fragmentary and incomplete. But as knowledge grows we see contradictions fading away and knowledge becoming more and more coherent or congruent. This implies, some idealists think, that there now exists an absolute, perfectly self-consistent Logos or God who is at the same time the universe. We note a few alleged weaknesses of the coherence theory as applied both to rational and to empirical knowledge.

a. COHERENCE AND RATIONALISM. Following Kant, let us take geometry as an instance of a rational or *a priori* branch of knowledge. All geometries, whether Euclidean or non-Euclidean, are perfectly consistent (congruent) within themselves. Given certain axioms certain conclusions follow of necessity and, within a given system, these conclusions never contradict each other. But there is contradiction between the different systems. In Euclid's system parallel lines never meet and the sum of the angles of a triangle always equals 180 degrees. In the non-Euclidean geometries the angles of triangles may give a total of more or less than 180 degrees, and parallel lines may always meet when extended, or may gradually approach each other but never meet. What is more, it is not so easy to decide which geometry is true to the realities. For centuries it was thought that Euclid's system was true to physical nature—which it is if one does not go beyond casual experience or even scientific knowledge at the Newtonian level. But physicists of today make startling suggestions to the effect that nature conforms best to a geometry of at least ten dimensions and that space is "warped" and non-Euclidean.

The points noted above suggest the difficulty of using congruence as the sole or even the chief test of truth. Many have concluded with Kant that all geometries are "mind-made." You get no more out of them than you put into them to start with in the form of axiomatic assumptions. Some of the elementary concepts of geometry clearly exist only in the mind. The notions of a point without area and of a line without width are purely conceptual, having no existence in the world of concrete things. Sir James Jeans somewhere expresses this thought somewhat as follows: Man believed that he had found a footprint on the shores of the unknown; but lo, the footprint turns out to be his own!

b. COHERENCE AND EMPIRICISM. Can the coherence theory of knowledge be applied to empirical knowledge? It seems sensible to hold that the truth of any material assertion is supported by its coherence with other material statements accepted as true. Newton's law of gravity is verified not alone by the behavior of falling bodies but by the movements of planets in their orbits, by the flight of projectiles, and by the rhythmic beat of the pendulum. The progress of science appears to depend on finding more and more coherent knowledge.

Difficulties arise when one seeks to establish the existence of a final and absolute coherence from the enumeration of finite instances of it. Most modern scientists are rather of the opinion that the order which science finds in nature has only a statistical, not an absolute rigor. According to this, knowledge can only *tend* to be congruent, and does not attain the absolute congruence to be found in a purely rational system like geometry.

Not all of the material findings of science are congruent with each other, even in a statistical sense. These lacunae *may* vanish as knowledge increases, but can we be sure of this in advance? For all we know, says the "radical empiricist," there may be unresolvable contradictions in the very fabric of reality. To be sure, as knowledge which is materially true increases, it grows in congruence. But the empiricist denies that one can reverse the situation and hold that if knowledge is congruent it must be materially true. But absolute idealists assume the existence of an absolute Mind or Reason where all facts are known and are seen to be in perfect congruence. Perhaps the Absolute Mind has such knowledge but this is His enlightenment, not ours! We poor mortals must base our conclusions on what *we* know. To accept the Hegelian Absolute requires an act of faith to support observation.

2. The Nature of Error

We perhaps would find it easier to accept the thesis that reality is identical with *truth* than Hegel's claim that reality is also identical with *thought*. It seems to us that sometimes we do not "think truly." There is error, and it seems strange to speak of erroneous thought as being identical with reality. Yet Hegel undoubtedly states that reality is identical with thought. Reality is an evolving process of thinking. Of course, erroneous thoughts do exist, and if existence is thinking, then false thoughts are as "real" as any. If these Hegelian notions seem strange to the reader this is in part because he has been reared in the belief that knowledge is distinct from reality, and that the function of knowledge is to *refer* to reality, not to *be* reality. We may at times declare that a certain bit of knowledge is "real," but we only mean to say that it is true to reality. But Hegel regards all reality as identical with thought. How then can there be a place for error in Hegel's system?

Hegel provides a place for error in at least two ways, although neither of these may satisfy the critic. In the first place, Hegel distinguishes between man's "natural logic" which he possesses by nature, and the "science of logic" which he says (note the typical Hegelian verbiage) is the "Knowing of the Thinking in its truth" (9, p. 98). The findings of the science of logic are identical with reality, but presumably man's "natural logic" leads to error.

Hegel's second way of providing a place for error is to treat truth and error as differences in *degree* rather than differences in *kind*. Truth is something which grows by becoming more and more inclusive, more and more universal. There is a grain of truth stated or implied by even the most erroneous statements. For instance, the assertion that "$2 + 2 = 6$" implies, correctly enough, that the sums of positive numbers are greater than such numbers taken severally, and that numbers are subject to the process of addition. The assertion that Chinese have green hair correctly implies that Chinese, hair, and the color green exist! (It might be argued that if teachers adopted the genial view that all erroneous statements contain truth in disguise it would lead to more justice to students than the "all or nothing" theory which is usually observed in grading examinations.) Hegel held that truth (reality) is growing—it gradually approaches perfection as it approaches inclusiveness and congruence. The ideal terminus of this process is the Absolute Truth.

3. The Evolution of Reality

For Hegel the universe is an unending process of dynamic development. Hegel has a number of terms which refer to reality as a whole. It is the *Absolute,* the *Spirit, God,* or *Logos.* The Absolute, which is the unity of all things, is engaged in an unending process of dynamic development or evolution. This process is called *dynamic* because it is a process of self-development. In evolving, the universe is realizing the plan or purpose already inherent in it. The goal of this evolution is to become conscious of its inherent mission and destiny. The laws of nature are thoughts but they occur on an unconscious level. The goal of the Absolute to become self-conscious can occur only in the mind of man. This is Hegel's tribute to the momentous importance of human selves.

The impatient realist may regard the notions sketched above as no more than "wooly-minded" mysticism! Yet it is faithful to the arresting picture of the universe which science portrays. A hot nebulous mass is thrown off by some central sun. After untold ages it solidifies and living forms appear which eventuate in a creature (man) who not merely *exists* but is *conscious of* and *reflects upon* his existence. If some sidereal upheaval puts an end to this, the process begins all over again—*a slow and inevitable groping toward consciousness.*

4. Status of the Concept of Time

Hegel's ideas raise troublesome questions regarding his view of the nature of time. Hegel speaks of God and the world as being in an eternal process of becoming. He has been called the modern Heraclitus because of his emphasis on the universality of time and change. There never was a time when the evolution of the Logos was not going on. So far, the reality of time is emphasized by Hegel. But there is a curious antagonism between the reality of time and the reality of persons and objects. Time appears "real" to us because persons and objects change—they come into being and pass away. If everything remained fixed time would become unreal. But persons and objects, on the other hand, seem more "real" the longer they last without loss of identity. It seems that a thing becomes perfectly real when it endures forever without changing. This "intuition of the heart," as we might call it, which is found in Plato's conception of the eternally real ideas, seems to be a universal intuition of mankind. Life begins to look shadowy and unreal the moment we reflect on its passing away. So far in our account of Hegel the eternal flow of evolution is so prominent that it negates the reality of everything else.

On the other hand, Hegel stresses the thought that reality is evolving only that which is potential or implicit in it. *The Absolute thus eternally becomes for itself what it is in itself*. It now appears that time and change are the illusions, and that the Absolute is timeless and unchanging. The problem of time and change is recondite for any philosophy or, for that matter, for any science. We need not pursue the matter further. Our aim is merely to note that Hegel is ambiguous on this matter. Hegel sought to overcome the dualisms between the phenomenal and noumenal worlds, between finite and infinite being as they are found in Kant and others. Hegel's own ambiguity regarding finite realities and the reality of the Absolute suggests that he has not solved the problem of harmonizing them.

5. The Dialectic of Development

Hegel held to a special view, which he owed in part to predecessors like Fichte and Schelling, regarding the way the Universal Mind develops. The universe follows the principles of *dialectical* development. The term *dialectics* refers to a part of logic which has to do with such things as the analysis of meanings and the modes and rules of reasoning. In a broad sense it refers to argumentation in which the main dispute centers on the meanings of the terms used, the ideas expressed, and the soundness of the reasoning. The philosopher Socrates taught his students by using the dialectical method. He would ask them to express their views on some problem and then, by means of clever questions, lead them to

realize their misuse of meanings and their errors in reasoning. This pedagogical method sharpens the wits and leads to truth by following the
course of thought to its logical conclusions.

Now Hegel conceived that all reality consisted in the development
of thought in the mind of the Absolute. All history, even natural history,
is like an argument developing into fuller knowledge. In all arguments
there are contradictions. Hegel held that the principle of contradiction is
at the root of all development. Everything tends to pass into or change
into its opposite. This development goes on until opposites are reconciled
by absorption into a larger truth. Cosmic Consciousness (God) develops
its thought (reality) through three stages: "to be," "to be denied," and
"to be transcended." That is to say, every assertion (to be) meets with
its contradiction (to be denied), and then returns to itself in a larger
whole (to be transcended). These three steps are respectively known as
the *thesis,* the *antithesis,* and the *synthesis.*

6. Examples of Dialectic

Since the application of idealism in education involves the pedagogical
use of the dialectical method it will be well to clarify it with some examples. Consider, for instance, the antithesis between human freedom
and compulsion. The individual desires freedom without the exercise
of compulsion. But this thesis encounters the antithesis that in order to
attain freedom we may have to use force, as in wars against aggression or
in the restraint of criminals. The synthesis comes in seeing that the use
of force to preserve liberty is not an evil. Liberty which uses force for its
own preservation "returns to its own" again in a more secure and precious
form—precious because a price was paid for it.

There is an interesting dialectic in the Christian account of salvation
which Hegel expands to cover all moral development. The thesis is that
the individual loves his own life and wishes to realize his own selfish
desires. The antithesis is that "He who loves his life shall lose it." Reconciliation is found as follows: By giving his life to God and serving
God's will the individual will indeed find that he gets his selfhood back
again, but much enriched. The reader will recall a similar solution of the
freedom of the individual versus the control of the state in the political
philosophy of Rousseau as stated and defended by Meiklejohn (Chapter
2).

Herbert Spencer supplied a nice example of dialectic in the sphere of
moral conduct—although Spencer, an empiricist, had no thought of
offering the example to support Hegel! Men seek to attain pleasure. This
thesis meets with the difficulty that to aim at pleasure directly is often to
miss it. To take a simple instance of this, the gourmet whose aim is to
enjoy his favorite foods finds that he must at first go without food so as to

increase his appetite! Hence, Spencer declared, attaining pleasure is like practicing archery on a windy day—in order to hit the target one has to aim at something else! If we will pursue ends in life other than pleasure we will find that pleasure comes to us unbidden (synthesis).

Hegel's dialectic of the virtue of innocence will be approved by those who deny that ignorance is bliss. Hegel taught that innocence (thesis) must encounter evil through temptation (antithesis) in order to rise to the tried and true virtue of innocence (synthesis).

7. The Dialectical Fate of Hegel's Thought

There is a self-destroying element in Hegel's logic which Jacob Loewenberg makes clear in an astute analysis. If Hegel's logic is valid it can never terminate in a supreme synthesis:

> His logic, playing the double role of uniting opposites and of providing a negative mate for the synthesis issuing from such union, suffers no philosophy to escape from the fate it decrees. Hegel's own method decrees that his own system be ultimately jettisoned (9, p. xiv).

8. A Liberal Version of Hegelian Dialectic

The unvarying hop-step-and-jump from thesis to antithesis to synthesis portrayed above seems entirely too wooden and inelastic to account for the flexible and resourceful nature of thinking. To go farther and seek to impose dialectical patterns on the events of physical nature becomes so awkward that the credulity of the realist is insufferably strained. The value of the concept of dialectic, especially for education, will be increased by simplifying it as follows: *Dialectical development of thought is its movement in the direction of greater completeness.*

This liberal conception of dialectic may be amplified as follows: All disputes and arguments, whether between individuals or groups, arise because knowledge is incomplete. In every dispute there are assertions and denials which serve as theses and antitheses. All disputes point to the condition of incomplete knowledge—either a dearth of evidences or a failure to see the conclusions to which evidences point. It may be said that in most of his own writings Hegel made use of just this version of dialectic—dialectic in the sense of movement in the direction of fuller knowledge. Hegel never tired of pointing out man's addiction to half truths, narrow prejudices, and partisan views. The only hope of arriving at agreement between individuals, social classes, or nations (to attain synthesis) is to transcend ignorance, to attain a fuller knowledge of the whole.

This version of dialectic is in nice accord with the growth of scientific knowledge. Contradictions and inconsistencies are always appearing which vanish when research makes further progress. When this happens old principles are not usually proved false, but are embodied in more sweeping generalizations. Hegel sometimes speaks as though there were a faraway or even now existing Absolute Mind in which all things find unity and where all contradictions vanish. The earlier scientist was hardly less a creature of faith in his belief that the universe is governed by absolute law although he had proved this to be the case only in part. The ultramodern conception that there are no absolute laws of nature but only laws of probability is also in part a commitment of faith for it also presumes to make present statements concerning what we will know when we know more!

⇕ C. Hegel's Theory of Morality

In the area of axiology Hegel wrote both on aesthetics and ethics. We will discuss his views on ethics since this subject bears on the fundamental question of the ends or aims of education. Hegel's views on morality also help clarify his theory of the state and legal rights.

1. First Interpretation: Hegel on Rights and Duties

The problem of facets in Hegel's philosophy, that is, the problem of choosing between two or more interpretations of him, becomes acute in discussing his ideas regarding morality. We first sketch a common interpretation of Hegel which is of ill repute because of consequences to which it has led.

Hegel held that *the same dialectical thinking which evolves nature, humanity, and all human institutions is the same dialectic (reason) which seeks to understand them.* This thesis is important for understanding Hegel's theory of rights and duties. It implies that we should direct our energy to discovering the course through which society and the state developed. We should try to know the state as it really *is* for only this reveals what it *ought* to be. Hegel declared that "the history of the world is the world's court of justice" (9, p. 468). Every nation has a great mission to fulfill in the evolution of the Absolute. It may serve its destiny as a "thesis" to be annihilated by an "antithesis." When one nation conquers another this suggests that the "idea constituting the victor" was greater than that of the vanquished. Whatever exists is rational—such is the conclusion of a philosophy which takes history as the working out of an inexorable logic!

What now about the rights and obligations of individuals? The state is a larger part of and hence enjoys fuller communion with the Absolute than is the case with any individual. Therefore, the individual must subject his conscience and his will to the state which better expresses universal reason. Hegel wrote: "Just as the spirit is superior to nature, so is the State superior to the physical life. We must therefore worship the State as the manifestation of the divine on earth . . ." (9, p. 447).

2. Consequences of the First Version of Hegel

The socialist Karl Marx, whose ideas serve as the present supports of communism in Russia and elsewhere, made use of the version given above of Hegel's theory of the state and of the duties of individuals. But Marx gives the dialectic of history a materialistic interpretation, whereas for Hegel history represents the spiritual development of God. As for political and economic development, Hegel saw it as a process of *accommodation* in which contradictory tendencies eventually find inclusion in a higher synthesis. This suggests the reconciliation of quarrels between groups and "due process of law." But Marx replaces the principles of accommodation with the principle of *revolution* (1, p. 40).

The interpretation of Hegel which makes the individual subservient to the state was also typical of Prussian ideology which reached the peak of its ravages under Hitler. Mussolini too sought Hegelian support in making the state in fascist Italy a superindividual, exacting complete obedience from the people.

3. Second Interpretation of Hegel on Rights and Duties

The account given above is but one facet of Hegel's theory of the state which was seized upon by dictators because it was congenial with their ambitions. We must in justice to Hegel take note of another interpretation which we have reason to suppose was Hegel's basic intention (9, pp. 443-446). Hegel wrote, "The true (real) State is the ethical whole and the realization of freedom" (9, p. 443). In the state the universal and the particular must be united. Hegel distinguishes abstract right in the sense of law as the thesis for which the inner conscience of the individual is the antithesis. The ethics of society is the synthesis of abstract right and individual conscience. Hegel notes that conscience is not an infallible guide. The ethics of the group, expressing the wisdom of history and embodied in social institutions is a better guide for the individual. One may venture to say that the latter statements harmonize very well with the place accorded in our democracy to social and individual judgments in matters of conduct.

Hegel held that in a "real" state, that is, in a state which is what it should be, the people have developed an organic totality, enabling them to express a common will. In such a state, says Hegel, the monarch is bound by the sovereign will of the people—he cannot act arbitrarily. We often say that an executive who implements the will of a group has to "sign on the dotted line." Hegel enjoins his sovereign to "put the dot upon the i" (9, p. 451). In Hegel's language, a state where the sovereign will of the people does not hold sway is not a "real" state—it only "exists." It is like a sick body which exists but is not the "real" body required by rational definition. Says Hegel: "A hand, which is cut off, still looks like a hand and exists, but it has no reality" (9, p. 446). The second version of Hegel just sketched harmonizes with our democratic outlook on the relations of the individual to his society. That this version of Hegel is the one he intended to convey is further supported by his utterances on education to which we turn later.

4. Criticism: The Idealist's Theory of Evil

The critic finds that absolute idealism encounters a difficulty with the fact of evil similar to the difficulty it has with the problem of error. The absolute idealist is prone to hold that if the whole of reality were fully known to man he would apprehend it as a realm of perfect beauty, goodness, and truth. To the mind of the Absolute, evil, like error, is only an appearance to finite man. This pious, other-worldly, and rather smug conception of evil fed the revolts against idealism of later pragmatic and realistic philosophers. The critic holds that man cannot know from his limited knowledge that a universal reason which views evil as illusory exists. Christian theology which posits an omniscient and omnipotent God shares with absolute idealism the problem of bridging the gulf between man's finite world with its black and cruel sufferings and God's infinite perspective where "everything is for the best."

⚡ D. Hegel's Thoughts on Education

As previously noted Hegel had experience as a tutor, as the director of a *gymnasium*, and as a university professor. Hegel's utterances on education are few, but they are based directly on his philosophy. We will consider Hegel's personal statements about education and also the educational implications of his philosophy as interpreted by others (10, 11). Hegel wrote:

> Pedagogy is the art of making man moral. It regards man as one with nature, and points out the way in which he may be born again, and have his first nature changed into a second spiritual nature, in such fashion that the spiritual nature may become habitual to him (2, p. 350).[1]

Hegel's conception of the basic process that takes place in education may be stated in dialectical form: The *thesis* states that the child begins life in a state of bondage to nature. That is, he is ruled by his

[1] William Boyd, from whose book this citation is taken, quotes it from Milliscent Mackenzie (10, p. 63).

senses, impulses, and emotions. The *antithesis* of this is the free life of the spirit which knows and accepts the Absolute Spirit. To reconcile these opposites (to achieve synthesis) "self-estrangement" is necessary. This is accomplished as follows: The individual, typically during adolescence, comes to realize that individual experience is incomplete and unsatisfactory. He begins to realize that his society and his state imply a larger whole, one that lies closer to the realities. The maturing adolescent should be taught and encouraged to renounce himself, to learn obedience and service to the social whole, and to learn reverence for its spiritual achievements. When self-renunciation is complete and is replaced by the individual's identification of his interests with those of the social whole, the individual enters upon a closer communion with the Absolute, and gets back a new self, much enriched. The reader will note the close parallelism between this scheme for educational salvation with the Christian doctrine of religious salvation.

We have said nothing so far about such practical questions as what we should teach, and when and how we should teach it. It is clear, however, that since Hegel wishes the child to appreciate the spiritual achievements of society as a step toward accepting them, a traditionalist curriculum is implied. The following chapters devoted to idealistic philosophers of education will fill in the broad outlines of Hegel's brief blueprint for education.

⋮̤ E. Prelude to Chapters 9 and 10

Chapter 9 is devoted to William Torrey Harris, greatest Hegelian philosopher of education in the United States, and to Herman Harrell Horne who applied religious versions of Hegel's idealism to education. Chapter 10 concerns the application of Hegelian idealism to education made by Giovanni Gentile in Italy.

Educators with idealistic convictions or at least with idealistic "slants" are numerous. The interested student will find it profitable to explore the following writers: William E. Hocking, student of Josiah Royce and professor of philosophy at Harvard, is a thinker of great repute in contemporary philosophy. Education is not Professor Hocking's leading interest, but he presents his ideas on the subject in various writings (6, 7). Theodore M. Greene, professor of philosophy at Yale University, writes thoughtfully and engagingly for Christian idealism (4, 5). J. Donald Butler is one of the most recent spokesmen for idealism in education (3). Butler was the student of the late Herman H. Horne, was much influenced by Horne, but holds to special views of his own and shows objectivity in considering the views of others. These three writers, like idealists in general, fuse idealism with religious thought. Professor Greene (5) cites further sources on religious idealism in education.

References

1. Bober, Mandell M. *Karl Marx's Interpretation of History*. Cambridge, Mass.: Harvard University Press, 1948.
2. Boyd, William. *The History of Western Education*. London: A. & C. Black, 1950.
3. Butler, J. Donald. *Four Philosophies and Their Practice in Education and Religion* (rev. ed.). New York: Harper, 1957.
4. Greene, Theodore M. *Liberal Education Reconsidered*. Cambridge, Mass.: Harvard University Press, 1953.
5. ———. "A Liberal Christian Idealist Philosophy of Education," pp. 91-136 in *Modern Philosophies and Education*, Part I (N. B. Henry, ed.). Chicago: University of Chicago Press, 1955.
6. Hocking, William E. *Human Nature and Its Remaking*. New Haven, Conn.: Yale University Press, 1918.
7. ———. *What Man Can Make of Man*. New York: Harper, 1942.
8. Hook, Sidney. *From Hegel to Marx*. New York: Reynal and Hitchcock, 1936.
9. Loewenberg, Jacob (ed.). *Hegel Selections*. New York: Scribner's, 1929.
10. Mackenzie, Milliscent. *Hegel's Educational Theory and Practice*. London: Swan, Sonnenschein, 1909.
11. Rosenkranz, Karl. *Pedagogics as a System*. St. Louis, Mo.: Studley, 1872.

§ *chapter 9*

AMERICAN IDEALISM IN EDUCATION:
WILLIAM T. HARRIS AND HERMAN H. HORNE

Living philosophies, although they may claim to voice unalterable truth, become adapted to the cultural climates to which they are transferred. They also modify the culture which they invade. Chapter 8 reviews the idealism of Hegel and sketches his ideas on education. We now follow the importation of German idealism into the United States, and will see how William T. Harris and Herman H. Horne adapted Hegelian idealism to the needs of education in a democracy. This chapter takes up three main subjects:

A. Early German Idealism in the United States
B. The Educational Idealism of William Torrey Harris
C. The Educational Idealism of Herman H. Horne

▽ A. Early German Idealism in the United States

1. Transcendentalism

The aspects of transcendentalism in German philosophy were altered by American idealists. In a broad and yet exact sense the transcendental is that which supposedly transcends human experience but not human knowledge about it. We may speak of a transcendental realm of being such as Plato's realm of eternal forms. Or we may speak of a transcendental theory of knowledge, as when Kant regards *a priori* knowledge as transcending empirical knowledge. In a looser sense, the transcendental is that which exalts the personal and divine as superior to the material and finite aspects of the world. It was largely in this second sense that transcendentalism took root in the United States.

German idealism first manifested itself in America in literary rather than philosophical spheres of interest. German influences arrived indirectly through English writers such as Coleridge and Carlyle. An indigenous American transcendentalism was voiced by such writers as Ralph Waldo Emerson, Bronson Alcott, and Henry David Thoreau. Being "literary," none of these transcendentalisms were systematically set forth and defended; but the flavors of personalism, independence, and self-reliance in them are unmistakable. Emerson, says Herbert W. Schneider, "literally saved himself by transcendental self-reliance" (12, p. 283). Emerson sought for the meanings which all things had for *him*, thus fashioning his own world and teaching others this new way of salvation. Thoreau expressed transcendentalism in the sense of the human spirit rising above enslavement to the material world and its monetary and political concerns.

2. Personalism and Voluntarism

Two features of post-Kantian idealism were not congenial to the democratic convictions of early American scholars. The idealistic emphasis on the *unity* or *oneness* of the universe in general and of human society in particular did not find favor in the American climate of thought because these ideas threatened the principle of a plurality of independent individuals. Secondly, the emphasis of absolute idealism on *fate* and *finalism* contradicted the voluntarism and freedom cherished by a people who wished to preserve the initiative of individuals. Accordingly, when German idealism came to our shores it was amended to suit the temper of the people.

In time, American academic philosophers also altered German idealism to suit the democratic temper of America. G. H. Howison developed an original pluralistic idealism on our West Coast. In the East, in New York, Thomas Davidson developed an idealism of the voluntaristic sort. The illustrious Josiah Royce at Harvard developed an idealism with a strong personalistic slant. At Boston University, Borden P. Bowne developed the personal idealism which was continued by Flewelling and Brightman.

3. Brightman's Personalistic Idealism

To secure a fuller sense of the flavor of current "Americanized" idealism a sketch of the views of Edgar S. Brightman will be of help (1, Chapter 15). Hegel's idealism contained the germ of personalism in the doctrine that the Absolute Mind attains conscious self-realization only in human individuals. Personalistic idealism accepts this as in harmony with the Christian conception that the self is spiritual in nature. But Brightman modifies the conception of the spiritual self in directions required by our realistic version of democracy. Hegel had identified knowledge with the object known. Brightman takes a step toward common-sense realism by holding that knowledge *refers* to its objects but is not indentical with them. All physical objects represent God's will in action. These statements imply that you can have no relations with other persons which are not personal because all persons are spiritual selves. You cannot even have purely impersonal relations with physical objects because they are manifestations of the will of God! Brightman makes the personal self distinct from the outer world in that the self exercises volition in the form of choice and effort.

☿ B. The Educational Idealism of William Torrey Harris

1. The Career of William T. Harris (1835-1909)

The fullest biography of W. T. Harris is given in a volume by Kurt F. Leidecker (9). An excellent account of Harris' views is given by John S. Roberts (11), but a more direct access to Harris' philosophy and his theory of education is afforded by his own writings (4).

a. THE EDUCATIONAL CAREER OF HARRIS. To be brief on matters of chronology we begin our account of Harris' career with his work at St. Louis, Missouri. Here Harris served as assistant superintendent of schools for ten years (1857-1867), and as superintendent of schools for eleven additional years (1867-1878). Harris then served as United States Commissioner of Education for seventeen years (1889-1906).

Harris' influence as commissioner was, as one would expect, very great. Harris opposed the old faculty theories and supported a more modern approach to psychological problems. Harris was largely responsible for giving the kindergarten, originating with Froebel, a firm place in the United States. One of the first American kindergartens had been established in Boston, but it did not last. Under the inspiration of Harris, Susan Blow established the first permanent American kindergartens in the schools of St. Louis (2, p. 406). Harris represented the United States at foreign expositions. His influence on other educators and on the public was exerted through extensive lecture tours and lectureships, some in universities; by his participation in numerous conferences; and by his voluminous correspondence with hundreds of individuals, great and small. Leidecker's biography of Harris gives one the impression that Harris was a dual personality of sorts. On the one hand he appeared to be an idealistic dreamer, on the other hand he was an energetic and practical Connecticut Yankee transplanted in Missouri.

On the administrative side of his work as commissioner Harris was the acme of efficiency, meeting and solving endless problems with dispatch and common sense. A mere sampling of his duties in the Washington office included the gathering of information from coast to coast, consolidating it, and disseminating it. There were annual reports to be made to the Secretary of the Interior on the state of education in the Union. Harris' reports were noted for their statistical clarity, made human and interesting. Practical problems were always rearing their heads such as those of the Land Grant Colleges, schools in the territories, the examination of teachers, dental practitioning, laws against bogus diplomas, and the system of grades in the schools. But Hegelian ideology was nevertheless present in Harris' educational practices. We will next take a glimpse at Harris as philosopher.

b. THE PHILOSOPHICAL CAREER OF HARRIS. Harris' influence was probably the chief factor which led to the establishment of philosophy as an independent profession in America. This was the result of his tireless efforts to introduce Hegelian philosophy to Americans. Jerome Nathanson says that Harris thus made the chief effort which removed philosophy from the control of the clergy (10, p. 5). Harris founded the St. Louis Philosophical Society. This society had great influence in promoting idealism in the United States. The spectacle of St. Louis threatening to eclipse Boston as the intellectual metropolis of America aroused mixed trepidation and amusement. Harris founded and edited the *Journal of Speculative Philosophy*. The phrase "speculative philosophy" has reference to Hegelianism. In 1890 Harris published his work entitled *Hegel's Logic* (3), which was accepted as authoritative by professional philosophers.

Harris' statements on Hegelian doctrine were so crisp and clear that a student familiar with the obscurities of Hegel might fail to recognize them! Yet Harris insisted on being guided by what Hegel himself had to say. Nicholas Murray Butler, former president of Columbia University, expressed the consensus about Harris in declaring that a knowledge of the work of Harris is necessary for a proper understanding of the development of American philosophy and education (9, foreword by Butler).

2. Harris' Idealistic Philosophy: General Principles

a. HARRIS' PSYCHOLOGY. Although Harris rejected faculty psychology in his *Psychologic Foundations of Education*, 1898 (4), his own work is not impressive when viewed as scientific psychology. Harris' psychology is leagues behind the work of some of his contemporaries; for example the two volumes of William James, *Principles of Psychology* (8), which was published eight years earlier than Harris' book. Harris' treatments of such subjects as neurology, the senses, memory, and even child psychology are quaint and outmoded.

It must be noted, however, that Harris did not offer his book as a system of *empirical* psychology—he considered it *rational* psychology. Empirical psychology, says Harris, makes an inventory of psychological facts and principles derived from phenomenal observation. Rational psychology, on the other hand, deals with the philosophical presuppositions of mind, with what mind must be on *a priori* grounds as determined by rational analysis (4, p. 3). Harris' psychology was modern in at least one respect. He rejects faculty psychology in the old sense of an inventory of mental powers which function in isolation. This view, says Harris, ignores the consideration that higher mental functions develop out of lower ones. For example, Harris regarded the function of conception not as existing on a par with perception but as including perception in a more complete form of activity (4, Preface, p. vi).

b. HARRIS ON MENTAL DEVELOPMENT. In harmony with his Hegelian point of view Harris considers all mental development as the development of thought. Harris distinguishes three stages of such development (4, pp. 8-10).

(1) *First Stage.* The first stage is that of sense perception which experiences all objects as existing in isolation without relations to other objects. Harris, in Aristotelian fashion, assumes that each stage of development persists, the later stages being added to it. It is true enough that both for the child and for the adult a primary function of the senses is to present objects in their isolation. We sometimes say that we see the "relations" between objects. But seeing objects in isolation is a precondition for seeing their relations. As the gestalt psychologist holds, the perception of the object as *segregated on a ground* is a primitive prerequisite for all perception—without this there could be no perception. The *spatial* relations between objects may appear in immediate perception but their other relations, such as *causal* relations, appear on a higher level of apprehension, which Harris sets above the first stage.

(2) *Second Stage.* This is the stage of *relativity* in which objects are understood in their causal and other relations to each other which do not appear on the perceptual level. The second stage represents the point of view of science, the level which is known as "field theory." At this level of thought, says Harris, *necessity is the ruling principle in nature.* From this point of view there is no freedom, no purposive self-determination.

(3) *Third Stage.* The third stage arrives with the mature insight that *the true nature of being is attained only when it is understood as a whole.* Reality as a whole is not dependent upon or related to an environment—no such environment exists for it! The whole, Harris held, is self-

determined—it becomes free through its self-activity. This true being of the whole manifests itself to us in our own self-conscious thinking and willing.

c. UNIVERSAL REASON AND THE INDIVIDUAL. The universal reason appearing in and to the individual during the third stage of development was implicit in the person from the beginning of his development (4, p. 63). The reader will notice that Harris, showing the usual bias of citizens of our democracy, plays up the individual actors to whom Hegel gave rather scant importance in the majestic dialectic of world history. What Hegel found implicit in the Logos from the beginning Harris now finds implicit in the individual. Universal Reason is present implicitly in sense perception long before the individual attains conscious awareness of it.

(1) *Reason as Implicit in Perception.* Despite his Hegelian bias, Harris often prefers to regard reason as manifesting itself in Aristotelian syllogisms rather than in dialectic. Harris proceeds to show, to his own satisfaction at least, that sense perception manifests the unconscious operation of syllogistic thinking. Suppose that you see a building looming vaguely before you in semidarkness. You note that it has a cross-crowned spire, and hence see it as a church. This perception embodies the second figure of the syllogism which may be stated in symbolic form as follows:

$$S \text{ is } M.$$
$$P \text{ is } M.$$
$$\overline{\text{Hence, } P \text{ is } S.}$$

Stated in material form we have:

All churches have cross-crowned spires.
This object has a cross-crowned spire.

Hence, this object is a church.

Harris held that in sense perception this reasoning process occurs on an unconscious level. Also, the second figure of the syllogism is invalid (undistributed middle term). The conclusion does not follow of necessity from the premises because buildings other than churches might have cross-crowned spires. Like most rationalists Harris will not trust sense knowledge without reservations. He goes on to show that the necessities which science finds in the world of phenomena must be validated by a level of understanding which goes beyond immediate perception (4, pp. 65-74). Empiricists would agree with this position.

(2) *Reason in Nature.* Harris held to the Hegelian thesis that all forms of life and the entire inorganic world show an implicit syllogistic structure (4, p. 63). But one notes that for Harris the glorious consumma-

tion of universal development appears at the third level when the individual becomes conscious of his identity with Universal Reason.

Harris' idealistic philosophy may well be, as he insists, derived from Hegel; but he alters the picture by retouching it here and there, especially to highlight individuality in it.

d. SOME CRITICISMS. The idealistic philosophy of Harris offers a heyday for philosophers engaged in their favorite pastime of questioning answers. The thesis against which most criticism is leveled is the notion that a person becomes *individual* and *free* by accepting his identity with and by pursuing the goals of a superindividual called "Universal Reason." The problem of personal freedom is not a difficulty peculiar to absolute idealism. Rousseau encountered it, and democratic society encounters it endlessly in reconciling the freedom of the individual with the authority of his society or state. In the case of the individual's relations to society and the state the problem of freedom is not so acute because the "whole" and the "individual" usually achieve compromise: The whole gives up some of its wholeness and the individual gives up some of his individuality. But presumably in Hegelian philosophy and in Christian theology the eternal Absolute does not drive such bargains with human individuals who insist that they must act willfully in some degree in order to be in some degree individual!

The accredited way out of this difficulty is to note that when the individual sees and accepts the purposes of his society, his state, or his God as his own purposes and even makes them his desires he is at once individual and free and yet identified with a larger whole. In support of this view one may note that freedom in the psychological sense does not require complete individual *originality* of action. The freedom of the student who decides to take up painting is not contradicted by the fact that Leonardo da Vinci "thought of it first." Perhaps the student wishes to paint *because* Da Vinci did—being free does not imply doing things for reasons which never before served as a motive for others. Besides, events which from an external point of view are *repetitions* may still be considered as *novelties* in individual psychological experience. Thus, the coming of Halley's comet is no novelty to the science of astronomy but each time it appears in the heavens it is a novel event to numerous individuals. Suppose that a poet of today were to compose the "Marseillaise" without a shred of acquaintance with the original. Would he be any less a creator than Rouget de Lisle who composed it the first time?

3. Harris' Philosophy of Education

a. THE CENTRAL AIM OF EDUCATION. The idealistic philosophy of Harris points unerringly to the chief purpose of education. This purpose is to bring the individual as completely as possible to the third stage of his mental development. The attainment of his mature level has the most momentous consequences for Harris. The validities of man's beliefs in God, human freedom, and immortality depend upon attaining the third level of development. At this level it is seen that the universe as a whole is spiritual in nature, that is, that God exists. Since the universe is a unified whole, it is seen that God is a Person. We are free and immortal like God to the degree that we understand ourselves as parts of the universal whole, i.e., as parts of God. Harris writes:

> The most important end of intellectual education, is to take the pupil safely through the world theory of the first and second stages—namely, the sense-perception and the relatively doctrine—up to the insight into the personal nature of the absolute (4, p. 9).

b. HARRIS ON RELIGION AND MORALS. It is clear that Harris' basic aim for education is tied up with religion. This is a quite constant feature of idealism whether or not it is applied to education. Harris accepts Christianity although he was often accused of being an "infidel" because of his ill-understood interest in German philosophy. In fact, many professional philosophers find it difficult to think of Hegel's Absolute, a system of universal logic, as God. Perhaps the religion of Harris was a bit cold and intellectual; which traits, according to William James, befit a philosopher. The God of Hegel is indeed unlike the God of Abraham and Jacob, capable of infinite mercy and terrible wrath. Leidecker gives us a glimpse of Harris' religion: "The Trinity (for Harris) is not the object of worship and prayer, and God is Reason more than he is Love; the proof of the existence of God is more significant than unquestioned devotion" (9, p. 563).

A passage previously cited from Hegel declares, "Pedagogy is the art of making man moral." In harmony with this, Harris held that of all branches of instruction ethics is the most practical (9, p. 555). Harris' school virtues were unoriginal but sound. The child must acquire such habits as punctuality, regularity, self-control, and industry. These virtues are for the child's own good, not merely, as with Hegel, the demands of the state validated by its being a larger portion of the Absolute!

Harris cherished education as the pupil's self-realization. But it must be remembered that on the third plane of development the individual also glimpses his identity with eternal Reason. Like Hegel, Harris thus finds that moral development has a cosmic aspect. For Hegel, as we have seen, individual salvation comes with self-renunciation and absorption by the *Volksgeist*. Harris followed this thought in holding that the function of education was to bring about the social development of the individual

—pedagogy is a branch of social science (9, pp. 281-282). But the society in which the pupil develops is democratic, not a Prussian state modeled after one version of Hegel.

c. SELF-ACTIVITY. Harris stresses the self-activity of the pupil as a major principle of education. Hegel had emphasized the doctrine that the Absolute is everywhere and eternally active. But for Harris self-activity is the source of the plurality of free individuals. The educational application of the principle of self-activity comes from Froebel, father of the kindergarten. Harris had a warm regard for Froebel. Harris must be counted with Froebel, Pestalozzi, and Colonel Francis Parker as a precursor of the activity-centered education of the later progressive movement. But Harris deplored the unbridled self-activity which sometimes appeared in the schools of his day. The child was not to be pleased and interested at all costs. Application to assigned study has its own worth, even without the zest of spontaneous interest (11, pp. 199-202).

d. THE DIALECTIC OF SELF-ACTIVITY. Following Hegel, Harris saw human development as a series of dialectical experiences. Harris made good educational use of the liberal but still authentic interpretation of dialectic as the movement of thought in the direction of fuller knowledge by the method of discussion. Harris held that when a problem is dissociated from other problems it is seen *abstractly*. This stands in the way of an adequate solution. A problem to be seen as a *whole* and dealt with *concretely* must be viewed as a dialectical development of thought (9, p. 283).

This conception of the dialectical development of thought has fruitful uses for education. The great examplar of its pedagogic use was Socrates, the "Gadfly of Athens." Socrates taught his followers by first accepting their statements and then by deft questioning convince them of the partial, superficial, and untenable character of their opinions and beliefs, thus leading them to fuller wisdom. Hegel applied the same sting against the complacency of a much later age. If men are to live together peacefully and with justice they must realize that their thinking is often blind, narrow, and egotistic.

In the "cold wars," "iron curtains," and propaganda in which man's world has been engulfed in recent times we witness the eclipse of the primary function of reason which is to see problems as wholes—in the light of the most inclusive knowledge. Propaganda is the very opposite of dialectical thinking, for propaganda seeks to establish beliefs on *partial* evidences. The critic may say that the heart of the difficulty is not man's failure to seek complete knowledge but rather his blind passions which drive him to cling to provincial, sectarian, and partial evidences in general. His knowledge may be complete enough but he brazenly denies or shuns it because he is driven by such things as jealousy, fear, and the thirst for power. This criticism voices the most common fault found with absolute idealism: namely, that it emphasizes too much the intellectual component of man's nature and exaggerates the evidences of reason as the essence of reality.

e. THE CURRICULUM. In keeping with his views on dialectical development as a device for instruction, Harris emphasizes the worth of wholeness and integration in the subjects of instruction (9, p. 555). Harris worked out five subjects as central "core" studies, to be organized for maximum logical integration and for the best psychological presentation. These subjects are: mathematics and physics; biology; literature and art; grammar, leading to logic and psychology; and history, leading to such studies as sociology and politics. Some work representing each one of the five groups should be present at each level of the curriculum, the particular course depending on the ages and previous training of the pupils. It will be noted that Harris may be classified as a liberal essentialist in his views regarding the curriculum. Following the thought of Hegel, Harris is impressed with the importance of history. History reveals the self-activity of the will of the social aggregate. This emphasis also appears in the thinking of Herman H. Horne, to whose views we now turn.

⩔ C. The Educational Idealism of Herman H. Horne

1. Career and Writings of Herman Harrell Horne (1874-1946)

a. CAREER. Horne's work as proponent of idealism in education came after the turn of the century when idealism in the United States was beginning to wane in favor of pragmatism and realism. Horne's work is considered by some as the most systematic presentation of the import of religious idealism for education. Horne was the student of Josiah Royce. Royce held to a personalized form of Hegelian idealism. That Royce was the chief influence on his philosophical beliefs is acknowledged by Horne himself (5, Preface, p. xi).

Horne was a member of the faculty at New York University for over thirty years, during which time he wrote on the history and philosophy of education. He also lectured on education at other institutions, such as Dartmouth College, the University of North Carolina, and at Harvard University.

b. WRITINGS. Horne's philosophy of education is set forth mainly in two books, although he published many articles on the subject in journals. The first book, *The Philosophy of Education*, 1909 (5), is still authoritative because Horne did not alter his views very much during his long career as educator. The second book, *The Democratic Philosophy of Education,*

1932 (6), is designated in the subtitle as "Companion to Dewey's *Democracy and Education.*" This book compares Dewey's pragmatic and Horne's idealistic views in education. As late as 1942 (four years before his death) Horne's writings show that his views remained essentially unchanged. He still looked upon the learner as a finite person who may be educated to grow in freedom and be worthy of immortality by becoming the image of his originator, God (7).

2. Outline of Horne's Philosophy

a. HORNE'S EPISTEMOLOGY.   Horne's theory of knowledge favors the rationalistic and speculative method usually favored by idealists. This does not mean that Horne excludes the data of science from consideration. His rationalistic bias appears, however, in his insistence that scientific knowledge must be examined with a view to discovering its "significance." Philosophy takes the facts from all areas of human experience and seeks to determine their *meaning.* There is thus a philosophy for every area of facts—a philosophy of art, of religion, of the state, etc. Philosophy of education is, so far, on a par with the others. But each field of experience is but a fragment of the whole of experience (5, pp. 257-258). Twenty-three years after publishing his first book Horne's preoccupation with the divine is less vocal but still real. In constructing a view of the universe man does not merely listen to reason, but also hears the voice of his emotional needs (6, p. 4).

b. HORNE'S METAPHYSICS: IDEALISTIC THEISM.   The key to Horne's conception of reality is *transcendentalism.* There is but one ultimate reality but due, so to speak, to the misfortune of man's ignorance, he gets the contrast between two aspects of reality arising from two perspectives. From the perspective of our mundane existence reality is a temporal process, full of the deplorable imperfections of the finite. But reflection upon our temporal and finite experience discovers the nontemporal and infinite reality of the Absolute Spirit (5, p. 260). The human mind is the flower of cosmic evolution and is the key to and part of a reality which is universal in scope. The temporal is man's inadequate experience of the eternal. Such is the fruit of a philosophy which does not search for more facts but extracts the "meaning" of the facts on hand.

Horne informs his reader that his view of reality is properly called *idealistic theism.* This view holds that God is not in nature and man, but *nature and man are in God.* Material objects are objectifications of the infinite consciousness (cf. Berkeley). This brings it about that man's environment is also God (5, pp. 270-271). These statements need some clarification. Hegel's philosophy was regarded as *pantheistic* in the sense that God and the universe are identical—the universe *is* God. Hegel's view allows no overlapping—neither the universe nor God extend beyond each other. Horne's idealistic theism clearly rejects this by making God a more extensive reality than the universe, which universe is part of God as far as it goes. This also rejects the view held by Spinoza that God dwells immanently in the world—the situation is rather the reverse of this.

3. Horne's Philosophy of Education

The philosophy of education, says Horne, has no new facts to present. It concerns itself with the significance of the facts now on hand by inquiry regarding their meaning. The meanings which Horne extracts for a philosophy of education are certainly not wanting in scope and grandeur.

a. THE NATURE OF EDUCATION. The reader will recall Hegel's dictum that "The history of the world is the world's court of justice." This elliptical remark is usually accepted as suggesting that since the coming into being of anything is itself the product of supreme reason, its being is also its justification. In order to determine what a thing *ought* to be we need only determine what it *is*. But do not be unduly alarmed by this seemingly grim view. For what a thing *is*, is not revealed by its brute factuality but by its *meaning*. The stage is clear for portraying all things as meaning what we wish them to mean whether they like it or not! It is in this way that Horne secures his ideal conception of education by speculative discovery. Speculation on the meaning of education yields several generalizations as follows:

"Education is the process of evolution become conscious of itself" (5, p. 261). The ordinary realist would be content to say that for man education is indeed a glorious undertaking but it has no more than human and terrestrial scope, causing no reverberations in the Milky Way. But Horne gives the education of man cosmic significance. We are reminded of the story James Jeans tells about the unimaginative sailors who concluded that God particularly had sailors in mind when He decreed that the world should have three dimensions—so that sailors could tie knots.

b. THE IMPLICATIONS OF EDUCATION. From the nature of education as conceived by Horne he derives three implications:

(1) *Implications Concerning the Origin of Man.* Man represents the most recent stage of biologic evolution, and the mind of man the very flower of such development. The great mission of education is to develop the mind. But education can do no more than actualize the potentialities already present in mind. Horne's learner, like Hegel's Absolute, is destined to "become" that which he "eternally is" (5, p. 264).

Horne holds that man is the only educable being. Lower animals can be *trained* but not educated. To be subject to education a creature must have the power of symbolic thinking, and man alone has this power. Animals cannot pursue consciously conceived ends (5, pp. 265-266).

Horne quotes William James in support of these views. Horne fails to stress the point that what the animal mind can and cannot do is a highly controversial question. In 1909 when Horne wrote, experimental work in animal psychology was barely started. The Darwinian doctrine that animals are man's blood relatives started a long and bitter controversy concerning the question of whether or not animals are capable of reasoning. This problem is by no means settled as yet. A central question is whether animals merely respond to *signals* (as in conditioned-response experiments), or whether they can also employ *symbols* or engage in conceptual thought. Gestalt psychologists like W. Köhler hold that animals are capable of *insight* in the human sense but in lesser degree. Horne's reservation of reason for man reminds us that in this respect he agrees with essentialists of the Neo-Scholastic type who support Aristotle on this point.

(2) *Implications Regarding the Nature of Man.* Here Horne develops his acceptance of voluntarism, a familiar tendency of American idealists. Horne was much influenced by the famous views of William James on the nature of will and of habit formation, set forth in *Principles of Psychology* (1890) and in *Psychology, Briefer Course* (1892). James held that the individual is capable of effective effort, and he is made free through his power to direct attention (make choices). Education, Horne held, is the result of the mind's efforts. Effort appears on the scene when the individual deliberately pursues goals despite the lack of present interest in them. Horne sanctions the idea, previously discussed in the case of essentialists, that the capacity for effort is good as an end in itself. Horne endorses the famous rule of James which enjoins us to keep alive the capacity for making efforts by exercising this function gratuitously every day. Horne is not suggesting that the teacher prescribe unpalatable tasks for developing the pupil's will power. The point is that when interest fails in a task which simply must be done, the capacity for effortful application will pay dividends. In general, education yields results proportionate to the efforts expended by the student (5, p. 274). Today we would add that the educational results depend a great deal on the pupil's level of intelligence and interest. Yet, no matter how intelligent or interested the student, effort can push achievements to higher levels or at least should yield accelerated rates of achievement.

(3) *Implications Concerning the Destiny of Man.* Horne considers it quite evident that education as an empirical process is never completed. In the hackneyed phraseology of the campus, the more you learn the more appalling the ignorance yet to be exorcised! Horne infers that man's development must be an infinite process (5, p. 281). The logic he offers in support of this conclusion is as follows: Either the universe must be pronounced irrational, if it allows the good work of education to get

started only to be interrupted by death; or, if the universe be considered rational, man must be immortal so that his education can continue (5, p. 281).

From the point of view of some students the universe might seem rather irrational to deny death as a way of escape from an education which requires immortality for its completion! This benighted opinion is of course beneath Horne's ardent love for enlightenment. Horne concludes that *if* the world order is rational and purposeful, as is suggested by science, art, and history, then man may hope for immortality and to complete his education (5, pp. 281-283).

c. HORNE'S PSYCHOLOGY. Horne does not confine himself to rational psychology although his first and third implications [(1) and (3)] indicated above are prime examples of speculative philosophy. Horne's 1932 book (6) is interlined with modern psychological principles. We confine ourselves to what Horne has to say about basic mental functions.

Horne rejects faculty theory for reasons similar to those offered by Harris (6, pp. 73-83). Such so-called faculties as observation, recollection, and thinking do not exist as original or native mental powers in the child. Instead there are a large number of original native tendencies (reflexes, instincts, impulses, etc.) which are grounded in the nervous system and hardly exist as mental functions at all. That is, their operation at first is automatic and unconscious. But training brings about the inclusion and coordination of these native elements of skill in higher functions. This implies that such higher functions as perception, memory, and reasoning develop gradually by a process of including partial functions in larger wholes. The consonance of this view with idealistic doctrines of evolution is apparent.

The chief weakness of faculty psychology according to Horne is its body-mind dualism. Body-mind dualism means the doctrine that the body and the mind, although possibly interacting with each other, are existences which differ in kind. The rejection of this dualism in favor of the view that matter and mind are ultimately facts of the same order expresses Horne's idealistic slant. It should be added that the "identity hypothesis" of body and mind is favored by others who do not regard themselves as idealists. Indeed the materialist, who is the arch opponent of idealism, also identifies body and mind as ultimately "the same thing." But in place of regarding matter as the "objectification" of the mind of God the materialist regards the mind as the "manifestation" of the material processes of the brain!

d. HORNE ON THE CURRICULUM. On the subject of the curriculum Horne speaks the language of liberal traditionalism and of Hegelianism as well. The aim of education is to take the child through the history of his race so that its achievements will be reflected in his own feelings, ideas, and behavior (5, p. 146). Here we see the façade of Hegelianism to be voiced again by Gentile in Italy. Human history is viewed as expressing the development of the Absolute in its most important phase—namely, the human. The essentialist, of course, may value history for its record of *human* accomplishments, but the Hegelian idealist values it as a record of the evolution of the *Absolute*.

The products of the race's mental life according to Horne fall into three classes: the theoretic, the aesthetic, and the volitional. The essentials of education for Horne must include material from these three components of racial achievement. The theoretic achievement is largely embodied in the sciences, the aesthetic is realized in the study of the arts, and the volitional is found in history as an expression of the human will. Horne suggests seven areas of prescribed study: physics, biology, psychology, mathematics, grammar, literature (as the most accessible of the arts), and history (as the most usable record of the expression of the human will (5, pp. 146-147).

These seven foundations are stable and broad enough to support any added superstructures in the forms of electives or professional studies. Horne compares his prescribed subjects with those of the Middle Ages, noting that he added to them science and history. These two basic areas became prominent since medieval life and the Renaissance (6, p. 147).

William James declared that philosophies are shaped by the temperaments of philosophers as much as by the facts of observation. Each individual seeks a view of the world and hence of education which makes life significant. Absolute reality conceived as Reason was the most congenial to the cool, orderly, and intellectual temperament of Harris. Horne, filled with religious fervor, sees the Absolute as the God of Christian theism. Chapter 10 which follows will be devoted to the idealism of Giovanni Gentile, an Italian minister of education during the rule of Mussolini. Gentile needed a philosophy of education which would be congenial to fascism. This he found chiefly in a conception of the political state which he derived from Hegel by means of that mixture of honesty and unconscious guile which James suspected in the hearts of all philosophers.

References

1. Brightman, Edgar S. "Personalistic Metaphysics of the Self: Its Distinctive Features." *Radhakrishnan* (Rev. W. R. Inge and associates, eds.). New York: Harper, 1951.
2. Brubacher, John S. *A History of the Problems of Education*. New York: McGraw-Hill, 1947.
3. Harris, William T. *Hegel's Logic*. Griggs Philosophical Classics (G. S. Morris, ed.), 1890.

4. ———. *Psychologic Foundations of Education*. New York: D. Appleton, 1898.
5. Horne, Herman H. *The Philosophy of Education*. New York: Macmillan, 1909.
6. ———. *The Democratic Philosophy of Education*. New York: Macmillan, 1932.
7. ———. "An Idealistic Philosophy of Education." *Forty-First Yearbook of the National Society for the Study of Education*. Bloomington, Ill.: 1942, Pt. I.
8. James, William. *Principles of Psychology* (2 vols.). New York: Holt, 1890.
9. Leidecker, Kurt F. *Yankee Teacher, the Life of William Torrey Harris*. New York: The Philosophical Library, 1946.
10. Nathanson, Jerome. *John Dewey; the Reconstruction of the Democratic Life*. New York: Scribner's, 1951.
11. Roberts, John S. *William Harris*. Washington, D. C.: National Education Association, 1924.
12. Schneider, Herbert W. *A History of American Philosophy*. New York: Columbia University Press, 1946.

⚡ chapter 10

IDEALISTIC PHILOSOPHY OF EDUCATION
IN ITALY: GIOVANNI GENTILE

Two prominent Italian philosophers, Benedetto Croce (1866-1952) and
Giovanni Gentile (1875-1944) were influential in Italian education. Both
Croce and Gentile were protagonists of a form of idealism which was
Hegelian in origin. We need not undertake the rather technical analysis
required to show their departures from strict Hegelianism. Their differences from Hegel do not materially affect the broad use made of idealistic thought in the educational philosophy of Gentile, who serves as our
spokesman.

The main divisions of this chapter are as follows:
A. The Careers of Croce and Gentile
B. Gentile's Theories of Reality and of Knowledge
C. Special Notes on Gentile's Metaphysics and Religion
D. Gentile's Theories of the State and of Morality
E. Gentile's Views on Education
F. Some Final Evaluations of Idealism in Education

⚡ A. The Careers of Croce and Gentile

Croce and Gentile were close friends, and collaborated in founding and
maintaining the journal *Critica*. Croce was a philosopher of international
repute. He served as minister of education in Italy in 1920-1921. He wrote

the introduction to Gentile's book, *The Reform of Education,* 1922 (2) from which the following details are derived regarding the educational philosophy of Gentile.

Gentile became a senator in the Italian government in 1918, and has been regarded as a philosopher of fascism. Butler observes that Gentile's ideas lacked the concreteness and expediency needed to make his fascism a force in education (1, p. 222). This judgment may be doubted, as will appear later. Gentile became Mussolini's minister of education when the latter came into power. Gentile carried out the reform of Italian education, stressing the development of the mind in Hegelian style and reviving religious teaching in the schools. Gentile was killed by an unknown assassin in 1944.

Gentile wrote profusely, chiefly on professional problems of philosophy. As early as 1900 Gentile wrote in defense of idealism in education. The one best source to Gentile's educational philosophy is his *Reform of Education* (2). This book contains a series of lectures delivered by Gentile to the teachers of Trieste. Another source for English readers is M. M. Thomson's work on Gentile (4).

⚥ B. Gentile's Theories of Reality and of Knowledge

Gentile's thoughts on education cannot be understood without certain concepts derived from Hegel. These basic ideas clash with our realistic habits of thought. This realistic bias, which is almost second nature to most of the readers of this book, consists in separating the *subject* (mind, ego, self) from the *objects* which it knows. Gentile identifies subject and object by means of three theorems and arguments in their defense. The three basic theorems are as follows:

1. You, like God, are a spirit.
2. Spirit is real only because it "becomes."
3. The becoming of the spirit consists in acquiring self-consciousness.

1. Theorem of the Spiritual Nature of the Self

The first theorem, which holds that the self or personality is spiritual, will be acceptable enough to most Americans, especially if we replace the word *spiritual* with the word *mental.* The term *mental* is less "sectarian," and does not imply certain claims which attach to the word *spiritual,* such as the implication of immortality. By speaking of the self as mental we mean that it is a nonmaterial entity. First, the operation of observing the mind is quite unlike the methods involved in observing material objects. We become aware of external objects through sense perception, but acquaintance with the mental sphere is secured through introspection.

Secondly, it may be admitted that there are material causes of the mental processes, at least in part. The necessary antecedents of mental activity are found in part in intricate neuro-chemical activities of the brain supported by other processes involving the entire organism. But the causal dependency of the mind on the body does not enable us to *identify* bodily and mental processes. On the contrary, to speak of the causal relation between two things implies their numerical difference. There is *causal* relationship between body and mind but not *constitutive* identity. When you are thinking, for example, that Gentile must have lived in the city of Rome, you have no direct awareness whatever of the electro-chemical impulses associated with this thought. Nor would the neurophysiologist who studies these electrical impulses expect them to look like the city of Rome if they could be seen! Most of us would thus accept Gentile's rejection of all materialistic conceptions of what the mind *is*.

2. Theorem of Spiritual Becoming

According to this theorem *the spirit is real only because it becomes*. This statement appears valid in the light of common experience as well as in psychological science. Mind is always a *process*—an intricate and restless *activity*. It never seems to exist as an arrested state of affairs. Even while one steadfastly holds a given image before the "mind's eye" activity is required to sustain this image. The more you "fix attention" while reading or thinking the less "fixed" are the mental processes involved! The desideratum that activities are real only while they occur holds even for the physical as well as the mental world. A stone is real enough while it is at rest, but the *falling of the stone* has reality only *while* it falls. One of the problems of faculty psychology which made it the target of Herbart's criticisms was the difficulty of conceiving of mental powers which existed during the intervals between activity. As for self-consciousness, it is so unstable and ephemeral that even megalomaniacs fail to sustain it for very long.

In addition to being a changing activity in itself the mind appears to be fed and nourished by the changing aspect of the world around it. Reason seeks for constancies in the world but the senses are aroused not by constant stimuli but by the onset and cessation of stimulation. The senses adapt themselves to constant levels of stimulation. We sense warmth, cold, odors, sounds, touch sensations when they first assail us. As these sensations continue we fail to notice them. This is in part because of "attentive neglect," but it is also due to the fact that the senses cease to respond. After adaptation to noise we hear the silence which follows. After being in a room where it is a bit cold or warm or where the air is sensed as stale these impressions fade away. The senses become inured to constancies and fail to respond to their existence. Bergson expressed this principle vividly by declaring that water is the last thing a fish of the deep sea will ever discover! Hence also the hackneyed truism that "Always to think the same thing is the same as thinking nothing."

But in saying that the spirit is real only when it "becomes" Gentile does not take the word *becoming* as synonymous with *change*. Becoming implies change but in addition it implies *growth* or *development*. This is in harmony with the Hegelian doctrine that all reality is developing in the direction of an all-inclusive Absolute Mind. Since such development is the essence of reality, the human mind which fails to "become" is to that extent regarded as "unreal." It is like Hegel's example of the political state which does not express the spirit of the people as a whole. It would be unreal because it failed to conform to what a proper state should be—which is the same thing for Hegel as what a proper state *is*. One can only say that a state which is not what it should be "exists" but has no proper reality. Similarly, Gentile would grant that a mind which failed to develop properly has existence but it would not be a real mind, for real (normal) minds develop.

3. Theorem of Self-Conscious Growth

We will have more trouble with Gentile's third theorem which holds that *the spirit becomes only to the degree that it acquires self-consciousness*. At first blush this assertion sounds like downright nonsense. We consider it a part of normal development to overcome self-consciousness, not to cultivate it! But never condemn a philosopher, especially a disciple of Hegel, until you have fully explored his definitions of terms. We begin with the fact that the mind can be conscious of itself. We may also grant that during an "attack" of self-consciousness we are *becoming* in the sense that change is going on. If the term *becoming* is defined as *growth* we also grant that self-consciousness may be a way of becoming since the self may grow as a result of having the experience of being self-conscious.

The difficulty lies in restricting either the activity or the development of the mind to the acquisition of self-consciousness. We may well object to this strange doctrine. We ask, "Does not the self also sustain its activity and develop by being conscious of objects in the outer world?" When absorbed in a book, a puzzle, or a game, the self is certainly active and growing although in these instances self-consciousness tends to vanish completely. The notion that the spirit "becomes in so far as it acquires self-consciousness" (2, p. 226) seems to express no more than monstrous egotism!

Gentile, however, is no advocate of egotistical self-absorption. The reader perhaps realizes that Gentile, like Hegel, *identifies subject and object.* The book, the puzzle, and the game of chess are ordinarily regarded as involving outer objects which stand in opposition to the self. But Gentile considers that when they are "known" they become part of the observer. These objects also have a spiritual existence. When, therefore, we become conscious of them we are experiencing self-consciousness.

▽ C. Special Notes on Gentile's Metaphysics and Religion

1. All Things Are Spiritual

The idealist's doctrine of the spiritual nature of all things might be passed over at this point except that Gentile adds some interesting thoughts on the subject. The student who has carried books from place to place would emphatically agree with the proposition that books are "material objects." Listen then to Gentile's demonstration that books are spiritual entities down to the very paper and glue of which they are composed! First, books are books because they contain symbolic records which *mean* something. The very alphabet of the book can become part of the reader's soul. The alphabet both has and conveys *meanings,* and meanings have existence only in the realm of mind (2, p. 186). That is to say, each letter of the alphabet is not merely a scratch in ink but is a symbol from a set of symbols which refer to sounds, which sounds refer to thoughts. A book or a whole library of them cannot be real books if the feelings, images, memories, and thoughts they convey do not become part of the reader's soul (2, p. 188). (The story is told that some savages watched the great Livingstone read a book. Wholly ignorant of what was going on, the savages decided that Livingstone was "taking an eye bath"! One is led to wonder how much of this optical hygiene is practiced in school libraries.) There is sense in Gentile's contention that a book is identical with the images, meanings, feelings, and attitudes it expresses. But this leads to the startling result that he who understands the book has literally engulfed it—has incorporated it in his spirit! As for the material substance of the book, its paper, its glue, string, weight, and shape—these too, according to Gentile, are what they mean. *All external things become for us what we understand them to be, and thus become part of the self.* You are then self-conscious not merely when you contemplate yourself: You are also self-conscious when you contemplate any external object of which you have true knowledge.

Psychologically considered there are certain evidences which support the idealistic thesis that knowledge becomes identical with the self which at the same time "has" it. Our memories, for instance, lie very close to selfhood. In cases of multiple personality, where there are two or more selves associated with the same body, there are also extensive amnesias or memory losses. Each such self has access to certain memory contents, although one personality may also have access to the memories of another secondary self. The relation of memory (knowledge) to personal identity is illustrated by the myth of a certain demon who promised a man eternal life under one condition, namely, that the man must agree to give up every earthly memory. The puzzle posed by the myth is whether the man who survived all his memories could really be said to have won survival for himself.

The view that acquired knowledge becomes a part of the self's identity has a certain lofty grandeur. It contrasts with the staid and callous attitude so common in American education which views knowledge as an alien thing, not part of the self, but rather an extraneous burden added to it. Hence the popular aphorism, "Ignorance is bliss." Knowledge is regarded as worth while as a *tool*, e.g., as a means for passing examinations and thus winning an academic degree, or as a means for earning a living.

2. The Finite and the Infinite

Like Hegel and like Horne, Gentile stresses the ever-changing and finite characteristics of the life of man. History advances as the human mind progresses. The school, like everything else, is caught in the current of growth, and must change its contents and methods with different times and places. But the ideal or transcendental reality is "that spiritual content which never changes as it passes through the various historical determinations" (2, p. 225).

3. Criticism of Idealistic Metaphysics

Since we have sketched only the broad outlines of Gentile's theory of reality which he shares with most other absolute idealists our criticisms will be essentially those which could be charged against any absolute idealism. Absolute idealism does not claim to be validated by intuition, by revelation, or by faith. Like most occidental philosophies, absolute idealism makes human experience its first source material, and uses human reason as guide in constructing a world view. Let it be assumed that human experience is limited and temporal, with evil, ugliness, and ignorance everywhere rampant. At the same time man has the experience of development in which growing knowledge reveals permanence in the midst of change and in which beauty and goodness relieve the somber tones of phenomenal experience.

Absolute idealism is that speculative philosophy which finds that man's experience and reason point to the existence of a transcendental and now existing reality which is perfect and unchanging, and which embraces all reality. By thus being all-inclusive, it embraces the whole of man's finite world. We thus get a universe which is somehow *one* and yet split into two parts, one of which is phenomenal, mundane, temporary, and imperfect while the other part has the opposite characteristics.

These two views of the world certainly have their uses if we can only forget the alleged virtue of consistency! The concept of the phenomenal world is useful because it harmonizes with innumerable details of human experience, with the vicissitudes of time and change in which insight and ignorance, good and evil, and numerous other contraries and contradictories form an appalling melange. At other times, as when we tire of striving against ignorance, evil, and ugliness and would fain regard all ideals as already achieved, we need only to exchange the idealist's "phenomenal aspect" of the world with his "transcendental one"!

But a philosophy which pretends to be guided by logic must ultimately reject the inconceivable. It is not inconceivable that man's thought is a developing dialectic of contradictions in which each assertion passes into its opposite, etc. But what is inconceivable is the notion that the assertion of two contradictory statements can both be true at the same time. This violates Aristotle's touchstone of valid thinking: namely that A cannot at the same time be *not-A*. Every attempt to disprove this principle asserts it. Applied to the absolute idealist's claims, the situation is simply that the entire universe as a single object cannot at the same time be finite and infinite, changing and unchanging, imperfect and perfect, etc.

In order to get rid of these patent contradictions the idealist's favorite device is to regard the world of the infinite as real and to treat man's phenomenal experience as an illusion. The dilemma now takes on another but scarcely less aggravating form: Human experience which at first is alleged to point beyond itself to the realm of the Absolute is now rendered illusory by that very Absolute and hence not to be trusted as pointing to anything! The predicament is indeed like that of the philosopher who dreamed that dreams are unreliable!

4. Gentile on Religion

Gentile revived religious teaching in the schools of Italy. His religious ideology, however, is rather intellectual, lacking the fervor and emphasis on the personal which one notes in Horne. For Gentile, as for Harris, intimacy with God appears to consist essentially in knowing Him, and this you cannot help doing if you learn anything at all since God is the sum total of all knowledge. Gentile holds that to enter upon the course of education is to open the soul to the Deity. Man's development is in fact God's development. "God is the very spirit of ours which at every moment prescribes its own law to itself and thus determines its own content" (2, p. 225).

D. Gentile's Theories of the State and of Morality

Mussolini realized with Marx the potential value of Hegelian philosophy as support for an authoritarian state, hence his appointment of Gentile as minister of education. There are good grounds for the suspicion that Mussolini thus hoped to capitalize on Hegelian philosophy to establish his fascist dictatorship. Gentile has been accused of deliberately selling his probity as a philosopher to become the agent of fascism. But Gentile had been a Hegelian philosopher before he was appointed minister of education, and Hegel's philosophy of the state does lend itself to interpretations which glorify the state (see Chapter 8). In the opinion cited from Butler, Gentile's version of idealism was judged as altogether too abstract to suit the expediency and opportunism needed by a dictator. On the other hand, the systematic indoctrination of children in the schools with Gentile's idealism could become an insidious weapon for a dictator. The arguments used by Gentile to identify loyalty to the state as loyalty to God show a considerable degree of subtle indirection well calculated to befuddle the unwary regarding their true import. The reader may judge whether Gentile's theory of the state and of morality imply an innocent utopian idyl or a blueprint for a condition of slavery.

1. The Abstract and the Concrete: Language

Gentile asks, what are we as concrete individuals? We are inclined to regard as concrete our daily empirical experiences of ourselves as separate personalities, pursuing goals of our own choosing. Gentile, however, declares the individual empirical self to be an *abstraction.* Things are seen abstractly when considered in isolation from other realities. We are inclined to think of our own egos or minds as shut up in our bodies in isolation from other egos. "Those of my fellow beings that are most intimately, most closely related to me seem yet as completely external to me, as thoroughly sundered from my spirit, as their bodies are from mine" (2, p. 19). Consider an audience during a lecture: It seems that no necessary ties exist between the various hearers. After the lecture each one goes away confident that he has lost no part of himself. This apparent isolation of selves is even impressive in successive generations of families. Our parents pass away and we continue our lives in isolation from them.

Gentile now argues that the notion of independent selves sketched above is a false abstraction. Consider language: We think of it as a tool with which we speak to ourselves (think) and communicate with others. But language is *social*—it would be of no use to anyone who lived alone. Even cryptograms are jargon until translated into a common language; only then do they communicate anything. Language thus shows that we are not isolated and abstract egos. We are one with a vast company of other spirits. The individual is *concrete* only as a member of society. The reader will notice that this result is quite the opposite of the conception of individual concreteness in a democracy. We feel that individuals lose their concrete individuality to the degree that they coalesce into a social whole like a hive of bees.

2. The Abstract and the Concrete: The Will

The notion of an individual will, says Gentile, is also an abstraction. This theme could be applied to daily life as follows: Suppose that Mr. X is trying to decide whether to invest his money in securing an education or use it to found a business for selling radios. If one is careful to stay on Harris' level of causal relativity of thinking, one can argue that Mr. X deceives himself in supposing that he is really deciding (willing) anything. Had it not been for the "great company of spirits" who lived before him there would be no college to go to that could further his education as he plans. And without Heinrich Hertz who discovered radio waves and the small army of other "spirits" that followed him there would be no radios to sell! Only the will of mankind in general, manifesting the will of God as revealed in history and embodied in the state, is concrete.

3. The Abstract and the Concrete: Criticism

The term *abstract* in its derivation means to draw from, to separate. There are two main ways of abstracting: (a) To separate something from other things *physically*, as when volatile oils are abstracted from certain substances. (b) To separate *mentally*, as when an *attribute*, such as the whiteness of snow, is considered in abstraction from the substance and other properties of the snow; or when any *object* is thought of as isolated from other things which are necessary for its existence and proper meaning.

Clearly, Gentile is using the term abstract in the second sense. To consider human beings as isolated from society is a vicious abstraction. Taking language and voluntary behavior as instances, Gentile tries to prove that the concrete individual having a real existence depends on relations with others in his social group for his meaning and even for his physical existence. From these simple considerations Gentile performs a miracle reminiscent of the incident of the five loaves and fishes. This miracle is the alleged proof that the individual is concrete to the degree that he has become one with the political state, to which he completely submits his will (see Section 4 which follows). This was Gentile's service to fascism.

In reply to Gentile's argument it may be conceded that the full meaning of an individual and even his continued existence depend upon his membership in and relations to a social group. The hasty superficiality of Gentile's analysis appears in his failure to note *that there are many ways of belonging to, being dependent upon, and related to groups, of which the fascist pattern is but one instance.* The citizen of a democracy also has membership in a group, depends on it, and sustains many kinds of relations with it, hence on this ground is no less concrete than Gentile's ideal citizen. In a democracy the individual's freedom, his right to personal initiative within certain limits, does not mean the negation of social relationships but rather their fulfillment. For *in a democracy the social group expects, may even demand, that the individual serve it by exercising independence of judgment,* as did Jefferson, *and by initiative in action,* as did Paul Revere. In place of this Gentile offers the preposterous notion that citizens become "concretely" real to the degree that they belong to a society modeled after a hive of bees!

There is again the consideration that a thing is objectively real if it makes a difference, and is individually real if it makes an individual difference. The *idea* of a loaf of bread is objectively unreal because it will not nourish a man. A thermometer has an "individuality" among other instruments in that, for one thing, it will measure temperature but will not measure time. But if we confine our "realm of discourse" to measuring temperature only, a society of perfect thermometers would lack individuality except in the sense that each one preempts the place where it is, and this is necessary for it to exist at all. The members of a fascist state who should perfectly echo and act upon the edicts of the dictator would be as lacking in individuality as the perfect thermometers obeying the "edicts" of the temperature. Hence, individuals are concretely real and individual in a democracy rather than in a fascist state.

4. Gentile on Morality

Gentile's moral philosophy proposes the slavish subservience of the individual to the will of the state. Since the state is the product of history and history is the unerring logic of God, it is not a question of what the individual's relation to the state *should* be. Rather, it is a question of what the relation of the individual to the true state *is.* "I am a citizen of a state which has power; this power, this will of the state expresses itself to me in laws which I must obey" (2, p. 27). The state depends on the inviolability of its laws for its very existence. To will to transgress one's country's laws is to will to destroy that which one should revere, as Socrates and Plato taught. "I then want what the law wants me to will" (2, p. 27). The will of the state determines both the limits of law and of individual conscience. We are thus wholly subject to the state, either by what it commands by law or by what it permits. (2, p. 28).

In the way of conclusion, then, it may be said that I, as a citizen, have indeed a will of my own; but that upon further investigation my will is found to coincide exactly with the will of the State, and I want anything only in so far as the State wants me to want it (2, p. 29).

5. Criticisms of Gentile's Views of the State and of Morality

Gentile's ideas about the state and the obligations of the citizen cannot be regarded as clearly validated by Hegel's authority. As was shown in Chapter 8, it is true that Hegel taught that the individual should identify himself with the *Volksgeist* and the state which it brings into existence. But Gentile's teaching disregards Hegel's view that in a real state the people act as a self-developed whole and that this tolerates no ruler who acts arbitrarily. Mussolini is clearly *persona non grata* in a genuine Hegelian state.

▽ E. Gentile's Views on Education

Gentile follows the pattern of Harris and Horne in giving his ideas about reality, our knowledge of it, religion, morality, and education in one package. We must then first extract his views on education from what has already been said about his philosophy as a whole, and then report on anything additional he has to say.

1. Implications of Gentile's Theory of Reality

Although there is a transcendental reality which never changes, man is concerned with the "historical determinations" through which the Absolute Spirit passes. This history consists in the development of knowledge which culminates in that human self-consciousness which sees the subject (self) and the object (the external world) as identical with the Absolute Spirit. This most assuredly gives scope enough for education: It says in effect that education is the basic process in the universe. Becoming (development) is the process by which the human mind engulfs (makes part of itself) the entire world. Since all things are ideational in nature to "engulf" them is merely to receive them as knowledge.

2. Implications of Gentile's Religion

Since reality and God are identical, to enter upon the course of education is to open the soul to the Deity. This formulation has the curious effect of making all instruction "religious" instruction whether or not it was so intended. One might study anything, guided by any plan or caprice, and yet have the assurance that the resulting instruction was "religious." But Gentile would probably add that for education to open the soul to God the pupil must be taught that this is what is happening when he studies. This easily converts any instruction into religious instruction.

3. Implications of Gentile's Theory of the State

Since service to the state is service to God, not much more remains to be learned about education from Gentile's theory of the state. To will to violate the laws of the land is to will to destroy something divine. Conscience is restricted to activities which are permissive in the sense that the citizen may indulge them if the state has issued no commands or prohibitions against them. It is clear that education in Gentile's ideal state is under the complete control of the state: without individual options or initiative except as the state "permits" them.

4. Interest and Discipline

Gentile calls attention to the conflict in education between the authority of the teacher and the free interests of the student. To solve this problem Gentile invokes once more the principle that the individual is not alone but is part of a community of minds. When the teacher catches the interest of the pupil the soul of the pupil becomes identical with the soul of the teacher—there are no longer two of them. The pupil's purpose becomes identical with that of the teacher, and all problems of discipline vanish. The freedom of the pupil is not violated since his purposes are being realized. Suppose, for instance, that the poems of Leopardi are being studied. The soul of Leopardi enters into the souls of the teacher and of the pupil. Individuality is nevertheless saved despite this fusion of souls because the Leopardi who enters each mind will be to a degree unique (2, pp. 40-62). This fusion of souls overcomes the barriers of time. Cultural knowledge in general is not a thing dug out of the past; it can only live in us in the present. Knowledge is not to be found beyond the bounds of the human spirit, which is identical with God. History thus "exists in a past which is in the present" (2, p. 87). Hence when we read history we are at one with those who thought before us, the spiritual creators of the past.

These concessions to individuality and freedom are rather surprising in view of Gentile's theory of the moral and political authority of the state over the individual. Presumably Gentile considers that he is here dealing with that "permissive" area in which the individual is free "until further notice." Presumably also the teacher will see to it that the poets to be studied will be carefully selected in advance. Besides, if what the poets put into their lines is disturbing, one can read between the lines by "interpreting" them.

The entire notion of the souls of the pupil, the teacher, and the author being studied "fusing" into one strikes one as hyperbole which is not intended literally. The realism of common sense would deny that there is any such "fusion of souls" except in a metaphorical sense. Having an identical interest or conviction with another does not give an identity of souls or selves. To say the least, each soul has many interests, urges, hopes, and memories; and the fusion with another individual with respect to one of these still leaves the others "out in the cold."

5. Emphasis on Self-Activity

Like Harris and Horne, Gentile stresses the dynamic role of the pupil in education. This led Harris to establish the kindergarten in American education to implement Froebel's activity-centered principle of education. Horne expresses the same general thought in emphasizing the role of effort in the student's self-education. Gentile developed a similar point of view by a more dramatic approach suited to his Latin temperament. He excoriates realism in education for assuming that knowledge exists in books, and that libraries full of them are indispensable. Let us suppose that one of these books, Dante's *Divine Comedy*, is selected for study. Does this book really contain the living thoughts of Dante? Gentile answers with an emphatic negation: "The book contains exactly what we find there, what we are capable of finding there, nothing more, nothing less. . . . Only that can come out of a book which the reader with his soul and with his labors is capable of getting out of it . . ." (2, pp. 81-82).

6. Integration of Knowledge and the Self

Gentile accuses realists in education of making knowledge a collection of isolated specializations. Such knowledge is abstract. Knowing about one thing becomes fuller and more concrete as it is seen in relation to other knowledge. The more universal it becomes the more concrete its reality (2, pp. 166-167, 188-191). Gentile also belabors as meaningless abstractions the separation of the intellect, the will, and action. Thought and action working together express the creative activity of the soul. The concrete individual is *one*—he is at once intellect, will, feeling, and actor. Hence in education it is a mistake to separate intellectual education from moral and character education (2, pp. 179-180 and elsewhere).

All philosophies of education agree that the excessive departmentalization of knowledge is an evil, and they are equally unanimous in blaming this evil on schools of thought other than their own! We recall that Hutchins deplores the fragmentation of knowledge which he attributes in part to the system of elective courses and in part to the "service-station conception of education." The realists in education are favorite scape-goats as regards the sin of departmentalized knowledge.

⚛ F. Some Final Evaluations of Idealism in Education

Critical matters concerning idealism as a philosophy were given in pre-vious pages in conjunction with presentations of idealistic points of view. Criticisms of details regarding the educational doctrines of idealism have also been covered in the same way. There remain certain broad bearings of idealism on education the discussion of which may serve as the ending for Book III.

1. An Exalted Conception of Education

According to idealists the teacher is engaged on a high mission fraught with the most momentous significance. One sees this in Harris who de-clares that education reaches sublime fruition at the third level of enlight-enment where the individual realizes the spiritual nature of all things, his union with God, and personal immortality. For Horne education is the activity whereby man shapes himself into the likeness of God—a task which requires eternal life for its fulfillment. Gentile's reverence for edu-cation is expressed on almost every page of his book. Sometimes he flowers into Latin eloquence on this theme:

> The school, this glorious inheritance of human experience, this ever-glow-ing hearth where the human spirit kindles and sublimates life as an object of constant criticism and of undying love, may be transformed, but cannot be destroyed (2, p. 59).

The idealist's stress on the momentous character of education stems from his exalted conception of man. The human mind according to Horne is the very flower of a long process of evolution. The educator, so to speak, practices the delicate art of garnishing the rose. It is no wonder that Gentile speaks with trepidation of the extreme importance of every word which the teacher addresses to his or her pupils (2, p. 180). For the idealist education overflows terrestrial significance and becomes the basic process going on in the entire universe. All finite growth in knowledge expresses the self-realization of the Absolute.

2. Comments on the Celestial Scope of Education

The disillusioned realist is likely to consider that idealists exaggerate the importance of man in the universe. It is bad enough for man to regard himself as the special "darling of the Deity," but to interpret himself *as* the Deity goes beyond the pale of proper modesty. If idealists are at fault in exalting the status of man, perhaps scientific realists sometimes commit the opposite fault by regarding man as a mere trifle in the cosmos. Thus, Harlow Shapley, Harvard astronomer, goes the length of referring to all living forms including man as an "infection" on the surface of a few planets.

It (life) is but one of many minor crustal phenomena at the surface of a planet; . . . Animal behavior is a trivial matter compared with the behavior of elemental gases. Human laws are transient, weak, arbitrary, and absurd, when contrasted with the impressive laws of physical science (3, p. 92).

Which is better, Gentile's exaltation of man or Shapley's depreciation? But surely it is not merely a question of which view is "better," as though beliefs were judged for their salutary value in the way we judge climates! J. Donald Butler, an idealist writing in defense of idealism in education, asks: "And what profit is there in philosophizing if one philosophizes himself out of the picture?" (1, p. 269). One might have supposed that the profit in philosophizing is the attainment of truth, however unpalatable it may turn out to be. Viewing himself against the awesome grandeur of the physical universe man may find a corrective for exaggerated claims regarding his importance in the sidereal scheme of things.

3. The Idealist's Stress on the Religious Meaning of Education

The stress on the religious aspects of education found in Hegel, Harris, and Gentile, and magnified by Horne and Butler would seem to go counter to our legal secularization of education. Horne saw this difficulty and proposed that it be solved by selecting teachers who will be good models of religious conduct. But would the practice of hiring only teachers who profess and practice religion be regarded as observing the spirit of the law which secularized religion? Also, having teachers who are model Christians still fails to solve the problem of restoring religious instruction in the schools. The plan of employing religious teachers would perhaps encounter the same difficulties met by the plan to give religious instruction in the schools. For example, a board of education in which one religious sect held the balance of power might not be willing to appoint teachers who profess other affiliations.

4. Effects of Idealism on Moral Instruction

Morality in the period of the Protestant Reformation was a morality of *duty,* requiring an austere and inflexible devotion to moral commands having religious sanction. Our early Puritans looked askance at all forms of self-indulgence—pleasures were the wiles of the devil. No doubt much of this moral rigor was necessary in colonial life. Life was so full of hardship that schooling in Stoicism helped to make it more tolerable. Also life in the colonies was precarious and dangerous and moral discipline had to be exacted of everyone.

The morality of duty in the colonies was grounded on religious authority and faith. Moral thinking was pervaded by the doctrine of the fall from grace, of man's original sin from which God alone could save him. The Calvinistic sects of early American life were especially beset by the doctrine of man's original sin. The Massachusetts law of 1827 forbidding the teaching of sectarian religions in the schools was largely the result of bickerings about Calvinistic doctrines. Horace Mann, selected to administer the law, wished to introduce the ideas of Pestalozzi into teaching. This was bitterly opposed because Pestalozzi accepted Rousseau's view (given in the *Émile*) that there is nothing corrupt in the child as it comes from nature and from God!

German idealism had some alleviating effects on the gloomy and fatalistic doctrines of Calvin, as may be shown by the influence of Kant's moral philosophy. Enlightened elements in early America found Kant's moral system appealing because it too was a morality of duty. Kant, however, sought to validate duty by appeal to *reason* and not by theological doctrine. Kant rejected the doctrine of "original sin." The young child is neither good nor evil. The child becomes a moral agent only when he can understand the moral imperative. Also, as we have seen, Kant deplored punishment for violations of the moral law. The child should be led to freely choose the moral imperative as his guide. In Kant's ethics "good will" is one thing that is incontrovertibly good. In education this means that the child's misconduct should be forgiven if it is evident that he meant well. In these ways Kant's ethics had beneficent effects on moral attitudes and ideals in education. Unfortunately, few would agree that a similar favorable pronouncement can be made regarding the authority of the state over the morality of the individual which derives from biased interpretations of Hegel.

5. From Idealism to Realism

In the dialectic of philosophy realism is the opponent of idealism but not its "antithesis." There are, in fact, no two philosophies which are completely antithetical to each other. All of them are presumably concerned with what may be inferred from human experience and reason. If two philosophies should then contradict each other on all major points or even on most of them we would rightly suspect them of sheer perversity. A philosophy is not like the "wonderful one-horse shay" of Oliver Wendell Holmes which, being equally sound in all its parts, did not collapse at all until all of it collapsed at once. The "new realism" of contemporary times astutely borrowed Platonic idealistic realism as one of its postulates—it depends on more than one vehicle of truth.

Book IV which follows sets forth realistic philosophy and its application to education. Although realism has ancient roots, such as the philosophy of Aristotle, we begin Book IV with John Locke (Chapter 11) because he set most of the problems for current realism and wrote at length on education. Then we move on (Chapter 12) to the realisms and educational thoughts of Herbart, Spencer, and Fiske. Current realistic thought is complex enough to require a separate chapter (Chapter 13) before examining its application to education as voiced by Whitehead, Russell, and others (Chapter 14).

References

1. Butler, J. Donald. *Four Philosophies and Their Practice in Education and Religion* (rev.). New York: Harper, 1957.
2. Gentile, Giovanni. *The Reform of Education* (D. Bigongiari, tr.). New York: Harcourt, Brace, 1922.
3. Shapley, Harlow. *The Universe of Stars* (rev.). Cambridge, Mass.: Harvard Observatory, 1929.
4. Thomson, Merritt M. *The Educational Philosophy of Giovanni Gentile*. Los Angeles: University of Southern California Press, 1934.

♀ *book 4*

REALISTIC PHILOSOPHY
AND EDUCATION

$\overset{\bullet}{\triangledown}$ *chapter 11*

HISTORICAL REALISM: JOHN LOCKE AND EDUCATION

Realism is as old as the naturalism and materialism of ancient Greece. Throughout the centuries realism developed into so many forms that Frederick Lange required three volumes for his *History of Materialism* (4). Even classifying types of realism is a difficult problem. There is irony in the circumstance that the attempt to prove the existence of independent physical realities should result in such a disonant chorus of realisms! It is apparent that the discussion of realism as the basis of education must be restricted in some way. Toward this end the realistic philosophy of John Locke and its bearing on education will be given a prominent place in this chapter. The following chapter will add to Locke the more recent historical realisms and educational thoughts of Johann Herbart and Herbert Spencer. After this there is a chapter on contemporary realism (new realism and critical realism), followed by a chapter on realistic philosophy in present educational thought and practice.

The present chapter includes the following main sections:

A. The Realism of Common Sense
B. Historical Idealistic Realism
C. Historical Materialism and Naturalism
D. The Realism of John Locke
E. Locke's Philosophy of Education

⚥ A. The Realism of Common Sense

Although common sense genially assigns different meanings to the same word as occasion requires it usually considers the term *realism* as having to do with what "actually exists." Yet novels and paintings are sometimes perversely described as "realistic" because they dwell upon and exaggerate the sordid and ugly aspects of life as though the seamy sides of things were somehow more real than their other aspects. Common-sense realism agrees with official realism of the schools when it holds to the belief that there is a universe of objective reality which exists independently of its being known. Realists in philosophy are glad to claim the support of the naïve realism found in ordinary folk.

Thomas Reid (1710-1796), noted Scottish philosopher, was the champion of the realism of common sense. His views are set forth in his *Inquiry into the Human Mind on the Principles of Common Sense* (1764). Reid held that man has dependable and immediate intuitive convictions regarding the existence of the external world, of moral truths, and of the existence of the soul. We have an immediate awareness, not only of external objects, but of the causal and other relations between them. Scottish realism had great influence in the United States due in part to its advocacy by James McCosh at Princeton University.

There are five main agreements between the realism of the layman and the realism of philosophers:

1. There is a realm of nature which exists beyond or outside of our minds.

2. Nature existed before we knew it, exists whether or not we know it, and will continue to exist after we pass away. The realist usually keeps nature in the neuter gender, and does not personalize or apotheosize reality in the romantic manner typical of idealists.

3. The attributes of physical objects exist just as we know them, except for errors of perception which are verifiable as errors. The true nature of a thing is not altered by the mere circumstance of its being known. Of course, our knowledge about a real state of affairs may induce us to alter it. But the process of its alteration and the subsequent state of affairs remain essentially if not entirely objective.

4. Experience is the touchstone of what is real—"Seeing is believing." Whenever the simple and direct experience of daily life cannot determine objective truth, then common sense, like official realism, puts its trust in scientific research. Always remember, however, that realists too are human; so that when it comes to special beliefs such as that God and free will are realities or that the doctrines of the Republican (or Demo-

cratic) Party are false and vicious, common sense may be guided by the logic of foregone conclusions rather than by the light of experience.

5. Such knowledge as man has shows that physical nature follows or manifests a network of laws. Such laws are usually regarded as external realities, independent of our minds and even independent of the physical world which "follows" them. In this fifth thesis we see some realists coming very near to the idealistic realism of Plato.

There are at least two main ways of conceiving the relation between the laws of nature and the objects of nature: (a) We may regard such laws as separate principles which "govern" phenomena or supply models or *forms* (Plato) which nature follows. Since such laws or forms are not themselves material entities, then they must be *mental* in their existential nature. To escape this involvement with Platonism, some official realists prefer a second conception of natural laws: (b) The laws of nature do not "govern" natural processes but only *express* and serve to *describe* such processes. The laws of nature are deduced from observations of how nature *does* act. Nature behaves in uniform ways but these uniformities are not prescribed from without. The laws of nature are not forces. The law of gravity does not *cause* bodies to fall—it is merely a generalized statement of the ways in which bodies *do* fall.

To sum up, common sense and official realism hold that we live in the midst of external realities which simply are what they are, and that the best wisdom is to inspect them without first dressing them up in favored guises. This realistic temper appears in all areas of a realistic culture. It invades art and literature. Thus, nineteenth-century French writers—Balzac, Flaubert, Zola, and others—made realism a basic theme in literature. Literary realism seeks to describe characters and events as they really are without idealization or sentimentality.

In daily speech, when we call a man a "realist," we mean that he never loses sight of the "brute" facts of a situation. The realistic moral hero usually manages to achieve his ideals despite adverse circumstances. If there are realities which cannot be altered, then the realist alters himself to suit them. The danger here is that the realist in pursuit of an ideal may yield to realities so fully that the ideal remains in Plato's heaven. This gives us the familiar and invidious sense of calling a man a "realist." The realistic politician may make promises which "realize" his election to office and nothing more. The advertiser may make claims for his wares which serve only the realistic aim of selling them. This realistic note often creeps into education, which is then "sold" with a great air of public philanthropy. It does not follow, however, that such malpractice in education and elsewhere is perpetrated only by realists.

⚥ B. Historical Idealistic Realism

Idealistic realism includes all views which hold that there is an independent world which is *mental* or *spiritual* in nature. This contrasts with *materialistic* realism which finds the world lying beyond man as purely physical in nature.

1. Platonic Idealistic Realism

Chapter 7 gives a brief account of Platonic idealism with a view of showing the kinship between Plato's thinking and the idealistic philosophies there discussed. Plato was an idealist in holding that there exists a realm of ideas or forms; but he was a realist in declaring that such ideas exist independently without being sustained by the mind of God or by the minds of men.

Having separated the minds of men from the eternal ideas, Plato faced the chronic problem of all dualistic realisms of how to get them together again! Plato sought to meet this problem by a "copy" theory of knowledge which has had a tempestuous career in the history of philosophy. Like the installment plan of buying, the copy theory of knowledge created about as many problems as it solved. Plato united the eternal realm of ideas with human experience by supposing that these ideas served as models or archetypes of all earthly things. All things experienced by us are imperfect copies of perfect forms existing on some transcendental plane. No draftsman, however skillful, has ever drawn a perfect circle. But the concept of the perfect circle nevertheless continues its objective existence and prescribes how the perfect circle must be drawn.

2. Scholastic Idealistic Realism

During the Middle Ages the schoolmen debated the question of whether general ideas or concepts existed only in consciousness or whether, in addition, they had an objective existence of their own. The schoolmen divided into two camps on this question. Those who were idealistic realists held that universal ideas or abstractions were objectively real. This would mean that all class concepts such as of triangles, furniture, trees, and even of debts are quite as real as their concrete instances. The *nominalists*, however, held that all class terms and principles were mere *names* or *designations*. This says, for instance, that there is no concrete reality corresponding to the generic term *stone*, but the Stone of Scone, Plymouth Rock, and any other particular stone is real enough. As we shall see, the modern new realists accept at least some universals as objectively real.

ᵛ̧ C. Historical Materialism and Naturalism

The Greek atomists are usually regarded as the first formulators of materialistic realism, a view which is about as old as human reflection. Thales, accounted the first philosopher, held that all things are made of water. Anaximander derived all things from an original chaos or gas, thus foreshadowing modern nebular theories of the origin of the universe.

1. Aristotle (384-322 B.C.)

Although a devout student of Plato's for two decades, Aristotle laid the foundations for later science with its pronounced strain of empiricism. Realists are confident that the best avenue to knowledge is the observation of the world of concrete particulars. This preference for empirical observation over Platonic rational reflection, which has separated realism from idealism for many centuries, was forcefully expressed by Aristotle in his *Physica* (2, Bk. II, Sec. I, 193ᵃ).

Aristotle did not reject Plato's eternal ideas but brought them down to earth. If there is a gulf between the forms and the world how can forms be impressed on things? Aristotle viewed the forms or ideas of Plato as properties or essences of existing things. Form and matter are necessarily joined together. The forms of things in our world are not merely the shadows of things existing elsewhere. Physical objects always have form, i.e., exhibit an idea or principle. A physical principle or form does not have existence apart from physical objects. This view prepares the ground for the scientific exploration of nature. The laws (forms) of nature are discovered by scientific inquiry.

Aristotle regarded the universe as an organic whole which develops in time. Each existing thing in the world moves toward an end which is its perfection. As our knowledge grows we rise from sense perception to universal concepts (laws of nature). We reach general principles last in our thinking but these principles were nevertheless in nature before we discovered them. Aristotle was thus a realist who accepted the objectivity of both principles and material things. Form and matter are distinguishable in our thought, but in reality they are inseparable.

2. St. Thomas Aquinas (1225-1274)

St. Thomas followed Aristotle rather closely, and also accepted a form of realism which is both ideal and material. Universals, he held, do not exist apart from particular bodies, but give bodies their essences or whatness. Although universal principles are necessary constituents of existing things, the presence of *matter* is also needed to account for the reality of objects. St. Thomas veiwed matter as the principle which accounts for the existence of *particular* objects, for the *multiplicity* of things. (We are particular persons because our souls are united with our individual bodies. Twins may have any degree of resemblance, but there are still two of them, one here, one there. Cut a piece of wax into two parts and you get two of them because you have divided their matter. But each object also has *form* and form gives it its *whatness*.)

But for St. Thomas there are some forms which can exist without union with matter. Angels and human souls are purely spiritual forms. God too is pure actuality embodied in pure form.

The ideas of Plato, Aristotle, and St. Thomas had some importance for the development of educational thought, as is indicated in Chapter 5. They have just now served to make clear the difference between idealistic and materialistic realism. The same philosopher may hold to both of them. We turn now to a fuller discussion of John Locke, who lived many centuries later. One reason for selecting Locke is that his ideas had great influence on modern education. These influences involved more of his philosophy than his brief writings on education. Our further interest in Locke is due to the fact that his philosophy raised issues and problems which current realism sought to solve.

⚥ D. The Realism of John Locke (1632-1704)

Locke, living in the England of Charles I and Charles II, was a gifted man who spent a rather uneventful career as a physician, secretary, educator and holder of public offices. Poor health led him to leave England. Locke used the period of his absence from England to write some of the works for which he became famous. His chief writing is the *Essay Concerning Human Understanding* (1690).

1. Locke's Theory of Knowledge

Locke is numbered with a group of British philosophers whose members usually belong to both of two related groups, the British empiricists and associationists. This group included Francis Bacon, John Locke, Thomas Hobbes, David Hume, and others.

a. LOCKE AS AN EMPIRICIST. Francis Bacon was concerned with scientific method, but Locke was content to be a philosophical forerunner of modern science. To show that all knowledge rests entirely on experience Locke denied the belief, which is as old as Plato, that we are born with certain innate ideas. Modern psychology agrees entirely with Locke in rejecting the notion that we are born with certain ideas, or any form of knowledge whatever. The psychology of today even denies that there is inheritance of definite action tendencies (e.g., instincts) and of specific emotional responses. Even reflexes go through a process of learning before they become definite and useful. Inheritance provides the normal child with a healthy brain but the child must, so to speak, furnish it himself.

Locke asks us to think of the mind as a blank sheet of paper upon which experience inscribes its lessons, primarily through sense experiences. In receiving sensory impressions Locke assumed that the mind remains quite passive and *receptive*. He speaks, however, of higher understanding or reason which organizes sense data, generalizes it, and draws conclusions from evidences. Locke regarded such rational reflection as *active*, not passive.

These ideas of Locke had great influence on education. The passive "blank tablet" theory of mind suggested that the child's mind was completely plastic and that education was therefore unlimited in its power to mold the child. John Dewey and others have severely castigated Locke for being a very unrealistic realist in his view that the infant and child is a passive recipient of impressions.

b. KNOWLEDGE OF THE EXTERNAL WORLD. Like all realists, Locke believed in the existence of an independent material world. What are the sources of our knowledge both of the world of external nature and of the mind?

Regarding our knowledge of the external world, Locke makes use of the distinction between *primary* and *secondary* qualities of objects. Locke mentioned extension, solidity, shape, position, and motion as primary qualities of bodies and regarded them as true characteristics of physical objects. Every physical object shows *all* of the primary attributes in some form or other. That is, every object has extension in space, some degree of solidity, occupies some position, and is either in motion or at rest; rest being, so to speak, the limiting case of movement.

The *secondary* qualities of objects are such sensory attributes as color, brightness, sound, smell, taste, touch, and temperature. Unlike the primary qualities, secondary attributes are not uniformly present in all perceptions. That is to say the sunset has colors and brightness but not odor or taste, and sounds have loudness and pitch but not warmth.

The attributes of physical things having been discussed, it must be added that our knowledge about them exists in the form of *ideas* which dwell in the mind. Locke held that all the mind's ideas come either from sense observation or from reflection. The physical world supplies the objects of sense perception. We have direct awareness of the existence of ideas through *introspection*. Locke thus gives us a forthright dualism of a mental world set apart from the physical realm, but with a relationship of knowledge between them.

c. LOCKE'S REPRESENTATIVE REALISM.   According to Locke's theory of knowledge we have immediate awareness, not of physical objects themselves, but of our *ideas* about them. Ideas are the residuals which sense perception leaves in the mind, to which the mind adds other ideas through reflection. The qualities of physical objects are known through perception that leaves ideas in the mind which we know through introspection.

A little "reflection about reflection" at once gives rise to uneasy doubts about Locke's scheme of things. It is true that the mental image which you today have of a scene of yesterday can only be known through introspection. The trouble is that your first perception of the scene, even while you were having it, also involves introspection. When you describe a visual experience which you are now having psychologists consider that you are giving an "introspective report." It seems obvious enough that perceptions coming from *within* the body, such as hunger, thirst, and pain, are introspective experiences. But reflection along Locke's lines shows that what you see with your eyes is no less a subjective experience. In describing a scene before you, you are "reading off" an inner experience. We appear to be shut up in our inner realm of ideas without direct contact with outer objects. What assurance have we that these subjective impressions report faithfully on the realities lying on the other side of the wall which appears to separate the mind from nature?

Locke's answer to this problem contains some ambiguities but is essentially as follows: The primary qualities, such as extension, figure, and motion really exist in the objects themselves. So far, we have a *presentative* theory of knowledge. But the secondary qualities of things, e.g., their colors, tastes, odors, and sounds are not in the objects but in us (5, p. 69). Locke mentions pain as a convincing instance of this: Everyone would agree that pain is purely mental having no existence in the external stimulus which caused it. But pain is none the less "real" because it is mental. (Even imaginary pain "hurts"—a circumstance which makes it rather inaccurate to call it "imaginary.")

How do physical objects cause us to become aware of their qualities? Locke spoke of certain "powers" which physical bodies possess that enable them to convey impressions to the senses. The powers of things that enable them to cause sensations in us reside in their primary properties. Objects also have the power of causing changes in other objects, as when the sun causes wax to turn white or when fire melts lead (5, pp. 71-72). These ideas of Locke are in harmony with present views of what happens in perception. The stimulus which arouses a sensation is regarded as showing the "power" of movement. Stimuli arouse the senses through *motion*, and often (if not always) this motion is vibratory in character. Light vibrations excite vision, air vibrations excite hearing, temperature sensations arise from molecular (heat) motion, and there is evidence that even smell and taste are aroused by vibratory motion in their stimuli.

Locke gave reasons for doubting that bodies possess the secondary qualities we attribute to them in unreflective experience (5, p. 69). Modern psychology could multiply reasons for such skepticism. Locke pointed to the variations of sensory experiences of the same object as between different observers, the changes in a given person's observations of the same thing at different times, and variations due to changes in the observer's perspective. To give simple instances of our own, one man describes the prevailing weather as warm, his neighbor says it is cool. When we are fatigued a given weight, which previously seemed light, now appears heavy. An oar extending partly in water appears bent, etc.

2. The Existence of Substances

What were Locke's views regarding the existence of matter "as such"? He does not much elaborate his views but says about the same thing as Berkeley. If we strip from a physical object all its secondary qualities we can form no clear idea of it. The object still has its primary qualities, but there is not much we can say in describing it because we have agreed to exclude the secondary qualities as descriptive terms on the ground that they are purely mental. How could we become aware of the spatial extent of matter, which extent is utterly empty of all secondary qualities? (5, pp. 155-156). Locke comes to the same conclusion regarding soul substance considered as existing apart from its particular determinations. If matter and soul "as such" exist, they remain unknowable and ineffable. But Locke warns us against concluding that material and spiritual substance do not exist because we can form no clear ideas about them (5, p. 157). No conclusions can be drawn from a mere condition of ignorance!

Locke, however, did not doubt the existence of God. Locke's proof of the existence of God is essentially rational. We may assume it as unquestionable that (a) we exist, and (b) every existing thing has an adequate cause. Mere nothingness cannot be a cause of positive effects. Retracing the causes of our existence, then, we inevitably come upon the idea of something that has always existed, which is all-powerful since it is the source of all power. This cause of all things must possess knowledge since it produced knowing beings. These considerations show that God is the all-powerful and omniscient cause of all things (5, pp. 310-332).

3. Locke's Moral Philosophy

Lock founded morality on religious authority tempered with reasonableness. We are under obligation to behave morally through God's commands. This is the ultimate sanction of morality. The rules of proper conduct are to be found in Scripture. Disbelief in God removes all sense of obligation. Therefore atheism deserves to be looked upon as a threat to morality. Locke, however, was tolerant and conciliatory by nature, as his influential "Letter Concerning Toleration" and other writings show.

The state is temporal and secular. Its task is to establish the rights to health, liberty, property, and so on. The state can compel obedience to its laws, but it has no right to interfere with religious beliefs, and no church has the right to force its creeds upon the unwilling. There are many versions of religious belief, and no church has the right to exact conformity of nonmembers.

Locke believed that the truth of Christian morality as expressed in the Bible is subject to validation. There are evidences in nature which demonstrate their validity to unbiased reason. But men are inclined to be immoral and intellectually lazy. Therefore it became necessary to recall them to God through authoritative revelation.

Locke's ideas on morality are further set forth in his *Treatise on Government* (1690). His views regarding the relations between religion, the government, and the individual were set forth in our Chapter 2 (Section G), together with Meiklejohn's criticisms. To recapitulate, Locke conceived an original state of nature provided by God where man was entitled to such rights as freedom, justice, and the ownership of property. But men violated these God-given rights by seeking their own selfish ends and by robbing and enslaving each other. To escape this situation men formed political groups in which each individual surrenders some controls over his natural rights in return for group protection. Locke limited such "social contracts" to *constitutional* forms of government. Free men could not sensibly set up a despotic government which might take away all of their rights and give little or nothing in return.

Locke's political theory regarding the relations between politics and morality have been severely criticized. Meiklejohn declares that it is empty to speak of "natural rights" which men themselves violate through natural perversity. Locke made the state a merely prudential arrangement. It performs a negative function in telling men what is *forbidden*. A positive morality should tell men what they *should* do. Of course, Locke conceived that God, speaking through Scripture and conscience, tells man plainly enough what he should do. Since the positive social and political morality favored by Meiklejohn is essentially identical with a morality founded on reason and Christian values, his quarrel with Locke may appear to many as a tempest in a teapot. It must be recalled, however, that Meiklejohn finds a positive morality founded on religion inadequate in a society which has legally secularized education.

4. Evaluation of Locke's Realism

Realists emphatically avow their sincere desire to know reality as it really is without either derogation or sentimental adoration. The philosopher is inclined to overlook the inadequate nature of reality provided his theory about it is satisfactory. This is like the scientist who may end up by loving his methods of discovery more than any truths he may discover by their means! But Locke's realism was beset with shortcomings which later realists valiantly sought to overcome.

First of all, Locke's system is not pure realism—it harbors idealism. His treatment of the secondary qualities makes them subjective. Another difficulty with Locke's ideas grows out of holding too literally to that cult of common sense which regards the objective world as existing independently of the mind. Once this dualism is assumed it becomes very difficult to bridge the gap between these two worlds with a theory of knowledge. Locke gets the mind shut up back of its curtain of ideas, whether of primary or secondary qualities. Of these, the secondary qualities are regarded as having no external equivalent at all, and the primary qualities were held to *resemble* the real properties of objects. Both kinds of properties *represent* external reality for the mind.

Now there is something incredible about comparing a mental idea with a physical object and finding that they "resemble" each other. For instance, since the idea of a heavy weight cannot tip the balances how can it "resemble" real weight? Besides, how is one to break through the wall of ideas in which reflection is confined and "mingle" with things in order to test the resemblances which ostensibly hold between ideas and objects? In Chapter 13 an account is given of the contemporary realist's answers to these questions.

⇕ E. Locke's Philosophy of Education

1. Locke's Writings on Education and Their Influence

In evaluating Locke's writings on education it must be kept in mind that his interest in education was secondary. Locke was first of all a philosopher, regarded by many as the moving spirit of his age. Locke himself regarded his writings on education as of secondary importance. His *Some Thoughts Concerning Education* (1693) was not at first intended for publication. It consisted of a series of letters to a friend giving advice for the education of the latter's son. This work was modified and lengthened in later editions. Locke's *Thoughts* went through six editions, and was translated into French, Dutch, Swedish, German, and Italian. Locke's second work on education was entitled, *Of the Conduct of the Under-standing* (1706). The *Conduct* was intended by Locke as a sequel to his famous work in philosophy, the *Essay;* and as an attempt to show how a young man might best develop his mind. An excellent book containing Locke's works on education, together with historical and analytical commentaries, was edited by John W. Adamson (1).

Locke's experiences as an educator were limited. His *Thoughts* was validated by Locke's experience as the tutor of the son and also the grandson of his patron, Lord Ashley, who later became Earl of Shaftesbury. Locke also served as tutor and teacher of Greek and rhetoric at Christ Church, Oxford (1661-1664). Locke's influence on education was great, both in England and in foreign lands. This influence was perhaps due to his great repute as a philosopher rather than to his educational writings as such. Locke, as Fellow of the Royal Society, as an advocate of the new empirical science of Bacon, as profound writer on the problems of knowledge, as public official and aristocrat, as cultured traveler, had influence which spread throughout Europe and America. During the eighteenth century much theorizing about education was current in such countries as Germany and France. This critical discussion concerned ideas to be found in Locke's theories of the mind and of knowledge. Locke's empirical approach to mental phenomena laid the foundations for modern experimental psychology. Rousseau's *Émile* (1762) was based on the fundamental view that the mind derives all of its knowledge from experience. Locke's authority supported the gradual drift of education from dogmatic and authoritarian belief toward the Baconian ideal of science as the basis of true knowledge. Locke also voiced the religious and Puritan spirit which continued along with the increasing accent on empiricism.

2. Locke on the Aims of Education

The first sentence in Locke's *Thoughts* declares that "A sound mind in a sound body, is a short but full description of a happy state in this world" (1, p. 25). This statement became a sententious slogan repeated *ad nauseam* in later educational utterances of others. This platitude is of course empty until it is made clear what a sound body and mind includes. Locke dwells on the care and hardening measures needed for maintaining the strength and vigor of the body, which he sometimes refers to as "the clay cottage." This emphasis on the importance of bodily health is perhaps what we should expect from a realist, especially from Locke, who was trained in medicine and whose own health was somewhat precarious.

Having provided advice on physical health Locke goes on to list and discuss, in the order of decreasing importance, the four major aims of education. The first aim is *virtue*. Locke conceives virtue in the puritanical way typical of his age. Virtue consists largely in the capacity for and habit of self-denial, the power to inhibit impulse and resist temptation. This makes possible a life governed by reason. The second and third aims of education are to acquire *wisdom* and *breeding*. By *wisdom* Locke does not mean, as we might expect, the love of knowledge. For Locke, wisdom is that shrewd and practical wit which enables one to manage one's affairs and property with success, and to be an experienced judge of men. Good *breeding* guides one in practicing the obligations and amenities of social life (1, pp. 109-114). *Learning*, the fourth aim of education, comes last!

3. Criticisms of Locke's Aims for Education

In view of Locke's own devotion to learning, his reader may well be astonished that Locke puts learning in the fourth place among the aims of education. This order is, however, no mere accident of enumeration; Locke clearly intended to put learning in the fourth place. Locke regarded learning as important but not as indispensable as are virtue, wisdom, and breeding. Other spokesmen for realism in education, such as Herbart and Spencer (see Chapter 12), also put virtue above learning. Very probably, common sense in general, which is said to express realism, would agree in putting sterling qualities of character above the mere cultivation of the intellect. In later chapters on pragmatism and education (especially Chapter 18) we will again find character and personality set above learning as aims for education.

Alexander Meiklejohn is a severe modern critic of Locke's subordination of learning as an aim of education (6, pp. 26-35). Meiklejohn contrasts Locke with John Amos Comenius, the great Czech educator who enjoyed international fame while Locke was a boy of nine or ten. Both Comenius and Locke were religious and admired the New Learning of Francis Bacon. Yet Meiklejohn finds that Locke compares with Comenius somewhat as a "shiver" compares with a "thrill," or the way a day of sunshine compares with a London fog (6, p. 27). Comenius puts learning *first* among his three goals of education: learning, virtue, and piety. Locke's aim in learning was to give the student a taste or sampling of exercises for his faculties, not to make an accomplished scholar, logician, or orator out of him. Locke seems to caution us not to take learning too seriously. Meiklejohn writes:

> How Lockian is our own worldly wisdom! "A boy goes to college to make friends, to learn to stand on his own feet, to meet his fellows from other parts of the country, to sharpen his muscles and his wits in the relatively harmless struggles of an undergraduate society. His chief business is to 'make good' in that. It makes little difference what he studies." The Americans who say such words as these today can find strong backing in *Some Thoughts Concerning Education* of the shrewd and cautious English thinker and public servant (6, p. 29).

Comenius made learning and intelligence the basis of the whole structure of education. For Comenius, learning, virtue, and piety formed a unified structure in which virtue and piety are grounded upon and enlightened by learning. Meiklejohn finds in Locke a basic confusion and split personality. On the one hand he is a puritan Christian who has faith in the other-worldly truths of the spirit, and yet he puts practical shrewdness in economic and business matters above learning. In the United States of the past and present we discern the same Lockian double-dealing and insincerity. Professions of Christian brotherly love go hand in hand with the individual aggrandizement inherent in capitalism and proclaimed as "rugged individualism."

Comenius believed unswervingly in education as the right of all children, irrespective of social or economic status. Locke shows the second aspect of his split personality in his profession of Christian love on the one hand and his being a deep-dyed aristocrat on the other. Locke's writings on education were intended for the upbringing of young men of family and property whose parents were able to provide tutors for them. What provision did Locke make for the education of the poor? He wrote his recommendations on this subject in 1697. He proposed that working schools be provided for pauper children who were between the ages of three and fourteen years. Locke suggested that such children be trained in whatever trades were current in a community. The income from such child labor was to help pay for this education. Religious training was the only education suggested by Locke for these children of the poor which went beyond manual training.

Meiklejohn's severe indictment of Locke's philosophy of education will be regarded by many as deserved. Also Meiklejohn's discovery of the Lockian virus in American culture must not be overlooked. It may be maintained, however, that the schism in Locke between religion and prudence, between equality and special privilege is not something inherent in realism. It was rather something inherent in the circumstances of Locke's age. It is not certain that the split referred to by Meiklejohn was part of Locke's character. For it cannot be doubted that in his own life Locke gave learning a place second to no other aim. His *Essay* alone was the product of about twenty years of hard labor and soul-searching reflection. Also, as William Boyd points out in detail (3, pp. 276-279), Locke has much more to say about learning than about the goals of education he puts above it. Locke regarded training in virtue as no more complicated than imparting sound ideas about God and the ordinary Christian virtues. His remarks on wisdom are also rather scanty. But when it comes to learning, Locke has many things to say, as will appear below.

4. Locke on the Principles of Learning

Locke's utterances on the principles to be observed in the attainment of learning remind one of current progressive education, to be discussed in Book V.

a. THE EDUCATION OF THE UNDERSTANDING. In the *Essay* Locke speaks of the mind of the child at birth as like a piece of blank paper, and in his *Some Thoughts* he refers to it as similar to wax to be molded into any desired shape. This notion of Locke's has been severely criticized. Observation of normal infants shows that they are dynamically active, not merely passive recipients of impressions. The careful student of Locke will realize, however, that the blank paper and wax analogies were chiefly intended to deny the doctrine that infants inherit *innate* ideas. All true knowledge, Locke held, comes from experience. It is true that Locke regarded the senses as passive recipients of impressions. But he viewed reason, which operates with the raw data supplied by the senses, as dynamically active.

Whether or not the senses are to be regarded as active or passive is largely an academic question depending on the way terms are defined. If by perception is meant the total activity involved when, for instance, a boy looks for his dog in semidarkness, then it is certainly active. It is quite possible, however, to say that most of the boy's activity occurs, not in sensory perception as such, but in the other functions which attend it. These associated activities in the case of the boy will include his running about, feeling anxious concern about his pet, trying to remember or conjecture where he might be, and in keeping attention fixed on the task in hand. Meanwhile, his eyes and ears remain relatively passive, quietly and impartially waiting, *not to act* but *to be acted upon*.

The scientist who waits for some faint visual or auditory cue similarly prepares to *receive* and not to *give*, and thus reads the scroll of nature for what it is. The senses, of course, do not act in isolation from other mental functions. But if one makes an *analytical* comparison, surely the senses are relatively more *receptive* and *passive* than reason. Since the infant is more a creature of the senses than of reason it seems appropriate to speak of the infant's mind as receptive rather than as active.

Locke put learning in the fourth place among the aims of education. But this is mitigated by the fact that, quite inconsistently, he devotes more space to learning and understanding than to any other topic. His work, *The Conduct of the Understanding*, shows Locke to be, so to speak, the Robert M. Hutchins of the seventeenth century. But in his practical recommendations for pedagogy Locke is more like a forerunner of John Dewey.

b. EMPHASIS ON PRACTICAL INSTRUCTION.   Although Locke ostensibly wrote on education for aristocrats, the courses of study he recommends are practical. English is to be studied at all times. Reading, writing, and drawing are "musts," and shorthand is added for some pupils. Geography, arithmetic, astronomy, geometry, history, ethics and law are Locke's fundamentals for a general education. Dancing, fencing, riding, and several manual occupations (e.g. gardening, carpentry) are added for good measure. As Boyd notes, if this curriculum is narrow it is because it leaves out certain cultural interests, such as literature and art, which are just the things we would expect in a "gentleman's" education (3, p. 277).

c. LOCKE ON INTEREST AND ROTE LEARNING.   In addition to his emphasis on utility in the choice of studies Locke sounds a modern progressive note in his emphasis on interest as opposed to rote learning. Locke revolted against the harsh practices of grammar schools where instruction in Latin and Greek was enforced by the "severity of the lash" (1, p. 69).

Locke also revolted against the sway of scholasticism at Oxford and against the narrow theology of the Puritans. Locke stressed the educational value of play. Numerous passages in *Some Thoughts* condemn the unnecessary use of compulsion and rote learning in education.

Locke condemned the practice in grammar schools of forcing lads to memorize long passages from authors as a method of teaching languages. He declared that languages are best mastered by the easy and pleasant method of reading and talking. In any case, Locke considered it ridiculous to teach a student to recite brilliant pasages which, by contrast, emphasized the poor quality of his own thought (1, pp. 142-143).

Learning things "by heart" has been defended as a way of developing memory power. It is interesting that Locke, anticipating William James, questioned whether memory could be strengthened by exercise. Locke inclined to regard memory capacity as constitutional. (This does not say that there are innate memory *contents*.) To expect memory to become more retentive due to practice would be like expecting a piece of lead to improve in retaining impressions because of its former use in this respect. If it is true that *memory* can be improved by practice, Locke held that life will exercise it plentifully enough without the special and dull rote learning of the grammar schools. Locke is not certain that he is correct in denying that memory capacity can be improved by practice. This notion, he says, is not yet established by reliable observation. Such remarks from Locke foreshadow modern experimental psychology (1, pp. 143-145).

One of the most remarkable achievements of Locke is pointed out by R. S. Woodworth (7, p. 41). In his *Essay* (4th ed., Book 2, Chapter

33, 1700), Locke clearly formulated the principle of the conditioned reflex some two hundred years before its rediscovery by the Russian physiologist, Ivan Pavlov, around 1905.

The conditioned reflex is a basic principle of association as follows:
If a given stimulus arouses a given response, any new stimulus which
occurs in conjunction with the effective stimulus will also, if sufficiently
repeated, elicit the response. Thus, a mild electric shock (stimulus) to
the dog's foot causes the dog to withdraw the foot (response) from the
electric grid. Any other stimulus, e.g., a light or sound which occurs just
before or while the shock is given, will cause the response despite the
absence of the electric shock. This seemingly simple principle manifests
itself according to various principles depending on various factors of the
experimental situation. A vast experimental literature has grown up on
the subject, and some contemporary students, such as behaviorists in
psychology, consider Pavlov's new science of reflexology as the basic explanation of all learning.

5. Summary and Prelude to Chapter 12

It is laudable to try to rid the mind of prejudices, but there is the predicament that we cannot get rid of some prejudices because we do not know
that we have them. Our American culture is steeped in wordless realism.
Attention has to be called to it before we realize that it exists. This chapter accordingly began by formulating the unexpressed realism of common sense. The doctrines of common-sense realism were then related to
three historical forms of realism: idealistic realism, naturalism, and materialism. We then considered in more detail the realistic and educational
views of Locke. The next task is to discuss both the realistic philosophies
and educational views of two other prominent realists of history, Johann
Herbart and Herbert Spencer. Chapter 13 will give an account of contemporary realistic philosophy. Chapter 14 gives an account of realistic
practices in current American education.

References

1. Adamson, John W. *The Educational Writings of John Locke*. Cambridge,
   England: Cambridge University Press, 1912.
2. Aristotle. *The Works of Aristotle* (W. D. Ross, ed.). Oxford: Clarendon
   Press, 1930, *Physica*, Vol. II.
3. Boyd, William. *The History of Western Education* (5th ed.). London: A. &
   C. Black, 1950.
4. Lange, Frederick A. *History of Materialism* (new ed., 3 vols.). New York:
   Humanities Press, 1950.
5. Locke, John. *An Essay Concerning Human Understanding* (abr. and ed. by
   A. S. Pringle-Pattison). Oxford: Clarendon Press, 1924.

6. Meiklejohn, Alexander. *Education Between Two Worlds*. New York: Harper, 1942.
7. Woodworth, Robert S. *Contemporary Schools of Psychology* (rev.). New York: Ronald, 1948.

chapter 12

REALISM IN EDUCATION: JOHANN HERBART AND HERBERT SPENCER

In his essay, "Crabbed Age and Youth," Robert L. Stevenson has a kind word for theorists. When assailed by the confusions and shocks of life it is better to invent a theory about one's troubles than to accept everything with stupid acquiescence (9, pp. 135-136). The attempt to explain the jars and inconsistencies of life is often the first step in rising above them. Knowledge about the nature of existence of an evil may lead to the destruction of the evil known. But the attempt to understand the ultimate nature of reality is often quite as forlorn as taking everything as it comes in wordless silence. Locke's realism, as was shown in the preceding chapter, has in it a note of skepticism, at least as regards such ultimate realities as matter and the soul. There is not much that can be said about matter if we strip from it all secondary qualities. The apple becomes a ghostlike entity which lacks all color, taste, odor, and other sensory properties. Under these circumstances we could not even perceive it, and would know of its existence only by its effects on other bodies.

The story of Locke's realism and philosophy of education may now be supplemented by similar accounts concerning Johann F. Herbart, Herbert Spencer, and Spencer's American disciple, John Fiske. Herbart and Spencer, like Locke, were realists who applied their philosophies to education. They were again like Locke in that, even more than he, they arrived at skepticism concerning the possibility of knowing ultimate things which lie beyond the veil of the phenomenal. The main sections of this chapter are as follows:

A. The Pluralistic Realism of Herbart
B. Herbart's Psychology
C. Herbart's Philosophy of Education
D. The Evolutionary Realism of Spencer
E. Spencer's Philosophy of Education
F. Fiske's Developmental Psychology

⋄ A. The Pluralistic Realism of Herbart (1776-1841)

1. Herbart's Career

Johann F. Herbart entered the University of Jena in Germany and became the student of the idealist Fichte. Idealism did not appeal to Herbart, and he expressed his opposition to it at the "tender" age of twenty-one years. His thinking turned in realistic directions. He served for three years as tutor to three boys, and this experience awakened his interest in education. Another event of importance was Herbart's visit with Pestalozzi. Herbart admired the ideas and personality of Pestalozzi, and wrote appreciatively about the latter's work. In 1809 Herbart was called to the chair at Königsberg made famous by Kant. At Königsberg Herbart's duties included lecturing in education as well as in philosophy. Herbart's interest in education was unflagging. He established a training school where his theories were tested, wrote on education, and worked out a system of psychology. He is credited with having developed the realistic trends in Kant's philosophy. Herbart is perhaps better regarded as a theorist in psychology and as an educator rather than as a philosopher of importance.

2. Herbart's Analysis of Phenomenal Knowledge

Herbart's principal philosophical writings were: *Principal Points in Metaphysics* (1806), *Textbook of the Introduction to Philosophy* (1813), and *General Metaphysics* (1828-1829). It will be recalled (Chapter 7) that Kant declared such "things-in-themselves" as matter and the soul as unknowable to pure reason. Deprived of particular determinations, matter "as such" escapes all phenomenal description, and becomes an unknowable noumenon. Kant, however, did not deny existence to such things. We learn of the existence of God, matter, the soul, and free will through the practical reason. Herbart in general follows Kant in his skepticism about ultimate things, the existence of which he too does not deny. This view, to which Locke was also inclined, appears again in Herbert Spencer's philosophy.

Herbart held that human thinking, whether that of common sense, scientists, or philosophers, is *self-contradictory*. The aim of philosophy is to revise and simplify our views of reality so as to overcome these contradictions. The master contradiction consists in regarding the objects of thought, whether they be physical objects or persons, as both one and many. This contradiction appears clearly in our belief in the persisting identity of a thing in spite of its changes. The green leaf of summer withers but we regard it as the "same" leaf. The infant grows into manhood, but his name survives and his identity is assumed to survive the enormous changes involved. Herbart considered that when we view the matter sensibly we will agree that the identity of a thing is altered by every change it suffers.

The self-contradictory character of human thinking is the consequence, so Herbart thought, of the phenomenal character of immediate experience. Such phenomenal experience gives us only appearances. How are we to penetrate appearances and reach the persisting actualities lying beyond them? To achieve this end Herbart puts his trust in logical analysis. His use of analysis is very similar to the scientist's atomic analysis. Herbart's realism consists in inferring the existence of realities lying beyond phenomenal experience.

3. Herbart's Realm of Noumenal "Reals"

To explain the contradictions of experience the best procedure is to assume or posit the existence of a plurality of "reals." We should think of all objects as complexes or patterns of reals. When an object changes, as when the leaf withers, it is because the reals composing it have altered in number and pattern. The reals themselves never change. For them there is no problem of the persistence of identity because they never change. The reader will recognize the similarity of Herbart's view to that of atomic science, which explains physical changes much in the same way. Herbart's theory of reals also resembles the earlier theory of *monads* held by Gottfried W. Leibniz (1646-1716).

Science, of course, recognizes many kinds of ultimate atoms (the elements), and can offer concrete evidences of their existence. Herbart's reals differ from atoms in striking ways. He held that the reals exist, not in objective space, but in "intellectual space" (thought). It is true that the atomic explanation of physical phenomena was accepted intellectually long before it was demonstrated as valid. Herbart's metaphysics raises many questions which we will not discuss since we are more interested in his phenomenal psychology and philosophy of education.

⚡ B. Herbart's Psychology

Herbart's main contributions to psychology are recorded in his *Text-Book of Psychology*, 1894 (4). In addition to the reals which compose physical nature there are the "soul-reals." That is, Herbart conceived that the soul of each individual is also a simple and unchanging real. Like other reals the soul as such is undifferentiated and unknowable. Hence Herbart's attack on faculty psychology which, so Herbart supposed, differentiated the soul into separate faculties. All souls are essentially alike. The nature of the soul is unknown and will remain unknown. What psychology studies is not the real soul. Psychology investigates the phenomenal processes and states of *mind*. What is the origin and nature of the mind?

1. The Origin of Phenomenal Mental Processes

All reals, whether mental or physical, are engaged in *self-preservation*. This part of Herbart's philosophy is obscure. He has said that reals do not alter each other. In fact, each real remains unchanging. In view of these assertions it is confusing to be told that the reals struggle for self-preservation. If reals do not affect each other, what threatens their existence? Herbart's notion on this point is enticing. He considered that although each real is not directly affected by other reals, the presence of neighboring reals arouses various degrees of self-preserving activity in each real. The reals of Herbart appear to behave very much like human personalities as we know them. Thus, my neighbor maintains a placid silence until someone else appears on the scene; whereupon he at once launches on the "self-preservative" defense of his political views or in other forms of self-assertion which we kindly view as "self-expression." The interaction of Herbart's reals are like behavioral responses. Although each real is unchanging this does not mean that remaining what it is does not involve self-preservation. The real, so to speak, has to work hard to remain what it is!

Herbart describes the soul-real as simple, timeless, spaceless, unchanging. It is like Locke's *tabula rasa*, with no ideas and no impulse to procure them. But the soul-real reacts to other reals. When the soul-real asserts itself in the presence of other reals a *sensation* arises. The sensation expresses the function of self-preservation. We are perhaps willing to grant that the capacity to have a sensation in response to an external stimulus is an aid to self-preservation. The retention and mutual association of these sense impressions is the cause which gives rise to all of the empirical contents and processes of mind which psychology investigates. Herbart anticipated later doctrines of an unconscious mind by holding that some mental contents and processes exist below the conscious threshold.

2. Herbart as Precursor of Mathematical Psychology

Herbart derived our inner mental life from two unknowns—an unknown soul-real reacting to unknown world-reals. All of us, including the most learned psychologists to date, are not sure about just what is reacting to what in such common experiences as seeing a rose. Hence, where all men are beggars, we must not call Herbart poverty-stricken! However mysterious the origin of consciousness, Herbart assumed that its processes followed exact laws. He sought to establish a mathematical psychology. Just as physics establishes a mechanics of particles, so Herbart thought that psychology could establish a mechanics of ideas. There is no free will. Mental processes follow exact laws of fusion, opposition, and association which Herbart considered subject to mathematical formulation.

Herbart's attempt to establish a mathematical psychology failed. But an unnumbered host of psychologists since his day have emulated his endeavor—and also, in large measure, his failure. To express mental processes in formulas is the supreme ideal of many psychologists of today. One great pioneer of these contemporary Herbartians was the late Edward L. Thorndike, a leader in the field of psychological testing.

3. Herbart on the Contents and Processes of Mind

Herbart held that mental contents, without exception, arise from experience (cf. Locke). The most primitive contents of consciousness are sensations. Herbart speaks of all mental contents as *presentations*. Once such a presentation exists in the mind it is permissible to think of it as an activity which interacts with other presentations. Some presentations are contraries. Thus, yellow and green conflict with each other when they appear as the color of an object. (Psychologists of today, using properly prepared stereoscopic materials, have reduced such phenomena of rivalry to law.) Other presentations readily fuse. Still others form patterns of association. Whenever the mind acquires new contents they are assimilated to the mass of mental contents already in existence. Herbart called this process of assimilating new knowledge to old knowledge *apperception*. This term persisted through many decades of psychology. Apperception amounts to asserting that the unknown is understood in terms of the known. One of the aims of education is to integrate new knowledge with knowledge already on hand. The "apperceptive mass" which absorbs new ideas is itself altered by them.

Herbart asks us to conceive that all presentations struggle to present themselves to attentive consciousness. Unless they encounter too much rivalry from competing ideas, they rise above the threshold of consciousness. The weaker ones sink into the unconscious. But this "struggle for the limelight" is not governed by the rule, "Each for himself and let the devil take the hindmost." Ideas form integrated groups and are thus able to rise to consciousness with greater ease. In the language of ordinary associationism, which Herbart does not entirely accept, we say that the more numerous the associative bonds between ideas the more easily they are retained and recalled.

Herbart's influence on modern psychology was very great. He aided in breaking the long and tyrannical reign of faculty psychology. Although Herbart's own attempts to establish a mathematical psychology did not bear much fruit, he set the example for a scientific approach to psychology which in time won over all contenders. The account just given of Herbart's psychology already gives intimations about his philosophy of education.

⩩ C. Herbart's Philosophy of Education

1. Herbart's Influence on American Education

Herbart's chief educational work is his *General Principles of Pedagogy Deduced from the Aims of Education* (1806). A good translation of Herbart's work was made by A. F. Lange, with annotations by C. De Garmo (5). About two decades after the Civil War Herbart's theories of education were brought to our shores largely by Americans who had studied under German scholars. Herbart's method of pedagogy was quickly taken up by American normal schools and thus made familiar to prospective teachers. As already noted, E. L. Thorndike (1874-1949) was Herbartian in his approach to psychology. Thorndike's theory of learning bears resemblances to Herbart's principles of apperception (11). Three other prominent Herbartians in America were Charles De Garmo (1849-1934), Charles McMurray (1857-1929), and Frank McMurray (1862-1936). The National Herbart Society, organized in 1895, published important yearbooks in education. Due to the decline of interest in Herbart, this organization altered its name, becoming the National Society for the Scientific Study of Education (1, pp. 233-234, 511, 530).

2. Herbart on Moral Education

Our three historical realists in education, Locke, Herbart, and Spencer, agree in making moral development the chief aim of education. Locke regarded virtue as the chief and first aim of education, and Herbart regarded moral instruction as the aim which includes all other aims. Education aims to produce good men, but the goodness of a man, said Herbart, is *many-sided*.

a. PSYCHOLOGY OF MOTIVATION. Moral behavior is goal-seeking, hence involves the psychology of motivation. Herbart's psychology of motivation differs radically from the type to be found in current psychology, psychoanalysis, and in the beliefs of the average layman. To be brief, the current view of purposive or teleological behavior is as follows: Each individual has within him dynamic elements which serve as drives or urges in the direction of certain ends. Some of these urges are definitely hereditary and sometimes grounded on the existence of specific bodily structures and their nerve connections. Hunger, thirst, sex drive, and pain illustrate such native urges. Training can alter the intensity of these urges and radically alter their mode of expression. In human beings training may alter means-toward-ends in very complicated ways. Consider, for example, the highly differentiated and yet integrated training of the student looking toward the goal of practicing medicine.

What roles do ideas play in this conventional theory of goal-seeking behavior? Ideas are regarded as playing an important role as means-toward-ends in practically all of human behavior, becoming very prominent in professional training. It is granted that ideas may even play a role in *selecting* the goals to be pursued. The student usually selects his life work on the basis of an aggregate of knowledge about what he has learned to like, where his talents lie, the opportunities presented by circumstances, etc. But in all of this *ideas (knowledge) are essentially viewed as instrumental, not as urgent*. Ideas can *guide* behavior, they may help select a goal, but they do not in themselves supply the urge or drive which sustains behavior.

Now Herbart's view differed radically from the scheme of things sketched above. For Herbart, ideas themselves are dynamic sources of urge. All ideas strive for self-preservation. They struggle to rise above the threshold of consciousness and crowd into the focus of attention. Feeling and willing arise from what Herbart called the circle of thought. He appeared to look with favor on the so-called ideomotor theory of action which William James upheld but which later psychologists, including even Thorndike, inclined to reject. The theory of ideomotor action holds that ideas in the mind which have reference to action tend to produce action. In James's picturesque language, ideas struggle to get out of one's head and into one's hands!

b. HERBART ON MORAL TRAINING. Herbart's theory of motivation indicates what his theory of moral education will be like. For Herbart, as for Socrates, virtue is founded on knowledge. Socrates held that man does not deliberately behave in ways which he knows to be wrong. Misconduct is always the consequence of insufficient knowledge. This may strike the reader as a strange and perverse view. It seems so obvious that some offenders are what they are, not because they lack rational insight, but because they are driven by "bad" impulses. But what if one should regard impulses themselves as modes of understanding? Then the selfishness of the thief and his inability to feel sympathy for his victim become a sort of "ignorance."

The conventional "moron" cannot pass an intelligence test because he lacks the rational insight required. But the criminal, to borrow a term from Emil Kretschmer, suffers from "affective dementia." That is, he is unable to solve a social problem which confronts him because he lacks the insight which love could give. These are not specifically Herbart's ideas, but Herbart found it impossible to separate ideas and impulses. All ideas are impulsive. Moral training will consist essentially in presenting the mind of the child with the proper moral ideas. Morality involves *judgments* of approval and disapproval. Aesthetics similarly deals with judgments regarding the beautiful and the ugly. All evaluation involves patterns of ideas—ideas which bear certain relations to each other.

There are five main types of ideas which serve as the foundation of moral character. It is the main business of education to inculcate them through education. Herbart lists these five basic moral ideas as follows: (a) The idea of inner freedom: This is the state in which the will of the individual (tendency to action) is in harmony with his inner convictions. The impulse to act agrees with the inner circle of ideas. (b) The idea of perfection: This is the harmonious relation between the various strivings of the will in the same person. The production of such harmony is one of the teacher's great responsibilities. Conflicts regarding behavior arise from conflicting presentations. Care must be taken to ensure the harmonious integration of the child's ideas about proper conduct. (c) The idea of benevolence: In this the individual adopts the idea of helping others to realize their worthy desires. (d) The idea of justice: In this the individual judges it right for the will of the individual to be superseded by the will of the group. (e) The idea of retribution: The idea that intentional acts, whether good or evil, should be recompensed (10, p. 484).

Upon critical examination Herbart's schema of moral training seems to involve more than imparting the right presentations. Thus, for the first "idea," it would seem to require much practice and habit formation to get the will to act in harmony with inner convictions. But for Herbart such practice merely strengthens the representations involved so that they will always hold sway. Again, granting for the sake of argument that moral education consists in imparting the five ideas, Herbart's proposals still strike the teacher as visionary. Herbart, the realist, appears all too unrealistic. How is one to convey to an immature child the ideas (virtues) of inner freedom, perfection, benevolence, justice, and of retribution or equity? Herbart would agree that all of this cannot be achieved with a child—nor in a day. Moral stature is the final product of a long-range program of education. The chief means toward this end is *instruction*. Morality presupposes knowledge of an appropriate kind. Virtue does not differ from enlightenment. But the enlightenment must be as many-sided as the moral behavior which society desires.

3. Herbart on the Psychology of Interest

Herbart derives interests directly from presentations just as he derives impulsive power from them. His doctrine of interest came into sharp conflict with later views of John Dewey and the progressive movement in education. According to progressivism the primary and spontaneous interests of the child arise from his existing needs—from his desired goals and the activity which they invoke. Interests attach themselves to ideas in so far as ideas are involved in the child's means-ends impulses. Thus, the little girl who desires a dress for her doll is easily induced to make the dress; and may thus be led to become interested in the weaving of cloth—its history, its raw materials, its processes.

Herbart, on the other hand, held that ideas are interesting in their own right. Interest implies the impulse to *attend* to something, to be self-active. Now all ideas by their very nature tend to struggle toward the focus of consciousness. The ideas that win, that capture attention, will be the ones backed by the strongest apperceptive mass of related ideas. This amounts to saying that from an initial interest in ideas the child turns to interest in the cognate action which the ideas suggest. Progressivism, on the contrary, says that we must lead the child from his natural interests in action to interest in the ideas related to them. According to Herbartian psychology, without ideas to start with the child would have no interests.

4. Herbart on the Contents of Education

Herbart's classification of interests designed to give "many-sidedness" will serve us in lieu of a detailed account of the curriculum he advocates. Herbart's remedy for Philistine indifference is the cultivation of many-sided interests, just as acquiring moral stature depends on the five-sided development of character. Herbart suggests two major forms of interest, each one having three main divisions. The *knowledge* interests form one major class, with three subdivisions as follows: empirical interests, covering factual branches of knowledge in general; speculative interests, concerned with general principles like those found in logic and mathematics; and aesthetic interests, satisfied by literature, music, and art. The second major category of interest is *ethical*. Its three main subdivisions are: sympathetic interests in other persons, social interests, and religious interests.

Herbart criticized the atomistic character of the curriculum of his day. To meet this problem of compartmentalized knowledge Herbart suggested a system of "correlation and concentration." The principle proposed was to teach each subject in a way that would bear upon and integrate with other related subjects. This principle is in harmony with Herbart's conception of knowledge as an integrated system of ideas which provides for the apperceptive assimilation of new knowledge. Teaching should be multilateral. Geography, history, and literature, for instance, have numerous mutual relationships which enrich them and make them more interesting.

Today this aspect of education is usually referred to as the problem of "integration," which is created by the evils of "concentration." The curricula of high schools and colleges of today are often inundated by a flood of courses the "correlation" of which would have filled Herbart with despair. Modern science has made possible this proliferation of courses, especially the narrow and technical courses of higher learning. The realists in philosophy, who avow their faith in science, are often held responsible for encouraging the virus of specialization which invades education. The realist may take comfort in the thought that Herbart, and after him Spencer, gave valiant service against this dreadful enemy.

5. Herbart's Pedagogic Methods

An account of Herbartian education is not complete without at least the enumeration of his once widely used but now largely historical technique of instruction. To secure the most efficient, that is, the most fully apperceptive education, Herbart worked out four successive steps to be observed in the classroom. After Herbart's death these steps were revised and were widely practiced in five steps as follows: (a) Preparation: The teacher begins the class by reviewing the knowledge which the learners already have that bears upon the day's lesson. The purpose is to evoke the ideas which can best assimilate the new ideas to be presented. (b) Presentation: The teacher presents the new material constituting the day's lesson. (c) Association: The purpose of this step is to bind the old and the new materials together with a network of associative bonds, which brings out every significant relation between the ideas. This is accomplished by lively and critical discussion over which the teacher is the presiding genius and moderator. (d) Systematization: The teacher presents the class with further instances which might be brought under the same principles as were covered in step c. Thus, if the lesson of the day concerned representative government in the United States, the teacher could "systematize" in the step d by describing the British government. (e) Application: The learners are given further problems to which they apply the knowledge acquired in steps c and d. For instance, the learner might be asked to make an analysis of representative government in France in critical comparison with the analyses already made for the United States and England. This sort of intellectualized classroom procedure became popular in the United States during the era of the National Herbart Society. Herbart's four steps are given in his *Outline of Educational Doctrine* with annotations by Charles De Garmo, mentioned earlier as an American leader of Herbartian education (5, 51-59).

The intramural observer of American education may well share Meiklejohn's disillusionment about it. Too many students go to college "to make friends" and "to learn how to influence people." Professing love of knowledge is sometimes piously voiced but not manifested in practice to the extent that might be desirable. More student's are "working their way through college" than are dreamed of by the statisticians—if one counts those that "work" their professors. But if it be granted that the acquisition of knowledge is at least one of the aims of education and that face-to-face instruction in the classroom (pending its final submergence by television) is still a chief means of instruction then Herbart's "steps" are still sound—sound for any age. Modern psychology might add some effective measures for learning, but Herbart's steps still remain important. They provide for *systematically organized* knowledge. After forgetting has wrought its havoc, as shown by the pathetic droop of the curve of forgetting, organized knowledge is seen as one of the last survivors. Herbart had faith in knowledge and faith that men want it. Ideas bear inner testimony to their worth; they are the primary repositories of interest. A child is governed by his appetites—this is because his head is still relatively empty. Experience also shows that ideas are keys to practical success. This is so true that students trained for the learned professions must follow a Herbartian scheme of education.

▽ D. The Evolutionary Realism of Spencer (1820-1903)

1. Biographical Notes

After a sojourn with Herbart in Germany we are back in England again to follow up Locke's application of realism to education with an account of the "transfigured" realism of Herbert Spencer. Spencer was a member of a family of teachers. He acquired a strong nonconformist attitude from his father and other relatives, who were followers of John Wesley and members of the evangelical movement. The boy Herbert got much of his education from his father, a cultured man who insisted on teaching his students how to think ably and independently. An uncle prepared Herbert for Cambridge; but the boy, not liking the course of studies offered, refused to attend. This spirit of independence appears in the stress on individualism in Spencer's philosophy and in his views on education. He assisted his father in teaching for a short period.

Spencer was the English equivalent of Abraham Lincoln in at least two respects: Both were stalwart defenders of freedom and both were self-educated. Spencer studied and mastered civil engineering and journalism. Later on with little benefit of academic guidance he mastered the thoughts of numerous scholars, penetrated the depths of speculation and, single-handed, set up an original realistic philosophy.

After an intermittent career as an engineer Spencer took up journalism and became editor of the *Economist,* investing his spare time in the rapid absorption of one subject after another. In 1852 Spencer gave up all other enterprises and spent the remainder of his life erecting his synthetic philosophy, set forth in ten volumes. This was an achievement of encylopedic proportions, especially in view of Spencer's chronic ill health since early boyhood. His published philosophy began with *First Principles* (1862). This work set forth the basic principles of Spencer's evolutionary naturalism. It must be kept in mind that Spencer's thinking on the subject of evolution was independent of the ideas of Charles Darwin whose *Origin of Species* appeared in 1859, after Spencer had already formulated his ideas.[1]

Following the volume of *First Principles* there were two volumes on biology, two on psychology, three on sociology, and two volumes on ethics. The works on ethics, published in 1879-1893, represented the climax of Spencer's realism. He regarded the earlier volumes as preliminary to his ethics. Spencer wrote about ten books other than the volumes comprising his synthetic philosophy. Spencer regarded his philosophy as "synthetic" in the sense that it attempts to set forth a consistent set of universal principles which can be verified empirically by the separate sciences. Our account of this ambitious undertaking must be very brief. Spencer's philosophy of education, although based on his evolutionary realism, does not demand full acquaintance with the latter.

---

[1] Later on, Spencer criticized Darwin, especially the part Darwin assigned to natural selection in the origin of the species. Spencer considered that Darwin exaggerated the role of natural selection. The organism adapts itself to the environment. This adaptation involves the exercise of certain functions entailing structural changes. Spencer thought that these structural changes could be inherited. Authoritative opinion is almost unanimously on the side of Darwin on this issue, the inheritance of acquired characteristics being denied.

2. Spencer's Theory of Knowledge

Spencer lived in the age of empiricism, but to his own thinking not all knowledge was to be regarded as the product of experience. Spencer was acquainted with the critical philosophy of Kant, and was impressed by Kant's defense of the thesis that there are *a priori* forms of understanding. Spencer accepted the Kantian idea that the mind has inherent ways of understanding which are prior to individual experience and which belong to "mind in general." There are primary capacities of thought, such as the apprehension of likeness and difference, which Spencer believed to be inherent in the mind. Indeed, it would be impossible to acquire knowledge without them. Spencer thought it plausible to suppose that the mind's tendency to follow certain logical modes of reasoning was the result of racial evolution. That is, certain ways of understanding experience have been repeated so often in countless past generations that they have become reflexes in the individual mind. In this way Spencer sought to reconcile the *a priori* and empirical aspects of knowledge.

3. Spencer on "Things-in-Themselves"

Locke had troubled doubts about man's ability to know the nature of such things as matter, the soul, and God. Spencer held to a frank skepticism about such matters, a skepticism so frank and bluff that it has the appearance almost of positive knowledge! Ultimate or absolute reality, Spencer held, is unknowable. Man's knowledge is always *relative*. Our conclusions are contingent—they depend on other things being true. Like Kant, Spencer believed that any attempt of reason to understand ultimate things will end in baffling contradictions. It is inconceivable that units of space or time are infinitely divisible, yet equally impossible to imagine that such units are not infinitely divisible. Like many others Spencer gave up the struggle with such conundrums as whether time and space could begin or end, whether or not one could exist without the other, what God might be like when not conceived in terms of man's finite notions.

Spencer's agnosticism about transphenomenal realities and his defense of the evolutionary theory of the origin of man made him unpopular, especially in religious circles. Kant had found a way to absolute things through the "practical reason." Since Spencer accepted only the guidance of observation and "pure" reason, his agnosticism about ultimate things was more final. Final, that is, if it is ever sensible to assert in advance that present ignorance will be permanent!

Spencer's unpopularity because of his alleged "atheism" was not deserved. He was an *agnostic,* but this view does not deny the *existence* of God or of any transfinite object; it merely denies that we can have knowledge of such things. Spencer pointed out that since science can form no verifiable conception whatever regarding God's nature, science can never conflict with religion. Science will never be able to deny traits imputed to noumenal realities. The fact that we can form no idea of God's nature is no reason for denying His existence.

Spencer goes on to assert that we are in fact driven to accept the existence of something absolute beyond our phenomenal experience. The absolute must exist as the *cause* of phenomena. Our knowledge is relative but relative to some absolute. If we had knowledge which was not relative, that knowledge would itself be absolute. Spencer concluded that the absolute required to account for all phenomena is *power* or *force*. Without this assumption it is impossible to explain the never-ending occurrence of dynamic processes in nature. Force as the "absolute," however, is encountered in our experience. We meet it in the resistances of physical objects to muscular strain.

Empirical phenomena point to the existence of force but we can also discover it through rational inference. To deny the existence of this force would land us in the irrational assertion that phenomena are causeless, that motion arises from nothing. Both logic and empirical observation show that primordial energy is also indestructible. To admit that it can be destroyed would be to say that something can change into nothing, that an existing cause can eventuate in no effects. The notion that effects can arise without causes and that causes could have no effects whatever is repugnant to reason. Reason also compels us to believe in a sphere of existence lying beyond consciousness. For Spencer this compulsion of reason is the result of ages of racial experiences which have become compelling necessities or intuitions in individual minds.

The reader will recognize the harmony of Spencer's views about universal energy with the doctrine of science that matter is a potential form of energy and that energy can be transformed but not destroyed. All processes of nature manifest energy and its transformations.

4. Spencer's Evolutionary Philosophy

Spencer compensates for man's lack of absolute knowledge by giving us a surfeit of relative knowledge—ten volumes of it! The main principles employed by Spencer to give order to the vast store of observations accumulated in the sciences were the principle of evolution and the opposed principle of dissolution. For Spencer evolution was the process whereby things which are indefinite and homogeneous pass into definite states of heterogeneity. Darwin confined his principles of evolution to plants and animals, but Spencer found his own laws of development and decay everywhere—in biology, psychology, sociology—even in the evolution of planetary systems.

There are three main phases of an evolutionary sequence. At first there are phenomena of *concentration* as in the formation of clouds, the contraction of nebulae, the accumulation of elements leading to the formation of elementary living cells. Secondly, there will be a gradual *differentiation* or specialization of structures which are so impressive in the evolution of organisms. Thirdly, there will occur *determination,* by which Spencer means the appearance of factors that maintain integration and unity, which sustain the wholeness that is threatened by differentiation. When these processes reach a certain point, a climax is reached. Differentiation becomes too complex and delicate. External forces will inevitably destroy it. Old age and disintegration and death ensue. Meanwhile the processes of evolution are beginning and continuing elsewhere.

To say the least, Spencer's "transfigured" realism, as he called it, offers a gloomy outlook which contrasts sharply with the optimism usually found in idealism. Arthur Schopenhauer, reputed to be the world's greatest pessimist, relates his tale of human woe with a bleeding heart and words of poignant pity for man's unhappy lot and hopeless fate. Schopenhauer was an idealist, but he found reality the expression of blind will rather than of benign intelligence. Spencer saw all finite processes as the expression of blind force or power.

Yet there is a vast difference between the blind will of which Schopenhauer speaks and the blind forces of Spencer's realism. Spencer expresses the temper of all realists in looking upon nature with awe but not with fear. Nature may not love us, but then neither does she hate us. Nature will not object to our seeking happiness. Her forces are subject to intelligent guidance on our part. We may not win eternal happiness but that does not make temporary pleasure any the less precious. Spencer held that the search for the good and the evolution of living forms are the same thing. All other investigations of the synthetic philosophy are preliminary to ethics. Ethics is the inquiry to which all inquiries lead. Spencer's story of evolution and dissolution occurs in ten volumes of cold, ponderous, and desiccated prose, but it is not told in the spirit of gloom.

5. Spencer's Ethics

The ultimate goal of Spencer's philosophy was to find a scientific basis for the distinction between right and wrong and for the general guidance of conduct. Toward this end he considered it necessary to examine the nature of the physical universe in which conduct occurs and to study all forms of conduct. Hence the volumes on biology, psychology, and sociology provide the materials for his *Data of Ethics.* The Darwinians conceived all animals as engaged in a perpetual struggle for existence, not merely against the nonliving environment, or against other species, but also against blood relatives. This theme of individualistic competition was taken up by the followers of Spencer. In his sociology Spencer saw the principle of survival of the fittest at work in political and economic development. This "social Darwinism," for which Darwin was not entirely responsible, led to the condemnation of Darwinism in general as a cult of ruthless individualism. But Spencer's own utterances in the *Data of Ethics* are benign rather than harsh, as we will now see.

Spencer regarded conduct as good to the degree that it makes life longer, richer, and happier for the individual, for his children, and for his social group. Moral evolution reaches its fulfillment in a society where there is durable peace and in which each individual achieves his desirable goals and aids others in achieving theirs. Spencer was a *hedonist* in ethics —*pleasure is the essence of the good.* Life approaches perfect goodness when it leads at once to present pleasure and to remote pleasure. Spencer's hedonism also served to define right and wrong. Conduct is right and just when it leads to pleasure for all, wrong when it entails avoidable pain and the deprivation of pleasure.

Spencer was an optimist in the sense that evolution itself moves in the direction of more pleasure for all living forms. The capacity for enjoyment increases with the appearance of organisms with greater "differentiation" and "determination." The human being is capable of more pleasure than is an animal. This note of optimism seems to overlook the consideration that the potentiality for acute suffering is also enhanced by evolution. But Spencer considered that evolution brings more capacity for happiness than for pain.

Spencer's deep sense of the worth of individual freedom and independence appears in his moral philosophy. *Happiness or pleasure is an individual experience.* There are no literal "group satisfactions." Society therefore exists in the service of its individual members. The pleasure of the group exists in terms of the pleasure of its individual members. What about the obligations of the individual to the group? Spencer held that during early stages of social evolution egotism must come before altruism. But as society evolves it will be seen that altruism is also necessary. Without it, egotism misses its goals. Egotism and altruism are thus complementary. (This reminds one of the remark of Sir Henry Maine that the individual's desire to possess property makes possible his appreciation of the property rights of others.) Spencer considered that in a perfectly developed society altruism will become primary and egotism secondary. In such a society the individual will wish to sacrifice his pleasures in the interest of other people but they will prevent him from doing this! The reader will perhaps agree that to begin with egotism and end with an altruistic Utopia is no small achievement of natural evolution—or of Herbert Spencer!

6. Spencer's Psychology

Spencer recognized two types of approach to psychology: the subjective and the objective. Subjective psychology (corresponding to the "mentalism" of today) approaches psychology from the point of view of introspection. Objective psychology (corresponding to a degree with modern behaviorism) investigates the outward behavior which is related to mental processes. Introspective psychology studies the units or elements of consciousness and their relations and laws. Spencer teased out the elementary sensations ("feelings") and showed how they are "compounded." The compounds form still higher aggregates, thus moving in the direction of greater "differentiation." Analysis broke the mind down into elements which were seen as bound together by associations. This "mental chemistry" became dominant in later decades but is now subject to severe strictures, especially those of gestalt psychology.

Spencer was not a materialist in the strict sense of the word. He felt obliged to confess that the essence of life cannot be conceived in terms of physics and chemistry. Spencer favored the "double-aspect" theory of body and mind, an earlier notion which we will encounter again in the speculations of current realism. The double-aspect theory holds that mental processes and nerve processes are ultimately two views of the same underlying reality. That is, what is outwardly considered as an organic nerve process is inwardly experienced as a mental process. This theory is a compromise between the monistic and dualistic ways of conceiving the body-mind problem. Spiritualistic monism asserts that the brain is no less a spiritual fact than is the mind. Materialistic monism regards material realities as the only ones. Common sense regards consciousness and nerve processes as entirely different realities. But common sense, "ignorant of its ignorance," fails to see the difficulties inherent in dualism. Spencer's "transfigured" common sense deemed it wiser to adopt the double-aspect theory which gives (in appearance at least) both a monistic and dualistic point of view for psychology.

⸖ E. Spencer's Philosophy of Education

Spencer's views on education are expressed in four essays or reviews written between 1854 and 1859 (7, 8). Spencer's style in these essays is forceful and vivid, quite unlike the ponderous Spencerian periods encountered in the synthetic philosophy. Spencer's remarks on certain practices in education are mordantly critical. His judgments are remarkably acute and sound and bear intimately on the educational problems of today.

1. The Aims of Education

Knowing the exalted place accorded to ethics in Spencer's philosophy we are not surprised to note that he makes moral training the most general aim of all education. All phases of education, whether concerned with bodily health, the intellect, or social training bear upon the "right ruling of conduct in all directions under all circumstances" (7, p. 30). Learning how to live morally embraces five subsidiary aims of education which will be discussed in section 3 below.

2. Moral Education in General

The general aim of moral education is to prepare the child for successful living where success is measured by the Spencerian theory of the good, which is to attain that most perfect pleasure for all which results from the harmonization of egotism and altruism. Spencer finds a principle for moral education in nature which he sets forth in detail. When a child violates a principle of nature, as when it carelessly falls, cuts itself, or experiences a burn it inevitably suffers *pain*. Pain serves as the best possible mentor for guiding the child away from suffering and toward satisfaction. Spencer held that we can do no better than to emulate this type of discipline found in nature. To be sure, the concepts of right and wrong do not have application to acts of nature as such. Nature does not aim to "punish wickedness" by causing bodily injuries to be painful. Pain and pleasure operate in nature as principles of survival rather than as rules of moral equity. But man's reason sees pure justice in the principle that individuals must bear responsibility for the consequences of their own acts. Parents and teachers can do no better than to teach right conduct by making this principle perfectly clear to the child.

The critic will point out that many of the pains and pleasures which man experiences rise out of his cultural rather than strictly natural environment. Nature will burn the fingers put into the flame but not the wayward fingers of the thief. Nature is much too myopic in her justice. We cannot depend on her to visit suffering (and hence perhaps reform) upon the perpetrators of crime, graft, and corruption. Society must therefore devise its own rules of justice and mete out rewards and punishments for social as opposed to biological sins.

In reply to this criticism it might be maintained that Spencer's philosophy implies that society and culture evolve "naturally," and their punishments of offenders will thus be "natural." Biological facts are in part the preconditions for social culture. If man's biological nature were such that he had no need for food and other forms of property it would be rather meaningless to talk about the "injustice" of depriving him of them. The evolutionist regards the pursuit of learning as a consequence of the biological survival value of intelligence. As for other higher cultural satisfactions such as art, it is always hazardous to try to prove that they have no biological roots and serve no biological needs. Even religion has brought about "adaptation" to biological aspects of life.

It could be maintained that to a large extent social justice operates "naturally" rather than through design. If the merchant charges too much for his goods he loses customers as a "natural pain" inflicted on his avarice, although this was not deliberately intended by society. The distinction between nature and society is not so clear as Spencer's critic may suppose. It is true that children and adults who receive social punishments in the form of physical pain may find the physical pain less hurtful than the social disapproval implied by it. But Spencer regarded such social anger and resentment against offenses as spontaneous and natural: they occur plentifully among animals.

We need not belabor the question of the universality of natural as opposed to cultural good and evil. Spencer in fact does not insist that man's justice is identical with nature's. He only urges that man should *emulate* nature in his treatment of good and bad conduct. First, such justice is *rational*. Even the child can understand that pain following the violation of a principle must be borne by the individual who is responsible for the violation. This principle will also be appreciated as pure justice (7, pp. 172-186).

Perhaps the basic axiom of man's emulation of nature should be that no act is good or evil in and of itself. Acts are good or evil solely in view of their consequences. Spencer declared that if theft were indeed to the benefit of both the robber and the victim, it would not be found in our catalogue of sins. But man's behavior can be *rational*—he can foresee evil consequences and thus enjoys insights which his animal nature does not in itself give to him.

Spencer gives wise counsel concerning the ways in which nature's "justice" can be emulated. Let the child suffer the consequences of violating principles regarding which he has knowledge. In some mild cases it will not be amiss to allow the child to learn a rule of conduct by experiencing the pain first rather than last. Such things as touching a hot object or eating green apples teach their wisdom in one lesson. Emulating nature could be applied on a grand scale in our system of penal justice. Spencer noted that prisons and reformatories are notorious for their failure to reform criminals. They would be more effective if all justice were guided by the simple rational principle, made clear to every offender, that the imprisonment of offenders is designed to protect society from them. The prisoner should be deprived of all profits from his misdeeds and should be required to earn his own living while in prison. Nature's justice is usually swift and invariable. Man's punishments follow too long after the offenses and are inconsistent and fickle.

When children break their own things let them suffer the natural inconvenience of not having them. If such objects are replaced let the child bear the cost of replacement. If a boy carelessly loses his knife or breaks its blade it is foolish for the parent to replace it. The child should earn the price of a new knife and replace things he destroys which belong to others. Let the child suffer any pleasures missed through his own careless tardiness. Let the child learn for himself that untidiness results in later difficulty in finding things. Spencer's system of natural justice follows Rousseau very closely although Rousseau is not mentioned by Spencer.

What is the proper role of emotion in administering punishments? Spencer does not deny that scoldings, threats, blows, and vindictive anger may be *relatively* effective in *some* social situations. The barbarous child in a barbarous home may respond only to barbarous punishments! In general, social practices will be as good as human nature in a given case permits. *But sympathy and love, not anger, are nature's favorite bond between adults and children.* Love has a natural history. Sympathy and love are effective agents of control. The child will learn to love and respect the parent or teacher who is unfailingly friendly and a good companion. When such a child is guilty of an offense it is only necessary to withhold love to bring about quick penitence. These ideas of Spencer are astute anticipations of modern psychological studies. Spencer concludes his remarks on moral education by noting that he said nothing about transcendental distinctions between right and wrong. The distinction between right and wrong can be founded empirically on observing the consequences of acts.

3. Subsidiary Aims of Education

Spencer clearly regarded moral education as the chief goal which embraces his five subsidiary aims of education. Briefly listed, these aims are: (a) Self-preservation (maintaining health, etc.), (b) training for self-support and for maintaining a family, (c) learning how to rear children (parenthood in general), (d) learning to be a good citizen, and (e) training for hours of leisure. Spencer lists these five aims in their logical and temporal order rather than in their order of value. That is, unless one attains and maintains vigorous bodily health the remaining aims cannot fully be attained. Spencer's emphasis on training for health, in which we see him in agreement with Locke, perhaps reflected his own lifelong struggle with poor health. Secondly, unless a man can support himself it is idle to expect him to support a family and to play an adequate role as a citizen (7, pp. 32-34).

It will be noted that Spencer does not provide a special aim or caption for *learning* or *knowledge* in education. Where do the intellectual contents of education come in? Spencer considered that training the student to fulfill the five practical aims also provided for general intellectual education. Each course of study should serve all of the aims of education. Spencer's five subsidiary aims appear so intensely practical that one might expect him to recommend only narrowly practical studies. On the contrary, Spencer recommends the systematic pursuit of wide branches of knowledge, such as the sciences, the humanities, history, and the fine arts.

4. Spencer on the Contents of Education

Two of Spencer's reviews on education are entitled. "What Knowledge Is of Most Worth?" and "Intellectual Education." These two reviews set very high standards of intellectual education which anticipated many current practices. As we would expect from a modern realist Spencer regards the sciences as the most important contents for education. The study of science provides for moral as well as for intellectual education. The pursuit of science demands integrity, self-sacrifice, courage, and other prized virtues. Science acquaints the individual with those laws of nature and society which lead to happiness when applied in practice. Science also disciplines reason. We here find Spencer at one with the essentialist's faith in intellectual discipline. Science provides learning of a high order of scholarship.

Comments on some of the specific studies recommended by Spencer will make clear how he hoped to achieve an education which is intellectual and general and yet intensely practical. Spencer's ideas very much anticipated those of John Dewey. Physiology is one of the sciences basic to the maintenance of health. Spencer says that many people who would blush when they mispronounce a word would not feel the slightest shame concerning gross ignorance about anatomy (7, p. 43). Earning a living in the professions and in business depends on training in the sciences. As for the rearing of children, Spencer bitterly assails the incompetent practices of his day, and makes an eloquent appeal for the study of psychology. He declared that historians of the distant future, examining the schoolbooks of Spencer's day, would conclude that they provided a curriculum for celibates! Spencer created an apocalyptic vision of the "enormous mischief" which is everywhere done to children by unscientific methods of rearing and educating them (7, pp. 55-56). Training for citizenship requires the vigorous mastery of the social sciences, such as sociology and history. Training for the enjoyment of leisure includes the study of such things as literature, painting, and music; but science is also an adjunct to the full appreciation of the arts.

5. Spencer on Pedagogy

John Dewey, commenting on Spencer's emphasis on the value of instruction in science, criticizes Spencer for assuming that scientific knowledge can be imparted "ready-made" (2, p. 258). Dewey means that instruction is conveyed "ready-made" when it depends solely on textbooks and classroom instruction. As against this Dewey favors the approach to science and other subjects through practical projects and laboratory work. Dewey's statement that Spencer favored "ready-made" forms of instruction is inaccurate. In fact, Spencer underscored the tenets of modern progressivism so forcefully that he might well be regarded, along with Rousseau, Froebel, and Pestalozzi, as a pioneer of progressive education (7, pp. 60-62, 103-105, and elsewhere).

Spencer regarded books as supplementary adjuncts to education. He stressed the importance of taking advantage of the child's own restless interest in the world about him. Only when the child's knowledge acquired in the home, streets, and fields becomes tolerably complete should books be introduced. All education must be based on psychology. For instance, the teacher must know that knowledge proceeds from the concrete to the abstract. Spencer, like Locke, excoriated the system of rote learning. Children must be required to deduce general principles for themselves. If such principles are given to them by the teacher they may be able to apply them as rules but still not understand them as principles.

Not to be outdone by Dewey and Kilpatrick, who may be regarded as his modern successors, Spencer insisted that "Every science is evolved out of its corresponding art." All study should therefore begin experimentally and should be followed by reflection. "Children should be led to make their own investigations, and to draw their own inferences. They should be *told* as little as possible and induced to *discover* as much as possible" (7, pp. 124-125).

F. Fiske's Developmental Psychology (1842-1901)

John Fiske, Spencer's leading disciple in America, was one of a number of scholars who made it their mission to introduce European philosophy of science to Americans, and to reconcile evolutionary theory with theological doctrines. Fiske's popular essays (e.g., *The Destiny of Man, The Idea of God, Through Nature to God,* and *Life Everlasting*) made some modifications of Spencer's hedonistic ethics and agnosticism and interpreted the synthetic philosophy in favor of the belief in God and immortality (6, pp. 322-325).

Fiske's little book, *The Meaning of Infancy*, became a classic in education and child psychology. This work, first published in 1883, set forth an evolutionary theory of infancy and childhood which we may regard as a contribution of evolutionary realism to education (3). Man is the only creature capable of cultural progress and he is the animal with the longest period of infancy and adolescence. These two familiar facts, says Fiske, are connected. Man as he is today was made possible by the lengthening of the period of infancy (3, p. 2). The lower the animal forms we examine the more we find that they are creatures who were "educated" before they were born. Man owes his capacity to be formed by individual rather than by racial experience to the length of his period of development. The capacity to be modified by training is due to the biological plasticity of the nervous system during the period of growth. But the *form* of the child's modifications is culturally rather than biologically determined. That is to say, without the development of culture and educational systems man could not make full use of the protracted period of infancy (3, pp. 11-12).

Fiske credits others for some of his basic ideas. Alfred Russell Wallace, co-discoverer with Darwin of the principle of evolution, made a brilliant advance on Darwin's ideas. This was Wallace's idea that when the period arrives in the course of evolution when variations in mental traits are more important for survival than bodily traits, then natural selection will favor the development of intelligence, while bodily structures remain essentially unchanged (3, pp. 23-24).

The very helplessness of human infants requires parents to give them more care than is the case with animals. Family life thus becomes emphasized in higher animals and man. Fiske conceived that in this way clans and larger social groups arose, giving rise to social transmission of culture, and generating the first germs of morality. Fiske finds in man's evolution a groping toward things lying beyond the sensory world and beyond history and culture. This is the search for God, for that Absolute Energy which Spencer too found beyond the realm of phenomena. But Spencer did not personalize and deify the energy which he inferred as the cause of all phenomena. Fiske's evolutionary realism, wholly apart from its coloring of religious idealism, served to exalt the importance of youth in education.

We have now completed our sampling of the main historical forms of realism. The systems of Locke, Herbart, and Spencer were sketched in some detail, and were followed by accounts of their philosophies of education. The next task is to examine contemporary realism in its two main forms, new realism and critical realism. In both of these contemporary realisms the problem of establishing a satisfactory view regarding an objective world which exists independently of being known becomes very acute.

References

1. Brubacher, John S. *History of the Problems of Education.* New York: McGraw-Hill, 1947.
2. Dewey, John. *Democracy and Education.* New York: Macmillan, 1916.
3. Fiske, John. *The Meaning of Infancy.* New York: Houghton, Mifflin, 1911.
4. Herbart, Johann F. *Text-Book of Psychology.* New York: D. Appleton, 1894.
5. ————. *Outlines of Educational Doctrine* (tr. by A. F. Lange with annotations by C. De Garmo). London: Macmillan, 1913.
6. Schneider, Herbert W. *A History of American Philosophy.* New York: Columbia University Press, 1946.
7. Spencer, Herbert. *Education, Intellectual, Moral, and Physical.* New York: D. Appleton, 1888.
8. ————. *Essays on Education and Kindred Subjects.* London: J. M. Dent; New York: E. P. Dutton, 1910.
9. Stevenson, Robert L. *Essays by Robert Louis Stevenson.* New York: Scribner's, 1918.
10. Thilly, Frank. *A History of Philosophy.* New York: Holt, 1914.
11. Thorndike, Edward L., and Arthur I. Gates. *Elementary Principles of Education.* New York: Macmillan, 1930.

⩔ chapter 13

CONTEMPORARY REALISM

The naïve realist seldom if ever doubts his assurance that he knows such things as sticks and stones for what they "really" are. He owes this assurance to the circumstance that he never examines the bases of his faith. But the professional realist, smitten by the virus of inquiry handed down by Socrates, undertakes to prove that his knowledge about the ultimate nature of things is valid. In the two preceding chapters three forms of realism were set forth with special attention to their consequences for the philosophy and practice of education. The mission of the present chapter is to bring the story of realism up to date, again giving special attention to aspects of it which are significant for education. Contemporary realism is mainly represented by two schools, but there are important realists in America and abroad who do not officially belong to these schools. The two schools in question are *new realism* and *critical realism*. Both are reactions against idealism and pragmatism, the latter to be discussed in the chapters of Book V.

New realism was launched first. About 1910 six American realists published an article setting forth their joint platform (4).[1] This cooperative project led in 1912 to a much fuller statement in the cooperative volume entitled *The New Realism* (5). Another group of realists joined

[1] The six participants were: Edwin B. Holt, Walter T. Marvin, William P. Montague, Ralph B. Perry, Walter B. Pitkin, and Edward G. Spaulding.

forces in 1916 under the banner of critical realism. In 1920 their manifesto was published under the title, *Essays in Critical Realism* (1).[2]

The moral and religious views of a philosophy have more importance for education than its theories of knowledge and reality. Morality and religion supply the aims of life in general, and these aims directly concern education. The reader will recall that the realists discussed in the preceding chapter—Locke, Herbart, and Spencer—made morality their chief concern in their philosophies of education. In order to avoid undue involvement with problems of knowledge and of reality only meagre attention will be given to them in this chapter. In fact, except for a footnote on a later page, the school of critical realism will be ignored. This omission would be inexcusable in a work on American Philosophy. But contemporary realists who have interested themselves in education (see Chapter 14) show more intellectual kinship with new realism than with critical realism.

The main divisions of the present chapter are as follows:
A. The Aims of New Realism
B. Reality and Knowledge
C. The Problem of Error
D. Realism and Religion
E. Realism and Ethics

▽ A. The Aims of the New Realism

The new realists sought for a point of view which would justify commonsense realism. First of all, the common man seldom doubts that the external world of objects and natural laws continue to exist whether or not they are known. Bishop Berkeley's view that the existence of an object depends on its being known seems strange if not fantastic to the layman. All idealisms follow Berkeley in seeking to identify the objects and laws of nature with our experiences or knowledge about them.

The new realist rejects this doctrine. He contends that knowledge is an *external* relation between the mind and the object it knows. An external relation is said not to affect the natures of the things it relates. Two houses, for example, remain what they are irrespective of their purely external relations—it does not matter which one is to the north or south. But an *internal* relation affects the things it relates. The relation of father to son, for instance, is *internal*, because the relata depend on the nature of the relation. Without the internal relation of parenthood, Billy

2 This second group had seven original members: Durant Drake, Arthur O. Lovejoy, James B. Pratt, George Santayana, Roy W. Sellars, Arthur K. Rogers, and Charles A. Strong.

Jones is not the son of William Jones, Sr. The knowledge relation, says the new realist, is of the external type. The objects and laws of nature continue to exist whether or not the knowledge relationship holds. The realist feels that the idealist tries to solve the mystery of how ideas are related to their objects by simply denying the existence of objects and regarding the idea about them as all that there is. In this case there is no problem of how objects are known, not because the problem was solved, but because it was "banished."

Secondly, in addition to justifiying the common man's belief in the independent existence of objects, the new realist wishes also to justify the common belief that *we often know objects as they really are.* It will be recalled (Chapter 11) that John Locke disputed the belief that the *secondary* qualities of things, such as their colors, odors, tastes, and temperatures are real properties of objects, but did consider that *primary* properties, such as form and bulk, are real characteristics of objects. The new realist hopes to show that the secondary qualities of things belong to objects quite as surely as do primary properties. This would achieve a completely *presentative* theory of knowledge, whereas Locke held to a presentative view only for the primary properties of things.

The two main aims of new realism sketched above are simple and clear in themselves. Unfortunately, these aims are very difficult to realize to the satisfaction of everyone. To follow out the new realist's solution of these problems would take us into quite advanced and controversial problems of science and philosophy, beyond the limited scope of this book.

ⱴ B. Reality and Knowledge

We shall now briefly examine the realist's program by means of which it is proposed to amend the beliefs of common sense so as to provide for a fully presentative theory of knowledge and still account for the existence of perceptual and conceptual errors. For an account of the main postulates by means of which the above objectives are to be reached we turn to the set of postulates set forth by William P. Montague (9):

1. Philosophers should follow the example of scientists and cooperate rather than work alone.
2. Philosophers should also follow the example of scientists in isolating problems and working at one problem at a time.
3. Some, at least, of the *particulars* of which we are conscious exist when we are not conscious of them.
4. Some, at least, of the *essences* or *universals* of which we are conscious subsist when we are not conscious of them.
5. Some, at least, of the particulars as well as the universals that are real are

apprehended directly rather than indirectly through copies or mental images.

With these five postulates serving as the platform of new realism we turn to a discussion of the theories of knowledge and of reality which they imply.

1. Science as the Method of Knowledge

Aristotle, classic advocate and practitioner of realism, regarded empirical observation as the original source of knowledge. Knowledge proceeds from the more obvious to the less obvious, which means that the observation of particular things leads to the establishment of general principles. This Aristotelian view has served throughout history as the model, not only for realism, but for related points of view such as naturalism and positivism.

Empirical observation has reached its most perfect form in science, and realists of all times have put their faith in science. This was evident in the sampling of historical realists (Locke, Herbart, and Spencer) presented in previous chapters. This tribute to science as opposed to dialectical argument appears in the first two postulates of new realism. The ideal procedure adopted by science and new realists alike is to make distinctions where there are differences, and not to overlook differences for the sake of attaining some unity which exists on some transcendental plane. Ernst Mach somewhere observes that it is always possible, although not sensible, to get simplicity by the simple expedient of ignoring differences. By overlooking enough differences a penny and the moon may be regarded as identical! The concern of science for concrete particulars begins with isolating different problems and working at them one at a time. Scientists do not work alone, but cooperate in research and in sharing the results of research. These are the methods favored by the new realists.

2. The Nature of Reality

The three remaining postulates offered by Montague clearly say something about both the nature of knowledge and of reality, but the latter is now our concern. Postulates 3 and 4 assert that some of the "particulars" and some of the "universals" we know about "exist when we are not conscious of them." By "particulars" Montague means the objects of sense perception, such as trees, stones, persons. By "universals" he means such things as general laws and general properties of things. Thus, the law of gravity is a universal, and has an existence independent of our knowing it; and $7 + 5 = 12$ is also a universal truth, quite as stubborn in its reality as a mountain. The mass (weight) of all material bodies, the whiteness of snow, and so on are also universal and abstracted properties of things which are what they are whether we experience them or not.

The new realist holds, as against Berkeley and even against Locke, that objects may have the colors, odors, and tastes which we experience them as having. The man with red-green color-blindness, of course, does not see the redness of the apples. But this does not prove that the apple lacks redness; it only shows that this man's visual apparatus fails to make him aware of it. We are here on the brink of one of those controversial problems which we must dodge if we are to get around to the doctrines of realism which have more significance for education. The reader will note that Montague is careful to say that only "some" particulars and universals of which we are conscious are real. This provides for the possibility of error. What is the new realist's explanation of error?

C. The Problem of Error

The problem of error is an abstruse one on any theory. To avoid protracted discussion we select Montague's view as an example of the kind of error theory to be expected from new realists (9, pp. 434-439). The reader will notice the nice harmony between Montague's theory of error and that of common sense. A brief and rather free exposition of Montague's view would be as follows: All false objects as experienced in illusions, hallucinations, and dream images may be identified by the observation that they have but one effect: namely, an indirect effect on the individual who experiences them. Thus, the insane man's hallucination of a black cat affects only him. This "cat" cannot be seen by other observers, it cannot be photographed, and it cannot upset a real vase! Normal illusions differ from dream images and hallucinations in that they can affect more than one observer. Thus, the oar in water appears bent to all onlookers. On the other hand, real objects have two effects: direct effects on other objects and indirect effects on observers.

These criteria may be applied to determine whether perception is false or true. The oar in water appears bent to all observers. Even the camera photographs it as bent! But in this instance both the camera and the eyes *portray special conditions of stimulation* as much as they portray the oar. The impression of the oar being bent fails to meet the tests of the other senses and *it signally fails to meet objective tests.* When checked against a straight object the false character of the bent appearance of the oar is revealed. In general, the oar fails to respond like a bent object in its relations with other objects. *The characteristics of objects are shown by their effects on each other, and not alone by their effects on us.* The existence and nature of an external object is in no case directly altered by our mere knowledge about it. Of course, knowing that there are weeds in the garden one may be led to destroy them. But to do this knowledge has to affect the object indirectly through the use of one's muscles, and these are themselves material objects.

What about proofs of the reality of universals? In postulate 4 Montague speaks of the "subsistence" rather than the "existence" of universals. This is because a universal does not exist in the same sense as a material object. The principle that equilateral triangles are also equiangular is not in itself a physical object which can be put on a shelf, but it is nevertheless real. It is as impervious against our wishes and wills as a stone. Indeed more so, for the stone can be crushed but no one can draw a triangle with straight lines and get less than three or more than three angles. Such realities are said to *subsist* to distinguish them from concrete things which *exist*. The proof of the subsistence of universals is about the same as the proof of the existence of concrete objects. Montague writes, "That $7 + 5 = 12$ is entirely explained by the natures of seven, of five, and of twelve, and not in the least by the nature of consciousness" (9, p. 426).

What, then, is error? Errors of perception arise when we take *all* of the impressions which objects have on us as true properties of the objects. Errors of judgment, such as adding seven and five and getting thirteen, are similar cases of missing the true effects of numbers on each other when they are added. Of course, false ideas "exist" in the sense of being just what they are. But when we call them "false" we mean that they fail to agree with that great realm of reality which is oblivious to what we are pleased to believe about it. This is the spirit of realism.

In making his emphatic claim that we can know external objects as they "really" are, the new realist comes very close to saying that when an object is fully known it will be identical with what is known about it. Now, this looks suspiciously like idealism, which identifies our perceptions and ideas with the object to which they refer. The realist wishes to avoid this identification at all costs. It is natural to suppose that the sizes and shapes of things are usually apprehended directly, but a little reflection uncovers perplexing problems. Do we literally perceive the height of a tree? But to know the tree's height literally implies that the tree's presentation in the mind is perhaps twenty feet high! On the assumption that the mind is in the brain there is literally not enough room for this "presentation."

An apparently simple way out of this difficulty is to say that the perceptual image of the tree and our later memory of it *represent* the tree. The mind gives the image, copy, or symbol of the tree the *meaning* of being twenty feet high. The new realist feels that the acceptance of any copy theory will result in skepticism. This is because on such a theory the mind will be shut up with its copies of things and will have no assurance that the copies are faithful to their objects; and even if faithful, they isolate the mind from the world of external reality.

The new realist rejects the copy theory of knowledge in favor of a quite unique view. The mind is regarded as "in" the brain only in the *functional* sense that the brain is necessary equipment for having mental processes. The new realist favors the view that the mind is "out there" with its object. This has become known as the "cross-sectional" theory of mind. It was originated by Edwin B. Holt and was favored by some of his fellow new realists (5, pp. 353-356). This theory supposes that the nervous system and its sense organs are something like a searchlight which plays upon external objects, revealing a cross-section of external things. The objects revealed depend upon the directions taken by the light. Mind is a cross-section of outer objects selected by the nervous system. We perceive the objects which the sense organs, acting like searchlights, reveal. But the responses of the senses take the mind out to its objects. When you sit idly contemplating the things in a room, your consciousness is out there with them. This is the reverse of the ordinary view which says that the senses carry impressions *from* the object *to* the mind.

New realists thus seem to come close to identifying external objects and our experiences of them. They favor the "double-aspect" theory of the mind and material nature. This view says that the mind and physical objects are the same "stuff" which has two different aspects, the mental and the physical.

The critical realists prefer a different solution. They seek to restore the inwardness of mind, separating it from its external objects. They regard the world as made up of two realities, physical objects on the one hand and mental states and processes on the other. This is metaphysical dualism, and accords well with the common man's belief that the inner world of consciousness and the outer world of things are not to be identified. But, having separated the mind from its external object, the problem of the critical realist is to get them together again! Commonsense thinking, with its genial habit of overlooking difficulties, agrees with the critical realist that our knowledge of external things only *represents* them and agrees with the new realist that external reality is literally *presented* when we know things truly.

When the layman turns philosopher he will understand why Herbert Spencer and others, by dwelling too long and searchingly on the problem of knowledge, turned skeptics regarding the nature and existence of such things as matter, motion, causation, time, and space. The realist layman is quite innocent of such thoughts as the following from Flewelling:

In the course of about thirty years we have advanced from the affirmation that the most certain of all realities is the atom (made by Lord Kelvin) to the contrary affirmation that the most certain of all certainties is the principle of uncertainty (3, p. 335).

Perhaps by this time the reader can appreciate the twinge of frustration in Flewelling's words. Clearly an apology for philosophy is needed, so here it is: The philosopher and scientist, like the layman, also live in the world of external objects. They are not deprived of this world by questioning it. But what is the use of raising questions which have not been answered despite centuries of effort? Because, in the first place, the fact that they have not been answered is not proof that they will never be answered. Physicists keep on trying to decide between the "particle" and the "wave" theories of light, or try to unite them. The answer to the problem may come any moment. Meanwhile, the attempt to answer this question throws light on other problems. But the best apology for philosophy and for inquiry in general is given by Robert L. Stevenson: It is better to invent a theory than to take everything as it comes in dumb acquiescence. The answer to a question is not the only reward for raising the question. To raise questions expresses the love of knowledge which is like the romantic love praised by poets—"It is better to have loved and lost than never to have loved at all." Inquiry always yields positive results. It yields the fun of inquiry, and if it fails to reveal the truth, it reveals the state of our ignorance.

It is important for the teacher to realize the depth of knowledge as well as its surface extent. The teacher who has struggled with "ultimate" questions is not likely to end up with a neat list of certainties. Disquieting questions loom up beyond the supposedly final answers. The "last analysis" turns out to be only the last one to date. Nevertheless, the teacher who emulates Socrates can serve the mental and moral needs of students better than one whose certainties rest on a vast ignorance. Democracy itself is born of thoughtful controversy.

▽ D. Realism and Religion

Since the realist, St. Thomas Aquinas, accepted the reality of both God and matter we shall not be surprised to find many modern realists who are deeply religious. Materialistic realism, to be sure, will favor atheistic views. Also many realists adopt an agnostic position which is to declare with Spencer that human knowledge can neither prove nor disprove the existence of a divine being. Setting aside atheistic and agnostic views, we turn to the religious gnostics to be found among realists.

As noted by William James, the religion of a philosopher is likely to have a pale and intellectual cast. While the idealist's approach to religion is likely to be rational, the approach of the realist inclines to be empirical. An empirical way of validating religion is through the "argument from design." The imposing orderliness and evidences of purposiveness to be found in nature cannot be regarded as the results of chance or of the blind physical laws of nature. Many realists of science would endorse the Platonic thought that a "God of numbers" is the moving spirit of all reality. Many scientists regard the world as the creation of a purposive intelligence. This argument is set forth by Lecomte du Noüy (2).

Some realists validate religion through the more direct examination of the facts about religion itself rather than by the roundabout way of establishing God's existence on evidences found in external nature. They note that religion has a long history of complex manifestations. The realist examines these religious phenomena in the same way in which he examines everything else. After making this examination it is concluded that man's experiences of God are just as direct as many of the evidences on which science is founded. The point here is that the scientist's pathway to reality is usually very indirect, and seldom if ever yields empirical principles that are absolutely true. The scientist thus cannot, and usually does not, denounce other claims to knowledge, such as the knowledge of God, as indirect and therefore unreliable.

The history of man shows that he has felt the presence of the divine as nearer than hands and feet. This belief is not like certain primitive superstitions which vanish as enlightenment grows. On the contrary, religious beliefs have grown in clarity with the advance of culture. Man may come to serve more immediate and enticing gods, such as power, repute, and pleasure. But when these are replaced by pain and suffering, man knows where to turn. Every instinctive desire implies the existence of the things that can satisfy it.

The essential harmony between realistic philosophy and religion is attested by many sources, among which is the remarkable symposium by fifteen realists entitled *Religious Realism* (6). The aim of the symposium, in harmony with a realistic outlook, was to establish belief in the existence of God and to verify ancillary beliefs regarding man's relations to God. The evidences supporting these beliefs are derived from reflections on general experience and on the special examination of religious experience. The arguments of the idealists in support of religious beliefs are excluded. As regards the certainty of the realist's evidences, some of the fifteen participants in the symposium find them adequate proofs in support of religious beliefs, while others find them sufficient for "a practically valuable and theoretically permissible faith" (6, Editor's Preface).

Two of the contributors to the symposium, J. B. Pratt and A. K. Rogers, were among the original founders of critical realism. W. P.

Montague represented the new realists. Montague's views regarding religion are tied up with his moral theories, which are set forth in the following section. We will there see with what force and cogency a realist can defend religion.

▽ E. Realism and Ethics

Like other philosophies, realism hopes to provide foundations for the moral guidance of mankind. The ideas of realists in the sphere of moral theory are too varied and complex to be fully sketched in this book. We have already encountered their tendency to variety in Locke's religious morality, Herbart's morality of ideas, and in Spencer's hedonism.

A central difficulty of any system of ethics is to do justice both to the absolute and the relative aspects of moral values. By an *absolute good* we mean one which is intrinsically and always good. We had an instance of this in Kant's categorical imperative which enjoins us to so live that the rule of our conduct could be adopted by all human beings irrespective of time and place. Again, Kant found "good will" an absolute good. On the other hand, many of the good things of life are *relative*, not absolute. There are numberless values which must be subordinated to other more inclusive and higher values. As Montague notes, no amount of happiness enjoyed by pigs can be equal to the happiness of a Socrates (7, p. 44).

Ralph Barton Perry's interest theory of value is among the best known of the relational theories of value held by realists (10). In our further sampling of realistic moral philosophies, William P. Montague will serve as representative for the new realists. Since the secularization of education we may no longer demand that a philosophy of education be devoutly religious; yet we do not welcome it with open arms because it is militantly atheistic. But since the development of good character is almost universally regarded as one of the main aims of education, we would most assuredly look askance at any philosophy of education which harbored amoral postulates. But all philosophies of education faithfully promise to lower the rate of immorality just as all respectable political parties promise to lower the tax rates. Our only problem is to decide which philosophy of education when put into practice by teachers will result in the greatest moral development of the student.

A Promethean Ethics and Religion

Traditional Christian morality is based on the validity of religion. Montague rather reverses this order: Morality is the prior branch of inquiry and the nature of religion is determined by its results. Montague says that if the things that man finds highest in his spiritual and moral life are deeply grounded in nature then we can have a true religion which can make our lives radiant (7, pp. 6-8). With such a religion we could have faith in the existence in nature of an urge or power that works for the ends which man regards as ideal. Such a Being in nature would have our allegiance, not because of His authority but because He shares our love of the ideal.

The Bible, says Montague, is no more than a folklore which has become a source of authority and credited as divine revelation. Whenever beliefs become merely dogmatic, then the false sin of heresy and the false virtue of orthodoxy arise. Those who cannot believe the dogma are accused of the sin of heresy. They are regarded as not only guilty of error but of a strange sin, the sin of being in error. Those who do believe the dogma have the credit of being intelligent and also of being virtuous. But, says Montague, you cannot blame a man for inability to see the truth; one might as well blame a blind man for his blindness (7, pp. 10-11). Whatever the reader thinks of this, he will perhaps agree with Montague that we should help those who are ignorant rather than blame them for being "sinful." This, at any rate, seems a wholesome attitude for teachers.

If founding religion and morals on authority is a primary error, a secondary one is the notion that goodness is only to be found in asceticism and other-worldliness. The sensible purpose of self-denial is to secure good things in the future which require such present self-denial. "We save in order to spend." We give up lesser goods in order to secure greater ones. But asceticism and other-worldliness carry self-denial to an absurd extreme.

Now the ascetic is the *miser* of the spiritual life. For just as the miser begins by saving as a means to spending, and winds up by regarding saving as an end in itself, so the ascetic begins by inhibiting some desires as a means to gratifying others, and winds up by regarding inhibition as an end in itself (7, p. 13).

Rejecting authoritarianism and asceticism in religion and ethics, Montague does not entirely reject supernaturalism. His ground for accepting supernaturalism is given by the fourth postulate of new realism which declares that some of the universals apprehended by the mind "subsist" irrespective of our consciousness of them. This is Platonic idealistic realism. For Montague, the sacred and supernatural nature of Jesus and his teachings do not depend on the trappings of miracles, signs, and wonders which load down the story of his career. It is enough that Jesus discovered the ideals of absolute beauty and love and declared them free to both the great and the humble. The divinity of Christ must rest upon factual observations of his actual life and of the ideals he pursued, not upon miracles and revelations (7, pp. 17-27).

After his observation of man's life Montague concludes that the *summum bonum* or supreme good is this: *To attain the maximum abundance of life.* This statement must now be given explicit content. It is a categorical imperative of sorts, but unlike Kant's. Professor George H. Palmer had interpreted Kant's categorical imperative as *the law that there shall be law.* Montague wholly rejects this interpretation of Kant. Montague's "moral imperative" is rather *to act in such a way that fixed law can never be established.* That is to say, life means creative growth. It moves, not in the direction of fixed law, but rather in the direction of creative variation toward an abundance of good things. Montague's ideas have a Bergsonian ring, and Bergson rates as an emergent realist. As long as life continues "it will never lose its yearning to be more than it is" (7, p. 97). Without this divine discontent which makes for growth, morality and religion will perish under the weight of fixed customs and rituals perpetuated by the sanctions of presumptive authority.

For Montague the prime virtues are *love* and *enthusiasm.* Love points the way to the richest variation of life. Love is measured by the number and breadth of its interests. Love leads one to identify oneself with the desires, aims, pains, fears, and hopes of all lives, past, present, and future. Love is the (Platonic) ideal which Christ and Buddha exemplified so perfectly. In the virtue of *enthusiasm* Montague includes every impulse in us that makes for hard and persistent efforts to actualize the sublime potentialities within us. Ideals do not actualize themselves. They must be actualized by the will of man (7, pp. 57-61).

Unlike many realists in science and elsewhere Montague boldly defends the doctrine of free will. A physical body behaves mechanistically because it is completely at the mercy of its relations to other material bodies. To be in external space is to be subject to the forces in external space. This is the meaning of externality. But living organisms partly escape a deterministic system of enforced states of rest and movement. They do this by remaining in the stream of *time* and *becoming.* A *conscious being acts in accordance with its history.* Its past exists in the present in the form of memory and habit and its future is in part determined by them.

But so far this does not give the sort of freedom which Montague considers genuine. Determinists sometimes hold that for a man to be determined in part by what he is, is the only kind of freedom possible for him. We are free, says the determinist, precisely because our future is in part determined by what we were and now are. Grant that a man's future is already given by his present nature. But, says the determinist, this is *his* nature and its future is *his* self-realization. (After some bodily injury the body immediately sets into motion a highly complex process of healing which is essentially fatalistic. The "will" of the man who suffered the injury has little to do with it. Yet these fated processes realize *his* purposes—it is his body that is being healed.)

Montague rejects this "freedom" which is determinism in disguise. To be determined by one's past history and one's present nature is not enough for a satisfactory theory of freedom. A man wants the ability to deny his past and present nature in some cases, wants to become something different and better than what he now is. "I want, in short, a degree of liberty that will permit me not just to do what I desire, but to do what I desire to desire, what I know that I ought to desire" (7, pp. 52-53).

William James made clear what true freedom implies. James noted that the higher motive is not always the stronger motive. For the higher motive to win when it is in competition with grosser but stronger motives, voluntary effort must be exerted in behalf of the higher motive (7, p. 53). (The determinist may say that if the higher motive wins this proves that in fact it was the stronger motive. But this is circular argument. The determinist waits to see which motive wins, and then labels it the "stronger" motive. This is like the *tour de force* of certain Darwinians. They wish to prove that the "fit" always survive in the "struggle for existence." They wait until *after* the struggle and then label whatever creature survives as "fit." In the case of free-will problems the evidences must come from the period of struggle, not after it. The drug addict who battles against and overcomes his morbid craving may rightly regard as nonsense the idea that his inner efforts had nothing to do with the outcome.)

Montague's philosophy of morals is grounded on Plato's idealistic realism. The great ideals, such as of beauty, goodness, and truth have an eternal existence of their own, independently of the existence of God and the finite world. Perfect beauty and goodness exist even though no earthly thing "imitates" them. Many realists reject this Platonic doctrine and favor the Aristotelian view that forms and their material embodiments are inseparable. Thus, unless there were physical bodies there could be no law of gravity. There is no disembodied elasticity which exists whether or not bodies manifest it. Similarly, such virtues as courage and honesty are not real unless men manifest them. Montague, however, is faithful to Plato. Let all men be cowards and liars, the ideals of courage and honesty are still real. (Let all men, except the youthful George Washington, be liars. This establishes no rule of proper conduct but only grounds for regret. The more numerous the liars, the more we long for honesty.)

Montague believes that there exists in nature and human nature evidences of a finite God who works with us to actualize the eternal ideals.

There are two senses in which Montague considers that the transcendental appears in moral experience: (a) The realm of Platonic ideals transcends this world, and (b) our love and adoration for these ideals is "disinterested." By *disinterested* Montague means that man's devotion to ideals is selfless and thus in a sense transcends the realm of biological necessities. Man views ideals from a distance in the way he views a great painting whose frame sets it apart from the world of contemplation. But it is man's privilege to pursue ideals in the life of action.

An ancient Greek myth tells the story of the hero Prometheus who stole fire from heaven and gave it to man. Zeus doomed Prometheus to eternal punishment until some immortal should consent to give up immortality in his favor. Chiron made this sacrifice to secure the release of Prometheus. Montague calls his own religion and system of morality "Promethean." The fire which Prometheus brought from heaven was knowledge of the eternal ideals. Prometheus taught man the use of fire, i.e., taught man how these ideals could be made real by the power of free intelligence. This won the enmity of the false God Zeus, whose dominance depended on power and authority. This is not the true God of Christianity, who stands for the ideals of eternal goodness, truth, love, and beauty. This God rules men's hearts through a common fellowship of devotion to the ideals. His own son, Jesus, set the example of devotion to love, the greatest of all the ideals. Plato is that philosopher without peer who proclaimed the two great truths upon which morality and religion rest: namely, the existence of supreme ideals and the power of free intelligence to make them real.

Traditional morality has been religious, and traditional religion has been authoritarian, with the result that almost the whole of human ethics has been poisoned by the subordination of right to might, and of the ideal to the materially real. To do the will of God and to interpret righteousness as conformity to supernatural power, has been the cardinal principle of religious ethics. It has given us a morality of commands instead of a morality of ideals. . . . Now, subsistential or Platonic Realism is the doctrine that ideals are real in their own right, that they require not the will of God, nor the might of nature, nor the edicts of society to make them better than they are. They demand of us to actualize whichever of them is pragmatically relevant to a given situation. But demands are not commands, and the appeal of an ideal to be realized on its own merits is as different as possible from the threats of nature, God, or government. . . .

It (the ideal) gives us an assurance that nothing can take away. For, let the course of existence be what it will, ideals remain unshaken because their nature and validity are eternal. . . . Should there turn out to be demons in control of nature, at least they will not be worshipped. The God of a Platonist will be a Prometheus, to be loved because he is good, rather than a Zeus to be reverenced because he is powerful. The present is a time not only of religious disillusionment, but of moral disillusionment as well. Those who have been brought up in an authoritarian religion believe that ideals have no intrinsic validity, and that their claims upon conscience depends upon supernatural power; when they lose faith in the existence of such a power, they lose interest in the appeal of ideals. They may seek to enthrone nature in place of their dead God, or to make the force of the state, either Fascist or Bolshevist, fill the role of commander of the conscience. Both substitutes are hopeless, because both are subordinations of right to might and of subsistent ideals to existent forces.[3]

Montague wrote very little about education. Had he done so, he would probably, like Locke, Herbart, and Spencer, have made morality the prime concern of education. Certainly, Montague's views on the meaning of morality are both lofty and profound. In Chapter 14 which follows, aided by acquaintance with realistic philosophy set forth in Chapters 12 and 13, we will consider two present-day realists, Whitehead and Russell, who wrote rather fully on education. With Whitehead and Russell, we will again encounter the paradox that those who aim to portray reality in its "true" aspects end up with highly individual views about it! This does not necessarily indicate the incompetence of realists as thinkers for reality, with a lordly disregard for consistency, may harbor many possible realities.

References

1. Drake, Durant (ed.). *Essays in Critical Realism.* New York: Macmillan, 1920.
2. Du Noüy, Lecomte. *Human Destiny.* New York: Longmans, Green, 1947.
3. Flewelling, Ralph T. "Personalism." *Twentieth Century Philosophy* (D. D. Runes, ed.). New York: Philosophical Library, 1943.
4. Holt, Edwin B., and associates. "The Program and Platform of Six Realists." *Journal of Philosophy, Psychology, and Scientific Methods,* 1910, Vol. 7, pp. 393-401.
5. ———, and associates. *The New Realism, Cooperative Studies in Philosophy.* New York: Macmillan, 1912.
6. Macintosh, Douglas C. (ed.) *Religious Realism* (a symposium). New York: Macmillan, 1931.
7. Montague, William P. *Belief Unbound. A Promethean Religion for the Modern World.* New Haven, Conn.: Yale University Press, 1930.
8. ———. *The Ways of Things.* Englewood Cliffs, N.J.: Prentice-Hall, 1940.
9. ———. "The Story of American Realism." *Twentieth Century Philosophy* (D. D. Runes, ed.). New York: Philosophical Library, 1943, pp. 419-448.
10. Perry, Ralph B. *General Theory of Value.* New York: Longmans, Green, 1926.

[3] Wm. Pepperell Montague, *The Ways of Things* (Copyright, 1940, by Prentice-Hall, Inc., Engelwood Cliffs, N.J.), pp. 279-280. Reprinted by permission of the publisher.

☿ *chapter 14*

CONTEMPORARY REALISM IN EDUCATION

In his novel, *The Magic Mountain,* Thomas Mann wrote, "The word, even the most contradictory word, preserves contact—it is silence which isolates." Schools of philosophy do not suffer much from the isolation of silence! This, of course, is as it should be in a democracy which thrives, as Madison held, on diversities of opinion freely expressed. To preserve the individuality of contemporary realists who have written about education we will follow the practice of earlier chapters of presenting the views of selected writers as integrated wholes. Educational practices, however, are affected by a pervasive realistic temper existing in unconscious attitudes rather than in systematic pronouncements. Accordingly, this chapter ends with a section on naïve realism in education.

All realisms find common ground in the postulate of an external realm of objects and principles which exist in independence of their being known. In popular usage, being a "realist" also implies preoccupation with opportunism and a crass prudential morality which is blind to spiritual values. The moral philosophy of Montague, sketched in the preceding chapter, shows that realists in philosophy give allegiance to high idealism, and are concerned with universals which extend beyond present realities. Why should a realist not be concerned with ideals which exist and influence observable events no less than the laws and objects of physical nature?

The main sections of the present chapter are as follows:

A. Whitehead and the Aims of Education

Alfred North Whitehead (1861-1947) has had a long career in education, mainly as a Fellow of Trinity College, Cambridge, England, and (since 1924) as Professor of Philosophy at Harvard University. His voluminous writings reveal a philosophy of extraordinary complexity. His general approach to philosophy, typical of realists, is by way of scientific method, leavened with abstruse speculations. He collaborated with Bertrand Russell in producing the notable three-volume *Principia Mathematica* (1910-1913).

Whitehead's realism is more closely allied with new realism than with critical realism. This is shown in his attempts to bridge the separation between nature and mind, rejecting the dualism which, in his opinion, has vitiated philosophy since Descartes (17, pp. 131-144). For Whitehead, real things are fusions of external nature and inner life. Life is at root a process of self-enjoyment or interest. This self-enjoyment occurs when a living being, through creative activity, appropriates and unifies the actualities and the potentialities of nature. It would be a lengthy task to set forth this philosophy fully. Suffice it to say that Bertrand Russell regards Whitehead's recent books as expressing realistic defenses of "a more or less Bergsonian metaphysic" (11, p. 228). We turn now to Whitehead's philosophy of education set forth in *The Aims of Education and Other Essays* (16).

Bare enumeration of the aims of education of various writers appears to show so much agreement that one may wonder why the disputes are so acrimonious and seemingly endless. The main reason for this is, as Sidney Hook discerned, that although the same general labels are used in listing the aims of education, such aims are really different because they are applied differently in practice. A steeplechase over Whitehead's chapter on "The Aims of Education" is thus quite deceptive. We will find him saying that education should cultivate activity of thought, knowledge, sensitivity to beauty and human feeling. But who would deny that education should pursue these aims? But specious agreements about such aims are secured by overlooking individual differences in defining and in applying them.

Even a careful reading of Whitehead's views on education may court deception. His statements about education are often quoted with ardent approval by pragmatists in education, whose ideas still remain to be set forth in Chapters 15-18. Suffice it to say at this point that pragmatic and progressive educators lay great stress on the present needs and interests of the pupil as opposed to pure traditionalism; and set great store by the rule of learning through practical living rather than through textbooks. Whitehead certainly indorses these aims of education but qualifies them in the direction of essentialism in education. We have encountered the tendency of realists in education to fuse essentialism and progressivism, as in Locke, Herbart, and especially in Herbert Spencer. This is not surprising because essentialism rests in part on realistic convictions reaching back to St. Thomas and to Aristotle.

1. The Past and the Present in Education

A well-known passage from Whitehead appears to reject traditionalism in education:

> I would only remark that the understanding which we want is an understanding of an insistent present. The only use of a knowledge of the past is to equip us for the present. No more deadly harm can be done to young minds than the depreciation of the present. The present contains all that there is. It is holy ground; for it is the past and it is the future (16, pp. 3-4).

Taken out of context this forceful endorsement of presentism is easily misunderstood as an acceptance of a practical vocational curriculum which prepares the child for an "insistent present" with its interests and needs. But Whitehead's emphasis on intellectual training, mental discipline, and other things shows that he is leagues apart from Kilpatrick, advocate of the projects curriculum, who also declares that the present aims and interests of the pupil should determine what he studies (see Chapter 18). To prepare the child for the present Whitehead wishes to give him a balanced intellect and character. To attain these laudable ends Whitehead stresses the values of traditional and intellectual subject matter, not projects in agriculture, textiles, shopwork, and cooking!

The present is "holy ground," but the student is prepared for it by the pursuit of literary, scientific, artistic, and technical culture (16, pp. 84 ff.). Whitehead speaks favorably of classic books and languages. The translation of Latin into English and vice versa give training in logic. The student should pursue the "triangle" of English, Latin, and French literature, adding Roman literature for good measure. To these Whitehead adds history and religion! As Whitehead notes, the student would need the life span of Methuselah to properly master the knowledge of the past to equip him for the present!

2. The Practical Aims of Education

Whitehead's statements to the effect that education must be useful are no less emphatic than his endorsement of presentism—and are just as misleading when taken out of context.

Pedants sneer at an education which is useful. But if education is not useful, what is it? Is it a talent, to be hidden away in a napkin? Of course, education should be useful, whatever your aim in life. . . . It is useful because understanding is useful (16, p. 3).

Whitehead's conception of a useful education does include practical utility, as is indicated by his fourth chapter devoted to technical education. He there declares that we must break down the false contrast between liberal education and technical education. Each pupil should leave school with something he knows particularly well and something he does well. These ideas are in harmony with those of John Dewey, the reputed defender of progressive education (see Chapter 16). Like Dewey, Whitehead attacks the false separation of mind and body, as we would expect from his rejection of dualism noted above. Teachers will come to grief if they forget that their pupils have bodies. Not all learning should be book learning. First-hand knowledge acquired in action lies near to the intellectual life. Again like Dewey, Whitehead finds the best source of first-hand knowledge in the technical laboratory.

For Whitehead, the proper ideal of technical training which prepares for earning a living is that work and play should become identical. This, of course, does not exist in today's world of work. The employer who should go on the assumption that work is play would encounter financial ruin within a week! How can one produce workers who enjoy their work? Pay will not do it. Also the adage that "Necessity is the mother of invention" is silly. Observation, says Whitehead, rather suggests that "Necessity is the mother of futile dodges" (16, p. 69). These ideas too are in harmony with strict Deweyism, although not with radical progressives whom Dewey himself castigates.

In his defense of "specialism" Whitehead is a true spokesman for realists with their inveterate stress on exact science. Specialization and selection are inevitable in education. Knowledge is vast and life is short. Life involves specialization in all its phases, hence to avoid specialization in education is to run counter to life. The appreciation and exact formulation of a general principle is made possible only by special study. The well-disciplined mind is at once abstract and concrete in its thinking. These sanctions of specialization, which we also encountered in Spencer, set realism in education apart from the ideal of essentialism (Hutchins and his friends) of a common and general intellectual education for all as required by our common humanity.

Despite Whitehead's "lip service" to technical training for earning a living, he reveals his inveterate intellectualism in what he regards as the most useful of utilities. The way to interest in work is through education for thought and aesthetic appreciation. There must be disinterested intellectual curiosity. The scientist (that model for all workers!) labors to appease his passion for discovery. He wants knowledge in order to make further discoveries. Once again we encounter the literary, scientific, and technical curriculum for breadwinners (16, pp. 74-84).

3. Integrated *Versus* Inert Knowledge

It has been observed that the legal prohibitions and moral taboos of any society point out the things which most tempt the people. The stronger the inclinations toward homicide the greater will be its condemnation and punishment. A "defense reaction" of this sort is shown by realists in education. Whether the charge is warranted or not, scientific realism is blamed for the great welter of highly specialized courses which are especially rampant in large universities. Such "specialism" is severely censured by essentialists as an offense against integrated knowledge. The scientific realist, feeling responsible for the possibility of many highly specialized courses, inclines to atone for it by stressing the virtues of integrated knowledge. This stress appears in Herbart's views on education. It appears very forcefully in Whitehead's condemnation of "scraps of information" and "inert ideas."

Ideas are *inert* if they are learned without being utilized. But Whitehead does not restrict the term *utility* to ideas which have practical usefulness as in vocational training, although such utility is included. The higher utility of ideas is rather found in their power to train the child to the activity of thought. Our life consists in the constant adjustments to each other of our perceptions, feelings, and judgments. An idea's higher utility consists in taking part in this inner experience rather than in outer practical concerns (16, p. 4). To save ideas from inertness they should not remain piecemeal but must be thrown into new combinations (16, pp. 1-2). Studies will be saved from inertness by following them out to their consequences. Thus, algebra makes clear the *quantitative* aspect of the world. Algebra is saved from inertness by showing that quantity is ubiquitous, pervading every sphere of interest. Quantity appears, not merely in the world of matter, but in the rhythms of poetry and music (16, p. 11). It must be said that in thus stressing the integration of different areas of study Whitehead also advocates a decrease in the number of studies. To avoid the "dryrot" of inert ideas studies should be few and thoroughly mastered. (Knowing that Whitehead condemns "inert ideas," and having made no further inquiries about it, it is easy to assume that he has in mind ideas which have no "earthly use"—which do not serve the needs of action. It is clear that Whitehead holds to a much broader conception of inertness. Algebra is not "inert" because it is of no use in baking bread. It can become inert merely because it is not contemplated as the aspect of quantity which pervades all life.)

⩗ B. Whitehead on the Stages of Education

In Chapters 2 and 3 of his book Whitehead touches on problems of mental growth and pedagogy, and again stresses essentialism and realism. Whitehead challenges the principle that easier subjects should precede the harder ones in all cases. (This is to challenge the psychological order of presentation stressed by progressives.) Children learn to speak very early, but from the point of view of difficulty learning to speak is an "appalling task." It is more sensible to arrange the subjects studied in their order of *logical* sequence.

Whitehead speaks of three stages of mental growth which continue in repeated cycles. These alleged stages are not likely to be described in modern works on child psychology, but they are very suggestive. In the stage of *romance* the child first apprehends subject matter in its novelty. The child's first encounter with knowledge will be vivid and interesting because his apprehension of it is incomplete. New ideas will have an enticing aura of half-revealed connections with things lying beyond them. This is much like Herbart's theory of interest. Interest is generated from an incomplete circle of ideas which reach out for fullness. An "apperceptive mass" of ideas seeks for completion. Education at this stage is not systematic, but is alive with the dynamic power of interest. All further education will consist in utilizing this initial ferment of romantic emotional involvement (16, pp. 27-29).

The second *stage of precision* sets the child's chaos of ideas and perceptions in order. This is the stage of *analysis*, both of the grammar of language and the grammar of science. New facts are learned but they are now those demanded by analysis (16, pp. 29-30). This analytical activity constitutes mental discipline. It requires the patient, unyielding, and sometimes plodding application which leads to mastery.

The third stage is that of *generalization*. It arrives at general laws and principles made possible by the stage of precision. Generalization makes possible the utilization and enjoyment of knowledge. For example, after the child has acquired precision of language through language study (analysis) he can utilize language for classifying objects and for enjoying them (16, pp. 30-40).

These stages overlap and repeat themselves. During adolescence there is a new upsurge of romanticism, the greatest the individual ever experiences. It leads to renewed analytical attacks on language, literature, science, history, commerce. University education moves toward still greater generalization without being divorced from concrete facts. If facts are not mastered in the stage of precision the grasp of the general principle will not be secure. Having mastered fundamental principles the student is now able to enjoy mental power. That is to say, he is now able to apply the principles critically and fruitfully. The cultivation of mental power implies acquisition of the ability to apply general principles rather than relying on a knowledge of routine and detail (16, pp. 41-43). This emphasis on acquiring mental discipline by mastering general principles once more links Whitehead with essentialism in education. It also links him with Dewey when properly understood.

C. Bertrand Russell's Philosophy

Bertrand Russell (1872-) will serve as our second British realist who has influenced educational thought. Russell's brilliant scholarship, extensive travels, and lectureships, together with the facile and pungent qualities of his writing, have made him an international figure for many years. His views are sometimes boldly unconventional and iconoclastic, but usually turn out, upon close examination, to reveal a solid common sense which spurns euphemisms. Russell's writings are voluminous. In addition to scores of journal articles, his bibliography up to 1944 includes fifty principal books including one entitled *In Praise of Idleness and Other Essays!*

Like all realists, Russell rejects the attempts of idealism to explain away the vast multiplicity of persons and objects and the realities of evil and error by means of an all-embracing monism of spirit. Russell was under the influence of Hegelian thought in his earlier years. He was inspired to attempt a series of books on the philosophy of science which were to encompass mathematics, social and political questions, and biology. This ambition is reminiscent of Herbert Spencer's synthetic philosophy discussed earlier. Russell's writings are indeed so encyclopedic in scope that his earlier ambition was and is still being fulfilled. Russell has won distinction for his contributions to mathematics and logic in collaboration with Whitehead. Like all realists, he has faith in scientific method and in the findings of science.

If one penetrates beyond the broad characteristics of Russell's realism given above it is discovered that, as in the case of Whitehead, his views are so individual that it is impossible to classify him. The intricacy of Russell's realism is made evident by a symposium on his philosophy by twenty-one scholars (14). Russell's chief complaint about this work was that all twenty-one of the contributors misunderstood him! (editor's Preface). Another complication is that Russell shows the commendable but confusing policy of freely altering his views from time to time as his insights develop or change. As one reader of Russell's works observed, it is well to record the dates when Russell expressed given views so that one Russell may not be mistaken for another! (See Russell's "My Mental Development" in the symposium mentioned.)

1. Russell's World Outlook

Like Spencer, Russell must be accounted an agnostic in religion. Although a "doubter," Spencer's attitude towards religion was sympathetic and "permissive." Russell declares that he knows of no conclusive evidence against the existence of God. Leibniz had argued that some evil in the world may be necessary in order that a greater good might exist. But Russell considers the opposite argument equally compelling. Perhaps some malevolent devil created the world but must tolerate the good in it in order to have greater evil! Far from expressing a callous contempt for religion, these statements express Russell's realistic perception of the insensate cruelties of war and the acute personal suffering they evoke in him. Russell further declines to accept man's need for God as proof of God's existence. The existence of hunger is not proof that the hungry will get food! (12, p. 726).

According to Russell's own testimony, his life has been a search for something which deserved reverence, and which lies beyond the merely human. After abandoning Hegel, Plato's realm of perfect ideals gave him some such satisfaction (compare W. P. Montague, Chapter 13). Russell even sought in mathematics the evidences of an orderly and sublime world existing in the fitful fever of man's world. Russell also finds himself unable to subscribe to a "religion of humanity."

In his eloquent and searching essay, "A Free Man's Worship," in his *Mysticism and Logic and Other Essays* (4, pp. 46-57), Russell grimly accepts the highly probable evidence of science that some day man and everything on earth he holds dear, even the earth itself, will go down in utter destruction. In the face of this awesome doom, Russell salvages what he can to make life endurable while it lasts. There will still be the pleasure of experiencing the splendor of the universe and the enchanting beauty of nature. The enjoyments of culture and of knowledge, the fascinations of thought and discovery can go on. But how is moral peace to be found in a universe in which eventual destruction is the common fate of all men? The only way to peace is through the renunciation of futile personal desires. Freedom will be found when we bow before the inevitable, accept it, and even make it part of ourselves. Having fully accepted fate, we rise above its threats. Having won resignation to fate, we are free to enjoy the pursuit of beauty and truth. But there will be a third pleasure in life: namely, to aid, comfort, and love our fellow men with whom we share a common doom.

2. Russell on Morality

Russell's world outlook sketched above includes, not a "religion of humanity," but an "ethics of humanity." An account of Russell's ethical views will greatly aid our later understanding of his views on education. Russell's thoughts on morality have a special flavor quite unlike those of other writers, even realists. This will appear in a comparison of the ethical views of Montague, sketched in Chapter 13, with the views of Russell. The two special characteristics of Russell's views on morality are: (a) his stress on the part played by primary desires and emotions, and by (b) individual preference in determining whether conduct is good or bad.

a. THE PLACE OF EMOTIONS AND DESIRES IN MORALITY. Russell has shown concern with the problem of individual happiness for many years. His writings on this subject are full of simple and kindly wisdom (9). We are here concerned with his basic postulate that ultimate ethical valuations are *subjective*. By an ultimate ethical valuation is meant a judgment which declares some object or goal as good or bad in itself. This is to be distinguished from judgments about *means* for attaining objects or goals. When there are disputes about moral questions the disagreement is usually about means-toward-ends.

One of Russell's illustrations is the familiar dispute about whether or not capital punishment is right or wrong. The dispute usually centers on the question of whether capital punishment acts as a deterrent. Such questions about *means* are either in fact or theory subject to objective tests. But to say that killing people is bad in and of itself is to express a subjective and personal aversion. (If one should say that killing people is bad due to its evil consequences, then killing is being judged as a *means*, and the evil consequences mentioned now become the personal aversions.) Assertions about questions of *fact* are subject to objective verification, but assertions about what ends are good in themselves are matters of personal desire.

The only universality which an ultimate moral valuation can have is that those who have it desire that others share their desire. In leading others to desire what we desire we use *persuasion* in place of *demonstration*. Such persuasion is quite different from logical proof, but for Russell it is equally legitimate (12, pp. 720-724). Common practice appears to support Russell on this point. We do use the art of persuasion in moral matters, as in sermons, by according praise or blame, and teaching good behavior by example as opposed to precept.

Russell holds that a code of ultimate goods cannot be validated by *a priori* reasoning. Actions are to be judged as good or bad as *means* by the results expected from them, but as *ends* they are subjective preferences whether of one man or an entire population (8, p. 268). Except for its consequences, the only proof that an absolute value is desirable is that it is in fact desired. (We may point out good or bad consequences of a value but such consequences have validity in the light of some other absolute value. The argument that alcoholism ruins health is convincing because health is desired. Health may be accepted as desirable in itself. To support it by further argument we can say that health promotes longevity but now remaining alive becomes the absolute good.) These views have the support of common beliefs. The common man, says Russell, believes that impulses of love and sympathy supply their own justification. A parent usually finds his love for his child justification enough for protecting the child. We doubt the kindness of a man who is kind in obedience to doctrinaire rules and nothing more. In any case, loyalty to such a rule is only another sort of love, and to love the object of kindness is usually felt to be better than merely loving a rule.

The critic will at once attack Russell's morality as subjective and inadequate. It will be noted that "love is blind," that many parents literally "love" their children into delinquency and spineless adulthood. Uncritical kindness may do more harm than good. It must be noticed, however, that Russell allows for *objective* criteria of moral conduct. Factual observation shows that excessive and blind parental love may produce selfish monsters. But this views love as a *means* which cheats one of another subjective preference, namely to have children who are not selfish monsters. Such means-to-ends reasoning is a genuine part of Russell's moral philosophy. It is legitimate to try to reform an evildoer by pointing out that his evil deeds violate some other end which he views as good.

Suppose that a man is about to betray a trust for the sake of personal gain and that he considers the personal gain the greater good. In this case it is rather futile to adduce proofs that the personal gain is a *means* which violates the good of being loyal to a trust. The only recourse left is emotional appeal (persuasion) which exalts loyalty to a trust. We can also, of course, use means-ends arguments. We tell the alcoholic that his habits will ruin his health. We tell the angry man that aggression invites retaliation. We tell the dishonest man that "Honesty is the best policy." But the good conduct produced by such appeals to self-interest has a meretricious or bogus quality. It is not the genuine goodness produced by persuasion which taps good impulses that come from the heart.

The moralists who support rational, empirical, or even *a priori* rules of conduct have a strong case. Doctrinaire rules of conduct produce *consistency* of behavior. They protect the holder from the blindness of impulse which Russell appears to sanction in his subjective view of moral valuation. We have seen, however, that Russell finds means-to-ends reasoning an objective criterion of moral conduct. Clearly, an adequate system of ethics needs to provide a place for both subjective and objective, for both absolute and relative points of view. Russell attacks systems of ethics which rest their cases on supposedly *a priori* absolutes which they regard as *objective*. We will find the root of Russell's distrust of such systems in their tendency to violate the precious values of *individuality*, although they may pay "lip-service" to such values. Absolute rules of conduct tend to become social and doctrinaire "imperatives." Far from always preventing evil conduct or producing good conduct such rules may penalize *harmless* conduct. The sorry tales of religious and political persecutions and the martyrdom of numerous heroes bristle with herd violations of harmless or even noble impulses. All that has been said so far about Russell's subjectivism in morals points to his faith in individuality.

b. RUSSELL AS INDIVIDUALIST.   Like Herbert Spencer, Russell is always waging war against the forces which threaten the inherent preciousness of individuality. These ideas are worth dwelling upon because they have momentous consequences for education. An aristocrat by birth, Russell is nevertheless the bitter enemy of special privilege entrenched in social, financial, and religious institutions. Russell is a democrat in the popular American sense. Government exists to protect individual rights, which rights are limited only by the rights of other individuals. As we are wont to say, "That government is best which governs least."

It is in the individuals, not in the whole, that ultimate value is to be sought. A good society is a means to a good life for those who compose it, not something having a separate kind of excellence on its own account. . . . To believe that there can be good or evil in a collection of human beings, over and above the good or evil in the various individuals, is an error; moreover, it is an error which leads straight to totalitarianism, and is therefore dangerous (13, pp. 73-74).

At the same time, Russell considers it very important to harmonize individual desires. But the harmonization of desires is better procured by persuasion than by arbitrary dictates or force. Our first approach to a man or *child* in the toils of an unwise desire should be one of sympathetic understanding. *This understanding derives from the realization that the very existence of a desire causes that desire to seem good to the man—* and even more to the child. In any case, our attitude should be that only the desire is bad, not the individual who has it. (Desires are not ourselves—they are our possessions. In fact, we are rather their "possessions." Fear is an alien force which, as James observed, "lends wings to one's feet," whether one wants to flee or not. Anger "moves us" like an alien force. But beware of the doctrinaire rule which says that all anger is bad. Bergson declared that there is enough anger in the world to right all wrongs—if properly directed!)

The harmonization of desires should begin in the schools, but we must avoid the zeal which leads to the inhibition of harmless desires. There is sound realism in the principle that if we learn to desire things which we can enjoy without injuring others, we are more likely to attain what we desire for ourselves. Why is love better than hate? Some people may get more of a "thrill" out of hating others than from loving them. But if two people love each other, both can be satisfied. But one of them is doomed to disappointment if they wish to murder each other without being murdered themselves. "Therefore marriage is better than murder, and love is better than hate" (12, p. 740). This reminds one of Spencer's declaration that if robbery benefited both the robber and the robbed, robbery would be a virtue.

▽ D. Russell's Philosophy of Education

Russell's views on the subjectivity of moral valuations and his defense of individuality serve as the main keys to an understanding of his writings on education. In addition to a score of articles and several chapters in books, Russell wrote two books on education. *On Education Especially in Early Childhood,* 1926 (5), also appeared in an American edition entitled, *On Education and the Good Life,* 1926 (5). The second book, *Education and the Social Order,* 1932 (10), also occurs in an American edition entitled, *Education and the Modern World,* 1932 (10). A severe criticism of Russell's philosophy of education by Boyd H. Bode and Russell's reply appear in *The Philosophy of Bertrand Russell,* 1944 (14).

1. The Spirit of Education

Russell criticizes the influence of Dr. Arnold on English education. This education was for aristocrats. It trained men for positions of power in England and in the colonies. Toward this end it cultivated the virtues of energy, stoical reserve, and loyalty to fixed convictions about rectitude. This education neglected the cultivation of critical thinking—which might give rise to doubts! It also failed to stress the development of kindliness—which would not do in governing "inferior" races in the colonies (7, p. 165).

Russell's convictions about individual worth suggest a very different attitude towards education. In a sound educational program pupils are regarded as *ends* (cf. Kant), not merely as means for attaining ulterior goals. The teacher must love children. She will then desire things for the good of the child rather than for alleged needs of the state or, still worse, some "imperative" presumed to have an eternal and unchanging validity. If the individual wants something that is harmless he is under no obligation to prove that securing it will further some purpose beyond himself.

Boyd H. Bode (1) criticized Russell's philosophy of education in that it sharply opposes the interests of individuals and those of society without solving this conflict except by regarding individuality as the supreme good but grudgingly admitting the need for social control. Russell holds that educating for individuality is best, but education for citizenship is expedient. Russell's emphasis on the individual psyche as the source of the supreme good leaves unsolved the rift which develops between the individual and his group.

Russell, however, held that education for citizenship must not be neglected. Russell's point is that *education in the direction of group conformity harbors possible disasters for harmless individual desires* and possible injury even to the social group. In his reply to Bode (12, p. 733) Russell notes that an excessive emphasis on citizenship may lead to the evils of an inordinate nationalism. If Hitler's Germany had given more heed to individuals the Second World War might have been averted. Where the respect for individuality is overshadowed, demagogues seize power. In the end we get individualism of the worst sort. The Germans, having lost their individual rights, became a danger to the rest of the world. To protect ourselves against them we also were forced to give up individuality in order to secure united action. Unbridled individualism is an evil. But let it not be imagined that the unbridled ascendancy of the state is anything better.

2. The Ends of Education

To fulfill the child's needs the educator requires clear conceptions of what Russell calls human "excellencies." Russell joins Locke and Spencer in extolling the importance of physical health and energy. Friendly feelings of the child should be cultivated. An industrial class which has more than its share of the wealth creates rivalry and hostility, and leads to the deplorable exaggeration of the material goods of life and of practical success. The enjoyment of beauty is another kind of excellence (8, pp. 269-288). We now turn to Russell's remarks on excellencies of a more academic and intellectual sort.

3. Knowledge, Intelligence, and Thought

The philosopher Leibniz conceived the world as composed of elementary spiritual beings or monads, each of which reflected the whole universe. As we have seen, this vision inspired Herbart's conception of a universe of outer reals which, by interaction with the inner real of the soul, generated knowledge. Russell too takes his cue from Leibniz. The ideal mind faithfully mirrors the whole world. Russell shares this glorification of knowledge with Herbart, Spencer, Whitehead, and other realists. The high rating which Russell gives to knowledge arises in part as one of those subjective valuations which he defends in his moral philosophy. Knowledge is something resplendent and to acquire it is human. This faith in knowledge can be supported by further arguments but it carries its own subjective validity. (If one does not care for knowledge, that is just the kind of person one is—until the persuasions of others, aided by the school's rules against truancy, lead to conversion.)

Knowledge is glorious but intelligence which discovers it is still greater. Traditional morality, says Russell, has underestimated the virtues of intelligence. He notes that the term *intelligence* properly refers to the capacity to acquire knowledge rather than to knowledge itself. Intelligence as an aptitude is acquired by exercising it, as is the case with other aptitudes. This statement rates as a concession to the claims of formal discipline. It is possible to teach pupils so that they will acquire knowledge without learning how to think. But Russell does not consider it possible to reverse this order and train the intelligence of the pupil without having him acquire information. Russell regards the cultivation of knowledge and intelligence as one of the major aims of education (7, pp. 183-184).

Having developed intelligence as a capacity and having acquired a glorious range of knowledge which mirrors the world as far as it can, *independence of thought becomes possible.* Russell wants independent thinking in individuals and this must become the gift of the many, not of a few favored individuals. Russell sees the power of independent thought as the epitome of man's courage and promise.

4. Interests

To possess interest and romance knowledge must be imbued with emotion. Like Herbart and Whitehead, Russell finds that ideas have their own intrinsic delights. The thirst for adventure which drives men to the South Pole or to the contests of warfare can be directed to creative thought which is not destructive and cruel. Russell rejects the belief that only a few people enjoy mental adventure. Make-believe and fantasy during childhood lead naturally to interest in adventures with ideas.

Where this inclination is weak in adults it is because education has largely killed it (6, p. 108).

5. Mental Discipline

A want of interest in knowledge will at least not stand in the way of acquiring mental discipline through study. Russell notes that higher education especially is able to develop the mental discipline which enables its possessor to concentrate upon any subject despite the fact that it is found difficult and boresome. This instrumental efficiency of the mind cannot be acquired except by forcefully directing attention to prescribed tasks. This valuable habit is usually hard to acquire without outside pressure (6, pp. 103-104). Coercion is sometimes necessary to ensure mastery of the elements of education. There should also be compulsion as regards such matters as cleanliness, punctuality, and respect for the property rights of others. Individuals have to live together in the same world. The individual urge for complete independence must be curbed. It is clear that Russell's individualism provides its own restraints. The individual rights of others set limits upon egotism (5: b, pp. 38-39, 236-237).

▽ E. Naïve Realism and Education

We come now to aspects of education which reflect an unconscious and pervasive realistic temper to be found alike in teachers, pupils, and citizens in general. This realism perhaps exists also in Russell as a "subjective valuation." His advantage is that he has stated his prepossession in words. Most American realists in education are naïve in that they practice their convictions without voicing their presuppositions. Few American writers have formulated realistic views in education in a direct and extensive way. One notable exception is Frederick S. Breed, whose *Education and the New Realism* (2) gives voice to American realistic attitudes in education.

American culture is steeped in realism. We breathe it so constantly from infancy onward that it goes unnoticed. If the reader wishes to test this assertion and is willing to be regarded as a victim of harmless lunacy, he or she needs only to ask the average citizen whether trees are really green, or whether they exist when not perceived! The layman secures assurance in his realism by the simple expedient of not prying too closely, if at all, into the grounds of his realistic beliefs. Philosophers insist on prying into such problems with the result that they raise more questions than they answer. The resulting ignorance, as has been observed by Pascal, is at least an enlightened ignorance. It has been said that one cannot rid oneself of genuine preconceptions because their existence is unknown. The answer to this is that preconceptions need not remain unknown.

The practitioners of philosophies of education other than realism are usually less naïve about their preconceptions. Essentialist teachers know that Hutchins and his friends support their practices, and may know that realism in education has roots extending back to St. Thomas and to Aristotle. Professional educators like Harris, Horne, and Gentile do not lose sight of Hegel's speculative philosophy. Progressive teachers know their dependence on the philosophy of John Dewey and his supporters.

1. The Nature of Learning

Realists are often blamed for the emphasis on rote learning in the traditional school. Dewey, as we shall see (Chapter 16), blames this on the realism of John Locke. Locke held that the mind is like a blank sheet of paper upon which routine learning inscribes its lessons. This is an incomplete account of Locke's views (see Chapter 11). The mind may be passive in receiving impressions. But when it comes to abstraction and generalization, when hypotheses and laws are formulated, the mind is dynamically active. It may be true that the traditional school emphasizes rote learning too much. On this point naïve realists have something to learn from vocal realists in education. Whitehead justifies the plodding mastery of facts provided it is followed by actively relating the facts, thus leading to general principles. General principles are not understood unless their exact relations to facts are seen. Herbart, Spencer, and Russell agree in condemning the mere rote learning of inert knowledge.

2. Departmentalization and Integration of Knowledge

Realism leans toward the ideal of the love of knowledge for its own sake. Truth is something wholly objective. Knowledge is a relation between the mind and its objects which leaves the objects unaltered. Truth exists before man discovers it—exists whether or not man discovers it. Montague declared that the statement that Mars is inhabited by intelligent beings is now either true or false. Truth does not wait upon verification. When verified it becomes man's knowledge of the truth. The realist, like his scientific companion-in-arms, therefore looks upon knowledge as something austere and awesome, before which man should bow in deep humility.

Knowledge, like the nature which it presents or represents, is intricate and yet orderly. Hence, in the schools knowledge must be acquired by the systematic study of a systematic curriculum. Realism is blamed for the excessive departmentalization which sometimes besets education, especially in the case of higher education. For instance, a 1952 report shows that in only four colleges in New York City (Hunter, Brooklyn, City, and Queens) there was a total of sixty-five fields of specialization (15)! There are thousands of different courses of study in the high schools and colleges. However glorious this may appear to the realist, the student knows that every one of these courses involves mental labor in one form or another!

Here is a difference between essentialists and realists: We recall how Hutchins condemns the proliferation of courses and the inevitable employment of specialists as teachers. The specialists get to the point of "specialism" where they cannot understand each other—even when in the same department. Such education, says the essentialist, neglects the needs of our common humanity. But Whitehead and other realists defend such specialism, especially in higher education which gives professional training. No generalization, Whitehead holds, is really grasped unless its relations to details of fact are fully understood. (Many students can "recite" Newton's law of gravity. But give them the relevant facts and ask them to *prove* that the earth's movements conform to the law!)

As though feeling a sense of guilt about the dissected state of knowledge realist teachers often seek to correct it by stressing *integration*. Herbart and Whitehead serve well as spokesmen in this enterprise. Attempts to secure integration, however, are usually half-hearted and not very effective. One device is to create interdepartmental majors. Comprehensive examinations will not yield very extensive integration if confined to a given field of specialization. Another plan for realizing integrated knowledge is to require each student to take basic "divisional" courses each of which covers broad areas, such as material science, biological science, the humanities, the arts. These divisional courses can be integrated by special integrating courses followed by comprehensive examinations.

The predicament is that when more time is given to integration, less time remains for acquiring knowledge to integrate. "Divisional" or "survey" courses are likely to be thin in content, pausing in many places only to move on again at once as though all partings were sad but long overdue! This conflicts with the ideal that every graduate should have something which he thoroughly understands and something related to it which he can do well. The same predicament arises if we set aside some colleges or college years for general education and others for professional training. As Whitehead notes, if students had the life span of Methuselah these difficulties would fade away.

The problem of a surfeit of specialized knowledge is met by some realists by recourse to essentialism and traditionalism. For the child, at least, Whitehead recommends that ideas introduced should be few and important (16, p. 3). He emphasizes knowledge which bears on an "insistent present." But this does not cut out traditional subjects, for Whitehead regards the present as including the past and the future! Moreover, the courses of study he recommends are mostly those exalted by traditionalists. Montague also defends a curriculum of traditional courses as against the modern rage for elective courses and an "over-emphasis of futurism."

To leave a child free to study any subject or none is simply to deprive him of his social inheritance. He cannot choose intelligently until he knows what there is to choose from. . . . The child is intellectually and culturally naked, and the only life he knows independent of our teaching is the forest life of his instincts. Why should we expect him in the name of "individuality" and "self-realization" to repeat all that the race has learned by generations of trial and error? To abstain from all compulsion and all prescription in the teaching of children is, we repeat, merely to rob them of their rightful social heritage (3, p. 142).

3. The Practical Value of Knowledge

We will take the term *practical* in the sense of that which serves some useful end through *action*. This does not deny the practical value of such things as contemplation, aesthetic enjoyment, and philosophical resignation when action is helpless against fate. The realist is in a secure position in holding that systematic knowledge of the scientific kind he favors will be the most practical. Without departments staffed with specialists in the universities we would not have competent doctors, surgeons, engineers, or even ministers of the Gospel. The realist may appear to agree with progressive education through vocational projects but this is only appearance. It is one thing to lead a child from a project in cooking to acquire a smattering of chemistry. The successful chemist is the product of systematic study of chemistry through a logical sequence of courses involving related disciplines. Suppose that medical students were trained by starting them on a project which they found interesting, and then coaxing them to study other things they will need for practicing medicine. This might succeed if we could triple the length of time now required to turn out a medical doctor. We will do better, the realist says, to *require* medical students to study an indispensable array of courses in a specified sequence *whether they like it or not.*

We have noted that realists appreciate the Platonic love of knowledge for its own sake. Realists are capable of courageous and selfless devotion, but it is devotion to truth not primarily inspired by the love of humanity. We may witness here a vindication of the Biblical statement to the effect that he who loves his life shall lose it. In the long run, the pursuit of "pure" knowledge for its own sake will benefit mankind more than a myopic preoccupation with immediate needs.

Michael Faraday, playing with an induction coil, made the invention of the dynamo possible. The non-Euclidean geometers concocted strange systems, outraging familiar beliefs about triangles and parallel lines. It is now considered, however, that certain of the new systems describe reality better than does Euclid's geometry. The radio was invented by Marconi—after Heinrich Hertz discovered the existence of "radio" waves. It was Burbank who created new plants, not the practical farmer. It is not easy to ban certain courses of study on the ground that they are not practical. For, no one can declare in advance what knowledge will and what will not be practical. When Arago talked about electrical conductors he was laughed at for his pains; now every boy of ten years knows about them. When Spencer declared that some day the air would be traversed with objects heavier than air, he was viewed by "practical" folk as an idle dreamer. History has an embarrassing way of revealing that practical people were often merely dreaming when they imagined themselves to be wide awake!

4. Measuring the Products of Education

Realism, both vocal and naïve, is considered responsible for the vast *testing movement* in education. Edward L. Thorndike, who shared some basic views with Herbart, is regarded as a pioneer in the testing movement. Thorndike declared that whatever exists, exists in a certain amount, and whatever exists in a certain amount is in theory subject to measurement. At present, psychometrics is a vast and intricate enterprise, with thousands of tests for measuring a multitude of aptitudes and achievements; and is accompanied by an elaborate growth of experimental and field-research methods and methods of statistical analysis.

An atmosphere of realism and science pervades this aspect of education. Tests must be *reliable* in the sense in which yardsticks, thermometers, and clocks are reliable. A test would be ideally reliable if it yielded the same scores when reapplied to the same testees. This aim encounters difficulties which the specialist in mental measurement attacks tirelessly. To say nothing about variations of score due to a long list of outer and inner situational factors, the living subject *learns,* making impossible the scientific ideal of repeating an observation under the same conditions. Undaunted, the psychologist tries to calculate the effects of learning and thus make an allowance for it in measuring mental capacities other than learning. But after all causes of score variance are measured which can be measured, the testee still insists on earning different scores at different times! But do not be discouraged. It is very doubtful whether one of the countless leaves which fall from trees ever fell in strict accordance with Newton's universal law!

Tests must also be *valid.* A test is valid if it measures what it was intended to measure. Specificity of measuring instruments appears in the exact sciences. Rulers measure length, not time; thermometers measure temperature, not weight. But in exact science too there is the problem of definitive measurement. An old-fashioned pendulum clock runs faster on warm days, so that it mixes measures of time and of temperature. But the material scientist is able to employ exact criteria for correcting false measurements. Such validating criteria for psychological and educational tests are not easy to find. Actual performance in a course of studies may be used to validate an intelligence test, but the agreements (correlations) are far from perfect. The problem of proving that a test measures the aptitude it was intended to measure may become acute. As G. Undy Yule observed, failing to measure that which was intended, the psychometrist may measure something else in place of it and forget the difference (18)!

5. Prelude to Book V

We turn now to a set of four chapters dealing with the educational theories of a vast company of modern educators. The philosophical grounds of this new movement are found in the pragmatic philosophy of William James, continued in altered form in the instrumentalism of John Dewey. Reared on the postulates of a transmuted pragmatism is a ramifying structure of educational principles and practices variously known as reconstructionism, experimentalism, the experience curriculum, progressive education, and the project method. The pragmatic philosophy of James is already a thing of the past, with few avowed defenders in the present. A number of serious weaknesses in James's philosophy were corrected in the instrumentalism of John Dewey. Upon this reinterpretation of pragmatism Dewey founded a theory and system of educational practice which spread rapidly through the United States and even to some foreign countries. The four chapters of Book V attempt a systematic account of pragmatism and instrumentalism and the educational theories and practices founded upon them.

References

1. Bode, Boyd H. "Russell's Educational Philosophy." *The Philosophy of Bertrand Russell* (P. A. Schilpp, ed.). Evanston and Chicago, Ill.: Northwestern University Press, 1944, pp. 621-642.
2. Breed, Frederick S. *Education and the New Realism.* New York: Macmillan, 1939.
3. Montague, William P. *The Ways of Knowing.* New York: Macmillan, 1925.
4. Russell, Bertrand. "A Free Man's Worship." *Mysticism and Logic and Other Essays.* New York: Longmans, Green, 1918, pp. 46-57.
5. ———. (a) *On Education Especially in Early Childhood.* London: G. Allen & Unwin, 1926. (b) *On Education and the Good Life.* New York: Boni & Liveright, 1926.
6. ———. "Education." (From *Why Men Fight.*) *Selected Papers of Bertrand Russell.* New York: Random House, 1927, pp. 37-110.
7. ———. "The aims of education." (From *Education and the Good Life.*)

Selected Papers of Bertrand Russell. New York: Random House, 1927, pp. 159-193.

8. ———. "Moral Standards and Social Well-being." (From *The Prospects of an Industrial Civilization*.) *Selected Papers of Bertrand Russell*. New York: Random House, 1927, pp. 263-294.

9. ———. *The Conquest of Happiness*. London: G. Allen & Unwin, 1930.

10. ———. (a) *Education and the Social Order*. London: G. Allen & Unwin, 1932. (b) *Education and the Modern World*. New York: Norton, 1932.

11. ———. "Philosophy of the Twentieth Century." *Twentieth Century Philosophy* (D. D. Runes, ed.). New York: Philosophical Library, 1943, pp. 227-249.

12. ———. "Reply to Criticism." *The Philosophy of Bertrand Russell* (P. A. Schilpp, ed.). Evanston & Chicago, Ill.: Northwestern University Press, 1944, pp. 681-741.

13. ———. *Authority and the Individual*. New York: Simon & Schuster, 1949.

14. Schilpp, Paul A. (ed.) *The Philosophy of Bertrand Russell*. Evanston and Chicago, Ill.: Northwestern University Press, 1944.

15. West, Leonard J. *College and the Year After*. New York: Board of Education, 1952.

16. Whitehead, Alfred N. *The Aims of Education and Other Essays*. New York: Macmillan, 1929.

17. ———. "Philosophy of Life." *Twentieth Century Philosophy* (D. D. Runes, ed.). New York: Philosophical Library, 1943, pp. 131-144.

18. Yule, G. Undy. Critical notice on the work of William Brown and Godfrey H. Thompson. *British Journal of Psychology, 1921-1922*, Vol. 12, p. 107.

book 5

PRAGMATISM, INSTRUMENTALISM, AND EDUCATION

§ *chapter 15*

PRAGMATIC PHILOSOPHY AND THE
INSTRUMENTALISM OF JOHN DEWEY

The establishment of daylight saving time was criticized on the ground that it lowered the respect of the young mind for the truth. This criticism appears playfully jocose because we reflect that the use of clock time is no more than useful convention having nothing to do with truth or error. Such things are matters of practical convenience. They sometimes take on the semblance of truth in that, in order to be useful, everyone must accept them. We turn now to pragmatic philosophy which defends the bold hypothesis that *the truth of any judgment or idea is tested by and consists of its success when applied to practical life situations.* In so far as ideas produce fruitful results when applied to experience they are true ideas.

The pragmatic movement in philosophy is indigenous to the United States and is said to express the practical, down-to-earth temper of Americans. This flair for the practical approach to experience is exemplified by the fabled Yankee from Missouri who meets all claims with the challenge, "Show me!" Pragmatic philosophy made its advent under the leadership of William James although the groundwork had been laid by Charles S. Peirce. It rallied to its banners a host of critics of idealism. Pragmatism found a stalwart leader in John Dewey, who reshaped it into his philosophy of instrumentalism. John Dewey was a great educator as well as philosopher. In time, still harboring the general ideology of pragmatism, instrumentalism became one of the main supports of that vast ferment in

American education known as progressive education and the project method.

Of the four chapters of Book V, Chapter 15 first gives a brief account of the pragmatism of Peirce and James followed by a fuller account of Dewey's instrumentalism. Chapter 16 gives an account of Dewey's philosophy of education based on his instrumentalism. Chapter 17 traces the European origins of child-centered education, its advent in the United States, and its gradual development as progressive education. Chapter 18 is devoted to a special aspect of progressive education inspired by William H. Kilpatrick, known as the project method, and reviews earlier and current criticisms of progressive education.

Following is an outline of the main divisions of the present chapter:
A. The Pragmatism of Charles S. Peirce and of William James
B. The Career of John Dewey
C. Transition to Dewey's Instrumentalism
D. Dewey's Instrumental Theory of Knowledge
E. Pragmatic and Instrumentalist Metaphysics
F. Dewey's Instrumentalism in Ethics
G. An Instrumentalist's Religion

⚡ A. The Pragmatism of Charles S. Peirce and of William James

Charles S. Peirce (1839-1914) was the first to use the term *pragmatism* in an article (22) which probably would have been forgotten had not William James in 1898 called attention to it and elaborated it as a method for attaining knowledge and as a theory of truth. But James made certain interpretations of the term pragmatism which Peirce rejected. Peirce coined the term *pragmaticism* for his own philosophy to keep others from confusing it with the pragmatism of James. (Peirce remarked that the ugliness of the term "pragmaticism" might deter someone else's stealing it!) It is therefore usually considered correct to say that James is the founder of pragmatism as it is generally understood. Without the zealous support of James it is doubtful whether pragmatism would have become an important movement in philosophy.

1. The Pragmatism of Charles S. Peirce

Peirce, a mathematician and logician of repute, held to a now rather familiar view regarding the main steps of scientific research. (a) Having an array of verified observations on some problem, the scientist formulates a hypothesis concerning them. (b) He next deduces what further consequences would follow, assuming the hypothesis to be valid. (c) The scientist now tests the consequences expected, and modifies this hypothesis, if necessary, in the light of the additional findings. The hypothesis, if modified, now serves as the first step in another triune of steps. This procedure may continue indefinitely.

Peirce's conception of pragmatism begins with a theory of *meaning*. What determines the meaning of a hypothesis, a proposition, an idea? Peirce's answer was that the meaning of our idea about anything is found in our notions of the *sensible effects* of the thing in question. Our conception of an object is determined by whatever consequences we anticipate the object will have, which consequences are objective and observable. Our conceptions of the sensible effects which the object of our thought may have is the *whole* of our conception of that object.

So far, this gives only the *meaning* of an idea the mind may entertain. What determines whether or not the meaning we assign to anything is *true* or *false?* This, Peirce said, depends on the results of experience, whether casual or experimentally designed. Our idea about an object will be true if the sensible effects we expect from it actually occur. It will be noted that such verification of the truth or falsity of an idea involves *action;* it involves doing something. This germinal idea is at the root of the project method of education, as will be seen in the later discussion of the application of pragmatism to education as made by John Dewey and a host of successors.

An important point to remember about Peirce is that he regarded the tests which determine truth or falsity of ideas as subject to *objective* and *public* verification. That is, your personal observations of the sensible effects of things and the results of your actions must be verified by external and public evidences before their truth claim is established. This principle reminds us of the views of realists, with which the pragmatism of Peirce has strong kinship. Montague held that the falsity of the insane man's hallucinations is shown by their failure to meet both physical and social tests of truth. The false objects this man claims to see cannot be photographed or weighed, and other observers fail to see them. In William James's version of pragmatism, as we shall see, some ideas are regarded as true despite the fact that their verification is entirely private.

So far we have seemed to confine Peirce's theory of meaning and truth to ideas about particular things. Peirce's intention, however, was to apply his pragmatic theory to *general principles and laws* as well as to particulars. For example, the statement, "This lemon is yellow and has a sour taste" is verified by visual perception and by tasting it. These ideas become general in the rule, "All lemons are yellow and are sour to the taste." All of the principles and laws of science are generalizations derived from particular perceptions and actions. From the practical point of view all such laws are rules of expectation and action. Knowing that all bodies fall we act accordingly in handling a fragile vase. Since we believe that such general laws are true, it may be said that *all beliefs are rules of action*. Now, beliefs lead to *habits*. The belief that bodies fall leads to numerous habits in dealing with them. *A habit is thus the bodily equivalent of an earlier idea which led to a belief*. Different ideas and beliefs are distinguished by the different actions and habits to which they lead. As applied by later pragmatic educators, this means that the task of education does not stop with imparting ideas (knowledge). The teacher's further task is to establish in the student the useful beliefs and habits of action he will need in life both in the school and later on.

The condensed account given above of Peirce's pragmatism may be clarified by some examples. What is the meaning of the idea of quinine? Peirce would say that its meaning lies in anticipated and observable effects which we believe quinine will have. For some individuals the word "quinine" is meaningless. It is not yet part of their meaningful vocabulary. After they look up the word in Webster's they will have some of the essential meanings of the word. The dictionary tells them that quinine is a bitter alkaloid got from the bark of species of cinchona which grow in Peru. Quinine is used to abate fever, etc. Every one of these details about quinine is potentially subject to verification through sense observation.

The meaning of things which become truths when scientifically verified vary in richness. Quinine has the richest meanings for one who is a combined pharmacologist, physiologist, chemist, and medical practitioner. The truth about quinine may not be exhausted for many years to come because it may yield sensible effects as yet unobserved. Perhaps its meaning can never be fully exhausted. Thus, the redoubtable soybean is famous for yielding more and more novel by-products as though it were as inexhaustible as the universe itself. Aristotle meant something like this when he said that matter was *pure possibility*.

Peirce's principles for determining meaning and truth are treasured as devices for steering science clear of numerous notions and disputes which are idle because they fail to suggest concrete ways of testing their truth or falsity. Again, sometimes there are disputes about rival theories, which, so far as is known, fit the facts of observation equally well. The sensible way for deciding between them is to set up a situation in which the sensible effects of the two principles would be different, and in this way decide whether we are confronted with two principles or with but one. If it is impossible to conceive an observable situation which might show a difference between two principles, then the principles must mean the same thing. *Every valid distinction must rest upon observable differences.* The agreement of popular opinion with these ideas is shown by the language we use. We describe any sound idea and the person who utters it as "sensible."

2. The Pragmatism of William James

James (1842-1910) was not always clear and consistent in stating his pragmatic philosophy. His utterances on moral philosophy were somewhat scanty, and his treatment of metaphysical questions was unsystematic. We shall give chief attention to James's pragmatism as a *method of acquiring knowledge* and as a theory of the *meaning of truth*. These are the two aspects of James's thought which will concern us most in our later and fuller account of Dewey's philosophy. All pragmatists, in fact, have been so concerned with the problem of how the mind knows reality that they tend to neglect the question of the nature of the reality known.

a. PRAGMATISM AS METHOD. James agreed with Peirce that pragmatism offered a method for answering questions without favoring any special answer in advance:

A pragmatist . . . turns away from abstractions and insufficiency, from verbal solutions, from bad *a priori* reasons, from fixed principles, closed systems, and pretended absolutes and origins (16, p. 51).

The reader will note the implied rejection of idealism in James's adverse remarks about *a priori* reasons and absolutes. Also, the many things that pragmatists "turn away from" to start with do not speak very well for the claim that pragmatism does not stand for any particular result! What should we "turn to" in testing the meaning and truth of an idea? We should turn, says James, to the observable consequences of an idea's being true. In the case of scientific ideas, the procedure is clear enough. We have but to try to make the observations which the idea suggests, and then accept or reject the idea accordingly.

b. JAMES EXTENDS THE PRAGMATIC METHOD. James made extensions of the pragmatic method which went beyond the intention of Peirce and which raised a veritable storm of controversy. James extended the pragmatic method to *moral* questions and to religion (14, 23). James held that the consequences which follow the application of a moral belief determine whether or not that belief is right or wrong, true or false. This completely rejects the attempt, as with Kant, to determine rules of moral conduct by *a priori* reasoning, made before the rules are applied to conduct. It also rejects the view that the rightness or wrongness of conduct is determined by mere authority or by revelation. This view of James, that morality has its basis in observing the effects of conduct, was defended by John Dewey—indeed, was common enough both before and after James's relatively scanty treatment of the subject.

James's application of the pragmatic method to religious beliefs went far beyond what Peirce intended, and far beyond good sense as conceived by the contemporaries of James or, for that matter, by most subsequent thinkers. James held that pragmatism was broader than ordinary empiricism. Empiricism usually confines itself to scientific questions about material phenomena. Peirce had held that observable results which may verify the truth of an idea are both objective (sensible) and public (subject to verification by others). James at times appears to grow restive under these restrictions. James was above all a psychologist and individualist. He had no prejudice against religion because some of its claims such as the existence of God, are not subject to direct objective verification. The inner good feelings which result from accepting religion are also observable effects even though they cannot be demonstrated objectively with laboratory equipment and are not verified by all observers. Solitary experience can also have its truths. (To make sure that a hot flame can cause pain do we have to burn more than one observer? Is it entirely meaningless and false to say that some person gives one "a pain in the neck" because the neck does not show any abrasions? Are we to suppose that Robinson Crusoe knew truth only because he had at least his man Friday to join in the verification of truth?) As regards religion, James held that if religious beliefs have value for life's practical struggles, if they give inner comfort and courage, then they *are* verified by experience and are to that extent true. Pragmatism, says James, could not deny the existence of God if belief in His existence satisfies the demands of one's inner experience. (It is not necessary to demonstrate God's existence by locating His position in the universe of stars.)

It must be noted, however, that *James warns us against the acceptance of beliefs which clash with other vital beliefs.* This statement is one of those wily devices which enable a philosopher to retreat from difficulties or to withdraw again the things he has given us! James notes that it is vital for us to believe that proofs are objective and public. The belief in God as an invisible being manifested to us privately clashes with the desire to verify beliefs objectively and publicly (16, pp. 77-78).

c. JAMES'S THEORY OF TRUTH. We shall have to speak of James's "usual" view of the nature of truth because he was not always consistent in his utterances. His usual view of truth will appear in clear relief when contrasted with certain conceptions of idealists and realists. In the naïve thinking of common sense contradictory notions of truth live together in peace. We sometimes follow the practice of absolute idealists and speak of "truth" in the singular as though separate truths belonged to one unified whole. Again, we join the realist (cf. Montague) in regarding truth as being quite as objective as the physical world to which truth refers. This is shown in the belief that truth is "discovered" by us, that it existed both before its discovery and after the discovery is forgotten. This is the tribute common-sense realism pays to Platonic realism.

Pragmatism, often hailed as the champion of common sense, differs so radically from the views of truth indicated above that common sense is inclined to repudiate it. James rejects truth in the sense of an eternal and unchanging whole. Truths are *plural*, are *made*, and are *changing*. Idealistic beliefs about truth are hypostatized abstractions. That is, idealists have made a *thing* out of truth and set it up as something existing objectively and independently. James said that we hypostatize health and strength in the same way. If a man eats and sleeps soundly, enjoys freedom from illness, and can work with great vigor, we say this is because he is full of "health." If he endures protracted toil we envy his reserve of "strength." Now health, says James, is not a *thing*, but a *process*. It is a manner of functioning of the bodily organs, a set of functional relations. Nor is the word *health* properly used in the singular unless we mean it in the collective sense (like a school of fish!). We have as many healths as we have different ways of efficient organic functioning. (To illustrate James's idea further, we may say that a victory in an athletic contest was due to "team spirit." But we do not think that this factor of success is something that could be isolated and weighed, injected into the players, and shed with their clothing. Team spirit is a functional relation between the members of the team which is nevertheless subject to the tests of observation.)

For James, truth is on about the same footing as health and strength. *Truth is a functional relation between our ideas and the sphere of our thinking, feeling, and action.* James prefers this to the realist's "copy" theory of knowledge. To be sure, you may speak of your mental images, as of a familiar house, a song, or a plunge in cold water, as "copies" of experiences. But how could an idea be a copy of the *sublimity* of the song, or of the thought that Greek is a more difficult language than Spanish? But truth can always be the normal and healthy relation between our ideas and our behavior—a true idea is one which "works in practice," just as a healthy heart performs its functions successfully (16, Lectures 5 and 6). James's functional account of truth clearly opposes the idea that truth is objective, and that truth merely presents or represents realities to us. James gives truth a functional and psychological status.

James's view of truth as a psychological function is reinforced by his view about the categories of understanding. James rejected the idea of Aristotle that the categories (such as of space, time, and causality) are characteristics of reality; and he also repudiated Kant's idea that they are *a priori* forms of knowing. James held that the categories are *invented* by the mind. They are not acquired either by discovery or by *a priori* endowment. The chief function of the categories is not to give understanding but to give aid in the control of experience. Such categories of common sense as *things, sameness, difference, body,* and *mind* are aids in dealing with experience. They are aids when we wish to communicate our experiences to others, and they are aids to action. Thanks to the category of causality we can set about at once looking for ways of removing the causes of evil things and for instituting the causes of good results (16, Lecture 5).

A final stock-taking will show the radical departure which the "radical empiricism" of James made from idealistic and realistic ideas favored by common sense. First, there is no longer an objective truth which is "discovered." Truth is only a successful adjustment between our ideas and needs on the one hand and the world on the other. Truths are therefore, to some degree at least, "made" or "invented." Ordinarily we believe that certain things are true whether man knows them or not. The Copernican system of astronomy was true long before Copernicus. The Ptolemaic astronomy was false even while men believed it to be true—false in spite of the fact that it can be used to predict the movements of plants.

Now according to the radical empiricism of James, propositions become true or false only after verification. Since man does the verifying, he in a sense aids in making truths and errors to be what they are. Truth and error are attributes of man's ideas, they are his attitudes toward his ideas. (The motorist's belief that he is the lord of the highway is true for him—until he collides with another motorist who holds the same opinion about himself.) The tests of experience "make" truth which did not exist before. This is why truth is precious—it is won through risks and painful toil. Education exists as an institution to reduce these hazards for the individual. Activity-centered education, which pragmatists favor, seeks to keep alive in the mind of the pupil the preciousness of knowledge and its full comprehension by asking him to seek it or "create" it with his own efforts.

Another thesis of radical empiricism is that *truths change.* A belief is true if it leads to successful ways of attaining desired results. Now ideas differ in the degrees to which they satisfy these requirements. The Ptolemaic astronomy *was* verified by such observations as could be made by the ancients. The movements of planets *could* be accounted for in terms of this system. The Ptolemaic system was therefore true. The astronomy of Copernicus represents a *growth* in truth because it fits many more facts of observation and makes astronomical descriptions and predictions easier. There was also a *change* in truth, since the theory of Copernicus is the opposite of the Ptolemaic theory in essential respects.

It was formerly believed that malarial fever was caused by sleeping in rooms with open windows. This belief was true as far as it went. We now believe that the open window merely lets in the malarial mosquito! Einstein's relativity theory does not show that Newtonian physics is entirely wrong: It includes Newtonian physics in a more complete system. The greater truth of the new physics arises from its fuller usefulness. This fuller usefulness includes its fuller conformity with observations. It provides better ways of both thinking and acting successfully. The platitude that "Knowledge is power" is pragmatic in spirit.

Who knows what the science of the next decade will declare as true? But changing truth may shrink as well as grow. If a man dies he cannot take his "bodily health" with him. Similarly, if we forget precious wisdom, precious because it can guide behavior, it ceases to exist for us. If the universe contains no more than brute matter there could be no truths even though this matter followed exact laws. There would be no truths because there would be no minds to evolve them. We here seem to encounter idealistic conceptions concealed in the framework of James's pragmatism. But the pragmatist is earth-bound. Truth grows in the minds of men: It is not the dialectical unfoldment "of itself to itself" of an Absolute Mind.

d. JAMES'S METAPHYSICS. So far, in James's "radical empiricism," truth is not something objective—it is made by the mind. What is left to supply the arena in which the experiencing individual "makes" truth? James seemed content to let our experience itself be our universe. His views on the nature of reality were quite incomplete, as they are for most pragmatists. We will discuss the metaphysics of pragmatism more fully in our account of Dewey's philosophy. For James, the universe was not itself a system, hence needed no system to portray it. Reality is a concatenation of many things and forces which show more plurality than unity. The world shows a great variety and mixture of good and evil things, freedoms and restraints, uncountable objects differing in kind, conflicts in the midst of harmony. The universe is at least partly indeterminate, and man is partially free. The world can then be made better through man's efforts (meliorism). Even God is limited in power. Yet God is friendly toward man, and we may by our labors further God's larger purposes (14).

Due to bad health which got worse after 1899 James could not have constructed a fully developed system of philosophy had he desired to do so. The thought of James contained strong realistic elements which influenced the revival of realism discussed in Chapter 13. In spite of his lack of "system," or even because of it, James continued to be America's dean of philosophers. His philosophy was concrete, a philosophy of life which Americans tend to manifest wordlessly in their struggles for spiritual and material progress.

3. William James and Education

The ideas just reviewed have signal consequences for education. Peirce's views of meaning and truth, and still more the views of his positivistic successors would make the exact branches of knowledge the basic curriculum. James opens the portals once more to the realms of imagination. He also makes inner feelings valid tests of the existence of their objects. Poetry, art, and religion bring adventures with truth as much as does science. Above all, knowledge has reference to man's needs and his actions in satisfying them. For James, not all needs are of the "bread and butter" variety. There are also the satisfactions of contemplation and of attitudes toward things. But the bearing of knowledge on man's biological and social needs was singled out for special emphasis by Dewey, as we shall see.

Except for a few special lectures and other writings James made no published contributions to the literature on education (15). His work in psychology, however, exercised tremendous although indirect influences on education. James established the first psychological laboratory in America (1876); and his two-volume work, the *Principles of Psychology* (1890), was translated into a number of languages and influenced college instruction in psychology for many generations. These two volumes were the result of about nine years of patient work, and are still considered as at once scientific and literary masterpieces. James's psychology expresses his pragmatic philosophy. We are thus able to say that James exercised a direct influence on the psychology of education and a rather indirect influence on the philosophy of education. Dewey testifies that his instrumentalist philosophy of education was much influenced by James's work in psychology.

We turn now to the life and work of John Dewey who, rather reluctantly, agreed to be called a pragmatist. He altered it and rechristened it *instrumentalism,* and made it the inspiration of a new and vast reform in education.

⍜ B. The Career of John Dewey

1. Early Career

Philosophers usually rate John Dewey (1859-1952) with William James and Josiah Royce as the three greatest American philosophers. Our biographical chronicle of Dewey will be brief. We give attention only to the aspects of Dewey's career which particularly influenced his later philosophy of education. William T. Harris, great leader of idealistic philosophy in education, exerted an early influence on Dewey. The young

Dewey sent some of his philosophical writings to Harris. Harris found merit in them and gave Dewey encouragement. This was an important factor in Dewey's decision on a career in philosophy (21, pp. 5-6). Shortly after this Dewey went to Johns Hopkins University to start his graduate studies under the guidance of George S. Morris. Morris strengthened Dewey's grounding in the idealism of Kant and Hegel, and interested Dewey in such British neo-Hegelians as Edward and John Caird and Thomas H. Green. During this early period Dewey was an idealist in his convictions, and wrote some books from the idealistic point of view.

2. Dewey's Experiences in the West

Dewey's career at the University of Chicago (1894-1904) was crucial for American education. At Chicago Dewey served as chairman of the Department of Philosophy, as director of the School of Education, and as head of an experimental school for children. This school was a model for what later came to be known as progressive or project schools. Later on (1904), Dewey became professor of philosophy in Columbia University, but by this time he had profoundly changed his philosophy, abandoning idealism and adopting the pragmatism of James (25, pp. 531-534).

While Dewey lived in the West the region went through a depression and recovery. Dewey was impressed by the courage and self-reliance of Westerners in the face of misfortunes. They preferred to guide their own destinies rather than enjoy the passive security of federal control. The people, only a few generations removed from the pioneers, were unconventional, caring little for the culture of the past except for certain religious, moral, and social concepts. Westerners lived largely for the present and were forward-looking. The students in Western universities exceeded their Eastern counterparts in "academic resistance" to the liberal arts. Western youths saw their destinies in a world of agriculture and in business and industrial progress. They wanted vocational and professional instruction, hence the large agricultural, engineering, and other departments typical of Western universities.

It is easy to see the pragmatic and democratic principles inherent in this Western culture. For Westerners, as for William James, experience is never fixed—it is a constant flow of change both repetitive and novel. The significance of life was found in the present and in the future. When the future dawns, it too must be reconstructed. Knowledge for its own sake was regarded with suspicion or with little more than mild respect. Knowledge was looked upon as a tool for advancing progress in its numerous aspects. The value of knowledge was tested by its practical fruits. In the West, Dewey got visions of the greatness which a self-reliant democracy might achieve. Dewey, a son of Vermont, was no doubt a social and political equalitarian at heart; and his sojourn in the West did no more than rouse him from his "idealistic slumbers." Dewey's conversion to pragmatism and his championship of pragmatic ideas won for him influence and popularity in the West which he lost to an extent in his later years at Columbia University (1904-1929).

Dewey has been accorded great honors, among which the following deserve special mention: He was selected to give the Gifford lectures in England, published as *The Quest for Certainty,* 1929 (5). He enjoyed international repute, especially as educational adviser to such countries as China, Japan, Russia, and Turkey. Dewey was at one time considered as a liberal party candidate for the presidency. His writings are profuse, but most of them fall into one or both of two categories, philosophy and education. His publications in philosophy include works in logic, ethics, aesthetics, and religion. His main works in education will be our concern in the two chapters which follow. We have now to sketch Dewey's instrumentalism in philosophy upon which his theories of education rest.

⬧ C. Transition to Dewey's Instrumentalism

1. Agreements between James and Dewey

Dewey accepted James's insistence that he (Dewey) was a pragmatist. In his *logic* (1938), however, Dewey expressed a preference for the term *instrumentalism* or *operationism,* which terms are free from some of the ambiguous and questionable elements in the pragmatism of James. Both pragmatism and instrumentalism are revolts against what Dewey considered to be the other-worldly abstractions which idealistic philosophers were defending as "concrete universals." Both James and Dewey find the meaning and the truth of an idea in its observable consequences. Both of them stress the importance of a forward-looking philosophy in a changing world. Dewey writes that for pragmatism general ideas "are the bases for organizing future observations and experiences. Whereas for empiricism, in a world already constructed and determined, reason or general thought has no other meaning than that of summing up particular cases, . . ." (10, p. 462). Both James and Dewey look askance at the doctrine of eternal knowledge. Truth has difficulties in remaining eternal, for the discovery of truth may lead to the destruction of the very reality which the truth asserts. Addison W. Moore, a forceful spokesman for pragmatism, gives a striking example of how a true assertion can lead to the negation of evidences upon which it rests and thereby destroy itself. When the dentist discovers the tooth which causes the pain this knowledge is the first step in eliminating the tooth and the truth that it is the cause of pain (20, p. 92).

2. Some Differences between James and Dewey

Although James held to rather unorthodox views regarding the nature of God and of the proofs of God's existence, he may be counted as a defender of religious faith and religious living. With Dewey, on the contrary, we get an unqualified "religion of humanity" in which all transcendental beliefs are rejected. Dewey's approach to all philosophical and educational problems is predominantly *social*. He goes the length of supposing that all problems of philosophy arise from man's social problems. This idea will be encountered later in Dewey's philosophy of education. James's orientation is more catholic—he submits all problems to the pragmatic test and sees numerous aspects of progress besides the social. Some have noted that Dewey is interested in the evidences of *unity* and *harmony* to be found and to be sought in the stream of experience. This tendency of Dewey, which will be encountered in his philosophy of education, is regarded by some as the lingering vestige of his earlier acceptance of idealism. James, on the other hand, is an unqualified *pluralist* who sees the world filled with a multitude of clashing and individual forces.

Dewey's most important departure from James concerns the pragmatic theory of truth: namely, that the truth of any idea or proposition is determined by its successful consequences—that an idea is true if it "works" in practice. There are at least three ways in which knowledge is practically useful: (a) It is useful if it promotes understanding, if it orders and explains observations. Any law of science has this type of usefulness. (b) An idea may be useful in our practical dealings with nature. Most of the laws of science, if not all of them, have this kind of usefulness. (c) An idea may be useful merely because it is emotionally agreeable or comforting, and hence enables one to live more effectively. James accepted all three of these tests of the truth of an idea. Dewey, like most critics of James, rejects the third test of truth. To accept the idea of God as true on the ground that it is satisfying goes beyond the pale of legitimate empiricism.

D. Dewey's Instrumental Theory of Knowledge

1. Darwin's Influence on Dewey

Darwin's theory of evolution set forth in his *Origin of Species* (1859) had immediate effects on social thought in America and elsewhere (12). Diverse interests, despite their mutual hostility, claimed the support of Darwin. Thus Karl Marx in 1869 hailed *The Origin of Species* as supporting his views concerning the class struggle in history. Militarists and imperialists saw in Darwin the justification of warfare as a means for furthering the dominance of the strong over the weak. Although Darwin had been talking about the struggle for survival among pigeons and other animals, militarists saw no inconsistency in applying it to man! But man, unlike an animal, finds the question of *how* he may survive dwarfed by the more baffling question of *why* he wishes to survive. The militarists who invoked Darwinism were guilty of the fallacy of ambiguous terms. By survival value Darwin meant *biological* survival value, which does not necessarily imply *moral* survival value. The ambiguity of terms appears in assuming that being able to survive in fact is the same thing as being worthy of survival.

This misuse of Darwinism also involves the fallacy of "genetic models." In fact, the principle of evolution itself makes it clear that living things cannot be defined in terms of their origin. Man is *not* an ape precisely because he *evolved* from them. Those who criticize Darwin make the same error as the militarists who accept him. Religionists consider that the notion of man's origin from apes belittles man. But more credit is implied by the thought that man rose from the apes than by the idea that he descended from the angels. John Dewey, fortunately, invokes Darwinism to serve a constructive purpose in his philosophy of education.

2. Dewey's Use of Darwinism

Before Darwin published his startling ideas, intelligence had not been viewed primarily as a biological function. We recall from Book II the acceptance by essentialists of Aristotle's view that men should exercise reason simply because they are rational creatures by nature. To be rational was to be human. The life of each creature manifests what it is by nature. At the same time Aristotle regarded rationality as the divine element in human nature. These Aristotelian thoughts continued through later history, appearing in Scholasticism and even in current times with Neo-Scholastic educators like Hutchins and Adler.

Darwin, however, viewed intelligence as a rather late product of evolution, developing gradually to reach its most potent form in man. Intelligence, like all other biological functions, came into existence as a tool in the struggle for existence. This reason for being reasonable is quite unlike Aristotle's view that reason should be exercised because it is human or even godlike to exercise it. The pragmatists, as we would expect, found the Darwinian outlook congenial to their own views.

Dewey was the first philosopher of education to make systematic use of Darwin's ideas. Dewey looked upon intelligence as one of man's chief tools for securing adaptation. But Dewey did not forget that man had to adapt himself to mankind as well as to nature. He did not forget the endless social and cultural problems faced by man which go far beyond the mere problem of biological survival. In Darwin's scheme of things there appears to be no aim of evolution except more evolution! It has been said that if bees formulated the goal of existence it would read, "The more bees, the better." But evolution also means growth to a new stature, to a richer and more rewarding kind of existence. Now Dewey saw that for man, education is the chief process by which growth into a more ample and significant life is made possible. Man does not evolve by hereditary transmission and natural selection alone, but by social transmission. Social transmission is mediated chiefly through the institution of education. But Dewey still regards nature as man's home. The child in school, no less than the animal in the forest, should learn to exercise its mind and body by encountering in school the concrete problems of adaptation which constitute living. Intelligence is an *instrument* of adaptation.

3. Psychological Influences on Dewey

Dewey approved some elements in the behavioristic psychology of John Watson. Watson's "stimulus-response" psychology was consonant with Dewey's view that the chief function of the nervous system is to coordinate the senses with motor responses for the purpose of securing adaptation (10, p. 464). It is not the function of hearing and vision to secure knowledge of the world merely for the sake of knowing. The senses lead to motor channels—nature intended the senses to guide action. The senses and muscles are *instruments* for successful living. Although Dewey accepted the general model of a stimulus-response psychology, he does not give it the mechanistic connotations typical of behaviorists. Dewey has no objections to "mentalistic" concepts such as purposes, feelings, satisfactions, and the like, which Watson and his school wished to exclude from the consideration of psychology because they are not objectively observable.

Dewey acknowledged the influence on him of James's *Principles of Psychology* (1890). Dewey was a member of the Chicago school of functional psychologists, like James R. Angell, Harvey Carr, and others, who held that all mental processes are tools of adaptation. In his *How We Think* (1933) Dewey develops this conception of the biosocial function of thinking. In his *Studies in Logical Theory* (1903) Dewey worked out a full experimental theory of logic. Dewey rejected as futile and unimportant the view of rationalists that the chief function of reason is to contemplate reality. He said that such contemplation is a legitimate source of satisfaction, but it is *aesthetic,* not intellectual (2, p. 397). The rules of correct thinking do not have *a priori* existence and validity. There are no transcendental ways of verifying the rules of logic. Such rules are revealed by an empirical study of how man actually thinks, and are validated by their success in meeting practical problems. Such empirical study of thinking shows that all ideas are plans of action. For Dewey, the value of an idea as an instrument of successful action establishes the truth of that idea.

▽ E. Pragmatic and Instrumentalist Metaphysics

The utterances of pragmatists about the nature of reality are so incomplete that they have been accused of having no metaphyiscs. This situation was due in part to the extensive attention given to pragmatism as a method of knowing. The thesis that the pragmatic method stood for no particular result may explain the differences among pragmatists themselves concerning the results. It is difficult to give a brief account of the pragmatic theory, or rather theories, of reality. A brief account would be so general that it would violate the ideal of concreteness held by pragmatists. We have little choice, if space is to be conserved, but to sketch a metaphysic which is in harmony with most pragmatists.[1] The main tenets of pragmatic metaphysics, some of them neither clearly stated nor agreed upon by all pragmatists, are as follows:

1. The Objectively Given

Knowing their unanimous objection to idealism we would expect all pragmatists to reject the view that objective reality ever becomes identical with our knowledge of it. They should join the realists and insist on the existence of an objective realm of things which is not identical with our knowledge about it. Like common-sense folk, pragmatists appear to have taken the existence of an objective world for granted. They neglected to order their ideas about it. Dewey said that his instrumentalism certainly assumed the existence of an independent reality. He declares that he has asserted *ad nauseam* the existence of realities which exist before and after we know them (24, p. 553). The trouble is that other statements made by Dewey are not so clearly realistic.

Dewey and other pragmatists often speak as though *experience itself* were the only reality. But experience has two aspects: *that* which is experienced and the *process of experiencing it*. If the process of experiencing, on which subject the pragmatists are voluble, is *identical* with that which is experienced, we get a view which looks suspiciously like Hegel-

[1] The reader interested in summary and critical material on the metaphysics of pragmatism will do well to study the chapter offered by John L. Childs, who is a pragmatist interested in its application to education (1, Chapter 3). Sidney Hook offers a volume on pragmatic metaphysics (13).

ianism. But there would still be the difference that the pragmatist confines experience to man in his mundane world, whereas Hegel universalizes it as an adventure of the Absolute. Yet Dewey often writes like an inveterate realist about things being "just what they are." Most students of pragmatism confess themselves at a loss in trying to understand what theory of reality this school accepts. The critics say that pragmatists waver between an idealistic and a realistic conception of reality. Pragmatists sometimes speak of an obdurate external reality, which is what it is irrespective of our experience of it, while at other times nature and its laws are regarded as reflections of the categorizing activity of the mind.[2]

2. The Multiplicity of Nature

Reacting against the alleged tendency of idealists to unify things to the point where all distinctions fade away, James stressed the plural aspects of reality. Reality is a great concatenation of a multitude of separable things and persons. There are, of course, lines of mutual influence between things as shown by physical science, and between individuals in a society. But it is not possible, short of the "blindness" of Hegelianism, to overlook the differences between such things as mind and body, the subjective and the objective, good and evil, beauty and ugliness, truth and error. The pragmatist has no need for discovering some all-embracing reality which lies beyond human experience. Dewey, as we have seen, manifests a greater tendency than does James to find unity in the world. The important point is that the unity found by Dewey is not one which *identifies* different things. The unity which Dewey finds is one of *functional* or *organic* relationships. The individual is not asked to identify himself with his social group—he cooperates functionally with his group.

3. Reality as a Changing Stream

Our experiences in the world suggest that it is not constant, given once and for all. It is a realm of insurgent change. So also the very minds with which we contemplate reality are streams—streams of consciousness, James called them. This thought also appeared in Peirce, who held that a belief is merely a temporary resting place. Growing experience is bound to alter beliefs and enlarge them. There is nothing permanent or static in

[2] Thus, Clarence I. Lewis, a pragmatic logician, holds to a definite realism. According to Lewis there are two aspects of physical things which are objective. First are their sensuous qualities (e.g., snow is white); and secondly, objective things are not altered by our mental attitudes towards them (18). George H. Mead, on the other hand, is not so sure that there are objectively given things which are clearly separable from our ideas about them (19).

reality as man knows it. The belief that there are eternally changeless realities in a transphenomenal world is not subject to any kind of pragmatic verification.

4. The World Is Precarious

The all-embracing stream of change which even alters solar systems becomes a whirlpool in man's unstable social world. There may be black and unseen abysses from which destructive forces may rush forth, engulfing man and his flimsy structure of civilization. Physical reality neither loves nor hates man, but he must foresee and prepare for her chameleon-like changes. Progress is not inevitable. Biological evolution shows the regressive mutations of plants and animals and the development of parasites. Human society finds no rest from its struggles against parasitism in forms more numerous in society than is revealed in animal biology. John Dewey wrote as follows concerning progress:

The direction, the quality of change, is a matter of individuality. Surrender of individuality by the many to someone who is taken to be a super-individual explains the retrograde movement of society. Dictatorships and totalitarian states, and the belief in the inevitability of this or that result coming to pass are, strange as it may sound, ways of denying the reality of time and the creativeness of the individual (9, p. 107).

5. Man's Freedom

Pragmatists do not show much unanimity about the nature of man's freedom. All of them would agree that man is free, but that his freedom is limited by numerous circumstances beyond his control, including some factors in his own nature. James came the nearest to holding to a psychological theory of free will (see his chapters on the will in the *Principles* and *Briefer Course*). James held that by fixing voluntary attention upon a weaker impulse to action it may be made to prevail over a stronger impulse. It is reason which tells us that a weaker but more ideal impulse *ought* to prevail. But it is the will, expressing itself through the activity of attention, which *actualizes* a weaker but better impulse. It will be recalled that Montague (Chapter 13) approved these ideas of James as meeting the requirements for true freedom. We are free, not merely because our existing desires are realized, but because we can desire and actualize what we *ought* to desire. (For instance, the embattled soldier, by fixing attention on the call of duty, may cause this acquired, weak, and yet ideal impulse to prevail over the biologically stronger impulse to flee the battle.) In the end, however, James tells his reader that the question of free will is a problem of philosophy, not to be solved on strictly psychological grounds.

Because the world is constantly changing, all pragmatists see in it the possibility of growth, of change in desired directions. Man can and does find opportunity to engage in experimentation and alter the "stream of experience" to his own liking. The passage cited above from Dewey clearly shows his belief in the reality of freedom and that the individual is its agent. In order to act freely man must exercise both intelligence and action. Intelligence can foresee desirable ends and plan their attainment, but without action most worth-while goals are missed. Dewey's religion of social morality (see Section G below) also shows that he regards the individual as free and responsible for his behavior. Like most common-sense folk whom they claim to represent, pragmatists find the proof of freedom in its practice. James found freedom in effort of attention. The individual who will make the effort will secure empirical proof that effort makes a difference—it aids in the attainment of the goal.

☿ F. Dewey's Instrumentalism in Ethics

Dewey's moral philosophy is chiefly recorded in *Human Nature and Conduct* (3), *The Quest for Certainty* (5), and in *Ethics* (6). Dewey rejects all views which regard moral values as being absolute, eternal, and as having *a priori* validity. Moral values are subject to perpetual *reconstruction* as required by increasing knowledge and social change. Values, however, have a *relative permanence*. The good is not merely good for a given day—it must be good in the long run. Also the good is not merely individual. A thing is not necessarily desirable because someone desires it, or satisfactory because someone finds it satisfying. *Behavior is satisfactory, good, and right only in the light of all foreseeable results for all persons involved.*

For Dewey, as for Hegel, the supreme good of the individual is related to the social good of the group. But Dewey looks for goods in *human communities,* not in the entire universe, as does Hegel. What are the relatively permanent values for Dewey? Without discussing them in detail one may perhaps venture the generalization that Dewey regards the democratic society as the most precious of all values, under which one can subsume those lesser values commonly revered in cultured democracies. Freedom of thought and of speech should be complete. Freedom of action should be restricted only when and to the extent that moral and legal considerations advise restrictions. The interested reader will find details regarding Dewey's democratic idealism in three of his books (4, 8, 11).

∇ G. An Instrumentalist's Religion

Dewey's most systematic statement about religion is given in his little volume, *A Common Faith* (7), consisting of lectures given at Yale University under the Dwight H. Terry Foundation. If the proper meaning of being religious is determined by tradition, then Dewey's "religious" individual is not religious at all. Being "religious" in Dewey's sense of the word does not require that one must believe in a supernatural realm and a deity. It does not imply the acceptance and practice of any form of worship of institutional religions. Dewey defines "religious faith" in terms of his instrumentalism.

1. Conflict between Religion and Growing Knowledge

Dewey claims that about the only common characteristic of various religions is the belief in a supernatural realm and in the divine. Dewey is at pains to point out the excessive variations of beliefs and practices of different religions, held together only by a tenuous common faith in supernatural things. Religions differ so much in their conceptions of God or of the Gods that if we eliminate the differences nothing is left except "the bare reference to something unseen and powerful" (7, p. 4). Also religions vary widely in their ways of expressing reverence for and obedience to their favorite powers. There has been worship of animals, ancestors, ghosts, and phallic symbols. Reverence has found expression in human sacrifices, sexual orgies, as well as in the humble prayers of Christians (7, p. 4). Even the moral motives of religion show great variation. Brotherly love for its own sake may exist along with good conduct inspired by fear or by the hope of heaven.

Opposed to all religions are those who consider that all beliefs in supernatural things are discredited by modern knowledge. Dewey offers his own point of view as a solution of the conflict between religion and atheistic unbelief. Dewey proposes, with the unbelievers, to reject all beliefs in supernatural realms and powers. Yet, there will remain a way of life, freed from superstition, which Dewey considers may be called religious.

2. Dewey's Biosocial Morality

After rejecting the realm of the supernatural we still have the visible realm of nature and of human association. Above all, we still have the moral values of human experience which have given us adaptation and security, and sustained us in periods of darkness and despair. There are three ways in which we secure adaptation to life. The first of these is *accommodation*. When we encounter bad conditions which are unalterable we find accommodation by altering ourselves (like Mohammed who went to the mountain which could not be brought to him). If this fails, we may accommodate by becoming inured or conditioned to the unfortunate circumstances and thus find them less trying. The second way of meeting difficulties, which Dewey prefers to call *adaptation,* consists in actively altering conditions to suit our needs. We *reconstruct* reality instead of accommodating ourselves to it. This dynamic type of behavior is a cardinal principle in Dewey's instrumentalism, which might better be called *experimentalism* or *reconstructionism.* In addition to the two modes of reaction described there is a more inclusive, permanent, and deep orientation to life which Dewey calls *religious* (7, pp. 14-17). What is the meaning and source of this inward religious orientation?

3. Dewey on the Meaning and Source of Being Religious

Dewey finds the sources of being religious in *imagination,* from which poetry and art also draw their strength. Science and empirical logic give us facts and principles duly formulated. These facts and principles, although they have pragmatic significance for the future, relate to knowledge of the past and present. But imagination projects us into a future which is partially indeterminate. We envisage in this future the actualization of things which are nascent possibilities in the present. The self by its very nature looks forward to good things lying in the future, but not so far away as eternity; The actualized values which imagination sees in man's prospective future are his present *ideals.* Our realization that these ideals may be made real by our efforts is *faith.* Ideals, for Dewey, are not states of affairs which are assumed to exist already in some transcendent sphere of their own. The reader will note that this rejects Plato's realm of eternal ideals and the absolute idealist's doctrine that from the point of view of the Absolute the universe is becoming that which it already is, that perfection already exists and that error and evil are but appearances.

Faith, for Dewey, is not mere belief resting on intuition or revelation. *Faith is, rather, the conviction that certain conditions and things could exist, should exist, and includes our willingness to devote all our intelligence and power to bring about their realization* (7, pp. 18-22).

Dewey's religion is clearly an idealized social morality. He states and defends it with seductive eloquence:

The ideal ends to which we attach our faith are not shadowy and wavering. They assume concrete form in our understanding of our relations to one another and the values contained in these relations. We who now live are parts of a humanity that extends into the remote past, a humanity that has reacted with nature. The things in civilization we prize most are not of ourselves. They exist by grace of the doings and sufferings of the continuous human community in which we are a link. Ours is the responsibility of conserving, transmitting, rectifying and expanding the heritage of values we have received that those who come after us may receive it more solid and secure, more widely accessible and more generously shared than we have received it. Here are all the elements for a religious faith that shall not be confined to sect, class, or race. Such a faith has always been implicitly the common faith of mankind. It remains to make it explicit and militant (7, p. 87).

Dewey's faith is ostensibly based on human experience. Even faith in things envisaged for the future is seen in terms of reasonable and realizable possibilities in the present. Human society offers precious ideals to be sought and attained, not in a hypothetical heaven, but on our familiar earth, which dispels distrust in its reality because it can be touched, seen, and validated in other instrumental ways.

Yet, for many realists it will seem that Dewey's "religious" individual will have to outdo religious saints in mustering courage against the irrationality and hopelessness of man's life as science sees it. For, consider that man's animal ancestry stretches back in time to some dim and unknown origin. Looking ahead, it is seen that each individual faces annihilation which will in time overtake the earth itself. The mind, as empirical evidence shows, depends on the continued normal functioning of the body. In short, we do not know where life came from, but evidences show that it hangs on a tenuous thread which will break and plunge each living creature into an unknown doom. In this extremity Montague turned to the vision of permanence in Plato's realm of ideals, and mankind in general turns to religious faith. As for Dewey's social ideals, which are for him the highest of all ideals, what becomes of them when humanity itself is eventually destroyed by some cataclysm of nature, perhaps even one released by man's own hand? Was it Dewey's empirical logic or an irrational yet sublime faith which led him to struggle so long and so effectively in the service of social ideals, while at the same time accepting the pragmatic method which shows that change is the essence of reality and that all things must come to an end?

References

1. Childs, John L. *Education and the Philosophy of Experimentalism.* New York: Century, 1931.
2. Dewey, John. *Democracy and Education.* New York: Macmillan, 1916.
3. ———. *Human Nature and Conduct.* New York: Holt, 1921.
4. ———. *The Public and Its Problems.* New York: Holt, 1927.
5. ———. *The Quest for Certainty.* New York: Minton, Balch, 1929.
6. ———. (with James H. Tufts). *Ethics.* New York: Holt, 1932.
7. ———. *A Common Faith.* New Haven, Conn.: Yale University Press, 1934.
8. ———. *Freedom and Culture.* New York: Putnam, 1939.

9. ———. "Time and Individuality." *Time and Its Mysteries* (Series II, Ch. 3). New York: New York University Press, 1940.
10. ———. "Development of American Pragmatism." *Twentieth Century Philosophy* (D. D. Runes, ed.). New York: Philosophical Library, 1943, pp. 451-468.
11. ———. *Problems of Men.* New York: Philosophical Library, 1946.
12. Hofstadter, Richard. *Darwinism in American Thought, 1860-1915.* Philadelphia: University of Pennsylvania Press, 1945.
13. Hook, Sidney. *The Metaphysics of Pragmatism.* Chicago: Open Court, 1927.
14. James, William. *The Will to Believe and Other Essays in Popular Philosophy.* New York: Longmans, Green, 1897.
15. ———. *Talks to Teachers on Psychology and to Students on Some of Life's Ideals.* New York: Holt, 1899.
16. ———. *Pragmatism, A New Name for Some Old Ways of Thinking.* New York: Longmans, Green, 1907.
17. ———. *The Meaning of Truth.* New York: Longmans, Green, 1910.
18. Lewis, Clarence I. *Mind and the World Order.* New York: Scribner's, 1929.
19. Mead, George H. *The Philosophy of the Act.* Chicago: University of Chicago Press, 1938.
20. Moore, Addison W. *Pragmatism and Its Critics.* Chicago: University of Chicago Press, 1910.
21. Nathanson, Jerome. *John Dewey, the Reconstruction of the Democratic Life.* New York, Scribner's, 1951.
22. Peirce, Charles S. "How to Make Our Ideas Clear." *Popular Science Monthly,* January, 1878.
23. Perry, Ralph B. *Essays on Faith and Morals.* New York: Longmans, Green, 1949.
24. Schneider, Herbert W. *A History of American Philosophy.* New York: Columbia University Press, 1946.
25. Wright, William K. *A History of Modern Philosophy.* New York: Macmillan, 1941.

$\overset{\circ}{\triangledown}$ *chapter 16*

DEWEY'S PHILOSOPHY OF EDUCATION

Henri Poincaré declared that familiar things are the most mysterious.
The very dust under our feet harbors inscrutable problems for the scientist. Pragmatism, the earth-bound philosophy, illustrates the maze of confusions aroused by the attempt to clarify daily human experience. This
is not to say that the idealist's search for transcendental realities is all
sweetness and light! We have now to consider Dewey's application of
instrumentalism to an earth-bound conception of education, and remind
ourselves that to act on a philosophy involves a calculated risk similar to
the faith in things unseen required by religion. In order thoroughly to
discuss the educational ideas of Dewey there will be little space left in
this chapter for other pragmatists in education. We give brief attention
in advance to Bode, Counts, Mead, and Childs.

Boyd H. Bode (1873-1953), perhaps the most lucid interpreter of
Dewey, was a competent defender of pragmatism. He wrote on philosophical and psychological subjects, and wrote several important books on
education (3, 4). Bode was important in the development of progressive
education (see Chapter 18). Together with John Dewey, Harold O. Rugg,
and others, Bode fought to save the new movement from various fads and
excesses which were contrary to the teachings of Dewey's instrumentalism.

George S. Counts (1889-   ) has been an important figure in
American education for many years. He served as professor of education
at a number of institutions including Yale, Chicago, and Columbia. He is
the author of over a dozen books dealing with many aspects of educa-

tion. His most searching books deal with the areas of the philosophy and sociology of education (9, 10).

George H. Mead (1863-1931) was primarily a social psychologist but also a leader of the pragmatic movement. He was a member of the small group of pragmatists and functional psychologists led by John Dewey at the University of Chicago. Mead has long been recognized as an important contributor to instrumentalism. Although Mead wrote very little on education, his ideas have so much importance for education that Alfred S. Clayton wrote a book on the subject (8).

John L. Childs, an exponent of Dewey's instrumentalism, is the author of a book setting forth the significance of instrumentalism for education (7). The educational philosophy and principles of practice of William H. Kilpatrick, representing certain modifications of Dewey's ideas in education, will be discussed in Chapter 18 on the project method.

The main aim of this chapter is to set up Dewey's philosophy of education as based on his instrumentalism. There are four main subjects to be covered, as follows:

A. The Autonomous Status of Education
B. The Aims of Education
C. Clearing Away Dualistic Obstructions to Continuity
D. Education as the Continuous Reconstruction of Experience

⚥ A. The Autonomous Status of Education

Dewey restricts education to the mundane world, but within these confines he gives it a place second to none. Education becomes, so to speak, the most significant activity on the surface of a relatively insignificant planet. Education is the chief agency for conserving, reconstructing, and transmitting the ideal fruits of human culture. Dewey claimed that philosophy in the large sense is a general theory of education. This means that philosophy seeks to discover the meaning of human experience and from this to determine how man should live. Philosophy thus supplies a general theory of education, which by common consent prepares youth for successful living. But if education is carried out according to Dewey's instrumentalism, it is itself a vital form of living. Therefore education is seen by some as the chief if not the sole determinant of what our philosophy of life should be! Hence the much exercised question of the autonomy of education.

1. Deweyism Implies the Autonomy of Education

Dewey regarded education as preeminently a social function. Gentile, overstressing Hegel's view of the state, put education under the complete authority of the state. Dewey, however, considers it false to infer that, because education is a social activity supported by society, it should be determined by social and political demands external to it. Educators should be free to determine their own ends, *coordinate* with political power, not subordinate to it (6, p. 623). The aim of society is not merely to enjoy the fruits of acquired culture, but to provide for its further development. Such reconstruction of experience, as Dewey prefers to call it, means social evolution achieved through individual growth. Now the educators, who in the universities also include leading scientists and scholars in other fields, are in the best position for determining what evolution and growth are like, what directions they should take, and the means which will realize them.

2. Critical Comments on the Autonomy of Education

Some American educators have advocated that educators should try to win political control and thereby exert political leadership in reconstructing society. George S. Counts, a leader of progressive education, made an exploratory attempt in this direction during the severe economic depression of 1929 (9). As a result of this and other incidents, some critics have suspected educators of the tendency to harbor subversive and totalitarian ideas. In Chapter 18 we shall see that this distrust has survived to the present day, and is especially directed against leaders of progressive education. Counts's venture to win political control for educators came to nought because, for one thing, educators could not agree on the form which a reconstructed society should take. Educators, rather indifferent about matters of personal salaries, are less complacent when their favorite theories are challenged. Plato declared that rulers of the state should be philosophers. In this case, however, only a single philosophical dictator is advisable—two of them would produce a chaos of ideological warfare.

ᯤ B. The Aims of Education

If Dewey's conception of the most general aim of education were expressed in brief compass it would be about as follows: The aim of education is to lead the learner, through his own spontaneous impulses and interests, to achieve growth through participation in and reflection upon the democratic ways of living. Also the learner should develop the capacity for elastic adaptation essential in a democratic society and should learn how to reconstruct experience to suit the needs for further growth in the present and for the sake of an idealized future.

The condensed formulation given above could be broken down into its main ingredients as follows:

1. The Learner Is Led, Not Driven

The learner should pursue the aims of education through the impulses, aims, and interests which he happens to have when he falls into the hands of an educator (or when an educator falls into his hands!). This cardinal principle of student-centered education will be discussed in full later on.

2. The Special Aims of Education Are Not Fixed

The essentialists and idealists, perhaps like laymen in general, first set up a goal of endeavor and then select means to suit the goal. But for Dewey the separation of means from ends is an invalid dualism. Upon close examination many so-called "means" yield more pleasure than the ends sought. Raising grain, building houses, or inventing machines is as much fun as eating the grain, living in the houses, and using the machines. Conquering the world, as Alexander the Great learned, is less desirable than having more worlds to conquer. Dewey had genuine insight into the zestful minds of the young, who are as happy to be on their way as to get there.

Darwin's ideology, which influenced Dewey, will explain Dewey's belief that aims grow out of experience—they do not direct all experience from without. The problem of an animal is to continue living: How this is done depends on the total situation. This is the way generals fight their battles. Darwin held that animals meet novel situations through natural variation and the survival of the fit. Natural variation occurs as an unconscious variation of gene structure. But human beings meet novel situations, not by waiting hopefully for a suitable natural variation, but by exercising reconstructive imagination which proceeds experimentally in discovering new adaptations. Man, unlike an animal, has the conscious desire, not merely to live, but to live well; he has the desire to *grow*. This may be regarded as a "constant" aim, but it is only a general and empty form, to be given process and content as the exigencies of life require.

3. Action Is Prior to Reflection in Time

Logically considered, thought and action are on an equal footing, but from the point of view of time Dewey gives action a certain priority. In ordinary routine living we engage in spontaneous action in the pursuit of felt urges. But sooner or later difficulties will be encountered. We are then driven to think—perhaps as a "last resort," as C. I. Lewis says. Applied to education, this means that we should first discover the pupil's impulses to action and then arrange to indulge them, perhaps setting the stage in advance for difficulties! The difficulties will lead naturally to reflection—the teacher's opportunity to educate the mind. This stress on action as prior to thought is basic in Dewey's experimental theory of thought and to the entire movement of progressive education.

4. Education Is a Social Process

The child's environment, even in most of its physical aspects, is *social*. His food, clothing, and shelter no less than his culture are in large measure the gifts of human nature rather than physical nature. The ideals the individual cherishes for the future of society are lofty enough to constitute his religious faith.

But before the minds of men can institute the process of education as it should be, Dewey believes that a number of false ideas must be swept away. These encumbrances which stand in the way of an integrated theory of education are certain false distinctions or *dualisms*, conceived and perpetuated by philosophers of the past.

ᐁ C. Clearing Away Dualistic Obstructions to Continuity

Dewey discusses the vices of dualism in his famous *Democracy and Education* (11).

1. Four Dualisms in Brief

The first dualism to be mentioned may perhaps be regarded as the parent of the other members of a disreputable quartet.

a. THE OPPOSITION BETWEEN DOING AND KNOWING. This is the idea that while acting one seldom if ever learns anything, and that in order to learn anything one has to stop acting and reflect—which is at the cost of not getting anything done! This is an error which at least has the repute of a long history extending back to classic Greek philosophy. We set this "parent" dualism aside for later treatment.

b. PASSIVE *versus* ACTIVE LEARNING. The first scion of the opposition of knowing and doing is the distinction between learning in terms of the knowledge which is learned and learning in terms of the development of the learner. Learning as *knowledge* is regarded as the result of passive (rote) learning. In learning as *development* the important thing is the activity of the student while learning. His activity develops him and beyond this is worth very little.

The reader will remember the struggles which traditionalists and formal disciplinarians had over this issue. The traditionalist, in the case of the study of Latin, insisted that it was valuable as subject matter. The disciplinarian valued it as a means for developing mental capacities. Socially, says Dewey, this dualism corresponds to the distinction between being guided by authority and being self-guided. Dewey wishes to remedy this dualism by coordinating the acquisition of knowledge under the teacher's authority with learning through which the student develops from within by self-activity under self-guidance. The critic of Dewey may maintain, however, that the student is quite as likely to need guidance and be reduced to a rote imitator when he is active in the workshop as when he is listening in the classroom and studying in the library.

c. SENSORY *versus* RATIONAL KNOWING. This is the familiar opposition of sense to reason as they exist within the individual. This is not to be confused with the dualism indicated in *b* above, which has to do with the passivity or activity of the student's attitude toward *external* tasks which confront him. Sense knowledge, the source of all empirical knowledge is supposed to impress itself on passive sense organs. Rational knowledge, on the other hand, is supposed to require mental activity. Dewey deplored all this as a false distinction. The scientist making empirical observations is dynamically active in using his ears, eyes, and other senses. Empirical knowing is not in Dewey's estimation inferior to rational thinking in its *dynamism*. Dewey's point is that the empiricist engaged in research both makes sensory observations and subjects them to rational analysis. The false bifurcation consists in the attempt to isolate the function of the senses from the higher intellectual functions. To accept the dualism of sense and reason is to accept an untenable faculty psychology.

Dewey attributes the dualism of sense versus reason in education to the influence of Locke. In defense of Locke as against Dewey, it may be argued that if we compare the work of the senses with the work of reason in the usual situations of daily life, the senses do seem to be relatively passive. While merely seeing or hearing, we feel that we are being *acted upon* rather than acting. But it is difficult to conceive of rational processes as passive. While reasoning we are *acting* rather than being *acted upon*. This is why reasoning is so laborious for the average person. Professor C. I. Lewis, veteran teacher of logic at Harvard, declared that people do not think by preference but only as a last resort! Feeble-minded subjects are below average in both concrete and abstract ways of thinking, but they are particularly weak in dealing with abstractions. *Concrete problems lie closer to the senses.* This is why the mentally deficient may succeed quite well in learning a routine trade but fail when they encounter the more abstract problems of science. Kurt Goldstein and his associates have shown that brain-injured children also earn relatively higher scores in concrete tests than in tests involving abstraction and classification. These evidences and other considerations show that reasoning is usually a more dynamic form of mental activity than is the case with sensing. The opposition of sensory to rational knowing is then not altogether a false dualism as Dewey supposes.

d. THE INTELLECT *versus* THE EMOTIONS.   The dualism which Dewey condemns consists in viewing the feelings and emotions in general as purely personal and private affairs having little or nothing to do with intellectual understanding. It is said that emotions "becloud" reasoning. They are concerned with the person's fortunes, his gains and losses, his successes and failures. The intellect, on the other hand, is regarded as pure and passionless light, with no aim other than to learn "the truth and nothing but the truth."

Dewey says that this dualism has unfortunate consequences for education. We try to give students essential knowledge without regard for their interests and other feelings. Teachers are even criticized for deviating from the logical order of instruction in order to appeal to the interests of students. Noah Porter, president of Yale (1871-1886), declared that two reasons why a student should study mathematics are: first, that he has a distaste for it; and second, that he has no conscious need for mathematics!

Dewey holds that as a direct result of an education which makes no appeal to interest we have to resort to the "time-honored paraphernalia of rewards and punishments," such as examinations, grades, prizes, and promotions. The irony of this is that even while denying that feeling has anything to do with the activity of the mind, we smuggle in pains and pleasures to goad or to lure the mind to activity (11, p. 391).

2. The Master Dualism: Doing *Versus* Knowing

The opposition of experience and true knowledge, the breach between doing and knowing, has a long history.

a. DOING *versus* KNOWING IN CLASSIC GREECE.   Plato and Aristotle identified "experience" with practical work. Experience implies activity intended to satisfy some desire or need. Knowledge, however, was considered as having to do with pure truth, with interests in ideal and eternal things. Those who pursued knowledge were motivated by the love of truth free from implications of bodily need (11, p. 306). Dewey held that at the root of this distinction between experience and knowledge was the Greek social system of freemen and slaves. Freemen were economically independent and had no need for the skills required by experience. Freemen were hence given that liberal education which involves the employment of reason and higher appreciations suitable for men of leisure. Slaves, on the other hand, did all the work and had need of experience.

To the extent that experience conveyed knowledge at all it was regarded as knowledge of an inferior sort. Empirical knowledge consisted of the routine and rule-of-thumb procedures of workers who had no need for higher insight. Even today a knowledge of routine is despised as purely utilitarian and without cultural worth. As Dewey notes, we are inclined to refer to someone who relies on blind trial and error as an "empiricist." (The current low opinion of practical knowledge of a supposedly routine character is shown by the unwillingness of colleges to give credit for such courses as bookkeeping, cooking, stenography, and applied art.) The Greeks depreciated practical knowledge because slaves and common people relied on it in their work. In addition, the senses had the disrepute of kinship with work on the one hand and on the other with the appetites of the body. There is accordingly moral danger inherent in the sway of the senses as expressed by the words, "sensual," "carnal," and "worldly." Reason and science, on the contrary, bring man into touch with immaterial or spiritual realities. Reason discovers the eternal verities while experience, relying on the senses, instigates contradictory beliefs. Reliance on the senses leads to sophistry which rejects all criteria of evidence and makes truth a matter of personal conviction or preference.

The opposition made by the Greeks between sense and reason influenced subsequent ideas about education. It accounts for the favor which was later accorded to mathematics and logic and the lesser respect for material science. Not too long ago or even now the practical arts and crafts are depreciated because they suggest preoccupation with the senses rather than with reflection. Teachers incline to offer courses which are practical as items of information without much reference to general principles or laws. Mathematics, on the other hand, is likely to be taught as a pure and abstract science remote from practical applications (11, p. 389).

Medieval philosophy continued the Greek dualism of the empirical and rational except that it gave the bifurcation a religious flavor. To know God and to establish contact with Him required prayer and contemplation, not active experience. Men fled from the world of experience and sought haven in monasteries. Experience had to do with profane and secular affairs which were necessary but inferior to the cultivation of reason (11, p. 310).

b. DOING AND KNOWING AND THE RISE OF SCIENCE. The rise of science in the seventeenth and eighteenth centuries gave an interpretation to the word *empirical* which was quite the reverse of the Greek view. Rationalism is now depreciated and appeal is made to sense observation. Rational principles were either regarded as empty forms until given content and validation by empirical observation, or they were treated as dogmas imposed by authority, such as the authority of the church (11, p. 311). The change from the Greek outlook was twofold: Sense experience ceased to be associated with the menial aspects of life and was given cognitive status. Secondly, the mind was conceived as purely passive or receptive in acquiring sense knowledge while reason was considered dynamically active. Dewey attributes the influence of the latter notions in education to John Locke and roundly condemns them.

3. Dewey on the Origin of Dualistic Conceptions

Dewey finds that the dualisms he condemns originated from *social divisions,* such as the rich from the poor, men from women, the ruler from the ruled (11, p. 377). Even the distinction between the mind and the body has reference to social cleavages. These views about dualisms in general illustrate the completeness and internal consistency of Dewey's thinking. He was a formidable champion of democracy. If the false dualisms are mainly if not entirely due to social cleavages, they should mainly or entirely vanish in a democratic society without social divisions. Since education will be hampered as long as the dualisms continue, it follows that only in a true democracy can education approach perfection. Learning is derived from action *and* reflection. This is to say that learning is derived from experience in which action and reflection are normally in functional interaction. The less restricted the experience, the richer its returns in the way of learning. Therefore the democratic form of society represents the most ideal situation for successful education. The dualisms which Dewey so trenchantly criticizes are at once an obstruction to a democratic society and to education. Also, to separate reason from sensation, reflection from action, and knowledge from emotion is to emasculate education and make a mockery of democracy.

4. Criticism of Dewey's Theory of Dualistic Origins

In criticism of Dewey's derivation of dualisms from social cleavages it may be urged that they also have other and perhaps even more important roots. For instance, a plausible defense could be made for the thesis that the dualisms in question arise from each individual's personal experience, irrespective of class membership. The distinction between knowing and doing could not escape an observant Robinson Crusoe who, despite his isolation from society, would notice that doing and thinking are quite different activities. The child will notice readily enough the contrast between the *passive* and rote method by which a poem may be learned and the perhaps painful *activity* required for writing a poem for oneself. As for the difference between rational and sensory processes, it could hardly escape a thoughtful individual, whether slave or freeman, that sometimes sensory impressions overwhelm attention, at other times the "pale cast of thought" blots out vision.

No appeal need be made to the existence of social classes to explain why reason is regarded as the revealer of the orderly and constant aspects of reality. It is quite obvious that knowledge of the constant laws which operate beneath the visible surface of nature and human nature are discovered through rational generalization. As regards the senses, it is an elementary principle of psychology that they respond to *change* rather than to constants. The visual threshold for detecting *movement* is much keener than for the detection of *location*. Sounds, odors, touches, tastes, warmth, and cold fade away with constant stimulation (adaptation). The world as we see it is a gloriously colorful panorama of change. These differences between reason and the senses could hardly escape the keenly observant Greek philosophers whether they were slaves or freemen.

But, it may be observed, Dewey's point was that the Greeks *seized upon* the distinction between reason and sense to support their social class structure. But this is to concede that the distinction between the senses and reason existed before it was "seized upon," the distinction operates as a *cause* rather than as an effect of social cleavages. There are grounds enough for the distinction between reason and sense even in a one-class society. Dewey would perhaps have granted that distinctions can be made between reason and sense, but he protested against carrying the distinctions to the point of a dualism, i.e., a complete functional separation. In Dewey's scheme of education reason and sense should work in the closest cooperation. Dewey is entirely sound on all of this except the notion that Greek and subsequent social cleavages were the sole or even the main causes of the distinction in question.

Following Dewey's way of thinking the body-mind dualism may be viewed as following the aristocrat-slave distinction of Greek civilization. That is, the aristocrat represents the "mind" and the slave represents the "body" of an undemocratic partnership. As a justification for the social division the analogy is about as cogent as the Easter myth in which the rabbit lays the eggs because both the rabbit and the eggs are symbols of fecundity. But, as the psychoanalyst knows, the human mind is able to support belief on such bizarre evidence, like the insane patient who believed that she was Switzerland because, like this country, she longed for freedom (from the asylum, in her case). It is more plausible to suppose that the distinction between body and mind grows out of the daily experience of every individual. While asleep, the mind appears to vanish or to wander elsewhere in dreams while the body remains in bed. In deciding on the ultimate kinds of "stuff" to be found in the universe one arrives naturally at the Cartesian dualism of mind and body, neither one of which seems reducible to the other. Of course, having distinguished between the mind and the body, it is not easy to see how they are united in one individual who is somehow both mind and body. According to these points the body-mind dualism arose as a philosophical problem quite irrespective of social stratifications.

Again, the distinction between mind and body, between reason and the senses, arises from *moral* experiences of individuals which cannot be escaped whether or not there are social hierarchies. The stress found in Christian religion on the opposition between body and spirit arises in large measure from the experience that the body with its senses is indeed the locus of urges and appetites; and is therefore the source of temptations that come into conflict with reason, which takes the "longer view" and sees the possible evils of immediate gratification.

5. Why Dewey Seeks for Unity

Let us reverse the problem: Instead of seeking with Dewey an explanation for dualistic thinking, let us ask why Dewey so ardently seeks unity. Unlike the pluralist, William James, Dewey seeks for unity, especially as between the individual and society and between society and nature. This explains Dewey's numerous polemics against dualisms and artificial separations in general. This search for unity is considered by some as the reverberation of Hegelian influences on Dewey, dating from Dewey's association with George S. Morris, an ardent idealist. Hegel regarded as false all attempts to separate mind from matter, appearance from reality, the finite from the infinite. *"Natur hat weder kern noch Schale."* In turning from idealism to pragmatism and instrumentalism Dewey does not entirely abandon idealism. But it would be a mistake to suppose that a lingering and unconscious influence of idealism is the sole or even chief cause of Dewey's strictures against dualisms. Dewey's positive philosophy of democratic education is at enmity with dualistic thinking, as will be shown in his *continuity* theory of education.

6. Dewey's Latest Views on Dualistic Thinking

In one of Dewey's latest books, with Arthur F. Bentley as co-author (13), Dewey still regards as ontologically false such separations as the knower from the known, the organism from its environment, and the subject matter of science from daily life. Although failing to correspond with reality, Dewey concedes that such dualisms "serve a useful, indeed necessary, function in the conduct of inquiry" (13, p. 325).

Dewey's meaning may be made clear by two illustrations he offers. The first has to do with the organism-environment distinction. The organism and its environment are normally so continuous that it is impossible to state the precise moment when, for instance, food ceases to be an external object and becomes part of the organism. When, however, something goes wrong, as when digestion is disturbed, it becomes necessary to "do something about it." To locate the source of the trouble we need to inquire whether there is something wrong with the food or with the organism's functions. For the purpose of this inquiry the distinction between the organism and its environment is useful or even necessary (13, pp. 323-324).

As a second illustration of a distinction which is practically valuable, consider the chemist's conception of water as H_2O and the water we "drink, wash with, and sail boats upon," etc. The chemist claims that H_2O is the only "real" water and the layman respectfully agrees. (But now "real" water, the H_2O, exists only in small quantities in the laboratory while the vast ocean upon which ships are carried cannot be called "water" without qualification because it is impure!) But the chemist's conception of water, although involving abstractions, is very useful practically. For example, it is at the root of the chemist's ability to split water into its elements and uniting the elements to form water or some other substance. The chemist holds similar views of all physical substances.

If the chemist could not treat water and all other substances in his analytical and abstract ways his researches would soon come to a halt and the great *practical* value of chemistry would be lost. The chemist's conception of water is only temporarily remote from reality. It is precisely because his conception of water is *abstract* that it can be so *practical.* Water conceived as H_2O relates it to the chemical nature of everything else. Chemistry thus provides the foundation upon which vast practical industries are reared.

In this, his latest utterance, Dewey still sees clearly that *abstract knowledge can be the most practical because it is the most general.* The proponents of the project method of education often accept Dewey as their champion but too easily overlook the great importance which Dewey attaches to knowledge of *general principles.* Although they may pay lip service to this principle, many who use Dewey's method of education through practical projects make their projects so narrow that the student learns a routine skill but misses the general principles involved.

⚡ D. Education as the Continuous Reconstruction of Experience

Section C gave an account of the more negative or critical phase of Dewey's philosophy of education. In turning to his positive ideas a fairly complete exposition of it can be given by covering its three main facets: the neurobiological, the psychological, and the moral-religious. These approaches should make clear the use Dewey makes of his principles of continuity, experimentalism, and reconstructionism in education.

1. Neurobiological Aspects of Education

The following citation from Dewey forcefully expresses the stress he places upon the biological priority of *adaptive action*, of which the senses and the intellect are integral aspects:

Knowledge is not something separate and self-sufficing, but is involved in the process by which life is sustained and evolved. The senses lose their place as gateways of knowing to take their rightful place as stimuli to action (12, p. 87).

The next passage is from Joseph A. Leighton, an idealistic philosopher. It singles out one of the chief criticisms which essentialists and idealists level against Dewey's philosophy of education, which is considered as giving exaggerated importance to the role of action in life.

Disinterested contemplation and enjoyment of beauty, grandeur, meaning, and order of things for their own sakes are for some human beings inherently worth-while functions of consciousness (14, p. 459).

The quotation from Dewey says that sense perception exists only to serve practical adaptive functions. Dewey notes that for an animal, sense perception is not idle knowledge but a stimulus toward action—implying that man should follow this model (12, p. 87). These ideas have aroused a chorus of protests like Leighton's. Other writings of Dewey, however, make it clear that he recognizes that man has aesthetic and moral needs which are more than merely biological. Dewey's point is rather that one must *act* even to get nonpractical needs satisfied. In general, Dewey seeks a normal balance between reflection and action, but allows the side of action to get more than its share of the weight in many of his utterances.

Stimulation and response have reciprocal effects on each other. The response to a stimulus determines what the next stimulus will be. Dewey gives as example the carpenter at work with his tools. Seeing the hammer is one of the preconditions for using it; using it leads to hearing sounds and seeing new results. Experimental animal psychologists use the same schematism here employed by Dewey. When a dog is conditioned to come for food when a bell rings, the first stimulus (bell) results in other stimuli, the sight and taste of the food. Dewey concludes that the function of the brain is to establish *continuity* between series of stimuli and actions which form an organic unity (11, p. 392).

a. THE ROLE OF INTELLIGENCE IN ADAPTATION. In the lowest animals stimuli arouse responses reflexly—there is a minimum of mental activity. With higher animals behavior becomes more complex. Associative or reflective processes intervene between stimuli and their responses. The resultant behavior is adapted to a more distant future. But in Dewey's view the function of intelligence is still to coordinate knowledge with action. Its effectiveness in doing this is the reason why it gives survival value in biological evolution. The fact that reason enables us to pursue remote ends does not mean that the more remote they are the better! Dewey would perhaps have agreed that only the philosopher shut up in his ivory tower, who is paid to think without the need for acting on his thoughts, would conceive such notions as the following: (a) Knowledge exists for its own inherent rewards and not as a tool for meeting the organic demands for survival. (b) The ends toward which life moves are so remote that they lie beyond the portals of infinity. (c) The perfections for which we strive exist already in some transcendental realm which has expropriated reality, leaving the appearances as man's share of the bargain.

In place of such perverse philosophies Dewey favors the pragmatic theory of knowledge (11, p. 400). It maintains that knowing is continuous with activity. The only worth-while knowledge enables us either to adapt our needs and aims to the environment or alter the environment to suit our needs and aims.

b. THE LESSON OF MODERN SCIENCE. There has been another revolution in science since the seventeenth century which teaches a better lesson than can be learned from British empiricism. The best knowledge does not result from passive observation followed by reflection upon it. Modern scientific research engages in *active* observation. That is, the conditions of observation are planned in advance so that there is thought before action occurs, thought while it is taking place, and after action has ended. The research worker is *bodily* active while observing; research involves the manipulation of situations or of intricate apparatus. This type of *practical action* is not opposed to knowledge—it validates knowledge (11, pp. 318-319).

We now come to one of the fullest of Dewey's conceptions of education. It is imperative that it be fully understood, for Dewey was obliged to censure his would-be followers for forgetting his carefully wrought structure for education. The essential principle to be kept in mind is that *education involves the integration of abstract intellectual principles with the pursuit of practical projects.* Dewey's severe polemics against abstract knowledge were solely directed against being content with abstract knowledge without going on to its practical use. It is true that Dewey considered active response which puts knowledge to use as the basis of education. But he never sanctions response which is not illuminated by intelligence. Also Dewey notes that knowledge and action perform reciprocal services: Knowledge guides response and response reveals consequences which increase knowledge (11, p. 317).

The bearing of contemporary science on a philosophy of education,

Dewey held, is self-evident. Practical activities will *not* be educative if they are purely *routine*. Education implies the illumination of experience with meanings. Meanings grow out of the connections observed between stimuli and our responses to them, between our responses and the new stimuli which they evoke (11, p. 320).

Practical life today offers far better educative material than was the case in the age of Plato and Aristotle, and far better than anything the eighteenth century had to offer. In ancient and medieval times practical activities were of a routine kind, often servile in nature, which called for strong arms rather than strong minds. But today numerous occupations from a bristling array of professional technologies down to such formerly simple things as gardening and housekeeping are rich in scientific content (11, pp. 321-322). To the principle of *continuity*, which unites artificial dualisms, we now add a second foundation for a philosophy of education —the principle of *experimentation*.

2.   Criticisms of Dewey's Emphasis on Darwinism

Dewey's use of Darwinian ideas might be summarized as follows: *Action is the primary requirement for biological survival*. Such action may be adaptive even though it be entirely unreflective, as is the case with instincts and reflexes. The function of thought, even the most sophisticated, should be to guide action. If action reciprocally extends insight, that is desirable because insight will guide subsequent action.

It is probable that Dewey's frequent accents on action were "retorts in kind" for correcting the immoderate accent on knowledge-for-its-own-sake made by traditionalists. Granting the soundness of Dewey's stress on knowledge for action, the liberal-minded reader will still approve Leighton's reservation: "Disinterested contemplation and enjoyment of the beauty, grandeur, meaning, and order of things for their own sakes are . . . inherently worth-while functions of consciousness." We may grant that man's intelligence and all other mental capacities arose through natural selection and gave man survival value. But nature has embodied means and ends in the same activities. The very processes which make survival possible include the very ones which make survival worth while.

> Eating, drinking, sleeping, and so on up to remembering, reasoning, creating, and appreciating: These activities may provide for survival, but for what reason would one wish to survive except to exercise these very functions? If life were not filled with these activities, with what would it be filled? (16, p. 238).

When Dewey belabors idle contemplation for its own sake he is not merely being an austere and puritanical critic who begrudges this way of having fun. On the contrary, he expresses regret that the sedentary intellectual should miss the greater fun of acting on his thoughts. Means can be self-rewarding and in this way deserve to be regarded as desirable ends.

Dewey's statement that the world of work of today offers far better educative material than was the case in the past may well be challenged. The intent of Dewey's assertion was to point out that today the child can be trained for a future vocation and at the same time cultivate higher intelligence. The pupil, so to speak, can belong to both the fraternity of the enlightened and to the ranks of labor—a fine ideal for a democracy. The critic, however, may question the notion that craftsmen living before the age of machine industry led a hidebound and rule-of-thumb existence when compared with the modern technological worker. Unfortunately, as a technology is perfected at a given level of development, the mechanization of work increases to the point where the operators of machines themselves become machines. In fact, the instruction given in college professional schools and departments tends to become so dehumanized and time-consuming that the student misses the cultural values of a liberal arts program—until the situation becomes so scandalous that a revolt occurs.

It must not be forgotten that very many of the graduates from our schools are destined to spend their lives working at lower-level and routinized jobs. One is therefore led to question Dewey's principle that the child's initiation in any activity should take its departure from his present spontaneous interests and urges. One might better follow the advice of Noah Porter, doughty president of Yale near the end of the nineteenth century. That advice was to inure the student for doing what he dislikes! The probability that such frustration-tolerance will be useful in an industrial society is high!

3. Dewey's Psychological Approaches to Education

The discussion of Dewey's use of psychology in education will parallel to an extent what has already been said about his neurobiological approaches to education. Instead of speaking in biological terms about the associations between the senses, the brain, and the muscles, one merely shifts to a partly altered terminology; one speaks of the relations of sense perception to the mind and of the mind to behavior. The "stimulus-brain-response" formula is favored by behaviorists, the "perception-mind-behavior" formula is favored by mentalists in psychology. Dewey has commended the behaviorist approach, but shifts easily to mentalistic points of view. This shift from neurobiological to psychological points of view is not reprehensible. On the contrary, as William McDougall observed, we should "work" both of these points of view for all they are worth.

There are two main psychological assumptions made by Dewey

which were not covered under the rubric of neurobiology. These assumptions call for special discussion. They are Dewey's theory of mental development and his theory of interest.

a. DEWEY'S DEVELOPMENTAL PSYCHOLOGY.   What is the general nature of the development of the mind as a whole? Our earlier discussion of the ideas of W. T. Harris and H. H. Horne touched on this question. Both Harris and Horne attacked a theory of mental development which they attributed to faculty psychology. Although Dewey's ideas on the subject appear to have developed independently, they are somewhat similar to those of Harris and Horne. The older view of mind, attributed to faculty psychology, held that *the minds of children and of adults are essentially alike.* Both are equipped with the same set of faculties. This view was sometimes qualified by the concession that some faculties, e.g., of sensation and memory, manifest themselves earlier than certain intellectual powers. This theory holds that the chief differences between the child and the adult are *quantitative* or matters of *strength.* The child's powers of observation, memory, and reasoning are regarded as on the average weaker than those of an adult. Measured by objective tests these differences in degrees of development show up as quantitative score differences.

Harris and Horne rejected this "strength-increment" theory of development, as we might call it. In place of it they favored the general view that the higher capacities of mind come into existence gradually by the selection and coordination of more elementary and original skills. Dewey also stresses the idea of the *emergence* of capacities at different age levels, but bridged with increments in strength. Dewey recognized three psychological ages: (a) The *play period,* extending to about the age of eight years, is essentially a period of spontaneous activity. During this period the child's studies should center on home life and its occupations. Since he has no clear conception of causes and effects, of means and ends, his instruction must be simple and imitative. However, as the child approaches the age of eight years, he takes interest in spheres outside the home; and he may now be inducted into the life of the farm, invention, reading, writing, geography, and other appropriate subjects. (b) The *period of techniques,* accented between the ages of eight and twelve, marks the child's ability to analyze, to distinguish between means and ends, causes and effects, and to follow simple principles of procedure in work. This is the age for acquiring motor skills and for pursuing differentiated studies, such as history, geography, and science. (c) The age of *reflective attention,* at age twelve and following, marks the development of powers of thinking to the point where more technical mastery of distinct studies is possible. The child now has the ability to work for more remote goals than was the case in stage b.

The bearing of stages of mental development on educational practice is that the instruction of the child at each age should be in harmony with his capacities at each age. Dewey had not fully developed his three stages, realizing that the study of this subject is in its initial stages. One principle is outstanding in Dewey's schema of development: This is *the priority of action over reflection*. The first urge of the child is to do something. Actions encounter obstructions—this is the way the first problems of life appear. To solve such problems, the child is led to reflection. It is contrary to the order of genetic development to train the young mind to think about a problem before it has encountered that problem as its own. The aim of education is to secure an eventual balance between practical skills and intellectual prowess, but the practical side takes precedence in time. This balance between practical skills and intellectual growth are best achieved, Dewey thought, through the *occupations;* moving gradually from those which demand little more than elementary motor control to those which involve technical control and abstract principles (5, pp. 400-403).

Modern psychology finds the question of genetic stages of development extremely intricate, both as regards its experimental and conceptual approaches. The facts about genetic development are far more complicated than was envisaged by any of the writers so far considered. In theory, the facts about development should have consequences for education, but the practical use of the facts is not so simple. Despite considerable research, most aspects of genetic development are not well understood. We will note some difficulties of research, some of the findings, and comment on the problem of applying the findings in practice.

b. MODERN PSYCHOLOGY AND GENETIC DEVELOPMENT. It is not easy to tease out the natural stages of bodily and mental growth because environmental influences and training obscure the picture which nature might present. To answer questions about growth the psychologist has no choice but to use carefully devised experiments and tests. We may study development in *cross-sectional* style. That is, one selects children representative of various ages, applies one's experimental tests, and thus seek to determine mental growth in the functions measured. A better procedure is to make so-called *longitudinal* studies in which the same cases are tested and retested at different ages.

But neither of these procedures will separate development in the sense of *growth* from development in the sense of training (2, pp. 145-199; 1, pp. 216-265). The growth curve obtained is adulterated with the accumulating effects of training acquired in school and more randomly in everyday life.

Suppose, now, that one suspects with Dewey that certain capacities appear or at least become pronounced at certain ages of the child. But how are we to determine the genetic history of even broadly defined mental capacities when we are not agreed concerning the number and identity of these capacities? This matter is discussed in Chapter 5, in which it is shown that the long search for the primary abilities of mind is far from a successful conclusion. But if distinguishable mental capacities exist we must know what they are before deciding whether they exist in infancy and merely grow in strength, or whether they appear in saltatory fashion. The latter would be regarded as quite unlikely by most psychologists, who would rather favor the view that such main abilities as sensation, perception, learning, recall, problem-solving ability are present during infancy or at an early age and undergo subtle forms of differentiation with increasing age.

Can we draw any conclusion about primary abilities and their growth by merely readministering a given test or equivalent forms of it at different ages? No, because different abilities are brought into play at different ages by the test itself. Thus, a form-board test which taxes spatial perception at age four may chiefly measure motor speed at age ten (1, p. 226).

Let it now be assumed that the primary abilities have been determined and that we have tests which will measure them separately. Also assume that we have determined at what ages the abilities appear or, more likely, what their comparative strengths are at each age. We now encounter another fact which frustrates the laudable attempt to teach children at each age the things they are best qualified to learn. This is the fact of *individual differences*. Children of any given age will show tremendous variations in their various abilities. What is worse, *the same child who is relatively mature in one function may be retarded in another*. The child psychologist has difficulty in even validating the distinctions between such gross stages of development as infancy, childhood, adolescence, and adulthood. We may define puberty as beginning with maturity of the sexual functions. But such onset of maturity varies from ages eight to twenty-six in girls and from ages eleven to seventeen in boys.

In conclusion, it is hardly necessary to dwell on the unpromising effects of the matters outlined above on the hope of attaining a perfect sequence of school studies which are synchronized in detail with the growth curves of mental, motor, emotional, and other aspects of development. *Individual differences*, however, may be regarded as pointing to *individual treatment* in education. Dewey's educational thought and the entire movement of progressive education have the merit that they do stress the differential education of individuals depending on their several needs and abilities.

C. DEWEY'S PSYCHOLOGY OF INTEREST. We have noted Dewey's idea that each project or program for educating the child should originate from some spontaneous aim, urge, or interest which the child feels. The clever teacher directs these interests into new channels which lead to more complicated skills and more intellectual studies. Dewey's theory of interest was of the type which traces spontaneous interest to natural urges, as in the hormic psychologies of William McDougall and of Sigmund Freud. Impulses in general are native, spontaneous, and outgoing impulses in the individual. They do not wait for stimuli to arouse them. On the contrary, they actively seek their appropriate stimuli. The task of the teacher is therefore not to coax the child to become interested in some lesson already scheduled. The worst practice is to *force* the child into activities which he finds uninteresting. The teacher's task is to find a desirable activity in which the child can show spontaneous interest—at least to start with. Dewey no doubt realized that older children can adapt their interests to the rational requirements of advanced courses of study. But as a rhetorical emphasis against the essentialists, Dewey sometimes speaks as though spontaneous interests are the only legitimate ones in education. Some later enthusiasts, especially the followers of William H. Kilpatrick, made it a cardinal principle not to require the child to take part in a project against his will.

4. Dewey on Moral and Religious Education

We recall (Chapter 15) that Dewey rejects all moral systems and religions which claim to rest on transcendental and *a priori* sanctions. Dewey's moral philosophy is an earth-bound strategy rather than a system. Moral rules have authority to the degree that their observance promotes the ideals of democratic living in which the maximum individual and social goods are attained. Moral principles, like all others, are subject to pragmatic tests. Dewey's religion is an idealized social morality directed to the future. Like most religions it looks forward to an Elysium; but Dewey hopes to achieve it, not beyond the River Jordan, but on both sides of the Mississippi, and then on all the continents of the earth. Dewey's "heaven" will not be a resting place for the weary. Those of the future who realize the heritage of democratic social culture which is our present projected faith, must conserve, reconstruct, and transmit that culture to others who will come after them.

a. DEWEY ON MORAL EDUCATION. Dewey looks askance at the belief that moral virtues can be conveyed to the individual by formal instruction. Those who hold that morality is a branch of intellectual knowledge validated by such things as *a priori* insight, revelation, or divine command, believe that virtues can be acquired by study. This belief harbors what Dewey considers the false Kantian dualism between reason and impulse. Dewey sharply attacks all attempts to restrict moral education to didactic lessons about conduct. Knowing moral rules of conduct will be effective only in authoritarian societies where rules of conduct are strictly enforced. The effective element is not the teaching of the rule but the practice of it which follows. "To attempt to get similar results from lessons about morals in a democratic society is to rely upon sentimental magic" (11, p. 411).

Dewey applies to moral instruction the same formula he applies to all learning: *learn by living*. Good moral traits are best acquired by participation in social life and work. Moral behavior is a complex of social impulse, insight, and skill. It is best acquired by being part of a democratic social group. Moral insight is acquired where studies are pursued in ways which reveal their social significance (11, pp. 413-414).

The view that moral education should be conveyed by living was, of course, held by predecessors of Dewey. Froebel taught that moral and religious ideals are best acquired through actual living in the home and community. He decried the punishment of the child for offenses of conduct. Froebel sought to get rid of undesirable behavior through the *atrophy of disuse*. That is, by filling the child's waking hours with desirable activities the undesirable ones will weaken and vanish through disuse. Colonel Francis Parker also anticipates Dewey's ideas about moral education:

The predominant condition, then, for moral training is community life, the society of the school. The common schools present a perfect means of moral training; order, work, and play all tending to the cultivation of true manhood (15, pp. 258-259).

Some of the criticisms made by Dewey and others against the view that virtues can be imparted by instruction are exaggerations. Let us take Kant as the "whipping boy" of such criticism. Kant did not, as is alleged, separate reason from impulse in his moral philosophy. On the contrary, he imbued the categorical imperative with the deep reverence which the human mind and heart instinctively feel for truths believed to be universal and unalterable. Kant certainly believed that obedience to the categorical imperative should spring from love and reverence, not from fear or from compulsion. This is why Kant deplored punishment for violations of moral rules. Also, catechetical instruction in Christian morals in Sunday schools need not appeal primarily to fear, but to the love of God. Kant realized that to know the categorical imperative is one thing and being able to apply it in practice is another. The child's good will, which in itself is absolutely good, must still find embodiment in practice through experience.

The rationalist in morals might in his turn apply critical strictures against the experience school of moralists. The rationalists may give too small a place to workaday morality, but Dewey gives too small a place to formal instruction in good conduct. Any employment which has an aim and involves cooperation, says Dewey, yields moral knowledge (11, pp. 413-414). It may be conceded that morality which is embodied in the individual's habits, attitudes, and other traits of character and personality is more valuable than mere intellectual knowledge *about* morals which does not reach practice. But it is far from certain that participation in any employment having cooperative aims will yield moral knowledge and virtues. If the group in question were a society of thieves there would be cooperative aims, but would there be morality? And if the pursuit of the cooperation and aims exists as unconscious habit and attitudes, could they be called "knowledge"? The basic advantage of conscious knowledge of principles (see Chapter 6) is their *generality* and hence their power to transfer from one situation to another. Society wants general and conscious honesty, not the local honesty restricted to next-door neighbors and not the unwitting honesty of a man to whom it has not yet occurred to be otherwise. The trouble with the latter case, if such a case exists, is that the idea of being otherwise may dawn any moment.

The realization that *all* men are brothers is not, as Dewey's statements imply, a dependable result of merely working as a member of a labor union or of the National Association of Manufacturers. Such groups, to be sure, have their cooperative aims, but these are pathetically local and often deserve to be regarded as vices rather than as virtues. The greater the cooperation within the group the less there is with others outside the group! Conceivably the industrialists and members of labor unions might eventually learn that "*all* men are brothers" and that there are cooperative aims which all men should pursue. Such rules are subject to conscious formulation, as is the case with the Sermon on the Mount, the "golden rule," and Kant's categorical imperative. This being the case, such rules might better have been learned at the beginning rather than at the end of the scruff of experience.

Education differs from real life in one respect—it may repeat the experiences of the race but it must abbreviate or epitomize them. Obviously, if the wisdom of the past is to be applied to living in the present and in the future, such past experience cannot literally be relived. The wisdom of the past must be condensed and this is accomplished through generalization, and only intelligence can grasp generalizations. Once intelligence has grasped a general rule of conduct it can express the rule in *all* behavior rather than in isolated situations. It would not be sensible to expect every student of algebra to discover its rules through his own ingenuity and effort. Then why should we expect the student to discover for himself the general principles of morality, which on all counts are more complicated than algebra? Surely both precept and practice are important in moral education. The charges and countercharges which rationalists and empiricists hurl at each other on this subject are rather academic, and have the aspect of a tempest in a teapot.

b. DEWEY'S RELIGION AND EDUCATION.   Unlike the idealists Horne and Gentile, Dewey accords no special place to institutional religion in his philosophy of education. In his Terry Lectures (see Chapter 15) Dewey does not claim to set up a religion, but a conception of a "religious man." His "religious man" is a devotee of a faith in the future ideals of social morality. Many critics will say that although true religion includes this faith it is in itself no true religion at all. Having no true religion Dewey does not need a place for one in his educational philosophy.

Although Dewey did not initiate the vast movement of progressive education, many consider him its main inspiration. Many will be startled and dismayed by the realization that the ideological genius of one of our dominant educational trends was an agnostic in religion. On the other hand, Dewey's philosophy of education, like pragmatism, is a *theory of practice*, with only tentative metaphysical ideas. As a leader of educational practice Dewey has the hearty approval of a crusading army of educators who are at the same time devout members of various religious denominations. There is a possibility that one can accept Dewey's views on educational practice without accepting all of his instrumentalism. The religionist may consider that Dewey restricts his instrumentalism to the terrestrial realm, and therefore can neither prove nor disprove beliefs about celestial realities. David Hume, also a famous empiricist, held that, since the truth of religion can neither be proved nor disproved by science, everyone is free to believe what he pleases about it! In any case, since the teaching of denominational religion is forbidden by law the teacher need hardly be concerned with Dewey's agnosticism.

Instrumentalism, whether or not it validates religion, will be regarded by many as a good philosophy of life. It is a militant philosophy for those who believe that realities are *made* as well as *discovered*. Dewey held the view that evil, ugliness, and error are not merely things to be understood, but to be fought. We seek to understand because we need to act. Our warfare against our triune of foes will be effective to the degree that we do understand them. Understanding and action go hand in hand.

Chapter 17 which follows pays a debt, long overdue, to the predecessors and contemporaries of Dewey in the development of child-centered education. In Chapter 17 we will also see Dewey at work as educator in his famous experimental school in Chicago. This school became the prototype of "experience" schools, not merely in the United States, but in other lands as well.

References

1. Anastasi, Anne. *Differential Psychology* (3d ed.). New York: Macmillan, 1958.
2. Bayley, Nancy. "Development and Maturation." *Theoretical Foundations of Psychology* (H. Helson, ed.). New York: Van Nostrand, 1951.
3. Bode, Boyd H. *Modern Educational Theories.* New York: Macmillan, 1927.
4. ———. *Progressive Education at the Crossroads.* New York: Newson, 1938.
5. Boyd, William. *The History of Western Education.* London: A. & C. Black, 1950.
6. Brubacher, John S. *A History of the Problems of Education.* New York: McGraw-Hill, 1947.
7. Childs, John L. *American Pragmatism and Education.* New York: Holt, 1956.
8. Clayton, Alfred S. *Emergent Mind and Education.* New York: Columbia University, Teachers College, 1943.
9. Counts, George S. *Dare the Schools Build a New Social Order?* New York: John Day, 1932.
10. ———. *The Prospects of American Democracy.* New York: John Day, 1938.
11. Dewey, John. *Democracy and Education.* New York: Macmillan, 1916.
12. ———. *Reconstruction in Philosophy.* New York: Holt, 1920.
13. ———. (With Arthur F. Bentley). *Knowing and the Known.* Boston: Beacon Press, 1949.
14. Leighton, Joseph A. *The Field of Philosophy.* New York: Appleton, 1923.
15. Parker, Francis W. *Talks on Pedagogics.* New York: John Day, 1937.
16. Weber, Christian O. "Homeostasis and Servo-Mechanisms for What?" *Psychological Review,* 1949, Vol. 56, pp. 234-239.

♀ *chapter 17*

THE DEVELOPMENT OF CHILD-CENTERED EDUCATION

Sand confined in an hourglass cannot start an avalanche, but the mere whisper of an idea may start one down the corridors of history. Ideas which start conflagrations often seem to take root in unlikely places. The France of Louis XIV seemed an unlikely place for ideas about liberty to spring up. It was a time of tyranny in which even the nobility and the church suffered under the rule of the Crown. But out of this condition grew the educational ideas of Jean Jacques Rousseau asserting the rights of children to the natural growth provided by the state of nature unde- filed by human hands. Upon reflection, this will not appear strange. Ideas arise when a crying need for them exists.

Rousseau is generally credited as being the originator of child- centered education, although the basic idea can be traced to an earlier dawn, as in the teachings of Jesus. This new theme in education slowly gathered momentum, was transplanted to American shores, spread in the kindergartens established by William T. Harris and Susan Blow, was given the support of an insurgent pragmatic philosophy, and the leader- ship of the stalwart John Dewey. Meanwhile, the Progressive Education Association arose to unite forces and implement the new ideas of Rous- seau which had reached the proportions of an avalanche.

The present chapter, devoted to the development of child-centered education, will discuss four main topics as follows:

A. European Antecedents of Child-Centered Education

⚡ A. European Antecedents of Child-Centered Education

Curriculum-centered education, although intended for the child's own good, finds the chief value of education *external* to the child, in an objective and universally valid knowledge. Child-centered education finds *development from within* more important. The psychological presentation of subject matter is more important than adherence to its logical organization. Appeal to interest is of more value than the prescription of required studies. The early European leaders of the new movement of child-centered education were numerous. Brief notes on the ideas and work of three leaders will suffice for our needs.

1. Jean Jacques Rousseau (1712-1778)

Rousseau, eloquent master of tirade rather than of logic, became one of the inspirations of the French and American Revolutions. Our interest centers in Rousseau as the firebrand of a new philosophy of education. Rousseau's revolt against deplorable social conditions in France was emotional rather than logical. His fellow revolutionist, Voltaire, based his satire on acute analyses of the disreputable state of affairs. Rousseau's chief sympathies were for those who suffered most from the tyranny of the Crown and its agents. Paris was full of slums where destitute humanity lived in ignorance and filth. Rousseau's first notable writing, the *Discourse on Arts and Sciences* (1749), was a biting tirade against all existing institutions. He attacked even the arts and sciences and the false civilization they represented. In his romantic novel, *New Héloïse* (1760), Rousseau, among other things, declared that men were not made to fit their stations in life, but that their stations should be made to fit them. This sense of the individual worth of man deepened as the misrule of France continued and other voices of revolt joined that of Rousseau. His famous *Social Contract* and *Émile*, both of which appeared in 1762, caused such a furore that Rousseau was obliged to escape from Paris and seek haven in Bern. In Chapter 2 something was said about the role of the *Social Contract* in formulating the American Constitution, and how Alexander Meiklejohn found in it a philosophy of education to meet the crisis of education secularized from the church.

We are here concerned with Rousseau's great educational work, the *Émile*. This book is beset with confusions and contradictions. The main constructive points made by Rousseau about education are as follows:

a. CHILD STUDY.   The first task of education is to study the child. All of the native traits of the child, as shown by his spontaneous impulses, must be investigated. Sex differences must be explored and taken into account in education. Also, differences due to age must be determined and put to use in education. These insights of Rousseau are realized today in a vast literature on child psychology, dealing with sex and age differences and bristling with research on numerous aspects of child development. Rousseau extended his prescriptions to the recognition by the teacher of *individual differences* between learners. The *Émile* is the story of the experiences of a tutor who seeks to educate the boy Émile. In the *New Héloïse*, Rousseau tells the story of three children raised in an ideal family which provides for individual growth by allowing each child to learn from its own experiences.

b. NATURE AS THE GUIDE TO NURTURE.   Rousseau's guide to the reform of education is expressed by the injunction, "Return to nature!" All insincere artifice should be replaced by natural interests and needs. Rousseau anticipated the belief of G. Stanley Hall (discussed later) that the child's development reproduces the development of the race. Rousseau made numerous suggestions for furthering the natural upbringing of the child. The restless child is not to be restrained, but given something to do. The teacher should follow the rule of giving the child natural *freedom*. Certain current American methods for dealing with problem children make use of what is known as the "permissive atmosphere." This method allows the little "permissives" to relieve tension by such activities as destroying equipment and venting wrath on the effigies of their enemies. This permissive technique, which may have remedial effects on frustrated neurotics and delinquents, was not sanctioned by Rousseau. He declared that as a child is given more liberty it has less right to domineer others.

c. LEARNING THROUGH ACTION.   As a consequence of education according to nature, Rousseau believed that a child should learn through his or her own active experience and "like it!" The child must learn to acquire knowledge for himself. He is to learn science, carpentry, and many other things through personal discovery. But in return for this autonomy the child is not to complain about the necessities imposed by nature. If he is late in arriving for some pleasant occasion, let him do without it. If he intentionally breaks something or indulges in any other deliberate mischief, let him be punished. Rousseau did not reject education in the sense of intellectual studies, but insisted that these be postponed until the child is old enough for them. He protested against the practice of his age of treating the child as though he rose to the age of reason as soon as he left his mother's breast.

d. THE PEDAGOGY OF INTEREST. Education should be guided by the child's own interests. We should not regard him as a small adult, ready to pursue the interests of adults. Rousseau believed that the child was born with native tendencies in which his interests were rooted. The reader will recognize the marked resemblances between Dewey's ideas and those held by Rousseau in the eighteenth century. Rousseau and others living in his time expressed the conviction that each child is entitled to a free education, and that education should be provided by the state with impartiality for all classes of society.

2. Johann H. Pestalozzi (1746-1827)

Pestalozzi had hoped to succeed in politics in his native Switzerland, but succeeded only in becoming known as a troublesome agitator. Mankind owes a debt to his earlier failures because Pestalozzi turned his attention to education. For a time Pestalozzi lived an obscure life trying to improve the lot of the poor. His efforts took the direction of training children to develop their abilities. He was an ardent admirer of Rousseau, whose ideas harmonized with what Pestalozzi observed for himself through practical experimentation. He saw a contrast between the education he himself had received as a child and the ideal education portrayed by Rousseau in the *Émile*. Pestalozzi's ideas were largely inspired by Rousseau's philosophy of a return to nature. Also, Pestalozzi's express aim was to "psychologize education." His most important book was a novel, *Leonard and Gertrude* (1781), which portrays how Gertrude, a mother, teaches her children in ways which anticipate the methods of modern progressive schools. The skills developed by Pestalozzi were those which belonged in the home, such as spinning and gardening. Arithmetic was made practical by applying numbers to objects. Practical science was learned through observing the natural properties of objects and processes—earth, fire, water, plants, animals, and the seasons. The publication of *Leonard and Gertrude* brought Pestalozzi to the attention of officials both at home and abroad. His book, *How Gertrude Teaches Her Children* (1801) was followed by a series of works written by Pestalozzi and his staff for parents and teachers.

Pestalozzi's reputation as a practical educator developed gradually. Schools based on Pestalozzi's methods helped Prussia in her recovery of strength after her defeat by Napoleon. In fact, they succeeded so well that in time the Prussian Junkers regarded them as a threat to their own power. The people were becoming too enlightened and were asking for too many reforms! The Prussian Crown and the ruling class took measures for restricting the powers and practices of the normal schools! History has seldom furnished more clear-cut evidence of the power of education as a bulwark of freedom. An education which makes use of propaganda and indoctrination will also support a totalitarian state, but less forcefully than true education will support a democracy. This is because a democracy better expresses what human nature *is*. The truth of this statement is evidenced by the fact that there has never been an en masse revolt against a genuine democracy. But the more "genuine" a totalitarian state becomes, the more certain the eventual revolt.

3. Friedrich W. Froebel (1782-1852)

Froebel at once selected education as his career after his teaching experience in the Pestalozzian Institute of Frankfort. After a career of further teaching, further studies of his own at the Universities of Göttingen and Berlin, and after some military service, Froebel established a school of his own. Froebel then turned to the education of preschool children, and opened the first kindergarten in 1840; which led eventually to the establishment of such schools, everywhere, including the United States.

Like Rousseau and Pestalozzi, Froebel emphasized the natural and spontaneous growth of the child; but Froebel held to an idealistic philosophy of education which went quite beyond the simplicities on which Pestalozzi relied. Froebel's idealistic principles of education are set forth in his only formal work on educational theory, *The Education of Man* (1826). Froebel's earlier study of Schelling accounts in part for the romantic idealism set forth in his book. Froebel saw all things as unified in God. God expresses himself both in physical nature and in man's spirit. Having such faith in unity, Froebel sought for *correlation* in education. God is an active spirit and the universe expresses His creative activity. God is triune, finding reality in Himself, in man, and in physical nature. Every object, therefore, whether plant, animal, stone, or human being, has a threefold nature. Each is individual and diverse, but is also universal because of the divine element in it.

From these ideas Froebel derives his philosophy of education. The child, like his Maker, is self-active. The child is incomplete, but his self-activity will result in growth. This growth, which envelops all things, becomes conscious and deliberate in the case of man. Perception and reason enable man to realize his own divine essence and to develop from within. It is the function of education to guide such development, which is subject to outer influences. The child's education depends primarily on the divine self-activity within him, but he needs guidance in retracing the cultural history of the race and to adjust to the society of which he is a member. *But the teacher is forbidden to interfere arbitrarily with spontaneous growth.* The teacher *presides* over growth, something like a gardener keeping a weather eye on his plants, and going into action when an emergency arises.

Being an idealist, Froebel found it easy to gloss over the weeds in the garden. We cannot but envy his ability to regard the child's activity as divinely inspired with none of it emanating from the nether regions. Following a dialectical paradigm which he owed to earlier idealists, Froebel found that all growth proceeds by the "connection of opposites." Growth involves the opposition of the inner to the outer. In order to grow, the outer must be made inner and the inner must become outer. To translate this cryptic idealistic jargon into intelligible language, Froebel means to say that in growing the child exercises his inner nature on the outer world and thus develops his inner capabilities. Froebel regarded play as very important for bringing about development. For in play, the child spontaneously engages in objective expression and thereby develops inwardly.

Froebel's views on moral education were religious rather than rationally grounded. His recognition of the divine element in human nature led him to challenge all notions claiming the existence of natural evils in the child which must be corrected by discipline. The child instinctively seeks union with God. To regard the child as "fallen from grace" or "lost" and needing salvation was profanation. In his educational practices Froebel sought to reinforce the child's sense of unity with the divine by making use of numerous symbols of such unity discoverable in the child's environment.

As against Kant, Froebel rejected the view that moral growth depended on knowledge of rules of conduct. The child has but to grow in unity with nature, humanity, and God. Moral character consists of attitudes, feelings, and habits; and these are best acquired through active living with others in the home and community. Realistic readers will agree with those who regard Froebel's founding of the kindergarten as better representing his influence on education than his romantic idealism.

⇕ B. Two American Leaders of Child-Centered Education: Francis Parker and G. Stanley Hall

The American influences of Rousseau, Pestalozzi, and Froebel, united with the work of American recalcitrants against so-called "formalized" and "intellectual" education, culminated in the Progressive Education movement launched in 1918. Before dealing with this revolt and its ideology, we will discuss three of the more important American supporters of child-centered education. These are Colonel Francis W. Parker, G. Stanley Hall, and John Dewey. Interest in Dewey in this chapter will center on his personal contributions to educational *practice* rather than in his philosophy of education.

1.   Colonel Francis W. Parker (1831-1902)

Parker greatly admired both Pestalozzi and Froebel. He approved the new theme that the child's own activity is more educative than systematic instruction in knowledge. Dewey says that Parker, more nearly than any other individual, was the inspirer of the Progressive Education movement. Parker declared that the aim of education was to teach children, not subjects (4, p. 204). Parker's work at Quincy, Massachusetts, occurring shortly after the Civil War, represents Froebel's great conquest in the New World. Parker ranks as an innovator, not merely as a transcriber of activity-centered education. His views on education, which are held in great esteem, are most fully recorded in his *Talks on Pedagogics* (9).

Parker's educational philosophy is an amplification of Froebel's ideas on self-expression and moral training. Parker's justification of self-activity in education was well-seasoned with sound wisdom. *The most precious power of the individual is the power to make choices.* This concept is basic in a democracy. Applied to the school this principle is bound to result in some disorder because children are not yet old enough to make wise and consistent choices, and have not as yet learned how to cooperate with others. In this situation, the "order" which is so dear to the heart (or personal convenience) of the teacher might be restored by discipline. But such *control from without* neglects the development of *self-control from within*. The latter can develop only in a situation in which the individual can make his own choices, act on them, and learn the consequences.

Parker's chief originality consisted in extending the principles of self-activity to levels beyond the kindergarten and primary grades, and to new areas of instruction. He extended it to manual training, speech, music, modeling, painting, drawing, and writing. Parker effected the integration of more elementary skills with complex and practical occupations. Writing and spelling were mastered, not in separate "lessons," but as parts of communicative activity. Reading was developed along with the study of history, science, and other courses of the curriculum. Motor skills were developed by manual training, modeling, drawing, and painting. This is *concomitant* learning. Parker's work in general may be regarded as the transition between Pestalozzi and Froebel on the one hand and Dewey on the other. Whereas Parker integrated narrower skills with broader courses of study, Dewey integrated courses of study with such practical activities as weaving, carpentering, cooking, and sewing.

2.   G. Stanley Hall (1846-1924)

Rousseau's thesis that sound educational practice must be based on a thorough understanding of child development was favorably received by his successors. Rousseau worked out a scheme of the main stages of child development, and Froebel offered a similar analysis. These endeavors were rather amateurish, lacking the new insights derived from Darwin on the nature of development and the scientific approach to the facts of child development. It remained for later psychologists to serve as pioneers of the child-study movement. G. Stanley Hall is generally considered the founder of scientific child psychology. His work marks the transition from philosophical to psychological theories, although the latter were rather speculative. Hall was trained at the University of Leipzig under Wilhelm Wundt, the founder of experimental psychology. Hall became a distinguished president of Clark University, to which he attracted graduate students in psychology who have since become important contributors to their science. The research work directed by Hall covered many systematic problems of child psychology and of education. His writings include hundreds of articles in scientific journals, which in part supplied materials for his books. Hall founded and edited the important journal, *Pedagogical Seminary* (now the *Journal of Genetic Psychology*). Hall coined the term "paedocentrism" to cover his joint interest in education and child study. His chief books on education and developmental psychology are *Educational Problems* (5), the two volumes on *Adolescence* (6), and *Aspects of Child Life and Education* (8).

a. HALL'S CONTRIBUTIONS TO RESEARCH METHOD. Hall attempted to put child study on a scientific basis through extensive series of investigations. He used the questionnaire method which was a new approach at the time. The questions were typically answered by adults who relied on their reminiscences of younger days. Another method consisted in studying the child by analyzing compositions written by him. Hall's critics look askance at the questionnaire method which, so some hold, might better be called the "question-and-error method." Hall's use of it suffered from serious violations of statistical requirements. He often failed to use representative samples of subjects and did not test the reliabilities of his results in terms of adequate statistical criteria. Added to this is the risk of error in accepting adult reports on childhood memories. Even the memories of yesterday are subject to wish-fulfilling suppressions and alterations. It is true that Hall and his followers used kinds of empirical data other than questionnaire returns, such as biographical records, measures of gross physical development, extensive studies of the maturation of physiological and psychological functions, and other data. Hall's great contribution to child psychology was to introduce the scientific approach in place of the exhortations of Rousseau and the mysticism of Froebel.

b. HALL'S PHILOSOPHICAL OUTLOOK. Hall held to a general philosophical outlook which was pragmatic in nature. It would be a forbidding task to tease out the ramifications of Hall's philosophy and genetic theory of development from a study of his voluminous writings. Fortunately, Dr. George E. Partridge has done this in an epitome of Hall's writings which Hall endorsed as accurate (10).

Hall's ideas represent one aspect of the pragmatic revolution in philosophy. For Hall, as for James and Dewey, theoretical problems are to be approached in terms of man's practical needs and interests. To pass as truth, philosophy must do more than satisfy the requirements of logic; it must serve man's practical needs. Hall stressed the functional relationships between thought and action, and the role of both in evolution.

But Hall's pragmatism lies closer to James's contention that feelings may serve as tests of truth. It will be recalled that James considered that the emotional satisfactions yielded by an idea (e.g., as in religion) were evidences of the truth of the idea. Hall regarded the intellect as a rather superficial function of mind. The great truths of ethics and religion arise from the feelings which give them durability whereas intellectual philosophies come and go. Poetry and folkfore are better avenues to enduring truths because they speak the language of feeling. The feelings voice racial experiences while the intellect is concerned with individual experiences (10, pp. 8-9).

c. HALL'S THEORY OF RECAPITULATION. Like Dewey, Hall was influenced by Darwin's theory of evolution. But Hall developed a theory of the nature of individual growth which Dewey and practically all other moderns reject. There are some evidences from embryology that the embryo shows a few growths which resemble structures found in earlier stages of animal evolution. These observations suggest the interesting thought that each individual in his own (ontogenetic) development goes through or repeats the bodily evolution of his species (phylogenetic development). The biological evidences in support of this analogy are rather scanty. They are not sufficient to give it the status of a scientific principle. Nevertheless, Hall ventured to add to this so-called principle of physiological recapitulation a psychological parallel. He held that the individual in his development passes through, not only the *biological,* but also through the *mental* and *cultural* stages of ancestral history. Hall proposed to use this principle as a guide for research in genetic psychology. His aim was to secure a complete natural history of the mind. Darwin and Dewey would sanction the view that man's mind as well as his body is the *result* of a long period of animal evolution. But to hold that the mind of man in its genetic development recapitulates the history of the race is quite bold and not founded on sufficient evidences.

Hall maintained that the mind of the individual contains factors which were there before he had any experience. Mind is more extensive than individual consciousness. We would so far agree to this—there are memories which are not now in consciousness. There are even memories which, according to the Freudians, cannot be recalled at all. But whether they can be recalled or not, they are memories which arose from our individual experiences. But Hall had in mind *racial* memories which exist in the unconscious and influence our thought, feeling, and behavior. Hall compares the behavior of an individual to that of some floating object with most of its bulk beneath the surface of the water. Such an object may move against surface winds, *but only because it is driven by hidden currents.* Each individual thus harbors unconscious mental contents which arose in earlier periods of racial history. These forces, hidden behind the scenes, are the prime movers of consciousness and behavior, far exceeding the influences of reason.

What are these mysterious echoes from the racial past which reverberate in our souls? They are essentially the *instincts* and *feelings* coming down to us from an unrecorded past. Both instincts and emotions have roots in unconscious residuals or remnants from man's archaic history. These residuals are *psychophysical;* that is, they consist of primitive neural structures associated with innate tendencies to feeling and action. Learning may attach instincts and emotions to new stimuli; but Hall, like many of his contemporaries, believed that certain stimuli are predetermined by heredity to excite certain instinctive and emotional responses. Hunger and the impulse to search for food, the sex impulse, laughter and play, the tendencies to feel fear, anger, pity, and even the impulse to religious worship are echoes in us of ancestral tendencies extending back to an immemorial past.

d. HALL'S GENETIC THEORY AND EDUCATION.   What is the bearing of Hall's principle of recapitulation on education? Each child passes through the main stages of racial evolution. The first task, then, is to determine what racial epochs correspond with various age periods of the child. We will expect that at one period the child will be a predatory fighter, hunter, and fisher. He will become a pastoral creature or a builder as determined by the order of biological history. It is the task of genetic psychology to determine these main stages of child development. Once acquired, such knowledge will have pedagogical applications. For one thing, it will enable the teacher to *understand* the child with sympathy in place of becoming an impatient and carping critic.

Each such ancestral interest of the child, if given free and innocent expression, will lose its force (catharsis), enabling the child to go on to higher modes of activity. Further, the ancestral feelings and urges to action represent the child's dynamic interests. The strategy of the teacher will consist in satisfying these urges while at the same time leading the child to more profitable activities. Thus, the craving of the boy to live with nature should lead to exploratory visits to fields, forests, lakes, streams, and to the rich experiences to be had from them. The opportunity to "graft" nature study on these moods of the child should not be missed. If the child feels interests which cannot be embodied in overt experiences, they may be satisfied *vicariously*, as when he hears, reads, or writes tales of adventure and heroism. When he reaches the age of adolescence he is ready to relive, in more scholarly fashion, his cultural heritage from the more recent history of the race.

e. HALL ON RELIGIOUS EDUCATION.   Hall's ideas about religion have a few things in common with the views of Dewey. For both of them the function of religion is to firmly establish in the individual the moral values achieved by the race and to amplify them for future needs. To live religiously means to undergo normal development which, biologically viewed, is unselfish devotion to the group. Religion gives life its deepest meaning. But here the agreements between Hall and Dewey end. Dewey rejects Hall's theory of recapitulation, and Hall goes beyond Dewey in making religion a conversion to God and the acceptance of Jesus as spiritual as well as moral leader.

In his two-volume work on the psychology of religion (7) Hall interprets religion from the point of view of psychoanalysis and the theory of recapitulation. Hall's aim was to show that being a true Christian does not require belief in the miracles which abound in Biblical stories of the life of Jesus. Hall finds the origin of Christian faith in projections coming from unconscious levels of the soul. The child repeats racial history in his religious development. He cannot be a Christian until he has passed through earlier stages in which persons and objects are the foci of religious awe and reverence.

The first deity of the child is his mother. He must live through the mystic moods and ineffable impulses which nature evokes in him. The moon and the sun, light and darkness, snow and rainfall, lurking mysteries in the depths of forests and streams—all these things touch the tender mind of the child. Some of the vague whispers which nature evokes in the child's fleeting fantasies are echoes of primitive animistic superstitions. Through the inner life of fantasy, in which the dim outlines of primitive animism, fetishism, and polytheism may be seen, the child arrives eventually at the conception of God as the stern giver of laws. If the child has feared thunder he will better understand the fear of God. The conception of God as the omnipotent ruler and inexorable dispenser of justice and retribution should not be replaced too soon with the adult's conception of God as the loving father, watching over man's needs and listening to his prayers. Hall regards religion as having the profoundest import for mankind. It would be better for a man who rejects Christianity to become a Buddhist or Confucianist rather than to become an early skeptic.

A quandary arises when it is asked, "What, for Hall, validates religion? What evidences make the belief in the existence of God true?" Hall's evidence is pragmatic in nature. Religious beliefs provide for the most effective pursuit of the moral life of the group, which is the source of life's greatest satisfactions. This is to say with James that beliefs are true if they satisfy needs. But the critic will declare that proving a belief to be useful is not the same thing as proving it true. To tell a sick man that he will recover may comfort him but it is not true if it is known that he will die of his illness. Hall's ideas about religion lead to a strange paradox. According to them the insane man's belief that he is Napoleon, the savage's belief in sprites, and the naïve Christian's belief in God are true for them, thanks to their benighted ignorance about psychoanalysis and Dr. Hall's principle of recapitulation. For them to become enlightened would seem to be the surest road to skepticism. Wishing to be "Napoleon," no sane man can bring this about by *intentionally* believing it to be true. In order to be believed it must be "unconsciously intended," which expresses a strange contradiction. There are, so to speak, two Stanley Halls: One is the intellectual scholar who views God as a projection conjured up by deep spiritual needs lurking in ancient substrata of the soul, the other is the believer who views God as having objective reality. How can both of these beliefs exist side by side and be sincerely accepted by the same individual?

f. EVALUATION OF HALL'S GENETIC THEORY. Hall's recapitulation theory aroused a chorus of protests. The chief criticism was voiced by John Dewey, among many others (3, p. 25). We will examine this basic criticism briefly, noting that Hall does not fully deserve it.

The basic charge is that biological evidences in support of the principle of recapitulation are scanty. To be sure, the growing embryo does show some structures which appeared in certain stages of animal evolution. But these evidences are too piecemeal to justify the belief that the growing infant and child strictly traverse the racial past. But Hall did not maintain that the individual went through the complete gamut of the history of the race, either organically or psychologically. This absurd supposition would be as hopeless as the fabled biography of Tristram Shandy, which required more than a day's writing to record the events of a single day! Hall did not regard the parallel between racial and individual development to be precise in detail. The ancestral stages of the child's growth were regarded by Hall as becoming fragmentary as development went beyond the embryonic period (10, pp. 28-30). It may be noted that in an earlier work Dewey expressed sympathetic regard for Hall's theory. "There is a certain nearness, after all, in the child to primitive forms of life" (2, p. 123).

The principle of *catharsis* used by Hall is as old as Aristotle, and recurs in current psychotherapeutic and rehabilitative psychology, under such rubrics as abreaction, release therapy, permissive therapy. The essential process of catharsis consists in relieving states of frustration or tension by expressing the emotional and action tendencies involved in them. Thus, Aristotle considered that in viewing tragedies and comedies the mind was purged of its emotional states. Hall proposed to allow children to relive the innocent and constructive experiences to be found in racial history, and then by pedagogical strategy to redirect energies into activities found to be more useful today. It may be observed, however, that the indulgence by the child of such things as hunting, fishing, camping, and nature study in general result in woefully incomplete "catharsis," for when he becomes an adult he still responds to these ancient allurements.

▽ C. John Dewey's Experimental School

In 1896, while at the University of Chicago, Dewey had the opportunity of applying his philosophy of education in an experimental school. This school became the model for many others which, increasing in number, became part of the sweeping revolution known as the Progressive Education movement. Dewey gives a full account of the University Elementary School at Chicago in his book, *The School and Society* (2).

Although the children entrusted to the school were instructed, the school was not governed by "ready-made principles" put into routine practice. In addition to teaching there were experimental objectives to be carried out. The aim of the school was to answer four initial questions which served as the problems for research.

1. The Four Problematic Questions

The four main problems might be resolved into one: "How can the pragmatic philosophy of education be successfully embodied in practice?"

a. FIRST PROBLEM.   Dewey felt that traditional schooling had become too preoccupied with developing intelligence and conveying information through "book learning." Before the era of modern industry this sort of education was not so bad because the child in the home and community took part in such practical occupations as farming, gardening, weaving, milling, building, and animal husbandry. But the child of today is largely cut off from the educative value of *doing things,* of developing self-reliance and resourcefulness in practical affairs. To sever knowledge from practice is a vicious dualism.

To elaborate on Dewey's sense of the artificiality of our lives, we might compare them with earlier times. The pioneers of America were truly independent. To take but one item, they raised the grain, made the flour, and baked the loaf of bread for themselves. This was largely true for almost every item of a feast. It held for the garments they wore, the tables at which they sat, the houses in which they lived. We live in houses built by contractors, eat from manufactured tables, and the feast from soup to nuts usually has its origin elsewhere. We serve and are served by strangers who may live far away and are never seen. We are developing an almost incorrigible habit of working for someone else. We are like the sailors who, being shipwrecked on an island, sought to restore a sense of being at home by washing each other's laundry! We do not even know what many of the commodities we use are made of or where they come from. Ordinarily, we are no more curious about such things than is the dog about the origin of his kennel. What the child studies at school is not functionally integrated with what he does at home.

The first problem then is, "What can be done, and how can it be done, to bring the school into closer relation with the home and neighborhood life?" (2, p. 116). The child should have the same point of view in the home as he has in the school. The school should offer the child the same opportunity afforded by the home of doing things that are self-rewarding and interesting. Children living in large urban centers are especially afflicted by the bifurcation of knowing and doing. Some fortunate children live in suburban and rural areas where practical activities in the home and neighborhood are still abundant. Their parents might testify, as against Dewey, that these children do not act as though such activities as weeding the garden, shoveling snow, and raking leaves are self-rewarding and interesting. Dewey would reply that these activities must be made the children's own projects, and they must be convinced that this is the case. Success, no doubt, will require a high order of salesmanship.

b. SECOND PROBLEM. Children are quite likely to find their courses of study uninteresting, and may pursue them only to avoid penalties or to win artificial rewards. This, says Dewey, is due to the circumstance that the problems studied by children are not made to be *their* problems. Hence, the second problem of the school is, how can the teacher introduce varied subject matter which will have significance and value in the life of the child? (2, p. 117). Dewey charges that too much time is spent in mastering the skills rather than the substance of learning. He believes that if the child is led to discover knowledge about the world in a way that is personally significant for him, reading, writing, and arithmetic will be learned without so much special attention to them.

For the elementary levels of schooling, Dewey's principle that "tool" subjects like reading, writing, and arithmetic are best acquired as integral to the study of subject matter is sound enough. Experts in remedial reading find that the avid reader seldom appears in the reading clinic. Most reading difficulties are due, not to special functional handicaps, but to sheer lack of zestful practice in reading (11). But for more difficult levels of reading, writing, and arithmetic direct attention to the "tools" saves the time and patience of both pupil and teacher.

c. THIRD PROBLEM. How can the mastery of basic academic skills and knowledge be achieved by means of everyday experiences and occupations? (2, p. 118). Dewey thinks that occupations will be excellent bearers of learning because they can satisfy strong personal interests.

d. FOURTH PROBLEM. This last problem is to give more individual attention to pupils (2, p. 119). The problem is solved by the use of practical activities which are personally selected and pursued by the pupil under the teacher's supervision. Supervision is to be as individual as possible, and hence will require more teachers per pupil than in the traditional school. Dewey's school had one teacher for each eight to ten children (2, p. 119). The generous teacher-pupil ratio required by the usual "experience curriculum" creates financial problems for the school. The progressivist replies that there are methods of administration which will reduce these costs; and that, in any case, the results justify the costs.

2. The Methods of the Experimental School

We must not fail to notice the strict conformity of the methods of teaching used in Dewey's experimental school with his instrumental philosophy of education. The basic aim is to break down the vicious separation of knowing from doing. But in uniting them Dewey does not at all propose to unite *particular* occupational skills with *particular* knowledge about them. On the contrary, Dewey regards *general* knowledge of laws and principles as at once the most intellectual and the most useful. Dewey's quarrel with the "intellectualists" in education is not because they teach abstract knowledge but because they do not at the same time teach the child how to apply such knowledge.

In Dewey's school there were several types of practical activities: shopwork with wood and tools, cooking, and textile work, such as weaving and sewing. The principle followed was to start the child at some activity which lies as near as possible to his own preferences. Then gradually, as practical problems arose, the child was led to acquire intellectual knowledge. Thus, cooking leads naturally to the study of chemistry. Shopwork leads to the study of arithmetic and geometry. Weaving and sewing lead to interest in geography and history. In this way education moves from the particulars of practical work to general knowledge. In this way Dewey's school developed its departments of instruction.

The social and moral development of the child was a by-product of the experience curriculum. The various groups of children were small and intimate, hence they could function as integrated groups. Since children worked for a common objective, discipline was unnecessary. Since a given project was shared by others, the child was made to feel personal responsibility and to learn cooperation. All of this is in keeping with a sound philosophy of democracy. The increasing enrollment of the school in spite of almost doubling the fees showed that parents were satisfied. Yet work, not amusement, was the prevailing attitude in the school.

♥ D. The Rise and Spread of Progressive Education

The revolt against alleged "formal" and "intellectual" education in the United States reached major proportions during the second decade of the present century. The chief although not only expression of this revolt was the launching of the Progressive Education Association (P.E.A.) in 1918 with headquarters in New York City. The period of chief influence of the P.E.A. lies between the two World Wars. Its annual meetings were crowded. The *Journal of the Progressive Education Association* was founded. Various foundations gave funds to P.E.A. for research work.

By 1941, however, the influence of P.E.A. was on the wane and essentialism appeared to gain ground. The rise of essentialism was due in part to the threats of a second world war which led the American people to feel the need for solidarity and faith in our democratic culture. This led naturally to traditionalism and essentialism of a realistic sort. At times of threat to national security the study of history ascends in importance because it gives the records of ideals and achievements which give a sense of unity to the people. Already in 1938 essentialism reasserted itself under the able leadership of such men as William C. Bagley and Hermann Horne. A new organization appeared, the Essentialist Committee for the Advancement of American Education. On the polemic side, the essentialists condemned what they considered to be the vagaries and evil consequences of progressive education and the projects method (1).

Our next sampling of progressivism will be an account of the projects method of William H. Kilpatrick contained in Chapter 18 which follows. This final chapter will also show that Dewey himself together with some of his conservative friends had to castigate certain developments in progressivism which they regarded as radical and as leading to retrogression in education.

References

1. Brickman, William W. "Essentialism Ten Years After." *School and Society,* 1948, Vol. 67, pp. 361-365.
2. Dewey, John. *The School and Society.* Chicago: University of Chicago Press, 1900.

3. ————. *Democracy and Education*. New York: Macmillan, 1916.
4. ————. "How Much Freedom in Schools?" *New Republic*, 1930, Vol. 63, pp. 204-206.
5. Hall, G. Stanley. *Educational Problems* (2 vols.). New York: Appleton, 1911.
6. ————. *Adolescence* (2 vols.). New York: Appleton, 1915.
7. ————. *Jesus, the Christ, in the Light of Psychology* (2 vols.). New York: Doubleday, 1917.
8. ————. *Aspects of Child Life and Education*. New York: Appleton, 1921.
9. Parker, Francis W. *Talks on Pedagogics*. New York: John Day, 1937.
10. Partridge, George E. *Genetic Philosophy of Education*. New York: Macmillan, 1922.
11. Weber, Christian O. "Reading Inadequacy as Habit." *Journal of Educational Psychology*, 1949, Vol. 40, pp. 427-433.

⯆ *chapter 18*

KILPATRICK'S PHILOSOPHY OF EDUCATION AND CRITICISMS OF THE NEW EDUCATION

Dewey's experimental school was followed by others, some of which departed radically from Dewey's model. William H. Kilpatrick (1871-   ) ranks as an eminent leader of modern progressivism. His views are selected for special exposition in this chapter. The second purpose of the chapter is to give an account of earlier criticisms of progressive education followed by an analysis of the current ferment of criticism directed against the "New Education." The main divisions of the chapter are as follows:

A. Kilpatrick's Educational Philosophy
    1. Kilpatrick's Pragmatic Philosophy
    2. Kilpatrick's Critique of Alexandrian Education
    3. Aims and Methods of the Project Method

B. General Criticism of the New Education
    1. Right-Wing Criticism against Left-Wing Progressives
    2. Current Criticisms of the New Education
    3. Experimental Defenses of the New Education
    4. James B. Conant's Constructive Proposals

▽ A. Kilpatrick's Educational Philosophy

Kilpatrick, now professor emeritus at Teachers College, Columbia University, has exerted great influence on the development of progressive education, both through his leadership and through his militant books. His *Foundations of Method* (12), published in 1925, was followed by other works. The book on which the following account of his ideas chiefly relies is his *Philosophy of Education* (13), published in 1951. Samuel Tenenbaum published a biography of Kilpatrick containing an appreciative foreword by John Dewey (23).

1. Kilpatrick's Pragmatic Philosophy

In his foreword to Tenenbaum's biography of Kilpatrick, Dewey pays tribute to Kilpatrick as an educator. In the foreword to his recent book (13), Kilpatrick states that the chief formative influences on his thinking are to be found in Darwin's *Origin of Species,* and in the philosophical works of Charles S. Peirce, William James, and John Dewey; the debt to Dewey being the greatest. Kilpatrick is generally regarded as more radical than Dewey in the theory and application of experience education. Dewey's introduction of education by projects was cautious and conservative, stressing more than does Kilpatrick the importance of continuity and intellectual content in education, and the importance of holding the pupil's interests and individuality in leash.

To give an account of Kilpatrick's general philosophy would be to repeat much that has already been said about pragmatism. A brief review of Kilpatrick's salient convictions will suffice. He rejects views of the universe which are derived from and satisfying to mere intellectual contemplation. He replaces these with the scientific models initiated by Galileo. Perhaps more than Dewey, Kilpatrick finds moral values the chief fruit of human experience. "Philosophy . . . is the critical study of the conflicting values of life to find out as best possible how to manage life in the face of these conflicts" (13, p. 32 and elsewhere). Kilpatrick's stress on the importance of moral development in education calls for further elaboration.

Man's morality is social and arises out of his interaction with and dependence upon others for survival, beginning with complete reliance on others during infancy. Each individual is indebted to a numerous company who have relieved the barrenness of mere survival with the fruits of culture. It is indeed by the grace of our social inheritance, largely embodied in social institutions, that we can lead decent lives at all. But this precious patrimony is man-made; it is a human achievement and exists to serve man. Institutions are justified to the degree that their advantages outweigh their disadvantages for living the life which is good to live for all members of a democratic society (13, pp. 33-50).

For Kilpatrick, moral evolution is the supreme goal of life. As applied to concrete living, Kilpatrick defines religion as one's attitude toward one's supreme value and the realization of that value in experience. Note that, like Dewey, Kilpatrick does not insist that religious faith must include the worship of a divine power. There are bad religions, says Kilpatrick, as well as good ones. Measuring all things by the "dollar yardstick" is an example of a bad supreme value or religion. The excessive devotion of Russians to Marxism may be regarded as faith in a false ideal or false religion.

What ideal deserves our supreme devotion and, when it is sought for in life, becomes the best religion? Kilpatrick's answer is that the "over-arching concern of each individual should be that all people shall have and enjoy the fullest and finest life possible" (13, p. 158). But what man has won is never fully secure, and further achievements are uncertain. In this situation our hope for saving what we have achieved and enriching it will depend on intelligent effort on our part. This combination of intelligent foresight with determined effort constitutes faith (13, p. 158). The reader will note the strong agreement of these ideas with those of Dewey, set forth in Chapter 15.

Kilpatrick's encomium on striving for "the fullest and the finest life possible" may seem as empty of concrete content as Kant's categorical imperative. In discussing moral questions it is easy to indulge in tautology and circular arguments, as when it is said that growth is good because it results in more growth, or that life is "good" because it is "fine." The problem of moral inquiry is not so much to prove that we should seek the good as rather to determine what constitutes the good. The criminal's devotion to evil is often "full" and he may consider it "fine." But Kilpatrick does specify the ways of life that are good. They are the lusty good things of a democracy: the satisfaction of getting what we want, of exerting effort in some interesting activity directed towards a favored end, the joy of serving others, and so on.

Various systems of morality, despite their opposition in theory, usually end up with Kilpatrick's ideals of conduct. Perhaps, as Russell holds (see Chapter 14), the true criterion of what is "fine" is initially subjective. Considered in itself, any line of conduct is "fine" if the individual finds it so—at least while the "fineness" lasts. But this does not mean that there are no superindividual criteria of the good. The good life acceptable to the group must be found good by as many individuals as possible. All moral theories are thus driven to discover what is good in the long run and for the social group. But for Dewey and Kilpatrick the "long run" does not extend to eternity and "those concerned" may be in practice rather local.

2. Kilpatrick's Critique of Alexandrian Education

Kilpatrick's philosophy of education, among other things, takes the reader on a sight-seeing tour of the errors of education. The New Education defended by Kilpatrick is based on what he considers the proper psychology of learning. Kilpatrick rejects what he calls the "Alexandrian conception" of education (13, Chapter 16, pp. 222-234).

Alexandria was made the intellectual center of the world by the rulers of Egypt following the death of Alexander the Great. Although Alexandrian education included some science, such as Ptolemaic astronomy and Euclidean geometry, it depended on Greek civilization for its philosophy and literature. Ancient Alexandria established education as the study of books. This conception of education was taken over by the Romans, was continued and applied in new ways by Christianity, and came down to us through the vicissitudes of the Protestant Reformation. Even now, says Kilpatrick, Robert M. Hutchins and Mark Van Doren defend an intellectual learning via books, which regards man as a mere intellect and which largely reduces intellection to memorization.

3. Aims and Methods of the Project Method

a. EDUCATIONAL AIMS. Kilpatrick holds that the aim of education is not to teach children what they do not know, but to *teach them how they should live*. Three steps must be followed to reach this desired end: (a) The school must provide the child with the opportunity to live, not merely to study. (b) Learning should result from the experiences provided by the school. (c) Character-building is the consequence of learning (13, p. 301 and elsewhere).

b. KILPATRICK'S PSYCHOLOGY OF LEARNING. Kilpatrick bases his strategy for teachers on a theory of learning. His theory of learning has a number of aspects, but two may be mentioned as crucial. First, one cannot "assign" problems to children. In actual practice such problems tend to remain teachers' problems. You cannot legislate purposes and interests (12, p. 349). A second principle of importance is that of *concomitant* learning. Learning by experience involves the whole person, and experience teaches many things simultaneously. The bookworm in the library may be exercising the function of memorization or even of intelligence, but he is neglecting his social nature, muscular system, and other equipment. But the child working with other children on some practical project develops his whole person: There will be many concomitant learnings besides the acquisition of knowledge.

C. CRITICISM OF KILPATRICK'S EMPHASIS ON INTEREST. The pragmatic educator's emphasis on the importance of present aims and interests of the learner, which cannot be "legislated," was discussed earlier in connection with Dewey's ideas. Kilpatrick regards it as unfortunate and usually harmful for the child to do things which lie outside his present interests. He declares that adults learn what they now need and what now interests them (13, p. 322). They may learn what they need for the future but seldom trust to rote knowledge, acquired in school upon the advice of others that they will some day need this knowledge.

These statements of Kilpatrick's express exaggerations. Without statistical information on the subject, the critic might well assert on the basis of general observation that adults characteristically learn things in the present for future use. Society, one would think, has the right to protest the slaughter that might be practiced by surgeons who, reared in projects schools, gave superficial attention to the study of anatomy in college because they found it "uninteresting." We expect adults to perform their tasks with competence whether they like them or not. Why is going to school, which ostensibly prepares for adult life, singled out as the one occupation in which interest is indispensable to accomplishment? The critic might also note that refusing to learn what is now not interesting is well calculated to develop a spineless hedonist rather than a "whole" person with sterling moral qualities. The morally mature person sees that the significance of knowledge is determined by its systematic and practical importance, not by the fact that it tickles momentary interests.

d. TEACHING PROCEDURE: THE PROJECT METHOD. In his earlier work Kilpatrick recognized four types of projects (5, p. 415). These represent an amplified development of the projects used in Dewey's experimental school: (a) A project which pursues a purpose expressing itself in some external activity, such as weaving, growing plants, giving a play. (b) Some aesthetic experience, such as listening to a story, listening to music, or viewing art materials. (c) A project which solves some practical problem by finding a scientific solution for it. (d) A project where the purpose is to master some skill or to acquire knowledge which fulfills present needs or interests. In his latest book Kilpatrick shows essential adherence to his earlier ideas. We begin with the child as he is and then graft instruction onto some manifest or latent interest of the child. Subject matter is not determined in advance as in the "old" system.

For the teacher, the procedure is as follows: Before the school term opens the teacher should prepare "maps" of what she hopes her charges will learn. These maps should be discussed with the superintendent and the teaching staff as a whole in order to secure coordination. But this group does not dictate the plans of the individual teacher. The primary aim is to bring about the character development of the child. There will be many learnings needed for living the good life, such as various skills, knowledge, and the attitudes which individual and social life require. Just when the aims of instruction will be pursued cannot be determined by the calendar. The teacher discusses with the pupils the question of what should be done first. This is her opportunity to show skill in utilizing the manifest and latent interests of children so as to lead them in the direction of development indicated by her map of values.

Educators have been bewildered by the various ways in which the project method has been defined. There has been such a melange of misrepresentation, rumor, and exaggeration about the method that Kilpatrick is justified in protesting against caricatures of it (13, pp. 319-320). Enthusiasts about the project method have stressed the dominating importance in it of the child's interests. Dame Rumor accordingly reports that the democracy maintained in the projects school is so rigorous that children are compelled to exercise their liberty! This leads to popular stories like the one about the child who asked his projects teacher, "Must we again do today what we want to do?"

e. THE QUESTION OF COERCION. In his *Philosophy of Education* Kilpatrick devotes a short chapter to the subject of "Coercion and Learning," in which he makes it clear that coercion is viewed as of doubtful value, and that it is possible to replace it with the better controls already outlined. But he does not say, as is often asserted, that coercion must never be used. There are occasions when compulsion may be required, such as to compel attendance at school or to enforce proper conduct while at school (13, pp. 269-270). The projects to be launched are decided by group discussion with the teacher as moderator. The project finally selected should be decided by the children if this is possible. Presumably the teacher, failing to arouse the interest of the children in the projects outlined in her map, could veto their projects on the ground that necessary equipment for them is lacking, etc. Once the project is selected, each child cooperates with the group in pursuing it. It is therefore not true that each child is free to follow his own unrestrained interest. The children, so to speak, discipline each other, a matter regarding which they are often more adept than either parents or teachers.

f. DOMAIN OF THE PROJECT METHOD. Kilpatrick calls the method of education by projects "general education." He recommends that the entire time of the elementary school be given to it. It should continue through the high-school years, but diminishing in amount to make room for specialization, as required by the division of labor in our society. In the high school, general education should also consist of "core work" or an activity program pursued along the same lines as in the elementary school. There should be no "subjects" as such, no courses of study adopted in detail and in advance. As in the earlier grades, activities should start with the spontaneous needs and interests of students, which can develop them for full living and its problems. Such "general education," says Kilpatrick, should be continued in college, again in diminishing amounts from the freshman through the senior year (13, pp. 325-329).

⩔ B. General Criticism of the New Education

Since progressive education is founded for the most part on pragmatic philosophy, it is appropriate to subject it to pragmatic tests. Is it justified by its practical fruits? The present section explores this question and examines the main charges against, and defenses of, current educational practices. A veritable rash of criticism of the schools is current at the present time. This deluge of fault-finding is so thorough in its coverage that progressive education is not its sole target. Since criticism covers more than progressivism we will say that current evaluations—or, rather, devaluations—concern the New Education, which for us shall include progressivism as well as some tendencies in education for which progressives are not directly responsible.

1. Right-Wing Criticism Against Left-Wing Progressives

We may expect that criticisms of progressivism coming from progressives themselves will be less captious than criticisms from outsiders. In this section attention is given to only six basic criticisms by the more conservative progressives against the insurgents. Even with only six main criticisms, overlapping is difficult to avoid. All of the criticisms indicated below as well as others are repeated again and again in the literature. One series of six evaluations of extreme progressivism was prepared under the auspices of the *New Republic* (3). Pedro T. Orata prepared another survey of progressive criticisms of progressive education (16).

a. THE NEGATIVISM OF SOME PROGRESSIVES. Dewey himself points out the tendency of some progressives to be negative:

There is always the danger in a new movement that in rejecting the aims and methods of that which it would supplant, it may develop its own principles negatively rather than positively and constructively. Then it takes its clew in practice from that which is rejected instead of from the constructive development of its own philosophy (11, pp. 6-7).

As Orata expressed it, the progressive who is merely negative does not object to riding off in several directions on several horses. He may feel that all paths are good provided they do not lead back to traditionalism (16, p. 578). Because tradition stresses required courses the progressive rebel is tempted to show his originality by refusing to require any·

thing. Kilpatrick, at least several decades ago, gave voice to such revolt. In his introduction to Collings' book (about which we will hear later on) Kilpatrick says that the teacher should not "put over" traditional subject matter by means of some "back-handed" method. The teacher should literally not care whether or not children get traditional subject matter. If they do not call for such material it is not needed by them. When they need it seriously enough they will call for it (8, p. xix).

b. THE CHILD AS A NEW ABSOLUTE.   Boyd H. Bode, like a true pragmatist, rejects all absolutes, except perhaps the absolute of experience which tests all things. But he is dismayed to find his progressive friends setting up new absolutes. The main absolute of the ultraprogressive is the child—his needs, interests, growth, and freedom. After all, says Bode, the study of the child's needs and capacities reveal only the raw materials with which the educator works (4, p. 39). Growth for the mere sake of growth, says Bode, is not a proper goal for education. As for the child's immediate interests and freedom, Bode declares that it should be our aim to enable the child to outgrow them (4, p. 58).

c. A NEW ISOLATIONISM.   Progressives have criticized traditional education for making the school an ivory tower where the pursuit of hoary tradition supplants the preparation of the child for the problems and perils of adult life. The radical progressive now finds himself accused of the same fault. The child-centered school may develop a willful habit of individual freedom that ill prepares the child for an adult life requiring self-sacrifice, patience, and obedience to many socially and legally imposed rules of conduct. Bode writes, "According to Dewey, freedom is achieved through the exercise of intelligence, whereas the less discriminating of his disciples understand him to mean that intelligence is achieved through the exercise of freedom" (3, p. 63).

Dewey joins in warning the new educators against the fault of isolationism and related errors (11). He has no patience with those who sanction the sentimental indulgence of the child's wishes. He declares that the child thus pampered is not prepared to encounter a world which requires self-control in overcoming obstacles (11, pp. 73-76). To illustrate Dewey's point, we may note that the child reared on an exclusive diet of interests will find that the tax collector, looming in his prospective future, does not share the charitable view of his projects teacher.

In defense of the teacher's right to exercise leadership, Dewey writes: "That children are individuals whose freedom should be respected while the more mature person should have no freedom as an individual is an idea too absurd to require refutation" (11, p. 66). The teacher should seek types of experience for her charges that go beyond the mere interests of the moment. Egotism, cockiness, impertinence, and other traits associated with excessive freedom are mainly due to the want of intellectual control in the experience curriculum (3, p. 205).

Conservative progressives maintain that criticisms which allege wholesale pampering on the part of progressive teachers are exaggerations. Education by projects does not mean complete individual freedom of the child and complete individual attention to him. Kilpatrick suggests one teacher for each class of from twenty-five to thirty pupils. Groups need to be moderately large to make social development possible (13, pp. 331-332). In such a group the child cannot work at projects dictated by purely individual interests since he must cooperate with others in deciding what the project is to be and how it shall be carried out.

d. DISORGANIZATION OF SUBJECT MATTER. Harold O. Rugg and Ann Shumaker, as early as 1928, criticized child-centered schools for their lack of design in instruction (18). Programs of instruction in such schools are often lopsided and poorly integrated. There is not enough *continuity* of work in successive school years. This is a serious fault in a philosophy of education which tediously voices the preachment that all natural development or growth is continuous.

e. THE INORDINATE STRESS ON "DOING." The fifth charge against radical progressives is that they place too much stress on physical activity, e.g., on doing things with the hands. Dewey regarded experimentation as the source and test of true knowledge, but he did not mean that experimentation confines itself to active trial and error. Experience is educative to the degree that discrimination accompanies action. Thought and action are *continuities*. In science, hypotheses and laboratory exploration go hand in hand. Dewey thus insisted that activity schools provide periods for reflection (11, pp. 72-73). Even the youngest pupils need such intervals for thought. Dewey did not reject intellectual activity—he rejected a *purely* intellectual education.

Essentialists will agree with Dewey's strictures against excessive motor activity in learning. Always to insist on action tends to confine the child to the narrow range of his personal experience. If the child is to be taught that the earth is round, should we carry activity-centered instruction to the length of sending him on a trip around the world? Herbert Spencer declared that reading is vision by proxy. Reading does not travel to see the world but watches the world go by. This sedentary way of experiencing the world is secondhand, but its great advantage lies in the vast amount of the world that can be covered in limited time.

f. VOCATIONALISM THREATENS DEMOCRACY. Vocational education is in harmony with the ideology of progressives, but they are not entirely responsible for the great vogue of work education in our schools and colleges. This trend in education was given federal support by the Morrill Act passed during the Civil War, by the Smith-Hughes Act of 1917, and by supplementary provisions like the George-Barden Act of 1946. Progressives have accused essentialists of favoring an education for "aristocrats," and claim that experience-centered education is more appropriate for the common man (see Chapter 4, section A). It is true that in the distant past a higher cultural education was the gentleman's prerogative. But modern essentialists claim adherence to democratic ideals because they wish to extend the so-called "gentleman's education" to all. Thus, Stringfellow Barr, formerly of St. John's College, holds that the true liberal arts are reading, writing, speaking, listening, and thinking. These skills are the best bulwarks of democracy. The citizen does not fully discharge his obligations to a democratic society by being a skilled worker. He must do his share of vigilant thinking to safeguard democracy. His opinions will be formed by what he hears and especially by what he reads in authoritative works on politics, economics, government, history, and the sciences. Acquiring such knowledge is not child's play.

To be a worthy citizen one must in reading and listening give attention to the great classics and to the traditional subject matter of our schools. This is the conception of education laid down in 1952 in the joint declaration of three of our leading private high schools and three leading universities, Andover, Exeter, and Lawrenceville, and Harvard, Princeton, and Yale (2). Oddly enough, these six institutions are usually regarded as belonging to the "aristocracy" of education. Yet they now appear as the defenders of liberal education and democratic freedom for everyone.

2. Current Criticisms of the New Education

Current criticism of education is so profuse and chaotic that an advance prospectus is needed for this section. Our main jurisdiction should be the pros and cons of criticisms directed against practices which may reasonably be attributed to progressivism or which are at least tangent to its principles. Current disputes about education mainly, although not entirely, reflect the earlier intramural disagreements among the philosophies of education covered in this book. Today, these disputes have merely spread to the public arena. One difference is to be noted. During the earlier academic stage of the debate each school impartially directed criticism against all other schools. But in the current stage of the dispute a loose alliance of essentialists, religious idealists, realists, and laymen is engaged in attacks on education with progressivism as a main target. Current disputes follow earlier cleavages. We hear renewed praise of intellectual education as voiced in earlier decades by Hutchins and his friends; the need for religious orientation in the schools as formerly urged by Gentile and Horne; and the virtues of an unremitting "grind" in mastering exacting areas of inquiry as defended in former days by realists (e.g., Whitehead and Russell).

We shall also try to limit consideration to matters which concern the aims, contents, and methods of education, thus excluding no end of quarrels about such things as school taxes, private versus public schooling, the salaries of teachers, the costs of buildings and equipment. (Even the school lunch, the Bermuda shorts of coeds, and the rights of janitors come in for polemical treatment these days!)

With the exclusions noted above, we still face a series of criticisms against education which we shall trim down by restricting attention to the main charges that are voiced with special frequency and vigor. The vigor of the critics is especially noteworthy. Philosophic calm has been shattered, especially by some Zarathustras intoning solemn pronouncements from their mountaintops.

a. THE ORIGIN, EXTENT, AND CAUSES OF CRITICISM. C. Winfield Scott and Clyde M. Hill prepared an excellent anthology of representative attacks upon and defenses of the schools (20). Their survey (in Chapter 1) of the rise and spread of criticism, gauged by various indexes, guides, and journals, shows that attacks on the schools became noteworthy in 1942 and steadily increased in volume. Criticisms, formerly largely expressed in books, professional journals and bulletins, and research surveys, now also appear everywhere in newspapers and popular magazines, showing the layman's interest in the schools and his tendency to join the chorus of critics and defenders of current education.

Although criticism is on the whole violent and bitter, it is easy to be misled about its extent. Defenses of education are abundant. No nationwide poll has as yet been made on the matter, but quite a number of large surveys indicate that the great majority of citizens are satisfied with the schools (20, pp. 208-222). Even the severe critics accord praise now and then. Classroom teachers are on the whole warmly commended.

Regarding the causes of criticism, the critic will invariably hold that his attacks on education are motivated by the hope of mitigating actual faults and abuses. But criticism is likely to be sincere even when invalid. We need to heed the warning of the Freudians, well supported by the work of psychologists, that the wish is often father to the thought. Needs and wishes, looking upon the laborious processes of logic with jealous impatience, incline us to draw conclusions first and then to search for plausible evidences to support them, or to select the facts which fit the theory instead of finding a theory which fits the facts. In such "rationalizations" the wish is presumed to act unconsciously. But deplorable attacks on education sometimes arise from a conscious and Philistine distrust of education or from conscious rebellion against the growing burden of school taxes. One suspects that some critics are driven by sheer impulses of literary genius, sometimes reaching remarkable levels of performance in terms of polished wit and mordant iconoclasm.

William C. Trow (24) and Douglas Rugh (19) suggest that attacks on the schools are sometimes projected aggressions arising from the widespread insecurity and frustrations of current times. A "projection," in psychoanalytic terms, is an inner mental state which subjects project or externalize, finding its cause in the environment. Individual aggressive impulses generated by frustrations, being helpless against powerful and often concealed causes, seek a defenseless scrapegoat and one regarding which evidences are scanty and unstructured. The schools and their staffs fit both requirements rather well. The schools, like local, state, and federal governments are made helpless targets of criticism on the ground that they are the personal possessions of everyone.

At the same time, wishful thinking flourishes on ignorance. No one will venture to challenge the proposition that two plus two equals four, but the most positive opinions are heard about things surrounded by the mists of uncertainty, e.g., the question of whether or not the soul is immortal, or whether the manufacturers or the labor unions are responsible for the high cost of goods. Evidences about the national status of education are insufficient even for the best informed, and the less informed are often astonishingly ignorant about evidences on record. Fault-finding about the schools tends thus to degenerate into the citation of instances, rumored if not witnessed, and discussed in anecdotal style. But sound generalizations are not reared on single observations. Socrates is not classified as an alcoholic because he once got intoxicated during a banquet of Plato's. If proof consisted merely in selecting supporting instances, it is easy to "demonstrate" the most incredible propositions, such as that only redheaded coeds have big feet. All schools are not discredited because some high-school principal at Champaign, Illinois, suggested that baking a good cherry pie is as much an achievement for a girl as the mastery of spelling (14, p. 46).

b. PROGRESSIVISM AND POLITICAL SUBVERSION. Mortimer Smith (21, pp. 91-94; 22, pp. 137-139) suspects some educators of favoring a "deification of the state" in Hegelian style. Earlier progressives, such as George S. Counts, Harold Rugg, and William H. Kilpatrick, favored the stepping-up of the powers of government, to the detriment, so it is sometimes thought, of individual freedom.

In order to evaluate current suspicions of subversive and communistic ideas among educators, we should at once reject charges growing out of loose analogical reasoning. Dewey's personal loyalty to democratic ideals is almost invariably conceded even by his severest critics. But the word "social" occurs with extraordinary frequency in his writings. This could be enough to convince some minds that Dewey was fomenting "socialism," which now easily could become "communism" by a further disregard for differences. Such abortive logic is like that of the braves of an American Indian tribe who held that the squaws should raise the crop of corn since they gave birth to new crops of Indians!

What is the true story about George S. Counts, alleged defender of coercive powers of government? Counts (1889-   ) was a leader of progressive educators, and belonged to a subgroup of "social reconstructionists." His revolt against child-centered education took place during the severe economic depression around 1929, and found militant expression in his work, *Dare the Schools Build a New Social Order?* (10). Counts charged that progressive education had no basic theory of social welfare. He believed that educators could lead America out of the then current depression and prevent the recurrence of similar tragedies. Counts sought to rally educators to the cause of formulating and implementing a "comprehensive theory of social welfare." He held that teachers, more than other groups, represent the abiding interests of all citizens. They have at their disposal high levels of intellectual competence and information, and include high-ranking scientists and scholars in many fields. Since they educate coming generations, they can establish a just and secure social order in the minds and hearts of the people. At least, their performance is not likely to be worse than what we have had in the past.

What was the outcome of Counts's proposal for the high destiny of teachers? It let loose a storm of controversy in which it appeared that neither citizens in general nor teachers agreed that educators should assume leadership of the social order. Those who agreed with Counts could not agree on the kind of social order which should be established. As is to be expected, a "brain trust" is sure to end with contradictory views. According to John Brubacher (6, p. 624), what Counts had in mind was a collective society similar to the New Deal of the Democratic Party.

It is true, however, that Counts urged educators to seek political power and wield it boldly. He held it abundantly evident that leaders of the past who altered destiny did not hesitate to use the power at their disposal. Counts, of course, believed that such power should be used in the interests of the people as a whole. But dictators almost invariably profess this laudable motive. Communistic dictatorships very likely believe that it would be good for us to be conquered by them!

This matter of winning and wielding power is the one point about the "social reconstructionism" of educators which justifies the warnings of Mortimer Smith and others. Reform usually starts, says Smith, with the method of persuasion but easily shifts to compulsion. "Confirmed do-gooders always end by doing good by coercion; their devotion to the end will blind them to the deviousness of the means employed" (21, p. 32). Education is one of the main defenses of a democratic state, and for this very reason must not be controlled by any class or professional group. Educational reforms concerning the aims and contents of education may be initiated by educators but *power* about such matters rests with the citizens.

C. THE "EDUCATIONIST BUREAUCRACY." Albert Lynd considers that professional educationists have established autocratic control of federal and state agencies of education to an alarming degree. They tend to dominate teachers colleges and so on down to the local schools (14, especially Chapter 2). Professors of education have established "one of the neatest bureaucratic machines ever created by any professional group in any country anywhere since the priesthood of ancient Egypt" (14, p. 36). Arthur Bestor develops a similar contention in two lengthy chapters concerning "The Power Politics of Educationdom," and "Policy-Making by Intimidation" (1). Mortimer Smith laments the "superprofessional racket" established by teachers colleges aided by the NEA. They have sought to induce every state government to enforce certification laws designed by their own closed fraternity, and even write most of the textbooks used in the schools. They usurp the powers of local communities in determining the philosophy of education which is put into practice (22, pp. 137-139, cited in 20, pp. 65-69).

These charges against the alleged "bureaucratic machine" of educators involve exaggeration. Citizens can and do exert control over the educational policies of their schools. If this control is waning, it is perhaps largely due to indifference on the part of citizens themselves. Although there are federal controls of education, extensive powers belong to the states. The states delegate powers to local communities, which are able to implement their wishes through school boards. The influence of citizens is given national scope through the National Citizens Council for Better Schools. The degree of local independence in matters of education is shown by the bewildering variations among our schools and their manner of control. James B. Conant declares that an attempt to summarize the manner of selecting school boards in the forty-eight states would end with encyclopedic differences in details (9, p. 9). Conant declines to try to answer the question, "How satisfactory is the typical American high school?" This is because the variations among our 21,000 public high schools are so great that it is doubtful whether a meaningful sample could be isolated (9, p. 16). Two influential organizations of educators have, in fact, drawn up resolutions defending the responsibility of local school boards in matters of school control. These are the Association for Supervision and Curriculum Development and the American Association of School Administrators (20, p. 344).

d. THE DECLINE OF ACADEMIC INSTRUCTION. The charge of teaching disorganized subject matter, made by Harold O. Rugg against his confreres in 1928, has now reached the proportions of an avalanche. The schools are accused of discarding standard courses of the past (sciences, languages, history, literature, etc.) in favor of a hodgepodge curriculum including courses on success in marriage, family-life values, the dance, automobile driving, occupational adjustment, and so on. Lynd (14), Bestor (1), Smith (21), and others dwell on these faults at length. Dewey's ideal was to educate youth for "real" life. Modern educators, accepting this injunction with great enthusiasm, have tried to provide an education which covers all of life's contingencies. Mortimer Smith declares that the only thing lacking is a course on "how to come in out of the rain" (21, p. 28). Protests against the vagaries of progressive education in the United States even come from Canada, as in Hilda Neatby's book, *So Little for the Mind* (15).

The alleged anti-intellectual diet pervading our schools is said by the critic to fail in preparing the student for adult life. Bernard I. Bell declares, "A good education is not so much one which prepares a man to succeed in the world as one which enables him to sustain failure" (20, p. 64). Harry J. Fuller (20, pp. 23-24) speaks of the dwindling tenacity of high-school students. Such flabbiness might be remedied by severe and protracted training in some vigorous field of academic study.

The principle of automatic promotion (defended by Kilpatrick and others) is attacked by a number of critics. Like the "life adjustment" courses, the policy of promoting students to higher grades irrespective of their actual accomplishments further isolates the school from the scruff of real life. In life outside the school rewards are won by accomplishments and hard work. Automatic promotion in the schools can only weaken moral fiber and lead to muddled ideas about morality.

Defenders of the principle of automatic promotion point out considerations which are often missed by those not engaged in actual teaching. We confine attention to one consideration out of several that might be offered. The most important change leading to the present state of education in the United States is the great increase in public school attendance, especially in the higher grades. The influx began after 1900, at which time not over 10 per cent of youths of high-school age were attending school. The number graduating from high schools each year was about 70,000. But by 1940 the annual number graduating from high schools rose to over one million, and the end is not yet in sight.

The schools of 1900 were somewhat more selective. We here set aside the moot questions as to whether the I.Q. levels of students were higher in 1900, or whether schoolwork at that time was more or less exacting than it is at present. But in 1900 more of the high school matriculants came from native and higher cultural levels. A larger share had college matriculation in mind. These factors provided the interests in academic learning which smoothed the path of the high schools of 1900. Lewis M. Terman has estimated that a minimum I.Q. of 110 is required for success with the traditional high-school course of studies, but 60 per cent of American youths fall below this level. It is apparent that as the high school population increases the average capacity for success diminishes. There is much truth in Paul Woodring's claim that much of the criticism of the schools may be attributed to these facts (25, pp. 11-12).

The "nonreader" is a special problem in trying to maintain the traditional intellectual high school. More youths of foreign parentage are going to our high schools, and most of them have a natural "language handicap" which shows up in reading requirements. The term "nonreader" is, of course, an exaggeration. None of them are quite as bad as the boy in Kipling's tale who tried to read the white portions of the page. But they are bad enough to cause a serious number of failures in passing the basic requirements for promotion. Refusing to "pass" a boy to the sixth grade gives him "seniority" in the fifth grade, but his gains in reading will be uncertain despite such "tenure."

What can the schools do in this predicament? Formerly the failures could be summarily "flunked," a measure which was not too devastating because the academic failures could go to work. But today laws require school attendance to certain ages (usually to age sixteen) and forbid the employment of minors. To "flunk out" a youth today is to sentence him to idleness and to the education afforded by street gangs. It is better, so many school men think, to keep him in school and at least give him vocational training which may be more to his liking and more suited to his "nonverbal" abilities. Instead of grading him in terms of the achievements of others, let him be graded in terms of his own improvements *in the light of his actual levels of aptitude.*

3. Experimental Defenses of the New Education

The allegation that current education, including progressive schools, is producing inferior results does not fully agree with experimental studies. Critics of the schools seem especially prone to ignore or gloss over this evidence. A few of these studies will be reviewed briefly. Comparisons of schools offering traditional curricula with progressive schools have shown conflicting results, but have tended to favor progressive schools.

a. THE ELLSWORTH COLLINGS EXPERIMENT. Ellsworth Collings (8) compared one projects school with two traditional schools, quite carefully equating the pupils for age, initial aptitudes, and socioeconomic origins. The experiment covered four years. Initial and final tests were given, covering aptitudes and accomplishments in reading, writing, spelling, arithmetic, composition, American history, and geography.

Children in the projects school produced final scores definitely superior to those in the two traditional schools. Thus, for common facts and skills, the projects group exceeded the others by about 38 per cent. A study was also made of eight ordinary measures of attitudes, such as records of attendance, tardiness, and the need for discipline. In these respects children of the projects school again showed improvements superior to those in the comparison schools. Collings notes that the critic may attribute the superior results of the projects school to its intensified attention to individual children and to the use of more extensive equipment (e.g., kitchens and shops needed for certain projects). Collings quite rightly replies that these features are essentials in the very definition of the project method and cannot be regarded as extraneous causes of the desirable results.

b. J. WAYNE WRIGHTSTONE'S STUDIES. Wrightstone (26, 27) compared "subjects" schools with "subjects plus projects" schools, using carefully equated groups of children. His work shows that the schools using both courses and projects were superior by significant amounts.

c. THE EIGHT-YEAR STUDY. The most extensive study to date of the comparative values of traditional and progressive methods is the Eight-Year Study made under the auspices of P.E.A. and the Carnegie Corporation (7). The main aim was to determine whether graduates of progressive high schools succeed as well in college as comparison students from conventional high schools. Graduates (1,475 in number) were drawn from thirty progressive high schools and were matched, student for student, with an equal number of students from ordinary high schools. The progressive students entered various colleges in a list of over a hundred colleges willing to take them. The first students under investigation entered college in 1936, the last ones in 1939.

This study bristles with detailed findings. The most general and impressive result was that the progressive students did somewhat better on the whole during college attendance than the comparison cases. This superiority was shown by such things as college grades, intellectual aptitudes, citizenship shown in college, and the like. It is admitted that the average superiorities of the progressive students over the "regulars" were rather small. The result generally regarded as the most significant is the indication that success in college does not depend on having had high school courses usually prescribed in the past and required for college admission.

4. James B. Conant's Constructive Proposals

This final section of the chapter gives a brief account of the proposals made by James B. Conant for solving or at least alleviating some of the dilemmas of current high school education (9). Conant's little book is a mine of information about our high schools. Our interest in it is confined to its bearing on current controversies. Conant and four collaborators made personal and careful field studies of over a hundred so-called "comprehensive" high schools located in widely distributed areas of twenty-six states.

Conant's constructive suggestions chiefly concern the comprehensive high schools. Such a school is comprehensive in the sense that it seeks to provide an education for *all* youths of its district. It contrasts with "specialized" schools which serve more limited functions, such as preparation for college or for vocational training. The comprehensive high school is the familiar type to be found in most small communities. The comprehensive high school is the one that generally lands in the predicaments indicated in earlier portions of this chapter. It is expected to prepare some students for college, to provide a general academic education for all, and to offer vocational training for those whose education will not extend beyond the high school. The small comprehensive school, Conant declares, cannot possibly discharge all the functions imposed on it except by expenditures which most communities cannot afford. Conant's solution for this problem is to consolidate neighboring high schools, thus enabling them to supply the buildings, equipment, and teaching staffs which his educational recommendations require. Conant makes twenty-one recommendations in all. We briefly indicate only the measures which promise help in solving two of the most vexing problems just discussed, although Conant's proposals cover many other difficulties.

The first problem is the alleged neglect of traditional courses in the schools. Conant's solution proposes a required program for all, including a careful pattern of "traditional" courses—English, social studies, science, etc. This program is to total nine or ten courses (out of the total of sixteen courses covered in the familiar four-year high school). The remaining six or seven courses will consist of further academic studies (preparatory for college or for anyone who wants them) and elective vocational studies.

The second sample problem is the issue regarding automatic promotion. Conant's compromise solution is as follows: students who take *advanced* academic courses will be summarily "failed" if they cannot meet minimum levels of proficiency. But this is not to hold for the elementary academic courses required of all. In such courses the student "passes" if he has worked to "full capacity." All get diplomas upon graduation, but they also get a record of all courses they have had and the grades earned in them. The existence of these records should be widely advertised so that prospective employers will ask to see them! Provision is also made for superior and gifted students, and a double aid is provided for improving reading skills. Every effort is made for avoiding invidious distinctions of class.

Conant's blueprint for education saves as best it can the "cultivation of the intellect" for all students, so dear to the minds of essentialists and realists. As for the increasing hordes of students seeking admission to colleges and universities, Conant's plan could provide a high school preparation completely devoted to intellectual training embodied even in the vocational courses. The consolidated schools envisioned will be able to provide the equipment and staffs necessary for providing intellectually superior vocational training, an ideal clearly held by John Dewey.

Essentialists, idealists, and realists, together with insurgent laymen, are fighting to implement in our schools the principle that intellectual training, having the higher utility of serving the love of knowledge, also best serves the utility of earning a livelihood. According to this view, a direct search for practical utility may end by missing it.

The crossroads of educational thought are thus pursuing different directions, after the manner of roads and philosophies. Just now the militant critics of the New Education are pressing on to reestablish convictions which have ancient roots in the wisdom of Aristotle:

It is evident, then, that there is a sort of education in which parents should train their sons, not as being useful or necessary, but because it is liberal or noble. . . . To be always seeking after the useful does not become free and exalted souls (17, pp. 322-323; *Politics*, 1337ª11-1338ᵇ4).

References

1. Bestor, Arthur. *The Restoration of Learning.* New York: Knopf, 1955.
2. Blackmer, Alan R. (Chairman). *General Education in School and College.* Cambridge, Mass.: Harvard University Press, 1952.
3. Bode, Boyd H. (and associates). "The New Education Ten Years After." *New Republic*, 1930, Vol. 63, pp. 61-64, 93-96, 123-125, 145-146, 172-176, 204-206.
4. Bode, Boyd H. *Progressive Education at the Crossroads.* New York: Newson, 1938.
5. Boyd, William. *The History of Western Education.* London: A. & C. Black, 1950.
6. Brubacher, John S. *A History of the Problems of Education.* New York: McGraw-Hill, 1947.
7. Chamberlin, Dean and Enid; Neal E. Drought; and William E. Scott. *Did They Succeed in College?* New York: Harper, 1942.

8. Collings, Ellsworth. *An Experiment with a Project Curriculum.* New York: Macmillan, 1923.

9. Conant, James B. *The American High School Today.* New York: McGraw-Hill, 1959.

10. Counts, George S. *Dare the Schools Build a New Social Order?* New York: John Day, 1932.

11. Dewey, John. *Experience and Education.* New York: Macmillan, 1938.

12. Kilpatrick, William H. *Foundations of Method.* New York: Macmillan, 1925.

13. ———. *Philosophy of Education.* New York: Macmillan, 1951.

14. Lynd, Albert. *Quackery in the Public Schools.* Boston, Mass.: Little, Brown, 1950.

15. Neatby, Hilda. *So Little for the Mind.* Toronto, Canada: Clarke, Irwin, 1953.

16. Orata, Pedro T. "Progressives Look at Progressive Education." *Educational Administration and Supervision,* 1938, Vol. 24, pp. 570-580.

17. Ross, William D. *Aristotle Selections.* New York: Scribner, 1927.

18. Rugg, Harold O., and Ann Shumaker. *The Child-Centered School.* Yonkers, N.Y.: World Book Co., 1928.

19. Rugh, Douglas. "The Scapegoat Value of American Public Education." *School and Society,* 1951, Vol. 74, pp. 20-22.

20. Scott, C. Winfield, and Clyde M. Hill. *Public Education under Criticism.* Englewood Cliffs, N.J.: Prentice-Hall, 1954.

21. Smith, Mortimer. *And Madly Teach.* Chicago: Henry Regnery, 1949.

22. ———. "The Failure of American Education." *The Freeman,* December 3, 1951.

23. Tenenbaum, Samuel. *William Heard Kilpatrick: Trail Blazer in Education.* New York: Harper, 1951.

24. Trow, William C. "The Public School a Scapegoat?" *The University of Michigan School of Education Bulletin,* 1951, Vol. 23, pp. 17-22.

25. Woodring, Paul. *Let's Talk Sense about Our Schools.* New York: McGraw-Hill, 1953.

26. Wrightstone, J. Wayne. *Appraisal of Newer Practices in Selected Public Schools.* New York: Teachers College, Columbia University, 1935.

27. Wrightstone, J. Wayne. *Appraisal of Experimental High School Practices.* New York: Teachers College, Columbia University, 1936.

SUBJECT INDEX
AUTHOR INDEX

SUBJECT INDEX

AUTHOR INDEX